Instructor's Manual
and
Test Bank

to accompany

Global Business Today

Charles W. L. Hill
University of Washington

Prepared by
Bruce R. Barringer
University of Central Florida

Irwin
McGraw-Hill

Boston   Burr Ridge, IL   Dubuque, IA   Madison, WI   New York   San Francisco   St. Louis
Bangkok   Bogotá   Caracas   Lisbon   London   Madrid
Mexico City   Milan   New Delhi   Seoul   Singapore   Sydney   Taipei   Toronto

Irwin/McGraw-Hill

A Division of The McGraw·Hill Companies

Instructor's Manual and Test Bank to accompany
GLOBAL BUSINESS TODAY

1 2 3 4 5 6 7 8 9 0 BKM/BKM 9 0 9 8 7

ISBN 0-256-26039-7

http://www.mhhe.com

TABLE OF CONTENTS

INSTRUCTOR'S MANUAL

CHAPTER 8: The Foreign Exchange Market

CHAPTER 9: The Global Monetary System

CHAPTER 10: Global Strategy

CHAPTER 11: Entering Foreign Markets

Sample Weekly Schedule
Global Business Today
Based on 15 Week Semester

Date	Topic	Assigned Reading
Week 1 - Class 1	Introduction/The Emerging Global Market	Chapter 1
Week 1 - Class 2	The Emerging Global Market (cont.)	
Week 2 - Class 1	Differences in Political Economy	Chapter 2
Week 2 - Class 2	Differences in Political Economy (cont.)	
Week 3 - Class 1	Differences in Culture	Chapter 3
Week 3 - Class 2	Differences in Culture (cont.)	
Week 4 - Class 1	International Trade Theory	Chapter 4
Week 4 - Class 2	International Trade Theory	
Week 5 - Class 1	The Global Trading System	Chapter 5
Week 5 - Class 2	The Global Trading System (cont.)	
Week 6 - Class 1	Individual Exam #1	Chapters 1-5
Week 6 - Class 2	Foreign Direct Investment	Chapter 6
Week 7 - Class 1	Foreign Direct Investment (cont.)	
Week 7 - Class 2	Regional Economic Integration	Chapter 7
Week 8 - Class 1	Regional Economic Integration (cont.)	
Week 8 - Class 2	The Foreign Exchange Market	Chapter 8
Week 9 - Class 1	The Foreign Exchange Market (cont.)	
Week 9 - Class 2	The Global Monetary System	Chapter 9
Week 10 - Class 1	The Global Monetary System (cont.)	
Week 10 - Class 2	Global Strategy	Chapter 10
Week 11 - Class 1	Global Strategy (cont.)	
Week 11 - Class 2	Individual Exam #2	Chapters 6-10
Week 12 - Class 1	Entering Foreign Markets	Chapter 11
Week 12 - Class 2	Entering Foreign Markets	
Week 13 - Class 1	Global Marketing	Chapter 12
Week 13 - Class 2	Global Marketing	
Week 14 - Class 1	Global Operations Management	Chapter 13
Week 14 - Class 2	Global Operations Management	Chapter 13
Week 15 - Class 1	Global Human Resources Management	Chapter 14
Week 15 - Class 2	Global Human Resources Management	Chapter 14
Final Exam	Administered During Final Week	Chapters 11-14 or Comprehensive

CHAPTER 1
THE EMERGING GLOBAL ECONOMY

Learning Objectives

1. Understand what is meant by the term globalization.

2. Be familiar with the main causes of globalization.

3. Understand why globalization is now proceeding at a rapid rate.

4. Appreciate how changing international trade patterns, foreign direct investment flows, differences in economic growth rates among countries, and the rise of new multinational corporations are all changing the nature of the world economy.

5. Have a good grasp of the main arguments in the debate over the impact of globalization on job security, income levels, labor and environmental policies, and national sovereignty,

6. Appreciate that globalization is giving rise to numerous opportunities and challenges that business managers must confront.

Chapter Summary

This opening chapter introduces the reader to the concepts of globalization and international trade, and provides an introduction to the major issues that underlie these topics. The components of globalization are discussed, along with the drivers of globalization and the role of the General Agreement on Tariffs and Trade (GATT) in lowering trade barriers. The role of technological change in facilitating globalization is also discussed, along with the role of multinational firms in international business.

The chapter also describes the changing demographics of the global economy, with a special emphasis on the increasingly important role of developing countries in world trade. This discussion is complemented by a description of the changing world order, which was brought on by the collapse of communism in Eastern Europe and republics of the former Soviet Union. The chapter ends with a candid overview of the pros and cons of the trend towards globalization.

Chapter Outline With Lecture Notes and Teaching Tips

1) Introduction

    a) Globalization - Refers to the trend towards a more integrated global economic system.

    Teaching Tip: The trend towards globalization has not gone unnoticed at many premier universities around the world. An organization called the Network of International Business Schools {http://www.bibsnet.org} provides a forum for schools with international business programs to discuss their curriculums. Consider visiting this web site, and providing your students some examples of how colleges and universities are integrating the realities of globalization into their business curriculums.

    Lecture Note: The top ten trading partners for the United States, in terms of total exports, are: (1) Canada, (2) Japan, (3) Mexico, (4) China, (5) Germany, (6) United Kingdom, (7) South Korea, (8) Taiwan, (9) Singapore, and (10) France.

2) What is Globalization?

  a) The Globalization of Markets - Refers to the fact that in many industries historically distinct and separate national markets are merging into one huge global marketplace.

  b) The Globalization of Production - Refers to the tendency among many firms to source goods and services from different locations around the globe in an attempt to take advantage of national differences in the cost and quality of factors of production, thereby allowing them to compete more effectively against their rivals.

  Teaching Tip: The globalization of markets has provided many opportunities and challenges for business organizations. To gain some additional insight into the types of challenges that global firms confront, visit Danfoss Corporation's {http://www.danfoss.com/get_into/c12chan.htm} web site. At this location, the company highlights some of the challenges involved with globalization in an article entitled "Globalization and Change."

  Teaching Tip: For more in-depth information and insight about globalization, an internet site sponsored by Seattle University provides a comprehensive list of sites dedicated to all aspects of globalization. This site {http://www.seattleu.edu/~parker/homepage.html#Business} is well worth a visit.

3) Drivers of Globalization

  a) Declining Trade and Investment Barriers - Refers to the decline in barriers to the free flow of goods, services, and capital that has occurred since the end of World War II.

    i) International Trade - The exporting of goods or services to consumers in another country.

    ii) Foreign Direct Investment - The investing of resources in business activities outside a firm's home country.

    iii) General Agreement on Trade and Tariffs - Treaty designed to remove barriers to the free flow of goods, services, and capital between nations: other referred to as GATT.
    Teaching Tip: A comprehensive overview of GATT is available at {http://itl.irv.uit.no/trade_law/documents/freetrade/wta-94/nav/toc.html}.

    iv) World Trade Organization - Agency established at the Uruguay Round (of the GATT negotiations) in 1993 to police the international trading system.

  Teaching Tip: The World Trade Organization maintains an excellent web site at {http://www.wto.org/}. This site provides information about recent trade disputes and "hot" areas of international trade.

  Lecture Note: According to the WTO, the volume of world merchandise trade increased by 4 percent in 1996. A modest increase in world trade is expected in 1997. In value terms, world merchandise exports exceeded the $5,000 billion mark for the first time.

  Lecture Note: As of April 15, 1996, there were 120 members of the WTO.

  b) The Role of Technological Change - While the lowering of trade barriers made globalization of markets and production a theoretical possibility, technological change made it a tangible reality.

    i) Microprocessors and Telecommunications - Since the end of World War II, there have been major advances in communications and information processing.

      (1) Moore's Law - Predicts the power of microprocessor technology doubles and its cost of production falls in half every 18 months. As this happens, the cost of global communication plummets, which lowers the cost of coordinating and controlling a global organization.

ii) The Internet and the World Wide Web - The Internet and the World Wide Web, which have experienced explosive growth worldwide, promise to develop into the information backbone of tomorrow's global economy.

iii) Transportation Technology - In addition to these developments, several major innovations in transportation technology have occurred since World War II. In economic terms, the most important are probably development of commercial jet aircraft and superfreighters and the introduction of containerization, which greatly simplifies trans-shipment from one mode of transport to another.

4) The Changing Demographics of the Global Economy
   a) The Changing World Output and the Changing World Trade Picture
      i) Changing Role of the U.S. - In the early 1960s, the U.S. was still by far the world's dominant industrial power. In 1963, for example, the U.S. accounted for 40.3 percent of world manufacturing output. By 1995 the United States accounted for only 21.9 percent. This decline in the U.S. position was not an absolute decline, since the U.S. economy grew at a relatively robust average annual rate of 2.8 percent in the 1963-1995 period. Rather, it was a relative decline, reflecting the faster economic growth of several other economies, most notably that of Japan.

      ii) Rising Importance of Developing Countries - Given the rapid economic growth now being experienced by countries such as China, Thailand, and Indonesia, further relative decline in the U.S. share of world output and world exports seems likely.

      iii) Future Trends - If we look 20 years into the future, most forecasts now predict a rapid rise in the share of world output accounted for by developing nations such as China, India, Indonesia, Thailand, and South Korea, and a commensurate decline in the share enjoyed by rich industrialized countries such as Britain, Japan, and the United States.

   b) The Changing Foreign Investment Picture
      i) Rising Importance of Developing Countries - As depicted in Figure 1.3 in the textbook, the share of world output (or the stock of foreign direct investment) generated by developing countries has been on a steady increase since the 1960s, while the share of world output generated by rich industrial countries has been on a steady decline. This trend is expected to continue.
         (1) Stock of Foreign Direct Investment - Refers to the total cumulative value of foreign investments.
         (2) Flow of Foreign Direct Investment - Refers to amounts invested across national borders each year. Among developing nations, China has received the greatest volume of inward FDI in recent years.

   c) The Changing Nature of the Multinational Enterprise - A multinational enterprise is any business that has productive activities in two or more countries.
      i) Non-U.S. Multinationals - The globalization of the world economy, together with Japan's rise to the top rank of economic power, has resulted in a relative decline in the dominance of U.S. (and, to a lesser extent, British) firms in the global marketplace. Looking to the future, we can reasonably expect the growth of new multinational enterprises from the world's developing nations.

      ii) The Rise of Mini-Multinationals - Another trend in international business has been the growth of medium-sized and small multinationals. These businesses are referred to as mini-multinationals.

d) The Changing World Order
   i) Eastern Europe and the republics of the former Soviet Union - Between 1989 and 1991 a series of remarkable democratic revolutions swept the Communist world. For reasons that are explored in more detail in Chapter 2, in country after country throughout Eastern Europe and eventually in the Soviet Union itself, Communist governments collapsed like the shells of rotten eggs. The Soviet Union is now history, having been replaced by 15 independent republics.
   ii) Latin America - As for Latin America, both democracy and free market reforms seem to have taken hold.

5) The Globalization Debate: Prosperity or Impoverishment?
   a) Globalization, Jobs, and Incomes - Although many influential economists, politicians, and business leaders believe that globalization is a good thing, one frequently voiced concern is that far from creating jobs, removing barriers to international trade actually destroys manufacturing jobs in wealthy advanced economies such as the United States. The basic thrust of the critics' argument is that falling trade barriers allow firms to move their manufacturing activities offshore to countries where wage rates are much lower. Supporters of globalization reply that the critics that share this view miss the essential point about free trade - the benefits outweigh the costs. They argue that free trade results in countries specializing in the production of those goods and services that they can produce most efficiently, while importing goods that they cannot produce as efficiently from other countries.
   b) Globalization, Labor Policies, and the Environment - A second source of concern is that free trade encourages firms from advanced nations to move manufacturing facilities offshore to less developed countries that lack adequate regulations to protect labor and the environment from abuse by the unscrupulous. Supporters of free trade and greater globalization express serious doubts about this scenario. They point out that tougher environmental regulation and stricter labor standards go hand in hand with economic progress. In general, as countries get richer, they enact tougher environmental and labor regulations.
   c) Globalization and National Sovereignty - A final concern voiced by critics of globalization is that in today's increasingly interdependent global economy, economic power is shifting away from national governments and toward supranational organizations such as the World Trade Organization (WTO), the European Union (EU), and the United Nations. As perceived by critics, the problem is that unelected bureaucrats are now sometimes able to impose policies on the democratically elected governments of nation-states, thereby undermining the sovereignty of those states.

   Teaching Tip: There is a fascinating web site dealing with global business ethics at {http://www.globalethics.org/}. One of the ongoing features of the site is a set of "ethical dilemmas" that companies face in conducting business overseas. The current ethical dilemma deals with the ethics of paying "bribes" to get lifesaving medicine into remote areas of Bosnia. The ethical dilemmas are set up as short case studies and end with the question, "What would you do?"

6) Managing the Global Marketplace
   a) International Business - An international business is any firm that engages in international trade or investment.
   b) Managerial Challenges - As their organizations increasingly engage in cross-border trade and investment, managers need to recognize that the task of managing an international business differs from that of managing a purely domestic business in many ways.

c) Differences Between Managing International and Domestic Businesses - In sum, managing an international business is different from managing a purely domestic business for at least four reasons.

    i) Countries are different.

    ii) The range of problems confronted by a manager in an international business is wider and the problems themselves more complex than those confronted by a manager in a domestic business.

    iii) An international business must find ways to work within the limits imposed by government intervention in the international trade and investment system.

    iv) International transactions involve converting money into different currencies.

Critical Thinking and Discussion Questions

1. Describe the shifts in the world economy over the last 30 years. What are the implications of these shifts for international business in

- Britain?
- North America?
- Hong Kong?

Answer: The world economy has shifted dramatically over the past 30 years. As late as the 1960s four stylized facts described the demographics of the global economy. The first was U.S. dominance in the world economy and world trade. The second was U.S. dominance in the world foreign direct investment picture. Related to this, the third fact was the dominance of large, multinational U.S. firms in the international business scene. The fourth was that roughly half of the globe - the centrally planned economies of the Communist world - was off-limits to Western international businesses.

All of these demographic facts have changed. Although the U.S. remains the world's dominant economic power, it's share of world output and world exports have declined significantly since the 1960s. This trend does not reflect trouble in the U.S. economy, but rather reflects the growing industrialization of developing countries such as China, India, Indonesia, and South Korea. This trend is also reflected in the world foreign direct investment picture. As depicted in Figure 1.3 in the textbook, the share of world output (or the stock of foreign direct investment) generated by developing countries has been on a steady increase since the 1960s, while the share of world output generated by rich industrial countries has been on a steady decline.

Shifts in the world economy can also be seen through the shifting power of multinational enterprises. Since the 1960s, there have been two notable trends in the demographics of the multinational enterprise. The first has been the rise of non-U.S. multinationals, particularly Japanese multinationals. The second has been the emergence of a growing number of small and medium-sized multinationals, called mini-multinationals. The final shift in the world economy has been brought about by the fall of Communism in Eastern Europe and the republics of the former Soviet Union. Many of the former Communist nations of Europe and Asia seem to share a commitment to democratic politics and free market economies. Similar developments are being observed in Latin America. If these trends continue, the opportunities for international business may be enormous.

The implications of these shifts are similar for North America and Britain. The United States and Britain once had the luxury of being the dominant players in the world arena, with little substantive competition from the developing nations of the world. That has changed. Today, U.S. and British manufacturers must compete with competitors from across the world to win orders. The changing demographics of the world economy favor a city like Hong Kong. Hong Kong (which is now under Chinese rule) is well located with easy access to markets in Japan, South Korea, Indonesia, and other Asian markets. Hong Kong has a vibrant labor force that can compete on par with the industrialized nations of the world. The decline in the influence of the U.S. and Britain on the global economy provides opportunities for companies in Hong Kong to aggressively pursue export markets.

2. "The study of international business is fine if you are going to work in a large multinational enterprise, but it has no relevance for individuals who are going to work in smaller firms." Critically evaluate this statement.

    Answer: This statement does not reflect the realities of the 1990s. Small and medium-sized companies are becoming increasingly involved in international trade and investment. In addition, even if a small firm is not actively involved in international business, it may compete against foreign firms for orders in its home country. As a result, to fully understand its competition, an understanding of international business is crucial.

3. How have changes in technology contributed to the globalization of markets and of production? Would the globalization of production and markets have been possible without these technological changes?

    Answer: Changes in technology have contributed to the globalization of markets and of production in a very substantive manner. For instance, improvements in transportation technology have paved the way for companies like Coca-Cola, Levi Strauss, Sony and McDonalds to make their products available worldwide. Similarly, improvements in communications technology have had a major impact. The ability to negotiate across continents has been facilitated by improved communications technology, and the rapidly decreasing cost of communications has lowered the expense of coordinating and controlling a global corporation. Finally, the impact of information technology has been far reaching. Companies can now gain worldwide exposure simply by setting up a front-page on the World Wide Web. This technology was not available just a few short years ago.

    The globalization of production and markets may have been possible without improvements in technology, but the pace of globalization would have been much slower. The falling cost of technology has made it affordable for many developing nations, which has been instrumental in helping these nations improve their share of world output and world exports. The inclusion of these nations, such as China, India, Thailand, and South Korea, has been instrumental in the globalization of markets and production. In addition, improvements in global transportation and communication have made it relatively easy for business executives from different countries to converse with one another. If these forms of technology, such as air-travel, fax capability, e-mail, and overnight delivery of packages were not available, it would be much more difficult for businesses to conduct international trade.

4. How might the Internet and the associated World Wide Web impact international business activity and the globalization of the world economy?

Answer: According to the text, the Internet and World Wide Web (WWW) promise to develop into the information background of tomorrow's global economy. By the year 2000, it is likely that not only will voice, data, and real time video communication such as videoconferencing will be transmitted through the WWW, but also a vast array of commercial transactions. This improved technology will not only make it easier for individuals and companies in different countries to conduct business with one another, but will also further decrease the cost of communications. These improvements will undoubtedly hasten the already rapid pace of globalization.

Another distinct attribute of the Internet and the WWW is that they act as an equalizer between large (resource rich) and small (resource poor) firms. For instance, it does not cost any more for a small software firm to gain visibility via the WWW than it does for a large software company like Microsoft. As a result, the WWW helps small companies reach the size of audience that was previously only within the reach of large, resource rich firms.

5. If current trends continue, China may emerge as the world's largest economy by 2020. Discuss the possible implications of such a development for:

- The world trading system.
- The world monetary system.
- The business strategy of today's European and U.S. based global corporations.

Answer: This question is intended to stimulate classroom discussion. Obviously, if China becomes the world's largest economy by the year 2020, much more international trade will have to be conducted on terms that are favorable to the Chinese. This will require adjustments in the world trading system and the world monetary system to facilitate an increasingly amount of trade that is conducted in Chinese currency. The business strategies of today's European and U.S. based global companies will also have to change to meet the challenge. For instance, more joint-ventures and strategic alliances between U.S. and European firms may have to be developed to achieve the economies of scale and the market prowess of Chinese competitors.

6. "Ultimately, the study of international business is no different from the study of domestic business. Thus, there is no point in having a separate course on international business." Evaluate this statement.

Answer: This statement reflects a poor understanding of the unique challenges involved in international business. Managing an international business is different from managing a purely domestic business for at least four reasons. These are: (1) countries are different; (2) the range of problems confronted by a manager in an international business is wider and the problems themselves more complex than those confronted by a manager in a domestic business; (3) an international business must find ways to work within the limits imposed by government intervention in the international trade and investment system; and (4) international transactions involve converting money into different currencies.

As a result of these differences, there are ample reasons for studying international business as a specific field of study or discipline.

Case Discussion Questions

1. How has Kodak helped to create a competitor in Fuji Photo Film?

   Answer: Kodak helped create a competitor in Fuji Photo Film in two ways. First, by pulling out of the Japanese market at the end of World War II, Kodak left a void in the Japanese market that needed to be filled. That void was filled by Fuji. Second, Kodak sold to Fuji the technology that Fuji needed to become a world-class photo company. That not only helped Fuji compete against Kodak in Japan, but has helped Fuji compete worldwide.

2. What critical catalyst led Kodak to start taking the Japanese market seriously?

   Answer: In the early 1980s, Fuji launched an aggressive export drive, attacking Kodak in the North American and European markets where for decades Kodak had enjoyed a lucrative dominance in color film. Fuji's onslaught was very damaging to Kodak, and the company retaliated by attacking Japan in its home market.

3. What have been the keys to Kodak's post-1984 success in Japan?

   Answer: There have been two key factors that have contributed to Kodak's post-1984 success in Japan. First, the company has taken steps to control its own distribution and marketing channels, which is extremely important when doing business in Japan. This step was achieved in part through a join venture with a Japanese firm. Second, Kodak came to the realization that to do business in Japan, it needed to think and act like a Japanese company. As a result, the majority of Kodak's employees in Japan are Japanese.

4. From the evidence given in the case, do you think that Kodak's charges of unfair trading practices against Fuji are valid, or are they simply a case of the kettle calling the pot black?

   Answer: This question is designed to stimulate class discussion. From the information provided in the case, it sounds like Kodak may be pressing its case a little to far, which may be why the U.S. government is not being more aggressive in arguing on Kodak's behalf.

Internet Exercise

1) Summary:
   a) The Internet Exercise showcases several of the companies that are mentioned in Chapter 1, and briefly explains how these companies use the Internet to demonstrate the extent of their global operations.

2) Additional Material:
   a) Internet sites serve many purposes, one of which is to showcase a company's global operations as mentioned above. In a deeper sense, however, Internet sites directly contribute to both the globalization of markets and the globalization of production.
      i) Globalization of markets – Companies have facilitated the convergence of tastes worldwide through appealing web sites that are easily accessed by people from all corners of the globe. For example, the following is a sample of the sites that are dedicated to Coca Cola products.

8

These sites and others help create a worldwide appeal for Coke products, which facilitates the globalization of the soft drink market.

(1) Coca-Cola Collections of Singapore {hppt://www.cyberway.com.sg/~bnguang/}.

(2) Coke Bottles of the World {http://pl8s.com/coke.htm}

(3) The Official Belgian Coca Cola Page {http://www.cocacola.be/}

(4) Coca Cola Japan {http://www.cocacola.co.ip/}.

Opening Case: Citicorp – Building a Global Growth Company

1) Summary:

   a) This feature describes the efforts of Citicorp to become a global banking company. Citibank believes that the global demographic, economic, and political forces strongly favor global banking. As a result, the company has taken decisive steps to become a global banking company. It has standardized its products and services, which provides its customers the same retail experience everywhere in the world. In addition, the company has standardized many of its processes, which has resulted in a reduction in operating costs. Today, Citibank services over 20,000 corporations in 75 emerging economies and 22 developed economies, and over 50 million individuals in 56 countries.

2) Suggested Discussion Questions:

   a) According to the case, Citibank believes that "global, demographic, economic, and political forces strongly favor such a strategy" (i.e. providing standardized services to customers around the globe). What is the underlying logic behind this statement? In what way do global, demographic, economic, and political forces presently support the notion of global banking?

   b) What specific steps has Citibank taken to make global banking a reality? Could Citibank have achieved its current status without having taken these steps?

   c) Visit Citibank's home page on the World Wide Web (address shown below). Does Citibank's web site convey the sense that Citibank is a global banking corporation? Explain your answer.

3) Citibank Homepage: {http://www.citibank.com}.

Management Focus: Getting the World Hooked on Fish and Chips

1) Summary:

   a) This feature describes Harry Ramsden's early experiences in international business. Harry Ramsden's, which is a chain of English Fish and Clip restaurants, decided to build on its domestic success by opening a restaurant in Hong Kong. The Hong Kong restaurant was a hit, prompting the company to pilot test a restaurant in Japan. Today, Harry Ramsden's is proceeding by investigating additional international opportunities. The owners are moving forward cautiously, with the goal in mind of making harry Ramsden's a "global brand?"

2) Suggested Discussion Questions:

   a) What would be a good "next step" for Harry Ramsden's? How should the managers of the company proceed in their efforts to make Harry Ramsden's a global brand.

   b) Do you believe that global demographic, economic, and political forces support the notion of a global restaurant chain? If so, why?

   c) Is it wise for harry Ramsden's to proceed cautiously, or should the company be more aggressive in its efforts to internationalize?

3) Hary Ramsden's Homepage: {http://www.harryramsdens.co.uk/}.

Country Focus: South Korea's New Multinationals

1) Summary:
   a) This feature discusses the historical and present status of South Korean chaebols. A chaebol is a diversified business group. Historically, South Korea's chaebols took advantage of low labor costs to export a wide range of goods to industrialized countries. In recent years, however, the costs of both land and labor in South Korea have risen sharply, nullifying important sources of the chaebol's competitive advantage in the global economy. The chaebols have responded to rising costs at home by expanding overseas, establishing factories in countries where direct labor costs are lower and employee productivity is higher than in South Korea.

2) Suggested Discussion Questions:
   a) The South Korean chaebols have responded to rising costs at home by expanding overseas into countries where direct labor costs are lower and employee productivity is higher than in South Korea. In your opinion is this a good strategy? Why or why not?
   b) Speculate on how globalization has affected the competitiveness of South Korean chaebols? What should the chaebols do to take advantage of the trend towards globalization?

3) Examples of South Korean chaebols:
   a) Samsung Homepage: {http://www.samsung.com/}.
   b) Hyundai Homepage: {http://www.hmc.co.kr/}.

Management Focus: Procter & Gamble in Japan

1) Summary:
   a) This feature depicts Procter & Gamble's (P&G) experiences in the Japanese market. P&G entered Japan in 1972, and had some early successes. For example, P&G introduced disposable diapers in Japan, and at one point commanded an 80 percent share of the market. P&G's success in Japan soon waned, however, largely as a result of the company's failure to customize its products to suite the tastes of Japanese consumers. Today, P&G is attempting to correct that problem and has started to appoint local nations to key management positions in its Japanese subsidiaries.

2) Suggested Discussion Questions:
   a) When is it appropriate to "standardize" products and when is it appropriate to "customize" products when selling in a foreign market? Earlier, we read about Citibank's efforts to establish a global bank by "standardizing" its products and services worldwide. Why wouldn't this approach work for P&G in Japan, and other parts of the world?
   b) What lessons do we learn from P&G's experiences in Japan? If you were a manager for P&G and you were entering the South Korean market for the first time, briefly explain how you would approach that market.
   c) Think of examples of foreign companies that sell products in the United States. Do any of these companies "customize" their products to suite the tastes of American consumers? If so, is this a vital part of their American strategy?

3) Web sites:
   a) Procter & Gamble Homepage: {http://www.pg.com/}
   b) Procter & Gamble in Asia: {http://www.pg.com/docAsiacareers/business/index.html}.

CHAPTER 2
DIFFERENCES IN POLITICAL ECONOMY

Learning Objectives

1. Understand how the political systems of countries differ.

2. Understand how the economic systems of countries differ.

3. Understand how the legal systems of countries differ.

4. Understand how political, economic, and legal systems collectively influence a country's ability to achieve meaningful economic progress.

5. Be familiar with the main changes that are currently reshaping the political, economic, and legal systems of many nation-states.

6. Appreciate how a country's political, economic, and legal systems influence the benefits, costs, and risks associated with doing business in that country.

7. Be conversant with the ethical issues that can arise when doing business in a nation whose political and legal system are not supportive of basic human rights.

Chapter Summary

This chapter focuses on how political, economic, and legal systems collectively influence a country's ability to achieve meaningful economic progress. The first half of the chapter focuses on the different political, economic, and legal systems that are influential in the world. It is made clear to the reader that these differences are significant, and must be clearly understood by the managers of international firms. The section that focuses on legal systems includes a discussion of intellectual property, including patents, copyrights, and trademarks. Protecting intellectual property is a particularly problematic issue in international trade.

The second half of the chapter focuses on the determinants of economic development. The author makes the point that a country's political, economic, and legal systems have a direct impact on it's economic potential. The importance of innovation, along with the types of systems that facilitate innovation, is discussed. Next, the author discusses the parts of the world that are transition from one political-economic ideology to another. Finally, the chapter ends with a brief discussion of ethical issues.

Chapter Outline With Lecture Notes and Teaching Tips

1) Introduction - Different countries have different political systems, economic systems, and legal systems. Cultural practices can vary dramatically from country to country, as can the education and skill level of the population. All of these differences have major implications for the practice of international business.

   a) Focus of Chapter - In this chapter we focus our attention on how the political, economic, and legal systems of countries differ.

      i) Political Economy - Political, economic, and legal system of a country.

2) Political Systems - By political system we mean the system of government in a nation. Political systems can be assessed according to two related dimensions. The first is the degree to which they emphasize collectivism as opposed to individualism. The second dimension is the degree to which they are democratic or totalitarian.

   a) Collectivism and Individualism

      i) Socialism (i.e. collectivism) - Political system that stresses the primacy of collective goals over individual goals. Socialists trace their intellectual roots to Karl Marx (1818-1883).

         (1) Communists - Followers of socialist ideology who believe that socialism can be achieved only through violent revolution and totalitarian dictatorship.

         (2) Social Democrats - Followers of socialist ideology who commit themselves to achieving socialism through democratic means.

      ii) Individualism - Political philosophy that an individual should have freedom over his or her economic and political pursuits. In contrast to collectivism, individualism stresses that the interests of the individual should take precedence over the interests of the state.

         (1) Two Central Tents of Individualism:

            (a) An emphasis on the importance of guaranteeing individual freedom and self-expression.

            (b) The welfare of society is best served by letting people pursue their own economic self-interest. In practical terms, individualism translates into an advocacy for democratic political systems and free market economies.

   b) Democracy and Totalitarianism - Democracy and totalitarianism are at different ends of a political dimension.

      i) Democracy - Refers to a political system in which government is by the people, exercised either directly or through elected representatives.

         (1) Representative Democracy - Political system in which citizens periodically elect individuals to represent them.

      ii) Totalitarianism - Is a form of government in which one person or political party exercises absolute control over all spheres of human life, and opposing political parties are prohibited. There are four major forms of totalitarianism in the world today.

         (1) Communist Totalitarianism - Form of totalitarianism that advocates achieving socialism through totalitarian dictatorship.

         (2) Theocratic Totalitarianism - Form of totalitarianism in which political power is monopolized by a party, group, or individual that governs according to religious principles.

         (3) Tribal Totalitarianism - Form of totalitarianism found mainly in Africa in which a political party that represents the interests of a particular tribe monopolizes power.

         (4) Right Wing Totalitarianism - Form of totalitarianism in which individual economic freedom is allowed but individual political freedom is restricted in the belief that it could lead to communism.

3) Economic Systems

   a) Market Economy - Economic system in which the interaction of supply and demand determines the quantity in which goods and services are provided.

   b) Command Economy - Economic system in which the goods and services produced, the quantity in which they are produced, and the government plans all the prices at which they are sold.

c) Mixed Economy - Between market economies and command economies can be found mixed economies. In a mixed economy certain sectors of the economy are left to private ownership and free market mechanisms, while in other sectors there is significant state ownership and government planning. Mixed economies are relatively common among the states of Western Europe, although they are becoming less so.

4) Legal System - The legal system of a country refers to the rules, or laws, that regulate behavior, along with the processes by which the laws of a country are enforced and through which redress for grievances is obtained. The legal system of a country is of immense importance to international business.
Teaching Tip: The Seamless Website is the name of a site that contains a broad base of information about international law and the legal systems of the countries of the world. This site is available at {http://msm.byu.edu/c&i/cim/ibd/Dir.htm}.

a) Property Rights - Refer to the bundle of legal rights over the use to which a resource is put and over the use made of any income that may be derived from that resource. Countries differ significantly in the extent to which their legal system protects property rights.

   i) Private Action - Refers to theft, piracy, blackmail, and the like by private individuals and groups. While theft occurs in all countries, in some countries a weak legal system allows for a much higher level of criminal action than in others.

   ii) Public Action - Public action to violate property rights occurs when public officials, such as politicians and government bureaucrats, extort income or resources from property owners.

b) The Protection of Intellectual Property - Refers to property, such as computer software, a screenplay, or the chemical formula for a new drug, that is the product of intellectual activity. The protection of intellectual property rights differs greatly from country to country. While many countries have stringent intellectual property regulations on their books, the enforcement of these regulations has often been lax. In addition to lobbying their governments, firms may want to stay out of countries where intellectual property laws are lax rather than risk having their ideas stolen by local entrepreneurs (such reasons partly underlay decisions by Coca-Cola and IBM to pull out of India in the early 1970s).
Lecture Note: In 1947, Intellectual Property comprised just under 10% of all U.S. exports. In 1986, the last year the government compiled statistics in this area, the figure had grown to more than 37% (U.S. Dept. of Commerce). Today, some estimates place the figure at over 50% of all exports.
Teaching Tip: A summary of U.S. Trademark law, which may be interesting to your students, can be found at {http://www.law.cornell.edu/topics/trademark.html}.

   i) Patent - Document giving the inventor of a new product or process exclusive rights to the manufacture, use, or sale of that invention.

   ii) Copyright - Exclusive legal rights of authors, composers, playwrights, artists, and publishers to publish and dispose of their work as they see fit.

   iii) Trademark - Designs and names, often officially registered, by which merchants or manufacturers designate and differentiate their products.

   iv) Paris Convention for the Protection of Industrial Property - International agreement signed by 96 countries to protect intellectual property rights.
   Teaching Tip: An excellent article on the protection of intellectual property is available on the Internet at {http://www.journal.law.ufl.edu/~techlaw/1/gikkas.html}. This site contains a copy of an article entitled "International Licensing of Intellectual Property: The Promise and the Peril." The article, written by Nicholas S. Gikkas and published in the Journal of Technology

Law and Policy (Vol. 6, 1996), examines the history, rationale, benefits, and dangers of international trademark licensing with consideration given to the hazards involved.

c) Product Safety and Product Liability - Product safety laws set certain safety standards to which a product must adhere. The competitiveness issue apart, country differences in product safety and liability laws raise an important ethical issue for firms doing business abroad.

d) Contract Law - A contract is a document that specifies the conditions under which an exchange is to occur, and details the rights and obligations of the parties to a contract. Contract law can differ significantly among countries, and as such it affects the kind of contracts that an international business will want to use to safeguard its position should a contract dispute arise. The main differences can be traced to differences in legal tradition.

    i) Common Law System - Legal system based on tradition, precedent, and custom that evolved in England over hundreds of years and is now found in Britain's former colonies, including the United States.

    ii) Civil Law System - Legal system based on a detailed set of laws, organized into codes, that is used in more than 80 countries, including Germany, France, Japan, and Russia.

5) The Determinants of Economic Development - One reason for looking at the different political, economic, and legal systems in the world is that collectively these different systems can have a profound impact on the level of a country's economic development, and hence on the attractiveness of a country as a possible market and/or production location for a firm.

a) Differences in Economic Development - Different countries have dramatically different levels of economic development.

    i) Human Development Index - United Nations-developed index based on life expectancy, literacy rates, and whether average incomes are sufficient to meet the basic needs of life in a country.

b) Political Economy and Economic Progress - What is the relationship between political economy and economic progress? This question has been the subject of a vigorous debate among academics and policy makers for some time.

    i) Innovation Is the Engine of Growth - Innovation is the process through which people create new products, new processes, new organizations, new management practices, and new strategies. There is broad agreement that innovation is the engine of long-run economic growth.

    ii) Innovation Requires a Market Economy - It has been argued that the economic freedom associated with a market economy creates greater incentives for innovation than either a planned or mixed economy.

    (1) Privatization - Process of selling state-owned enterprises to private investors.

    iii) Innovation Requires Strong Property Rights - Strong legal protection of property rights is another requirement for a business environment conducive to innovation and economic growth.

    iv) The Required Political System - In the West, we tend to argue that democracy is good for economic growth. However, there are examples of totalitarian regimes that have fostered a market economy and strong property rights protection and experienced rapid economic growth. However, given all the facts, it seems likely that democratic regimes are far more conducive to long-term economic growth than a dictatorship, even one of the benevolent kind.

    v) Economic Progress Begets Democracy - While it is possible to argue that democracy is not a necessary precondition for the establishment of a free market economy in which property rights are protected, it seems evident that subsequent economic growth leads to establishment of democratic regimes.

6) States in Transition

   a) Eastern Europe and the Former Soviet Union - The post-Communist history of this region has not been easy. A recent study by the World Bank suggests the post-Communist states that have been most successful at transforming their economies were those that followed an economic policy best described as "shock therapy." (i.e. tight monetary policy and the privatization of state-owned industries)

   b) Western Europe - In Western Europe, there is a continual move towards privatizing state owned enterprises.

   c) Asia - During the 1980s and early 1990s significant changes were also occurring in Asia. A shift toward greater political democracy occurred in the Philippines, Thailand, Taiwan, and South Korea. *Teaching Tip:* MITI is the acronym for the Ministry of International Trade and Industry, a very powerful governmental agency in Japan. MITI promotes Japanese industry in a number of ways. MITI maintains a web site at {http://www.miti.go.ip/index-e.html}.

   d) Latin America - Latin America, too, shifted toward greater democracy and a greater commitment to free market economies during the late 1980s and early 1990s. The largest shift occurred in 1989 when Mexico, then run by the civilian government of President Salinas, moved toward a more free market economy.

   e) Africa - Africa is also moving toward more democratic modes of government and free market economies.
   Teaching Tip: A number of countries and regions maintain an international "Chamber of Commerce" to disseminate current information about their respective country or regional of the world. These Chambers of Commerce are an excellent "first stop" when conducting research on the market potential of a particular country or area. An index of the Chambers of Commerce available on the Internet can be accessed at {http://www.serraintl.com//morelink2.html#cofc}.
   Teaching Tip: The U.S. State Department produces a series of annual "Country Reports" to acquaint American businesses with other countries. Each report contains nine sections: (1) Key Economic Indicators; (2) General Policy Framework; (3) Exchange Rate Policies; (4) Structural Policies; (5) Debt Management Practices; (6) Significant Barriers to US Exports and Investments; (7) Export Subsidies Policies; (8) Protection of US Intellectual Property; and (9) Worker Rights. Information about obtaining these reports is available through the United States Stated Dept. at {http://www.state.gov/www/issues/economic/trade_reports/96_toc.html}.

7) Implications for Business

   a) Attractiveness - The overall attractiveness of a country as a market and/or investment site depends on balancing the likely long-term benefits of doing business in that country against the likely costs and risks. Next, the text covers the determinants of benefits, costs, and risks.

      i) Benefits - In the most general sense the long-run monetary benefits of doing business in a country are a function of the size of a market, the present wealth (purchasing power) of consumers in that market, and the likely future wealth of consumers.

         (1) First-mover Advantages - Advantages that accrue to early entrants into a business market.

         (2) Late-mover Advantages - Handicap suffered by late entrants into a business market.

      ii) Costs - The costs of doing business in a country are determined by a number of political, economic, and legal factors.

iii) Risks - As with costs, the risks of doing business in a country are determined by a number of political, economic, and legal factors.

    (1) Political Risk - Likelihood that political forces will cause drastic changes in a country's business environment that adversely affect the profit and other goals of a business enterprise.

    (2) Economic Risk - Likelihood that economic mismanagement will cause drastic changes in a country's business environment that adversely affect the profit and other goals of a business enterprise.

    (3) Legal Risk - Likelihood that a trading partner will opportunistically break a contract or expropriate property rights.

iv) Overall Attractiveness - The overall attractiveness of a country as a potential market and/or investment site for an international business depends on balancing the benefits, costs, and risks associated with doing business in that country.

b) Ethical Issues - Country differences give rise to some interesting and contentious ethical issues. One major ethical dilemma facing firms from Western democracies is whether they should do business in totalitarian countries that routinely violate the human rights of their citizens.

Teaching Tip: The Carnegie Council on Ethics and International Affairs maintains a very substantive and thought-provoking website at {http://www.cceia.org/}. This site contains publications that comments on many of the ethical issues that surround globalization and international business.

i) Foreign Corrupt Practices Act - U.S. law enacted in 1977 that prohibits U.S. companies from making "corrupt" payments to foreign officials for the purpose of obtaining or retaining business.

Critical Thinking and Discussion Questions

1. Free market economies stimulate greater economic growth, whereas command economies stifle growth. Discuss.

Answer: In a market economy, private individuals and corporations are allowed to own property and other assets. This right of ownership provides a powerful incentive for people to work hard, introduce new products, develop better advertising campaigns, invent new products, etc., all in the hopes of accumulating additional personal capital and wealth. In turn, the constant search on the part of individuals and corporation to accumulate wealth enriches the entire economy and creates economic growth.

In contrast, in a command economy, private individuals and corporations are not allowed to own substantial quantities of property and other assets. The objective of a command economy is for everyone to work for "the good of the society." Although this sounds like a noble ideal, a system that asks individuals to work for the good of society rather than allowing individuals to build personal wealth does not provide a great incentive for people to invent new products, develop better advertising campaigns, find ways to be more efficient, etc. As a result, command economies typically generate less innovation and are less efficient than market economies.

2. A democratic political system is an essential condition for sustained economic progress. Discuss.

Answer: This question has no clear-cut answer. In the West, we tend to argue that democracy is good for economic progress. This argument is largely predicted upon the idea that innovation is the engine of economic growth, and a democratic political system encourages rather than stifles innovation.

However, there are examples of totalitarian regimes that have fostered a market economy and strong property rights protection and experienced rapid economic growth. The examples include four of the fastest growing economies of the past 30 years – South Korea, Taiwan, Singapore, and Hong Kong – all of which have grown faster than Western economies. However, while it is possible to argue that democracy is not a necessary precondition for the establishment of a free market economy, it seems evident that subsequent economic growth leads to establishment of democratic regimes. Several of the fastest-growing Asian economies have recently adopted more democratic governments.

3. During the late 1980s and early 1990s, China was routinely cited by various international organizations such as Amnesty International and Freedom Watch for major human rights violations, including torture, beatings, imprisonment, and executions of political dissidents. Despite this, in the mid-1990s China was the recipient of record levels of foreign direct investment, mainly from firms based in democratic societies such as the United States, Japan, and Germany. Evaluate this trend from an ethical perspective. If you were the CEO of a firm that had the option of making a potentially very profitable investment in China, what would you do?

Answer: This question is designed to stimulate classroom discussion and/or encourage your students to "think" about this difficult issue in preparing a written answer. There are two ways to approach this issue. One school of thought argues that investing in China strengthens the current political regime, and will in the end help perpetuate the abuses mentioned in the question. Moreover, the people that subscribe to this school of thought argue that without foreign investment, the Chinese government will eventually fall (due to poor economic conditions) and be replaced by a more democratic set of leaders.

In contrast, a second school of thought argues that by investing in China, the Chinese economy will be strengthened and a strong economy will encourage political reforms. People that champion this point of view go on to say that China can only be changed from within, and that political reforms have the best chance of happening if the country is economically strong rather than economically weak.

Both of these schools of thought have merit. As a result, a firm must decided for itself whether it will or will not pursue business opportunities in China.

4. You are the CEO of a company that has to choose between making a $100 million investment in either Russia or the Czech Republic. Both investments promise the same long-run return, so your choice of which investment to make is driven by considerations of risk. Assess the various risks of doing business in each of these nations. Which investment would you favor and why?

Answer: I would invest in the Czech Republic rather than Russia. The overall attractiveness of a country as a potential investment site depends on a balance of the benefits, costs, and risks associated with doing business in that country. Today, the political stability of Russia is tenuous. Economically, Russia has not fared well since it broke away from the former Soviet Union. In 1993, the inflation rate was 841 percent. In addition, the graph in Figure 2.4 shows that the real percentage GDP growth for 1990-1994 in Russia has fluctuated some but in general has declined. As a result of these factors, Russia is not a hospitable site for foreign investment. The Czech Republic has faired better. It seems to be more stable politically than Russia. Its economy is growing and the inflation rate is relatively low, making it a more attractive investment site. The graph in Figure 2.4 shows a steady increase in the Czech Republic's GDP, compared to Russia's poorer performance.

Case Discussion Questions

1. What is the exact nature of the problems encountered by Trinity Motors in Russia? Are these problems due to deficiencies in Russia's political system, economic system, or legal system? What

will it take to correct these problems?

Answer: The problems depicted in the case stem from Russia's political system, economic system, and legal system. The political system has been compromised by state bureaucrats that take bribes. The economic system is hurting the country's efforts towards achieving economic growth by placing steep duties on imports, thus restricting free trade. The economic system is also apparently unable to control the appropriateness of the products that are imported into the country (e.g. GM cars imported into Russia by the Mafia aren't those designed for the Russian market). Finally, the legal system is not able to protect expatriate managers (i.e. Mark will only travel with a body guard) and is apparently unable to rid the country of pervasive organized crime.

The best vehicle for correcting these difficult problems is meaningful economic reform and economic growth. As the public becomes more economically secure, it will demand political and legal reforms.

2. Until the problems that Trinity is facing are corrected, how should Mark Thimming deal with them?

Answer: He should proceed in the manner that he has. From the case, we get the indication that Mark is trying to run a good, ethical businesses in the midst of the corruption that is so pervasive all around him. If Mark establishes a reputation for being fair, honest, and trustworthy, perhaps those attributes will be rewarded when economic reform is realized in Russia and more people have the financially ability to purchase a car.

3. Does it make sense for Trinity to tough it out in Russia until the current problems are revolved?

Answer: Probably. If Mark is willing to submit to the personal and financial risks of doing business in Russia, he may be rewarded handsomely for his efforts when economic reforms are finally realized. Based on the information provided in the case, however, this may take a substantial amount of time to accomplish.

4. How long do you think it will be before Russia resembles a stable Western democracy?

Answer: This question is designed to stimulate classroom discussion and/or encourage your students to "think" about this difficult question in preparing a written response. It is clear that Russia will not resemble a stable Western democracy anytime in the near future. How long it will take, if ever, is a matter of personal speculation.

Internet Exercise

1) Summary:
   a) The feature discusses the international problem of software pirating. According to the Software Publishers Association, which is an international software trade group, practically one-half of all business software in the world is pirated. The feature provides several Internet site addresses that address this difficult issue. The exercise portion of the features asks the reader to research the SPA and BSA Internet sites, and describe the similarities and differences in their anti-piracy policies.
2) Addition Material:

a) For individuals with a particular interest in business ethics Business Ethics Magazine, formally available only in hard copy, has just gone online. Selected articles each month will be offered online at {http://condor.depaul.edu/ethics/bizethics.html}.

Opening Case: General Electric in Hungry

1) Summary:

a) This case recaps General Electric's experiences as the majority owner of Tungsram, a Hungarian manufacturer of lighting products. In the heady days of late 1989 when Communist regimes were disintegrating across Eastern Europe, the GE company launched a major expansion into Hungary with the $150 million acquisition of a 51 percent interest in Tungsram. GE was attracted to Tungsram by Hungary's low wage rate and by the possibility of using the company to export lighting products to Western Europe. The majority of the case focuses on GE's disappointments with the Tungsram acquisition. GE's ambitious plans and corporate ideology have clashed with Tungsram's imbedded culture of waste, inefficiency, and indifference about customer service and quality. In retrospect, GE has admitted that the company underestimated how long it would take to turn Tungsran around and how much money it would cost. GE believes that it has now turned the corner, but getting there has been a painful experience for all parties involved.

2) Suggested Discussion Questions:

a) Was General Electric naïve in thinking that it could turn Tungsram around quickly? What could GE have done prior to the acquisition to get a better idea of how long it would take to revitalize Tungsram?

b) If a country switches from a command economy to a market economy as a result of abrupt political reforms, does that mean that the average worker in the country has changed his or her attitudes towards work? Does GE's experiences in Hungary provide us insight into how to answer this question? Why or why not?

c) What can other companies that are thinking about investing in Eastern Europe or the republics of the former Soviet Union learn from GE's experience? Make your answer as substantive as possible.

Management Focus: Microsoft Battles Software Piracy in China

1) Summary:

a) This feature focuses on Microsoft's entry into the Chinese software market and, in particular, Microsoft's frustrations with software piracy in China. In 1995, over 90 percent of the software used in China was pirated. Microsoft is a prime target of this activity. Most Microsoft products used in China are illegal copies made and then sold with no payment to Microsoft. Incredibly, one of the biggest offenders is the Chinese government itself. Not only does the government use pirated software in its offices, but has been reluctant until recently to enforce its own intellectual property rights laws. Fortunately, for Microsoft, the situation may be improving. The United States government has gone to bat for Microsoft and has made inroads in pressuring the Chinese government to create a more equitable environment for Microsoft in China.

2) Suggested Discussion Questions:

a) What is "intellectual property?" What can companies do to help protect the intellectual property of their products and services in foreign markets?

b) Discuss Microsoft's efforts to deal with software piracy in China. Has Microsoft done all that it can do? Do you believe that Microsoft's recent initiative to work with the Chinese Ministry of Electronics to create a Chinese version of the Windows 95 operating system is a good move? Why or why not?

19

c) In your opinion, will Microsoft's frustrations with software piracy in China be satisfactorily resolved in the near future? Explain your answer.

3) Microsoft Homepage: {http://www.microsoft.com/}

Country Focus: The Changing Political Economy of India

1) Summary:

    a) This features focuses on the evolution of India's economic system from 1947 to today. After gaining independence from Britain in 1947, India adopted a democratic system of government. However, the economic system that developed in India was a mixed economy characterized by a heavy dose of state enterprise and planning. The feature discusses many of the attributes of India's mixed economy, such as high tariffs, limited foreign direct investment, and an oppressive bureaucracy. Under this system, the Indian people did poorly. Fortunately, in 1991 the government of Prime Minister P.V. Narasimha Rao embarked on an ambitious economic reform program. The results have been impressive. India's economy is now expanding, and much of the bureaucratic red tape that inhibited business growth is gone.

2) Suggested Discussion Questions:

    a) Explain what is meant by the term "mixed economy." Does a mixed economy inhibit business growth? Explain your answer.

    b) How long do you believe that it will take for India to have a market economy that resembles those found in Western Europe and North America? Describe the benefits of a market economy. Will India's movement towards a market economy help or hurt its globalization efforts?

    c) When India does establish a genuine market economy, do you believe that the companies that have had bad experiences in India (e.g. IBA, Coca-Cola, and Mobile) will come back? Why or why not?

3) Additional Information About India: The following web sites provide additional information about India's economic progress:

    a) Links to Sites Focused On India's Economy: {http://webhead.com/WWWVL/India/india205.html}

    b) The Indian Economy Overview: {http://www.m-web.com/ieoindex.html}.

    c) All About India: {http://www.indiaintl.com/about.html}.

CHAPTER 3
DIFFERENCES IN CULTURE

Learning Objectives

1. Understand that substantial differences among societies arise from cultural differences.

2. Know what is meant by the term culture.

3. Appreciate that culture is different because of differences in social structure, religion, language, education, economic philosophy, and political philosophy.

4. Understand the relationship between culture and the values found in the workplace.

5. Appreciate that culture is not a constant, but changes over time.

6. Appreciate that much of the change in contemporary social culture is being driven by economic advancement, technological change, and globalization.

7. Understand the implications for international business management of differences in culture.

Chapter Summary

This chapter begins by introducing the concept of culture. The determinants of culture are identified, which include religion, political philosophy, economic philosophy, education, language, and social structure. The first half of the chapter focuses on the influence of social structure, religion, language, and education on culture. The section on religion is very thorough, and explains the economic implications of Christianity, Islam, Hinduism, Buddhism, and Confucianism.

Geert Hofstede's model of how a society's culture impacts the values found in the workplace is presented. According to Hofstede, cultures vary along the lines of power distance, individualism versus collectivism, uncertainty avoidance, and masculinity versus femininity. The concept of ethnocentric behavior is introduced. Finally, the author reiterates the point that the value systems and norms of a country influence the costs of doing business in that country.

Chapter Outline With Lecture Notes and Teaching Tips

1) Introduction - Two themes run through this chapter. The first theme is that operating a successful international business requires cross-cultural literacy. The second theme is that a relationship may exist between culture and the costs of doing business in a country or region.

2) What is Culture - Culture is a system of values and norms that are shared among a group of people and that when taken together constitute a design for living.

   a) Value and Norms - Values are abstract ideas about what a group believes to be good, right, and desirable, and form the bedrock of a culture. They provide the context within which a society's norms are established and justified. Norms are the social rules that govern the actions of people toward one another. Norms can be subdivided further into two major categories:

   i) Folkways - The routine conventions of everyday life.

   ii) Mores - Norms that are seen as central to the functioning of a society and to its social life.

b) Culture, Society, and the Nation-State - We have defined a society as a group of people that share a common set of values and norms; that is, a group bound together by a common culture. But there is not a strict one-to-one correspondence between a society and a nation-state. Nation-states are political creations. They may contain a single culture or several distinct cultures.

c) The Determinants of Culture - The values and norms of a culture do not emerge from nowhere fully formed. They are the evolutionary product of a number of factors at work in a society.

3) Social Structure - A society's social structure refers to its basic social organization. Two dimensions stand out when explaining differences between cultures. The first is the degree to which the basic unit of social organization is the individual, as opposed to the group. The second dimension is the degree to which a society is stratified into classes or castes.

a) Individuals and Groups - A group is an association of two or more individuals who have a shared sense of identity and who interact with each other in structured ways on the basis of a common set of expectations about each other's behavior.

i) The Individual - In many Western societies the individual is the basic building block of social organization.

ii) The Group - In contrast to the Western emphasis on the individual, in many other societies the group is the primary unit of social organization. In Japan, for example, the social status of an individual is determined as much by the standing of the group to which he or she belongs as by his or her individual performance.

b) Social Stratification - All societies are stratified on a hierarchical basis into social categories, or social strata.

i) Social Mobility - Extent to which individuals can move out of the strata into which they are born.

(1) Caste System - Closed system of stratification in which social position is determined by the family into which a person is born, and change in that position is usually not possible during an individual's lifetime.

(2) Class System - Form of open social stratification in which the position a person has by birth can be changed through his or her achievement or luck.

ii) Significance - From a business perspective the stratification of a society is significant insofar as it affects the operation of the business organization.

(1) Class consciousness - Refers to a condition where people perceive themselves in terns of their class background, and this shapes their relationships with members of other classes.

4) Religion - May be defined as a system of shared beliefs and rituals that are concerned with the realm of the sacred. While there are thousands of different religions in the world, five dominate: Christianity, Islam, Hinduism, Buddhism, and Confucianism.
Teaching Tip: Duke University's Department of Religion sponsors a web site that offers links to and brief descriptions of four of the most comprehensive sites for religion on the Internet. These are excellent sites that provide a broad array of information to augment the information about religion provided in the textbook. The site is available at {http://www.duke.edu/web/CIS/}.

a) Christianity - Is the most widely practiced religion in the world.

i) Economic Implication of Christianity: The Protestant Work Ethic - In 1904 a German sociologist, Max Weber, made a connection between Protestant ethics and "the spirit of capitalism."

b) Islam - Islam is the second largest of the world's major religions.

i) Islamic Fundamentalism - The past two decades have witnessed a surge in Islamic fundamentalism. Fundamentalists demand a rigid commitment to religious beliefs and rituals.

ii) Economic Implications of Islam - In general, Islamic countries are likely to be receptive to international businesses as long as those businesses behave in a manner that is consistent with Islamic ethics.

c) Hinduism - Hinduism has approximately 500 million adherents, most of whom are to be found on the Indian subcontinent.

i) Economic Implications of Hinduism - Max Weber, who is famous for expounding on the Protestant work ethic, also argued that whatever its spiritual merits, the ascetic principles embedded in Hinduism do not encourage the kind of entrepreneurial activity that we find in Protestantism.

d) Buddhism - Buddhism was founded in India in the sixth century BC. Because Buddhists, like Hindus, stress spiritual achievement rather than involvement in this world, the emphasis on wealth creation that is embedded in Protestantism is not found in Buddhism.

e) Confucianism - Confucianism was founded in the fifth century BC.

i) Economic Implications of Confucianism - There are those who maintain that Confucianism may have economic implications that are as profound as those found in Protestantism, although they are of a different nature. Three values are central to the Confucian system (of ethics): loyalty, reciprocal obligations, and honesty in dealing with others.

5) Language - One obvious way in which countries differ is language. By language, we mean both the spoken and the unspoken means of communication. Language is one of the defining characteristics of culture.

Teaching Tip: There are a number of resources available on the Internet to help international executives overcome "language" barriers in doing business in other countries. An entire menu of these resources is available at {http://www.csuchico.edu/cedp/export/global/protocol.htm}.

Teaching Tip: For individuals with a particular interest in Language, the Human-Languages Page {http://www.june29.com/HLP/} is a comprehensive catalog of language-related Internet resources. The over 1600 links available at this site include links to other Internet sites that focus on online language lessons, translating dictionaries, native literature, translation services, software, and language schools.

a) Spoken Language - International businesses that do not understand the local language can make some major blunders through improper translation.

b) Unspoken Language - Unspoken language refers to nonverbal communication.

6) Education - Formal education plays a key role in a society. Formal education is the medium through which individuals learn many of the language, conceptual, and mathematical skills that are indispensable in a modern society. From an international business perspective, education plays an important role as a determinant of national competitive advantage. The availability of a pool of skilled and educated human resources seems to be a major determinant of the likely economic success of a country.

7) Culture and the Workplace - For an international business with operations in different countries, a question of considerable importance is how does a society's culture impact on the values found in the workplace? The question points to the need to vary management process and practices to take different culturally determined work-related values into account.

a) Hofstede's Model - The most famous study of how culture relates to values in the workplace was undertaken by Geert Hofstede. Hofstede isolated four dimensions that he claimed summarized different cultures. These were: power distance, individualism versus collectivism, uncertainty avoidance, and masculinity versus femininity.

   i) Power Distance - Focused on how a society deals with the fact that people are unequal in physical and intellectual capabilities.

   ii) Individualism Versus Collectivism - Focused on the relationship between the individual and his or her fellows.

   iii) Uncertainty Avoidance - Measures the extent to which different cultures socialize their members into accepting ambiguous situations and tolerating ambiguity.

   iv) Masculinity Versus Femininity - Looks at the relationship between gender and work roles.

b) Evaluating Hofstede's Model - Hofstede's results are interesting for what they tell us in a general way about differences between cultures. However, one should be careful about reading too much into Hofstede's research.

8) Culture Change - Culture evolves over time, although changes in value systems can be slow and painful for a society. Social turmoil is an inevitable outcome of culture change.

9) Implications for Business

   a) Cross-Cultural Literacy - One big danger confronting a company that goes abroad for the first time is the danger of being ill-informed. International businesses that are ill-informed about the practices of another culture are unlikely to succeed.

      i) Ethnocentric Behavior - Acting on the belief in the superiority of one's own ethnic group or culture.

   b) Culture and Competitive Advantage - For the international business, the connection between culture and competitive advantage is important for two reasons. First, the connection suggests which countries are likely to produce the most viable competitors. Second, the connection between culture and competitive advantage has important implications for the choice of countries in which to locate production facilities and do business.

Critical Thinking and Discussion Questions

1. Outline why the culture of a country influences the costs of doing business in that country. Illustrate your answer with examples.

   Answer: One theme that continually surfaced in this chapter is the relationship between culture and national competitive advantage. Put simply, the value system and norms of a country influence the costs of doing business in that country. The costs of doing business in a country influence the ability of firms based in that culture to establish a competitive advantage in the global marketplace. For example, we have seen how attitudes toward cooperation between management and labor, toward work, and toward the payment of interest are influenced by social structure and religion. It can be argued that the class-based conflict between workers and management that we find in British society, insofar as it leads to industrial disruption, raises the costs of doing business in that culture. Many similar examples exist across a broad spectrum of cultures.

2. How do you think business practices in an Islamic country are likely to differ from business practices in the United States?

    Answer: Although the United States and the Islamic countries both share a pro-free enterprise philosophy, there are a number of differences between the countries in terms of business practices. One major difference is that Islamic countries prohibit the payment or receipt of interest, which is considered usury. Although there are ways that Islamic countries have attenuated the consequences of this rule, it does vary from the U.S. tradition of the payment and receipt of interest. Islamic countries are also critical of businesses that profit through the exploitation of others, and hold businesses in high esteem that undertake charitable acts to share their profits with the poor. These aspects of business are not as pronounced in the U.S.

3. What are the implications for international business of differences in the dominant religion of a country?

    Answer: For an international business with operations in different countries, a question of considerable importance is how does a society's religion impact on the values found in the workplace. This question points out the need to vary management processes and practices to take different religious values into account. A miscue in this area could be very offensive to a group of potential foreign customers.

4. Choose two countries that appear to be culturally diverse. Compare the culture of those countries and then indicate how cultural differences influence (i) the costs of doing business in each country, (ii) the likely future economic development of that country, (iii) business practices.

    Answer: This question is designed to stimulate classroom discussion or to encourage your students to "think" about this challenging question in preparing a written answer.

Case Discussion Questions

1. How can ABB's culturally diverse management team be a source of competitive strength?

    Answer: By bringing different perspectives to bear on a particular problem or decision making context.

2. What barriers are likely to stand in the way of Percy Barnevik's attempt to make his culturally diverse management team a source of competitive strength?

    Answer: Differences in cultural backgrounds may cause people to behave in a manner that is misunderstood. These misunderstanding may result in less than optimal decision making along with inter-firm bickering and tension. Also, decision making may be slowed down as a result of language and other cultural barriers. This may work to the firm's disadvantage if quick decisions are required in a fast moving industry.

3. What do you think that Barnevik means by the need to acknowledge cultural differences without becoming paralyzed by them - to work with those differences? What does working with cultural

differences at a global company such as ABB actually mean?

Answer: It is easy to become paralyzed by cultural differences, and to develop a mindset that basically says, "Ten people in a room that all speak different languages, prefer different foods, have different customs, and come from different religious backgrounds could never accomplish anything meaningful." For something with this perspective, cultural differences represent a problem rather than an advantage, and cultural differences are an insurmountable thing to overcome. Conversely, Barnevik and others adopt a very different type of perspective. While they acknowledge that differences in language, customs, religious background, etc., are issues that must be overcome, they approach the issue much differentially and might think, "What an opportunity – by having people in a group from ten different countries we can get ten totally different perspectives on how to solve our problems and capitalize on our opportunities." This is what Barnevik means by the need to acknowledge cultural differences without becoming paralyzed by them."

Working with cultural differences at a global company such as ABB means being sensitive to individuals from other cultures, being open to a variety of opinions, being respectful of the beliefs of others, and being open to learning things that help the company as a whole function.

4. How can ABB increase the cross-literacy of its management cadre?

Answer: By providing its managers overseas assignments in a variety of countries, by putting its managers through cross-cultural training programs, and by placing its managers in work teams with peers from other cultures.

Internet Exercise

1) Summary:
   a) This feature focuses on how the Federal Aviation Administration and the National Aeronautics and Space Administration are using Geert Hofstede's research on employee attitudes and values to better understand how employees from different cultures interact with one another in different job settings. For instance, NASA has supported projects studying astronauts' and pilots' national and organizational culture, personality and performance, and measures of individual and team performance. The FAA has supported studies to evaluate cultural issues in air crew performance, human factors in training programs, human factors in air traffic control, and attitudes toward flightdeck automation. The exercise portion of the feature asks the reader to read the FAA and NASA studies and discuss how Hofstede's research is cited.

2) Additional Material:
   a) For those individuals with a particular interest in the work of Geert Hofstede, Dr. Hofstede has written a book entitled Cultures and Organizations: Software of the Mind. Drawing on 25 years of research and consulting and offering data from 50 countries, Hofstede's book examines the effects of national cultures on work, family, education, and politics. A brief review of the book can be accessed at {http://hoshi.cic.sfu.ca/ipress/book.58.html}

Opening Case: Euro-Disneyland "Where Are the French?"

1) Summary:

a) This feature focuses on Disney's efforts to open and operate a "Disneyland" type theme part in France. Despite the initial euphoria surrounding the opening of the park, Disney's early experience in France were not positive. Park attendance did not reach early expectations, and the French seemed to resent rather than enjoy the American flavor of the attractions in the park. In addition, Disney was surprised by how its European guests reacted to many of the amenities associated with the park. The hotels that were built next to the park stood half empty most of the time. In addition, the guests in the park did not stay at late into the evening as Disney anticipated and Disney had trouble managing the breakfast and lunch rushes. As a result of all of this, by the end of 1994, Euro-Disney had cumulative losses of $2 billion.

2) Suggested Discussion Questions:

a) Was Euro-Disneyland a clash between American and European cultures? Why or why not?

b) What could Disney have done to better anticipate the challenges that it faced at Euro-Disneyland? What could the French have done to better prepare Disney for what to expect?

c) Are you optimistic about the future of Euro-Disneyland? Why or why not?

3) Disney Homepage: {http://www.disney.com/}.

Country Focus: Islamic Dissent in Saudi Arabia

1) Summary:

a) This feature focuses on the cultural of Saudi Arabia and on the Islamic dissent that exists in the country. The feature traces the Saudi government from the founding of Saudi Arabia in 1935 until the present time. In addition, the feature comments on the relationship between Saudi Arabia and the Western democracies of the world. Western governments have gone out of their way to curry the favor of Saudi Arabia, a cynic might say, because the country sits on top of more than a quarter of the world's oil reserves. As a result of this and the involvement of the West in the Gulf War, there is growing dissention in Saudi Arabia against the ruling family.

2) Suggested Discussion Questions:

a) Describe the basic beliefs of Islamic fundamentalists. Would the relationship between Saudi Arabia and the West change if Saudi Arabia shifted more towards a culture of strict Islamic fundamentalism? Explain your answer.

b) In your opinion, will Saudi Arabia remain a stable trading partner of the West. Why or why not?

3) Saudi Arabia Websites: {http://www.yahoo.com/Regional/Countries/Saudi_Arabia/}.

Management Focus: Hitachi and Japan's Changing Culture

1) Summary:

a) This feature focuses on the changes that have taken place over the years for the employees of Hitachi Corporation of Japan. Hitachi was founded in 1911 by Namihei Odaira. By 1965 Hitachi was one of the giants of Japanese industry. For many years, Hitachi was a typical Japanese company. Managers and their workers worked under a system of consensus decision making, the employees of the company lived in company housing, and everyone ate their meals in a company cafeteria. Two forces changed all of this – prosperity and globalization. Today, the company dorms and cafeterias have given away to private homes for the company's employees. Consensus decision making is no longer stressed to the extent that it once was. The top executives of Hitachi have encouraged these changes, recognizing that changing times require changes in work environments.

2) Suggested Discussion Questions:

a) In your opinion, have the changes that have taken place in the lives of Hitachi's workers resulted more from prosperity and globalization at Hitachi, or changes in Japanese society itself? Explain your answer.

b) Has Hitachi done a good job of allowing the lives of its employees to change in accordance with the changes in its business environment? In your opinion, what would have happened if Hitachi had tried to maintain its old culture despite its growing prosperity and move towards globalization?

c) How has Hatchi's prosperity change the lives of its employees? What can other companies learn from how Hatchi has handled its prosperity?

3) Hitachi Homepage: {http://hitachi.co.jp/}

Learning Objectives

1. Understand why nations trade with each other.

2. Be conversant with the different theories that have been offered to explain trade flows between nations.

3. Understand why many economists believe that unrestricted (free) trade between nations will raise the economic welfare of all countries that participate in a free trade system.

4. Be familiar with the arguments of those who maintain that government can play a proactive role in promoting national competitive advantage in certain industries.

5. Understand the important implications that international trade theory holds for business practice.

Chapter Summary

This chapter focuses on the benefits of international trade and introduces several theories that help explain the patterns of international trade that are observed in practice. The discussion begins with an explanation of the theory of mercantilism, and then proceeds to discuss the theories of absolute advantage and comparative advantage. Four additional theories are discussed, including the Heckscher-Ohlin theory, the Product Life Cycle theory, the New Trade theory, and the theory of National Competitive Advantage. Each of these theories help explain why certain goods are (or should be) made in certain countries.

The chapter ends by discussing the link between the theories of international trade and (1) a firm's decision about where (in the world) to locate its various productive activities, (2) the importance of establishing first-mover advantages, and (3) government trade policies.

Chapter Outline With Lecture Notes and Teaching Tips

1) Introduction – This chapter has two goals. The first goal is to review a number of theories that explain why it is beneficial for a country to engage in international trade. The second goal is to explain the pattern of international trade that we observe in the world economy.

2) An Overview of Trade Theory – Free trade refers to a situation where a government does not attempt to influence through quotas or duties what its citizens can buy from another country or what they can produce and sell to another country. Adam Smith argued that the invisible hand of the market mechanism, rather than government policy, should determine what a country imports and what it exports.

   a) The Benefits of Trade – The great strength of the theories of Smith, Ricardo, and Heckscher-Ohlin is that they identify the specific benefits of international trade.

   b) The Pattern of International Trade – The theories of Smith, Ricardo, and Heckscher-Ohlin also help to explain the pattern of international trade that we observe in the world economy. For example, why does Japan export automobiles and Ghana export cocoa?

c) Trade Theory and Government Policy – Before discussing these theories in more detail, the text points out that although they all agree that international trade is beneficial to a country, they lack agreement in their recommendations for government policy.

3) Mercantilism – The first theory of international trade emerged in England in the mid-16th century. Referred to as mercantilism, its principle assertion was that it is in a country's best interest to maintain a trade surplus, to export more than it imports. Consistent with this belief, the mercantilist doctrine advocated government intervention to achieve a surplus in the balance of trade.
Teaching Note: A historical perspective of Mercantilism is available at the following site sponsored by the University of California at Davis {http://ps.ucdavis.edu/classes/pol129/SWE/mercan.htm}.

a) Flaw in Mercantilism – The flaw of mercantilism was that it viewed trade as a zero-sum game. It was left to Adam Smith and David Ricardo to show the short-sightedness of this approach and to demonstrate that trade is a positive-sum game, that being a situation in which all countries can benefit, even if some benefit more than others.

4) Absolute Advantage – In his 1776 landmark book The Wealth of Nations, Adam Smith attacked the mercantilist assumption that trade is a zero-sum game. Smith argued that countries differ in their ability to produce goods efficiently, and that a country has an absolute advantage in the production of a product when it is more efficient than any other country in producing it. According to Smith, countries should specialize in the production of goods for which they have an absolute advantage and then trade these goods for the goods produced by other countries.
Teaching Tip: An overview of the ideas and philosophies of Adam Smith, from which his idea of absolute advantage emerged, can be accessed at: {http://www.stg.brown.edu/projects/hypertext/ landow/victorian/economics/smith.html}.

5) Comparative Advantage – David Ricardo took Adam Smith's theory one step further by exploring what might happen when one country has an absolute advantage in the production of all goods. Smith's theory of absolute advantage suggests that such a country might derive no benefits from international trade. In his 1817 book Principles of Political Economy, Ricardo showed that this was not the case. According to Ricardo's theory of comparative advantage, it makes sense for a country to specialize in the production of those goods that it produces most efficiently and to buy the goods that it produces less efficiently from other countries, even if this means buying goods from other countries that it could produce more efficiently itself. The textbook provides a detailed example to explain the rationale of this theory.
Teaching Tip: An overview of the ideas and philosophies of David Ricardo, from which his theory of comparative advantage emerged, is available at {http://www.stg.brown.edu/projects/hypertext/ landow/victorian/economics/ric.html}.
Teaching Tip: A more complete description of Ricardo's theory of international trade can be accessed at {http://dylee.keel.econ.ship.edu/intntl/ecn321/lecture/Ricardo.htm}. Lecture Note: An excellent source of material on Ricardo's theory of comparative advantage is available at a site sponsored by the University of California at Davis. The site contains the transcripts of lectures on this topic. The web site address is : {http://ps.ucdavis.edu/classes/pol129/SWE/compadv.htm}.

a) The Gains from Trade – The basic message of the theory of comparative advantage is that potential world production is greater with unrestricted free trade than it is with restricted trade. Moreover, Ricardo's theory suggests that consumers in all nations can consume more if there are no restrictions on trade.

b) Qualifications and Assumptions – Although Richard's theory must be understood in the context of a number of assumptions (articulated in the text), research data support the basic proposition of the Ricardian model – that countries will export the goods that they are most efficient at producing.

c) Trade and Economic Growth – It is apparent that opening up an economy to trade is likely to generate dynamic gains. These dynamic gains are of two sorts.

   i) First, free trade might increase a country's stock of resources as increased supplies of labor and capital from abroad become available for use within the country.

   ii) Free trade might also increase the efficiency with which a country utilizes its resources.

6) Heckscher-Ohlin Theory – Heckscher and Ohlin argued that comparative advantage arises from differences in national factor endowments. As a result, the Heckscher-Ohlin theory predicts that countries will export goods that make intensive use of those factors that are locally abundant, while importing goods that make intensive use of factors that are locally scarce.
Teaching Tip: A more complete description of the Heckscher-Ohlin theory is available at {http://dylee.keel.econ.ship.edu/intntl/ecn321/lecture/hotheory.htm}.

a) The Leontief Paradox – Using the Heckscher-Ohlin theory, Leontief postulated that since the U.S. was relatively abundant in capital compared to other nations, the U.S. would be an exporter of capital intensive goods and an importer of labor-intensive goods. To his surprise, however, he found that U.S. exports were less capital intensive than U.S. imports. Since this result was at variance with the predictions of the theory, it has become know as the Leontief Paradox.
Teaching Tip: A more complete description of the Leontief Paradox is available at {http://dylee.keel.econ.ship.edu/intntl/ecn321/lecture/leont.htm}.

7) The Product Life-Cycle Theory – Raymond Vernon initially proposed the product life-cycle theory in the mid 1960s. The product life-cycle is based on the following:

a) Early in the life cycle of a typical new product, while demand is starting to grow in the U.S., demand in other advanced countries is limited to high-income groups. The limited initial demand in other advanced countries does not make it worthwhile for firms in those countries to start producing the new product, but it does necessitate some exports from the U.S. to those countries. Over time, however, demand for the new product starts to grow in other advanced countries. As it does, it becomes worthwhile for foreign producers to being producing for their home markets. In addition, U.S. firms might set up production facilities in those advanced countries where demand is growing. Consequently, production within other advanced countries begins to limit the potential for exports from the U.S.

b) As the market in the U.S. and other advanced nations matures, the product becomes more standardized, and price becomes the main competitive weapon. One result is that producers based in advanced countries where labor costs are lower than the United States might now be able to export to the U.S.

c) If cost pressures become intense, the process might not stop there. The cycle by which the U.S. lost its advantage to other advanced countries might be repeated once more as developing countries begin to acquire a production advantage over advanced countries.

d) The consequences of these trends for the pattern of world trade is that the United States switches from being an exporter of the product to an importer of the product as production becomes more concentrated in lower-cost foreign locations.

e) Evaluating the Product Life-Cycle Theory – How well does the product life-cycle theory explain international trade patterns? Historically, it is quite accurate.

8) The New Trade Theory – The new trade theories argues that due to the presence of substantial scale economies, world demand will support only a few firms in many industries. This is the case in the commercial jet aircraft industry; estimates suggest that, at most, world demand can profitably support only three major manufacturers.

a) First Mover Advantages – New trade theorists argue that in those industries where the existence of substantial economies of scale imply that the world market will profitably support only a few firms, countries may export certain products simply because they have a firm that was an early entrant into that industry. Underpinning this argument is the notion of firms-mover advantages, which are the economic and strategic advantages that accrue to early entrants into an industry.

9) National Competitive Advantage: Porter's Diamond – Porter's thesis is that four broad attributes of a nation shape the environment in which local firms compete, and that these attributes promote or impede the creation of competitive advantage (see Figure 4.5 in the text). These attributes are:

a) Factor Endowments – A nation's position in factor of production such as skilled labor or the infrastructure necessary to compete in a given industry.

b) Demand Conditions – The nature of home demand for the industry's product or service.

c) Related or Supporting Industries – The presence or absence in a nation of supplier industries and related industries that are internationally competitive.

d) Firms Strategy, Structure, and Rivalry – The conditions in the nation governing how companies are created, organized, and managed and the nature of domestic rivalry.

e) Porter's Diamond – Porter speaks of these four attributes as constituting the diamond. He argues that firms are most likely to succeed in industry segments where the diamond is most favorable.

f) Additional Variables – Porter maintains that two additional variables can influence that national diamond in important ways: chance and government.
Lecture Note: According to the U.S. Commerce Dept., the greatest commercial opportunities in international business over the next decade will be found in what the department calls the ten Big Emerging Markets (BEM). These markets are: the Chinese Economic Area (including China, Hong Kong, and Taiwan), India, South Korea, Mexico, Brazil, Argentina, South Africa, Poland, Turkey, and the Association of Southwest Asian Nations (ASEAN: including Indonesia, Brunei, Malaysia, Singapore, Thailand, the Philippines, and Vietnam.

10) Implications for Business – There are at least three main implications of the material discussed in this chapter for international businesses: location implications, first-mover implications, and policy implications.

a) Location Implications – One way in which the material discussed in this chapter matters to an international business concerns the link between the theories of international trade and a firm's decision about where to locate its various productive activities. Underlying most of the theories is the notion that different countries have particular advantages in different productive activities. Thus, from a profit perspective, it makes sense for a firm to disperse its various productive activities to those countries where, according to the theory of international trade, they can be performed most efficiently.

b) First-Mover Implications – The new trade theory suggests the importance to firms of building and exploiting first-mover advantages.

c) Policy Implications – The theories of international trade also matter to international businesses because business firms are major players on the international trade scene. Because of their pivotal role in international trade, business firms can and do exert a strong influence on government trade policy.

Lecture Note: The top ten countries with which the U.S. has a trade deficit with (in order of the dollar value of the deficit) are: China, Japan, Taiwan, Mexico, Canada, Germany, Malaysia, Venezuela, Italy, and Indonesia. This list is updated periodically by the United States Census Bureau at {http://www.census.gov/foreign-trade/www/deficit.html}. The top ten countries with which the U.S. has a trade surplus (in order of the dollar value of the surplus) are: Netherlands, Brazil, Australia, Belgium, Argentina, United Arab Emirates, Egypt, United Kingdom, Chile, and Hong Kong. This list is updated at {http://www.census.gov/foreign-trade/www/surplus.html}.

Teaching Tip: For information about foreign governments and their approaches to international trade, visit the Electronic Embassy at {http://www.embassy.org/}. This site provides links to all of the foreign embassies located in Washington D.C.

Critical Thinking and Discussion Questions

1. "Mercantilism is a bankrupt theory that has no place in the modern world." Discuss.

   Answer: Mercantilism, in its purest sense, is a bankrupt theory that has no place in the modern world. The principle tenant of mercantilism is that a country should maintain a trade surplus, even if that means that imports are limited by government intervention. This policy is bankrupt for at least two reasons. First, it is inconsistent with the general notion of globalization, which is becoming more and more prevalent in the world. A policy of mercantilism will anger potential trade partners because it will exclude their goods from free access to the mercantilist country's markets. Eventually, a country will find it difficult to export if it imposes oppressive quotas and tariffs on its imports. Second, mercantilism is bankrupt because it hurts the consumers in the mercantilist country. By denying its consumers access to either "cheaper" goods from other countries or more "sophisticated" goods from other countries, the mercantilist country's ordinary consumers suffer.

2. The "Country Focus" reviews the arguments of those who suggest that Japan is a neo-mercantilist nation. Do you agree with this assessment? Can you think of cases in which your country has taken a neo-mercantilist stance to foreign competition?

   Answer: This question is designed to stimulate class discussion and/or to force your students to "think" about this complex issue in answering the question in a written format. By the examples provided in the country focus feature, it is easy to jump to the conclusion that Japan is a neo-mercantilist nation. However, encourage your students to think deeper, and argue both sides of this issue. Also, encourage your students to think about cases of neo-mercantilism in the United States. Sugar subsidies, for example, artificially inflate the price of sugar products for U.S. consumers and effectively block the import of sugar products into the United States. For instructors that want to use this example in their classroom discussion, more information about sugar subsidies can be found at the following:

   - Time Magazine article entitled "Sugar's Sweetest Deal." The article was published in the April 8, 1996 edition of Time.

   - Web site entitled "Ending Sugar Subsidies" at {http://www.nsda.org/}.

3. Using the theory of comparative advantage to support your arguments, outline the case for free trade.

   Answer: In a nutshell, the theory of comparative advantage argues that it makes sense for a country to specialize in the production of those goods that it produces most efficiently and to buy the goods that it produces less efficiently from other countries, even if this means buying goods from other countries that it could produce more efficiently itself. This is a somewhat complicated statement that can be simplified through following the example provided on page 131 of the text. The point of the example pertaining to the production of rice and cocoa in Ghana and South Korea, is that even though Ghana is more efficient at producing both rice and cocoa relative to South Korea, Ghana is comparatively more efficient at producing coca than it is at producing rice, so both Ghana and South Korea benefit it Gahan focuses on producing coca and actually imports rice from South Korea. This approach benefits both countries, which illustrates the inherent advantages of free trade. By engaging in trade, the two countries can increase their combined production of rice and cocoa, and consumers in both nations can consume more of both goods.

Generalizing from this example, the basic message of the theory of comparative advantage is that potential world production is greater with unrestricted free trade than it is with restricted trade.

4. Using the new trade theory and Porter's theory of national competitive advantage, outline the case for government policies that would build national competitive advantage in a particular industry. What kind of policies would you recommend that the government adopt? Are these policies at variance with the basic free trade philosophy?

    Answer: Porter's theory of national competitive advantage argues that four broad attributes of a nation shape the environment in which local firms compete, and that these attributes promote or impede the creation of competitive advantage. These attributes are: factor endowments, demand conditions, related and supporting industries, and firm strategy, structure, and rivalry. Porter goes on to argue that firms are most likely to succeed in industries in which the diamond (which are the four attributes collectively) is favorable. Porter adds two factors to the list of attributes described above: chance and government policy. The New Trade theory addresses a separate issue. This theory argues that due to the presence of substantial scale economies, world demand will support only a few firms in many industries. Underpinning this argument is the notion of first-mover advantages, which are the economic and strategic advantages that accrue to early entrants into an industry.

    One could argue that when the attributes of a nation are conductive to the production of a product, and when the manufacturers of that product have experienced some "chance" events that have provided them first-mover advantages, the governmental policies of that nation should promote the building of national competitive advantage in that particular area. This could be accomplished through government R&D grants, policies that favor the industry in capital markets, policies towards education, the creation of a favorable regulatory atmosphere, tax abatements, and the like. Ask your students whether they think this policy is at variance with the basic free trade philosophy. One could argue that it is, because the government intervention is creating the basis for comparative advantage. Conversely, one could argue that if a country establishes a comparative advantage in a particular area that is based on a unique set of attributes (such as Swiss production of watches), world output will be favorably impacted by letting that country pursue its area of comparative advantage.

5. You are the CEO of a textile firm that designs and manufacturers mass-market clothing products in the United States. Your manufacturing process is labor-intensive and does not require highly skilled employees. Currently you have design facilities in Paris and New York and manufacturing facilities in North Carolina. Drawing on the theory of international trade, decide whether these are optimal locations for these activities.

    Answer: Underlying the theories of international trade is the notion that different countries (or areas within a country), have particular advantages in different productive activities. Thus, from a profit perspective, it makes sense for a firm to disperse its various productive activities to those specific locations where they can be produced the most efficiently. If design activities can be produced most efficiently in Paris and New York, then these activities should remain in those locations. Similarly, if the manufacturing of the textile products can be conducted most efficiently in North Carolina, then the manufacturing operations should remain there. If the firm has better alternatives in other geographic locations (all other things being equal), then appropriate changes should be considered.

6. "Policies designed to limit competition from low-cost foreign competitors do not help a country to achieve greater economic growth." Discuss this statement.

Answer: This is an excellent question that will help you as a teacher determine whether your students understand the material in this chapter. Free trade, even if it results in low-cost foreign competitors to compete in a domestic market, can generate dynamic economic gains. These dynamic gains are of two sorts. First, free trade might increase a country's stock of resources as increased supplies of labor and capital from abroad become available for use within the country. Second, free trade might also increase the efficiency with which a country utilizes its resources. By not having to produce low cost goods, for example, a country could dedicate its efforts towards the production of higher-cost, higher-quality products.

Case Discussion Questions

1. To what extent does the theory of comparative advantage explain the rise of Italian tile firms to global preeminence in the tile industry.

Answer: As a result of the effort dedicated toward tile production in Italy, Italian firms became better at producing tile than any other location in the world. As a result, it made sense for the Italian firms to specialize in the production of tile, and import other products from other countries (or other parts of Italy). This scenario is consistent with the theory of comparative advantage. Even though firms in other countries produced tile, the Italian firms were comparatively better at producing tile than the other firms. As a result, the Italian firms reached global preeminence in this area.

2. To what extent does the Heckscher-Ohlin theory explain the rise of Italian tile firms to global preeminence in the tile industry.

Answer: The Heckscher-Ohlin theory argues that comparative advantage arises from differences in national factor endowments. Factor endowments can include a wide variety of things, from land, natural resources, capital, labor, and intellectual capital. In the case of the Italian tile firms, the Heckscher-Ohlin theory is instructive in that the area of Italy in which the majority of the tile manufacturing took place included the world's largest concentration of intellectual capital pertaining to the tile industry. This created a snowball effect. Because the intellectual capital for tile production was concentrated in the Sassuolo region of Italy, the region attracted an increasing number of tile firms. In America, the same phenomenon has occurred with computer production in California's Silicon Valley.

3. Use Michael Porter's diamond to analyze the rise to global preeminence of the Italian tile industry. What does this analysis tell you about how firms gain a competitive advantage in the world economy?

Answer: According to Porter's theory, tile production caught hold in Italy because the diamond (i.e. Porter's four attributes of a nation) was conductive to tile production. Porter's four attributes include: factor endowments, demand conditions, related and supporting industries, and firm strategy, structure, and rivalry. In terms of factor endowments, Italy has a historic competence in the area of tile production, dating back to the 13th century. As a result, the infrastructure for tile production was also well developed. In terms of demand conditions, the Italian people preferred tile floors, as a result of the Mediterranean climate in Italy. In terms of supporting industries, in the Sassuolo region there are hundreds of firms involved in the ceramic tile industry and in various supporting industries such as the manufacture of glazes, enamels, and ceramic tile production equipment. Finally, in terms of firm strategy, structure, and rivalry, the vigorous domestic rivalry in the Italian tile industry forced the Italian firms to become better and better at what they did, which increased the international competitiveness of Italian tile firms.

Porter's theory tells us that the degree to which a nation is likely to achieve international success in a certain industry is a function of the combined impact of factor endowments, domestic demand conditions, related and supporting industries, and domestic rivalry.

4. Which of the above theories – comparative advantage, Heckscher-Ohlin, or Porter's gives the best explanation of the rise of global preeminence of the Italian tile industry? Why?

Answer: This question is designed to stimulate classroom discussion and/or to force your students to "think" about the merits of the different international trade theories in providing a written answer to this question.

Internet Exercise

1) Summary:

   a) The article discusses the availability of material about the work of Wassily Leontief on the World Wide Web. Several internet addresses are provided that supply a broad array of information about Leontief and his work.

2) Additional Material:

   a) For more information about the life and work of Wassily Leontief, an autobiography of Dr. Leontief can be found on the World Wide Web at {http://www.nobel.se/laureates/economy-1973-1-autobio.html}

Opening Case: The Gains from Trade: Ghana and South Korea

1) Summary:
   a) This feature compares the results of an "inward-oriented" trade policy in Ghana versus an "outward-oriented" trade policy in South Korea. In 1970, both Ghana and South Korea had roughly the same standard of living. In the ensuring years, Ghana developed a very inward-oriented trade policy and South Korea developed a very outward-oriented trade policy. The results, in terms of economic well-being for the two countries, have been dramatically different. While the South Korean economy has prospered, the economy in Ghana has stagnated, and the country's trade and domestic policies have greatly reduced the effectiveness of Ghana cocoa trade, which at one time was the country's greatest strength.

2) Suggested Discussion Questions:
   a) What did the government of Ghana do wrong? What did the government of South Korea do right? What should the government of Ghana do at this time to improve its international competitiveness?

b) Using Porter's theory of competitive advantage, explain why Ghana's cocoa production waned in the 1960s and 1970s. Is it possible for Ghana to reclaim its leadership in world cocoa production? How can this be done?

c) What country specific factors provided South Korean a comparative advantage in the production of manufactured products?

Country Focus: Is Japan a Neo-Mercantilist Nation?

1) Summary:
   a) This feature explains the basis for the allegation that Japan is a neo-mercantilist nation. Several examples are provided which furnish evidence that the Japanese government works hard to ensure that Japan has a positive balance of trade, even if it has to resort to formal and informal trade barriers to achieve this objective.

2) Suggested Discussion Questions:
   a) In your opinion, is Japan a neo-mercantilist nation? Support you answer.

   b) Today, the trade imbalance between the United States and Japan is $60 billion (meaning that the United States imported $60 billion more in goods from Japan than it exported to Japan). Does this fact alone suggest that Japan is a neo-mercantilist nation? What other reasons could have created such a large trade imbalance between the two countries?

   c) Should the United States government fight back by imposing stricter import quotas on Japanese good coming into America? Discuss the wisdom of this suggestion.

Management Focus: The Rise of Finland's Nokia

1) Summary:
   a) This feature is about the growth of the cellular telephone equipment industry, and more specifically, about the rise in competitiveness of Nokia, a Finnish cellular telephone company. The feature explains the reasons that Nokia was particularly well positioned to take advantage of the growth of the global cellular telephone industry.

2) Suggested Discussion Questions:
   a) Using the New Trade Theory and Porter's theory of National Competitive Advantage, describe why Nokia emerged as a leading competitor in the global cellular telephone equipment industry.

   b) Explain why the cellular telephone industry caught on in Finland and the other Scandinavian countries faster than the rest of the world.

   c) Why didn't the development of the cellular telephone equipment industry take place in Mexico or another Central or South American country rather than Finland, Sweden, and the United States? Base your answer of the international trade theories described in Chapter 4.

   d) Nokia's Homepage: {http://www.nokia.com/}

CHAPTER 5
THE GLOBAL TRADING SYSTEM

Learning Objectives

1. Be familiar with the various policy instruments that governments use to restrict imports and promote exports.

2. Understand why some governments intervene in international trade to restrict imports and promote exports.

3. Appreciate the position of those who argue that government intervention in international trade can be self-defeating and typically fail to produce the gains that advocates of intervention claim.

4. Be familiar with the evolution, purpose, current status, and future prospects of the global trading system as embodied in the General Agreement on Tariffs and Trade and the World Trade Organization.

5. Understand the important implications for business practice of government intervention in international trade and of the current global trading system.

Chapter Summary

This chapter begins with a discussion of the six main instruments of trade policy, including tariffs, subsidies, import quotas, voluntary export restraints, local content requirements, and administrative policies. This section is followed by a discussion of the merits of government intervention into international trade. The author provides a balanced view of this difficult issue.

The second half of the chapter focuses on the development of the global trading system. A historical context is provided, along with a view of the global trading system as it exists today. The author acquaints the reader with the General Agreement on Trade and Tariffs (GATT) and the World Trade Organization.

Chapter Outline With Lecture Notes and Teaching Tips

1) Introduction – In this chapter we explore the political and economic reasons that governments have for intervening in international trade.

2) Instruments of Trade Policy – In this section, the text reviews six main instruments of trade policy. These are: tariffs, subsidies, import quotas, voluntary export restraints, local content requirements, and administrative policies.
   Teaching Tip: An excellent site on tariffs and quotas, containing case studies and a role playing example, is available at {http://ps.ucdavis.edu/classes/pol129/SWE/tariffs.htm}. The role playing example in particular may stimulate good classroom interaction.
   a) Tariff – A tariff is a tax levied on imports.
      i) Specific Tariffs – Taxes levied as a fixed charge for each unit of a good imported.
      ii) Ad Valorem Tariffs – Taxes levied as a proportion of the value of the imported good.
      iii) Who Suffers and Who Gains? – The important thing to understand about a tariff is who suffers and who gains. The government gains, because the tariff increases government revenues. Domestic producers gain, because the tariff affords them some protection against foreign

competitors by increasing the cost of imported foreign goods. Consumers lose since they must pay more for certain imports.

b) Subsidies – A subsidy is a government payment to a domestic producer. By lowering costs, subsidies help domestic producers in two ways: they help them compete against low-cost foreign imports and they help them gain export markets.

c) Import Quotas and Voluntary Export Restraints:

   i) Import Quota – An import quota is a direct restriction on the quantity of some good that may be imported into a country.

   ii) Voluntary Export Restraint – A voluntary export restraint is a quota on trade imposed by the exporting country, typically at the request of the importing country's government.
Teaching Tip: A review of the role of voluntary export restraints in world trade is available at {http://ps.ucdavis.edu/classes/pol129/SWE/restrain.htm}. This site is well worth a visit if you plan to emphasize this topic in your lecture.

d) Local Content Requirements – A local content requirement demands that some specific fraction of a good be produced domestically.

e) Administrative Policies – Administrative trade policies are bureaucratic rules that are designed to make it difficult for imports to enter a country.

3) The Case for Government Intervention – In general, there are two types of arguments for government intervention, political and economic. Political arguments for intervention are concerned with protecting the interests of certain groups within a nation (normally producers), often at the expense of other groups (normally consumers). Economic arguments for intervention are typically concerned with boosting the overall wealth of a nation (to the benefit of all, both producers and consumers).

a) Political Arguments for Intervention

   i) Protecting Jobs and Industries – Perhaps the most common political argument for government intervention is that it is necessary for protecting jobs and industries from foreign competition.

   ii) National Security – Countries sometimes argue that it is necessary to protect certain industries because they are important for national security. Defense-related industries often get this kind of attention.
Lecture Note: In the United States, the Bureau of Export Administration enhances the nation's security and its economic prosperity by controlling exports for national security, foreign security, foreign policy, and short supply reasons. The Bureau of Export Administration maintains a web site at {http://www.bxa.doc.gov/}.

   iii) Retaliation – Some argue that governments should use the threat to intervene in trade policy as a bargaining tool to help open foreign markets and force trading partners to "play by the rules of the game."

b) Economic Arguments for Intervention

   i) The Infant Industry Argument – According to this argument, many developing countries have a potential comparative advantage in manufacturing, but new manufacturing industries there cannot initially compete with well-established industries in developing countries. To allow manufacturing to get a toehold, the argument is that governments should temporarily support new industry (with tariffs, important quotas, and subsidies) until they have grown strong enough to meet international competition.

   ii) Strategic Trade Policy – There are two components to the strategic trade policy argument. First, it is argued that a government can help raise national income if it can somehow ensure that the firm or firms to gain first-mover advantages are domestic rather than foreign

40

enterprises. Thus, according to the strategic trade policy argument, a government should use subsidies to support promising firms that are active in newly emerging industries. The second component of the strategic trade policy argument is that it might pay a government to intervene in an industry if it helps it's country's domestic firms overcome the barriers to entry created by foreign firms that have already reaped first-mover advantages.

4) The Revised Case for Free Trade – The response to the strategic trade policy argument constitutes the revised case for free trade.

a) Retaliation and Trade War – Krugman argues that strategic trade policy aimed at establishing domestic firms in a dominant position in a global industry are beggar-thy-neighbor policies that boost national income at the expense of other countries. A country that attempts to use such policies will probably provoke retaliation.

b) Domestic Politics – Governments do not always act in the national interest when they intervene in the economy. Instead they are influenced by politically important interest groups. Thus, a further reason for not embracing strategic trade policy, according to Krugman, is that such a policy is almost certain to be captured by special interest groups within an economy, who will distort it to their own ends.

5) Development of the Global Trading System

a) From Smith to the Great Depression – This period market a protectionist period in American history.
   Teaching Tip: A review of the causes of the great depression, including a discussion of the role of tariffs, is available at {http://ps.ucdavis.edu/classes/pol129/SWE/depress.htm}.

b) 1947-79: GATT, Trade Liberalization, and Economic Growth – After the debacle of the Great Depression, opinion in the U.S. Congress had swung strongly in favor of free trade. As a consequence, under U.S. leadership, GATT was established in 1947. At the time, GATT had 23 member states, mostly advanced industrialized nations.

   i) GATT – GATT was a multilateral agreement whose objective was to liberalize trade by eliminating tariffs, subsidies, import quotas, and the like. In its early years GATT was by most measures very successful.
   Teaching Tip: A full review of GATT, containing an actual copy of the agreement, is available at {http://itl.irv.uit.no/trade_law/documents/freetrade/wta-94/nav/toc.html}.

c) 1980-1993: Disturbing Trends – During the 1980s and early 1990s the world trade system erected by GATT began to be strained as protectionist pressures arose around the world.

d) The Uruguay Round and the World Trade Organization – The Uruguay Round reached a successful conclusion in December of 1993. The Uruguay Round agreement has the following effects:

   i) Tariffs on industrial goods will be reduced by more than one-third.
   ii) Agricultural subsidies will be substantially reduced.
   iii) GATT fair trade and market access rules will be extended to cover a wide range of services.
   iv) GATT rules will also now be extended to provide enhanced protection for patents, copyrights, and trademarks (intellectual property).
   v) Barriers on trade in textiles will be significantly reduced over 10 years.
   vi) GATT rules will be much clearer and stronger.
   vii) World Trade Organization will be created to implement the GATT agreement.

e) The Future of the WTO: Unresolved Issues – The 1994 deal still leaves a lot to be done on the international trade front. Substantial trade barriers still remain in areas such as agriculture, financial services, broadcast entertainment, and telecommunications – although these seem likely to be reduced eventually. Talks on further liberalization of agricultural trade are due to begin in 1999, and a fresh round of talks on services is scheduled for 2000.
Lecture Note: There are presently 120 members of the WTO.

6) Implications for Business

   a) Trade Barriers and Firm Strategy – First, trade barriers raise the cost of exporting products to a country. Second, voluntary export restraints (VERs) may limit a firm's ability to serve a country from locations outside that country. Third, to conform with local content requirements, a firm may have to locate more production activities in a given market than it would otherwise. All of the above effects are likely to raise the firm's costs above the level that could be achieved in a world without trade barriers.

   b) Policy Implications – It is probably in the best long-run interests of the business community to encourage the government to aggressively promote greater free trade by, for example, strengthening the WTO.

Critical Thinking and Discussion Questions

1. Do you think the U.S. government is correct to use a "get tough" approach in its trade negotiations with Japan (see opening case)? What are the risks of such an approach?

   Answer: This question is designed to elicit classroom discussion or to force your students to "think" about this challenging issue. There are good arguments on both sides of this question. On the one hand, it is entirely appropriate for the U.S. government to come to the aid of American firms if they are being treated unfairly by a bilateral trade partner. Free trade between two nations depends upon good faith being exercised by both of the countries involved. If one country behaves in a "mercantilist" manner and violates the spirit of free trade, it must be forced to back down and allow a free trade atmosphere to be restored. Unless this happens, the rewards of the bilateral relationship will flow to the offending nation in a disproportionate manner. On the other hand, a "get tough" approach invites retaliation and a deterioration in the relationship between the United States and Japan.

2. Whose interests should be the paramount concern of government trade policy – the interests of producers (businesses and their employees) or those of consumers?

   Answer: This question does not have an easy answer. It is easy to argue that the interests of consumers should be protected first, because consumers represent the largest constituency in any nation. There are a number of ways that a government's trade policy can protect its consumers. By lowering tariffs and eliminating subsidies, governments allow the world market to dictate the prices of goods, which almost always works to the advantage of consumers (who are naturally looking for the most competitive price). In addition, the elimination or reduction of subsidies to domestic producers saves a government money, which in the end will lessen the tax burden on consumers. On the other hand, there are special circumstances that dictate a protection of producers at the possible expense of consumers. Governments often protect industries that are vital to national security. For example, even if other countries could refine oil cheaper than U.S. companies, it would be unwise for the U.S. government to let oil production totally cease in the U.S. Oil and all of its by products (e.g. gasoline, jet fuel) are vital for our national defense. In addition, the "infant industry" argument stipulates that countries at times may have a comparative advantage in the manufacturer of a particular product, but cannot initially compete with comparable industries in developed countries. As a result, the advocates of infant industries argue that to allow manufacturing to get a toehold, governments should temporarily support new industries (with trade barriers, import quotas, and subsidies) until they have grown strong enough to meet international competition.

3. Given the arguments relating to the new trade theory and strategic trade policy, what kind of trade policy should business be pressuring government to adopt?

    Answer: According to the textbook, businesses should urge governments to target technologies that may be important in the future and use subsidies to support development work aimed at commercializing those technologies. Government should provide export subsidies until the domestic firms have established first mover advantages in the world market. Government support may also be justified if it can help domestic firms overcome the first-mover advantages enjoyed by foreign competitors and emerge as viable competitors in the world market (as in the Airbus and semiconductor examples). In this case, a combination of home market protection and export-promoting subsidies may be called for.

4. You are an employee of a U.S. firm that produces personal computers in Thailand and then exports them to the United States and other countries for sale. The personal computers were originally produced in Thailand to take advantage of relatively low labor costs and a skilled workforce. Other possible locations were Malaysia and Hong Kong. The U.S. government decides to impose punitive 100 percent ad valorem tariffs on imports of computers from Thailand to punish the country for administrative trade barriers that restrict U.S. exports to Thailand. How do you think your firm should respond? What does this tell you about the use of targeted trade barriers?

    Answer: The only choice that your company has is to stop exporting computers from your factory in Thailand to the United States. You can still use your factory in Thailand to export to other parts of the world. However, you will have to find an alternative site (or hire a subcontractor) to manufacturer computers to be exported to the United States.

    This case illustrates the unfair nature of targeted trade barriers. The computer firm in this example is an innocent bystander that is caught in the middle of a trade dispute between the U.S. and Thailand.

Case Discussion Questions

1. What does this case teach us about the relationship between politics and international trade?

    Answer: The case teaches us that while governments have a role in facilitating trade, they should be extremely careful to remain "above board" in all of their activities. Even the hint of inappropriate or unethical acts on the part of government officials to promote a trade deal that benefits a company in their country can cause significant tension in international trade relationships.

2. You are the CEO of a British company that now faces the loss of a lucrative contract in Malaysia because of the dispute. What action should you take?

    Answer: This is a question that is designed to stimulate classroom discussion and/or to encourage your students to "think" about this challenging issue when preparing a written response to this question. There are several things that the CEO of the British company could do. First, the CEO could pressure his or her government to "make things right" with the Malaysian government. Second, the CEO could make a direct appeal to the Malaysian company to set their contract "aside" from the dispute resulting from a separate set of issues.

3. How do you think the British government should respond to the Malaysian action?

Answer: By telling the truth. If government officials are at fault, they should be dealt with in an appropriate manner. If government officials were not at fault, every effort should be made to demonstrate to the Malaysian government the facts pertaining to the matter. In all dealing, the British government should act in good faith and treat the Malaysian government in a respectful manner.

Internet Exercise

1) Summary:

   a) This feature describes the presence on the Internet of organizations that are instrumental to the effectiveness of the global trading system. Web site addresses are provided for GATT, the World Trade Organization, the Uruguay Round negotiation, and a number of related links. Also, an exercise in "global surfing" is provided, which illustrates the depth of information available on the World Wide Web about global trade organizations.

2) Additional Material:

   a) Along with information provided by World Trade Organizations such as GATT and the WTO, there are a number of international trade periodicals that can provide managers valuable information about trade related issues. A bibliography of export periodicals is provided at {http://tradeport.org/ts/biblio/per.html}. The periodicals in the bibliography include AgExporter, Business America, Export Today, and others.

Opening Case: Anatomy of a Trade Dispute

1) Summary:
   a) This case depicts the growing tension that has been building between the United States and Japan over the state of the bilateral trade between the two countries. Many Americans see the U.S.-Japan relationship as lopsided, as a result of Japan's $60 billion trade surplus with the U.S. The case describes several of the disputes that have arisen between the two countries. Each dispute has focused on U.S. firms trying to gain broader access to Japanese markets. The Japanese government has made concessions, but they have only come after intensive lobbying by the U.S. government and threats of retaliatory action.

2) Suggested Discussion Questions:
   a) If you were advising the American government on its trade policy with Japan, what would you tell the government to do? Should the government accelerate its pressure against Japan, stay the course, or back down, recognizing, however, that a "get tough" policy may trigger a trade war with Japan.
   b) In your opinion, is the Japanese government negotiating in good faith, or is the Japanese government trying to appease the American government without making an effort to enact meaningful trade reforms? Explain your answer.

c) Should the U.S. government take its complaints to the World Trade Organization? In your judgment, would this be a positive step in resolving the U.S.-Japanese dispute?

Country Focus: The Costs of Protectionism in the United States

1) Summary:

   a) This case illustrates that although American trade negotiators are quick to suggest that the U.S. economy is an open one with few import tariffs, import tariffs imposed by the U.S. government still exist. The case illustrate the adverse impact of these tariffs on the U.S. economy. A study conducted by the Institute for International Economics looked at the effect of import tariffs on economic activity in 21 industries that the U.S. protected most heavily from foreign competition. The study found that while the import tariffs saved about 200,000 jobs in the protected industries that would otherwise have been lost to foreign competition, they also cost American consumers about $32 billion per year in the form of higher prices, or over $50,000 per job saved.

2) Suggested Discussion Questions:

   a) The case illustrates the downside of subsidies. Looking at this situation from a different perspective, who benefits from subsidies? Are there occasions when subsidies are appropriate? Explain your answer.

   b) Draw upon the material presented in Chapter 5 to describe the destructive nature of tariffs. Does the information provided in the case support or hinder your arguments?

Management Focus: Toyota's Response to Rising Protectionist Pressures in Europe and the United States

1) Summary:

   a) This feature describes the emergence of Toyota on the world stage as an auto producer. Until the 1960s, Toyota was viewed as little more than an obscure Japanese automobile company. As a result of its world-class design and manufacturing skills, Toyota grew dramatically during the 1970s and 1980s, and is now one of the most productive auto companies in the world.

   The case also focuses on the challenges that Toyota has experienced in its export operations. For most of its history Toyota has exported cars from its plants in Japan. However, by the early 1980s political pressure and talk of local requirements in the United States and Europe forced an initially reluctant Toyota to rethink its trade policy. The trade policy that Toyota has adopted is to produce an increasingly number of cars in its major export markets. The case reviews that challenges that Toyota has faced in implementing this strategy.

2) Suggested Discussion Questions:

   a) In your option, would the United States government have imposed increasingly stringent tariffs and import quotas on Toyota if the company had not decided to build manufacturing facilities in the U.S.? From Toyota's perspective, what was the advantage of acting proactively rather than waiting for tariffs and quotas to be imposed?

   b) Explain the concept of "voluntary" export restraints. What role have voluntary export restraints played in Toyota's trade policy with the United States?

   c) Based on the information provided in the case, do you think that Toyota has been a good trade partner with the United States? Explain your answer.

3) Toyota Homepage: {http://www.toyota.com/}.

CHAPTER 6
FOREIGN DIRECT INVESTMENT

Learning Objectives

1. Be familiar with the forces underpinning the rising tide of foreign direct investment in the world economy.

2. Understand why firms often prefer direct investment as a strategy for entering a foreign market over alternatives such as exporting and granting foreign entities the right to produce the firm's product under license.

3. Appreciate why firms based in the same industry often undertake foreign direct investment at the same time.

4. Understand why certain locations are favored as the target of foreign direct investment activity.

5. Appreciate how political ideology influences government policy toward foreign direct investment.

6. Be conversant with the costs and benefits of foreign direct investment to receiving and source countries.

7. Have a good grasp of the different policy instruments that governments can use to restrict and encourage foreign direct investment.

Chapter Summary

This chapter focuses on the topic of foreign direct investment (FDI). FDI occurs when a firm invests directly in new facilities to produce and/or market a product in a foreign country. At the outset, the chapter discusses the growth in FDI, particularly by medium-sized and small firms. The theoretical underpinnings of FDI are discussed, which describe under what circumstances it is advantageous for a firm to invest in production facilities in a foreign country.

The chapter also addresses the different policies that governments have toward foreign direct investment. Some governments are opposed to FDI and some governments encourage it. Three specific ideologies of FDI are discussed, including the radical view, the free market view, and pragmatic nationalism. The chapter also provides a discussion of the costs and benefits of FDI from the perspective of both the home country and the host country involved. The chapter concludes with a review of the policy instruments that governments use to regulate FDI activity by international firms.

Chapter Outline With Lecture Notes and Teaching Tips

1) Introduction – This chapter is concerned with the phenomenon of foreign direct investment (FDI).

   a) Foreign Direct Investment – Occurs when a firm invests directly in new facilities to produce and/or market in a foreign country.

   b) Multinational Enterprise – Company that conducts business in more than one country.
   Teaching Tip: Each year Fortune magazine publishes a list of the 500 largest global corporations in the world. Fortune calls its list the "Global 500." This list, along with the article that accompanies the 1997 list, can be accessed at {http://pathfinder.com/fortune/1997/specials/g500/intro.html}. The article contains an excellent discussion of the role of global firms in the world economy.

Teaching Tip: Another web site that provides an excellent discussion of the role of multinational corporations in the world economy is available at {http://ps.ucdavis.edu/classes/pol129/SWE/multinat.htm}.

2) Foreign Direct Investment in the World Economy – When discussing foreign direct investment, it is important to distinguish between the flow and the stock of foreign direct investment.
   Teaching Tip: An excellent web site, sponsored by the University of California at Davis, provides a full array of information about Foreign Direct Investment. The site is available at {http://ps.ucdavis.edu/classes/pol129/SWE/direct.htm}.
   a) Flow of Foreign Direct Investment – Amount of FDI undertaken during a given period.
   b) Stock of Foreign Direct Investment – Total accumulation value of foreign-owned assets at a given time.
   c) Outflows of Foreign Direct Investment – Flow of FDI out of a country.
   d) Inflows of Foreign Direct Investment – Flow of FDI into a country.
   e) The Growth of Foreign Direct Investment – Over the past 20 years there has been a marked increase in both the flow and stock of FDI in the world economy.
   f) Changes in the Source of Foreign Direct Investment – Not only has the flow of FDI been accelerating, but its composition has also been changing. For most of the period after World War II, the U.S. was by far the largest source country for FDI. By 1990, however, the U.S. share of FDI outflows had slumped to 10.3 percent, pushing the U.S. into second place behind Japan.
   g) The Recipients of FDI – The leading recipient economies for FDI between 1985 and 1995 are summarized in Table 6.1 of the text.
      i) Host Country – Country that is on the receiving end of FDI.
      ii) Home Country – Country that is the source of FDI.
         Lecture Note: China is a major recipient of FDI by the United States and other Western countries. The Asian Wall Street Journal provides a "China Newsflash" each week on the Internet at {http://www.aial.com.hk/flash.html}. This site provides up-to-date information on international trade issues pertaining to China.
   h) FDI by Medium-Sized and Small Firms – FDI used to be associated most exclusively with multibillion-dollar corporations. In practice, however, the globalization of world markets has been accompanied by the rapid growth of FDI by small and medium-sized firms.

3) The Theory of Foreign Direct Investment – In this section of the text, several theories of foreign direct investments are discussed. These theories attempt to explain the observed pattern of foreign direct investment flows.
   a) Why Foreign Direct Investment – Why do so many firms apparently prefer FDI over either exporting or licensing?
      i) Limitations of Exporting – The viability of an exporting strategy is often constrained by transportation costs and trade barriers. Much foreign direct investment is undertaken as a response to actual or threatened trade barriers such as import tariffs or quotas.
      ii) Limitations of Licensing – There is a branch of economic theory known as internalization theory that seeks to explain why firms often prefer foreign direct investment over licensing as a strategy for entering foreign markets. According to internationalization theory, licensing has three major drawbacks as a strategy for exploiting foreign market opportunities.
         (1) First, licensing may result in a firm's giving away valuable technological know-how to a potential foreign competitor.

(2) Second, licensing does not give a firm the tight control over manufacturing, marketing, and strategy in a foreign country that may be required to maximize its profitability.

(3) Third, a problem arises with licensing when the firm's competitive advantage is based not so much on its products as on the management, marketing, and manufacturing capabilities that produce those products. Such capabilities are often not amenable to licensing.

   iii) Advantages of Foreign Direct Investment – It follows from the above discussion that a firm will favor FDI over exporting as an entry strategy when transportation costs or trade barriers make exporting unattractive. Furthermore, the firm will favor FDI over licensing when it wishes to maintain control over its technological know-how, or over its operations and business strategy, or when the firm's capabilities are simply not amenable to licensing.

   Teaching Tip: An article entitled "Constructing a Market Economy: A Guide to Countries in Transition" by Raymond Vernon (the author of the Product Life Cycle theory), discusses, among other things, the role of foreign direct investment in building a strong economy. The site is available at {http://www.cipe.org/e20/ver_E20.html}.

b) The Pattern of Foreign Direct Investment

   i) Following Competitors – One theory used to explain foreign direct investment patterns is based on the idea that firms follow their domestic competitors overseas. First expounded by F.T. Knickerbocker, this theory has been developed with regard to oligopolistic industries. An oligopoly is an industry composed of a limited number of large firms.

   ii) The Product Life Cycle – Vernon's view is that firms undertake FDI at particular stages in the life cycle of a product they have pioneered.

c) The Eclectic Paradigm – The eclectic paradigm has been championed by the British economist John Dunning. Dunning argues that in addition to the various factors discussed above, location-specific advantages are also of considerable importance in explaining both the rationale for and the direction of foreign direct investment.

   i) Local Specific Advantages – Advantages that arise from using resource endowments or assets that are tied to a particular location and that a firm finds valuable to combine with its own unique assets.

   ii) Externalities – Knowledge spillovers that occur when companies in the same industry locate in the same area.

4) Political Ideology and Foreign Direct Investment – Historically, ideology toward FDI has ranged from a radical stance that is hostile to all FDI to the non-interventionist principle of free market economies. Between these two extremes is an approach that might be called pragmatic nationalism.

a) The Radical View – The radical view tracts its roots to Marxist political and economic theory. Radical writers argue that the multinational enterprise is an instrument of imperialist domination. They see MNEs as a tool for exploiting host countries to the exclusive benefit of their capitalist-imperialist home countries. By the end of the 1980s, the radical position was in retreat almost everywhere.

b) The Free Market View – The free market view argues that international production should be distributed among countries according to the theory of comparative advantage. The free market view has been embraced by a number of advanced and developing nations, including the United States, Britain, Chile, and Hong Kong.

c) Pragmatic Nationalism – The pragmatic nationalist view is that FDI has both benefits and costs. Recognizing this, countries adopting a pragmatic stance pursue policies designed to maximize the national benefits and minimize the national costs.

d) Shifting Ideology – In recent years the center of gravity on the ideological spectrum has shifted strongly toward the free market stance.

5) Costs and Benefits of FDI to the Nation State
   a) Host Country Effects: Benefits
      i) Resource-Transfer Effects – FDI can make a positive contribution to a host economy by supplying capital, technology, and management resources that would otherwise not be available.
      ii) Employment Effects – The beneficial employment effect claimed for FDI is that FDI brings jobs to a host country that would otherwise not be created there.
      iii) Balance-of-Payments Effect – The effect of FDI on a country's balance-of-payments accounts is an important policy issue for most host governments.
         (1) Balance-of-Payments Account – Record of a country's payments to and receipts from other countries.
         (2) Current Account – Record of a country's export and import of goods and services.
   b) Host Country Effects: Costs
      i) Adverse Effects on Competition – Host governments sometimes worry that the subsidiaries of foreign MNEs operating in their country may have greater economic power than indigenous competitors because they may be part of a larger international organization.
      ii) Adverse Effects on the Balance of Payments – The possible adverse effects of FDI on a host country's balance-of-payments position are twofold.
         (1) First, set against the initial capital inflows that come with FDI must be the subsequent outflow of capital as the foreign subsidiary repatriates earnings to its parent country.
         (2) A second concern arises when a foreign subsidiary imports a substantial number of its inputs from abroad, which results in a debit on the current account of the host country's balance of payments.
      iii) National Sovereignty and Autonomy – Many host governments worry that FDI is accompanied by some loss of economic independence.
   c) Home Country Effects: Benefits – The benefits of FDI to the home country arise from three sources.
      i) First, the capital account of the home country's balance of payments benefits from the inward flow of foreign earnings.
      ii) Second, benefits to the home country from outward FDI arise from employment effects.
      iii) Third, benefits arise when the home country MNE learns valuable skills from its exposure to foreign markets that can subsequently be transferred back to the home country.
   d) Home Country Effects: Costs – The most important concerns center around the balance-of-payments and employment effects of outward FDI. With regard to employment effects, the most serious concerns arise when FDI is seen as a substitute for domestic production.
   e) International Trade Theory and Offshore Production – When assessing the costs and benefits of FDI to the home country, keep in mind the lessons of international trade (Chapter 4). International trade theory tells us that home country concerns about the negative economic effects of "offshore production" may be misplaced.

6) Government Policy Instruments and FDI

a) Home Country Policies:

    i) Encouraging Outward FDI – Many investor nations now have government-backed insurance programs to cover major types of foreign investment risk.

    ii) Restricting Outward FDI – Virtually all investor countries, including the United States, have exercised some control over outward FDI from time to time.

b) Host Country Policies:

    i) Encouraging Inward FDI – It is increasingly common for governments to offer incentives to foreign firms to invest in their countries.

    ii) Restricting Inward FDI – Host governments use a wide range of controls to restrict FDI. The two most common, however, are ownership restraints and performance requirements.

7) Implications for Business

a) The Theory of FDI – The implications of the theories of FDI for business practice are straightforward. First, the location-specific advantages argument associated with John Dunning helps explain the direction of FDI. However, the location-specific advantages argument does not explain why firms prefer FDI to licensing or to exporting. In this regard, from both an explanatory and a business perspective, perhaps the most useful theories are those that focus on the limitations of exporting and licensing.

b) Government Policy – A host government's attitude toward FDI should be an important variable in decisions about where to locate foreign production facilities and where to make a foreign direct investment.

    Teaching Tip: A site entitled Business Monitor has a section that provides information about the regulations involving foreign direct investment in almost every country in the world (you have to look for the information in each country's profile). The site can be accessed at {http://www.businessmonitor.co.uk/trading_blocks.shtml}.

    Teaching Tip: A very extensive directory of country specific web sites is available at {http://msm.byu.edu/c&i/cim/ibd/Country.htm}. These sites cover a wide variety of international business issues in regard to international business.

Critical Thinking and Discussion Questions

1. In recent years Japanese FDI in the United States has grown far more rapidly that U.S. FDI in Japan. Why do you think this is the case? What are the implications of this trend?

Answer: Currently, the U.S. has a $60 billion trade deficit with Japan. As a result, the U.S. government has been under protectionist pressure to impose tariffs and/or quotas on Japanese goods coming into America to rectify the trade balance. Given the threat of increased tariffs or quotas on good produced in Japan and exported to the U.S., Japanese firms have moved aggressively to set-up manufacturing facilities in the U.S. For example, Toyota now produces cars in California and Kentucky and Sharp produces microwave ovens in Tennessee. Both of these initiatives, along with many more, have resulted in a substantial amount of foreign direct investment on the part of Japanese firms in the United States.

Because the trade deficit is lopsided in favor of Japan, the Japanese government (with several notable exceptions) has not threatened U.S. firms with substantially increased tariffs or import quotas. As a result, there is not as much pressure on U.S. firms to invest in Japan as there is on Japanese firms to invest in the United States.

Challenge your students to assess the implications of this trend. Some people have made the remark that the Japanese are "buying up America?" Is this a fair statement? Should the amount of foreign direct investment by Japanese firms in America be regulated? These are important questions that can lead to stimulating classroom discussion.

2. Compare these explanations of FDI: internalization theory, Vernon's product life cycle theory, and Knickerbocker's theory of FDI. Which theory do you think offers the best explanation of the historical pattern of FDI? Why?

Answer: Internalization theory seeks to explain why firms often prefer foreign direct investment over licensing as a strategy for entering foreign markets. According to internationalization theory, licensing has three major drawbacks as a strategy for exploiting foreign market opportunities: licensing may result in a firm giving away proprietary technology, licensing does not permit a firm to maintain tight control over its activities, and licensing is not appropriate when a firm's competitive advantage is based not so much on its products as on the management, marketing, and manufacturing capabilities that produce those products.

Vernon's product life cycle theory argues that firms undertake FDI at particular stages in the life cycle of a product they have pioneered. They invest in other advanced countries when local demand in those countries grows large enough to support local production. They subsequently shift production to developing countries when product standardization and market saturation give rise to price competition and cost pressures. Investment in developing countries, where labor costs are lower, is seen as the best way to reduce costs.

Finally, Knickerbocker's theory of FDI suggests that firms follow their domestic competitors overseas. This theory had been developed with regard to oligopolistic industries. Imitative behavior can take many forms in an oligopoly, including FDI. An excellent example of how imitative behavior affects FDI in an oligopoly is provided on page 206 of the textbook.

The second part of this question is designed to stimulate classroom discussion and/or force your students to think through these theories and select the one that they feel provides the best explanation for the historic pattern of FDI. Vernon's product-life cycle theory seems to be the most robust and most descriptive. Opinions may vary, however, relative to this answer.

3. You are the international manager of a U.S. business that has just developed a revolutionary new personal computer that can perform the same functions as IBM and Apple computers and their clones but costs only half as much to manufacturer. Your CEO has asked you to formulate a recommendation for how to expand into Western Europe. Your options are (i) to export from the U.S., (ii) to license a European firm to manufacture and market the computer in Europe, and (iii) to set up a wholly owned subsidiary in Europe. Evaluate the pros and cons of each alternative and suggest a course of action to your CEO.

Answer: Exporting is a viable option in this situation. Because world demand for this product is likely to be high, a major advantage of exporting is that it would permit the firm to manufacture the product on one location or a few locations in its domestic market and by doing so capture substantial economies of scale. The disadvantage of exporting is that if too many computers go into a particular foreign market, jobs in the host country's computer will be threatened and the host country government may erect trade barriers to protect its domestic computer industry.

Licensing is out of the question. Because the computer is based on new technology, licensing runs the risk of giving away too much of the firm's proprietary technology to a foreign company. The only advantage of licensing in this case is that it may reduce the firm's expansion costs, but the tradeoff is not tenable.

Setting up a wholly owned subsidiary in Western Europe is another viable alternative. Through FDI, the firm would maintain greater control over the product and would provide jobs in the local economies (thus minimizing the threat of trade barriers). Since this is a revolutionary new product, the control issues may be particularly salient. The company could control the product through all stages of production, marketing, and, possibly, distribution. Another advantage of setting up the wholly owned subsidiary is that it would provide some of the firm's managers with overseas work experience. Developing a cadre of experienced managers may be particularly important if the firm attempts to open subsidiaries in other parts of the world. The disadvantage of setting up a wholly owned subsidiary is higher costs.

The arguments in favor of setting up a wholly owned subsidiary in Western Europe are the most compelling. This is the course of action that I would recommend to the CEO.

4. Explain how the political ideology of a host government might influence the process of negotiating access between the host government and a foreign MNE.

Answer: Host countries adopt policies designed both to restrict and to encourage inward FDI. It is increasingly common for governments to offer incentives to foreign firms to invest in their countries. Such incentives take many forms, but the most common are tax concessions, low-interest rate loans, and grants or subsidies. Incentives are motivated by a desire to gain from the resource-transfer and employment effects of FDI. In the United States, for example, state governments often compete with each other to attract FDI. If Honda announced that it was looking for a site to build a major new auto factory in the U.S., many states would offer incentives to Honda to attract Honda to their location.

On the other hand, host government also use a wide range of controls to restrict FDI. The two most common are ownership restraints and performance requirements. Ownership restraints require that a certain percentage of the foreign subsidiary be owned by a domestic company. For example, no foreign company can own more than 25 percent of a U.S. airline. Performance requirements are controls over the behavior of the local subsidiary of an MNE. The most common performance requirements are related to local content, exports, technology transfer, and local participation in top management.

As illustrated by the above descriptions, the political ideology of a host government can range from open arms to creating a very unfavorable environment for FDI. Clearly, the political ideology of the foreign government that a particular firm is dealing with will have a dramatic impact on the nature of the negotiations.

5. "Firms should not be investing abroad when there is a need for investment to create jobs at home!" Discuss.

Answer: This question is designed to stimulate classroom discussion or force your students to "think" about this provocative issue. International firms walk somewhat of a tightrope in managing their affairs. For instance, it would be easy for a Japanese citizen to say that Toyota should not be investing in manufacturing facilities in the U.S. when there are Japanese people looking for work. However, as mentioned in the textbook, Toyota has been compelled to invest in the U.S. to avoid the imposition of more stringent trade barriers on the part of the U.S. government to limit Toyota's exports into the United States. So what Toyota is doing by investing in the U.S. is protecting rather than sacrificing Japanese jobs by ensuring that the U.S. market will remain open to Japanese imports.

There are a number of other reasons that might compel a firm to engage in FDI. For instance, even though an American pharmaceutical company could license the production of a promising new drug to a foreign company rather than investing in the country by setting up a subsidiary, it might lose very valuable proprietary information through licensing that it could protect through owning and operating its own subsidiary. As a result, the American firm may be faced with an either or decision; either it sets up a foreign subsidiary or does not sell the drug in that particular country. As a result, if the company sets up a foreign subsidiary, the jobs would not replace American jobs for the reason described above.

Case Discussion Questions

1. What are the benefits to the Russian economy from Conoco's investment?

    Answer: Conoco's investment in Russia can make a positive contribution to the Russian economy by providing it capital, technology, employment, and management resources that would otherwise be unavailable.

2. What are the risks that Conoco must bear in investing in Russia?

    Answer: The risks for Conoco are enormous. Due to the unstable nature of the political and economic environment in Russia, the attitude of the Russia government relative to Conoco's presence in Russia could change at any time. If Conoco were asked to leave Russia, the company could lose all of its nonrecoverable investment in the Russian venture. In addition, there appears to be an unending number of administrative trade barriers that Conoco has to deal with to get its oil out of Russia. At some point, these barriers may become so oppressive that Conoco simply "gives up" and exists the Russia market on its own initiative.

3. Is there any way Conoco can reduce these risks without significantly curtailing its investment in Russia?

    Answer: One thing that Conoco could do is to bring more partners into the venture. For example, Conoco could build a consortium of American and European firms (e.g. Texaco, Shell, Mobile, Chevron) to joint venture with the Russian firm. This would reduce the exposure of each individual firm in the consortium. The downside of this strategy is that Conoco looses some control over its operations, and it lessens its profit potential if the venture works out.

Internet Exercise

1) Summary:
    a) This feature describes the Internet sites that provide information on the foreign direct investment of countries throughout the world. The exercise is focused on using the site sponsored by the Organization of Economic Development to review the foreign direct investment trends of a particular country.
2) Additional Material:
    a) Along with the sites mentioned in the exercise, there are an interesting collection of sites available on the web that are jointly sponsored by two or more nations that promote trade and foreign direct

investment between the nations. An example is the site sponsored by the United States-Mexico Chamber of Commerce {http://www.usmcoc.org/}.

Opening Case: Electrolux Invests in Asia and Eastern Europe

1) Summary:

   a) This case focuses on the growth plans of Electrolux, a Swedish producer of household appliances. Historically, the company depended primarily upon Western European markets for the majority of its sales. However, by the mid-1980, these markets had matured, and Electrolux had to look elsewhere to sustain its impressive growth rate. Electrolux decided to pursue markets in Asia and Eastern Europe. The case describes Electrolux's options in terms of entering these markets.

2) Suggested Discussion Questions:

   a) According to the case, Electrolux, General Electric, Whirlpool, and Bosch-Siemans, four major competitors in the global appliance market, were all moving at the same time to enter markets in Asia, Eastern Europe, and Russia. Which theory of foreign direct investment describes why global competitors seem to move in concert in regard to foreign investment patterns? Do you agree with this theory? Explain your answer.

   b) Electrolux decided to establish wholly owned subsidiaries in Russia, Poland, and the Czech Republic. Speculate on why Electrolux decided upon this foreign market entry strategy rather than exporting or licensing. Did Electrolux make the right decision? Why or why not?

3) Electrolux Homepage: {http://www.electrolux.com/}

Management Focus: Nissan in the United Kingdom

1) Summary:

   a) This feature focuses on Nissan's automobile factory in Britain. Nissan's investment in Britain was originally motivated by fear that rising protectionist pressure in Europe would make it increasingly difficult for Nissan to serve the European market through exports from Japan. In 1984, Nissan announced that it has selected the United Kingdom for the location of a major automobile factory. Initially, the countries on the European continent were critical of Britain for offering generous financial incentives to Nissan to lure the plant to British soil. One of the main criticism was that the plant would be nothing more than a "screwdriver plant" assembling cars from parts and components imported from Japan. Over time, however, the critics have been proven wrong. Today, the majority of the component parts used by the plant are provided by European suppliers. The plant has made a positive impact on the British economy, and has contributed to economic growth in other parts of Europe as well.

2) Suggested Discussion Questions:

   a) In your opinion, was Nissan's decision to invest in a manufacturing facility in Britain prudent? What type of retaliation could the EU have imposed on Nissan if it had persisted in a policy of strictly exporting cars from Japan to Europe?

   b) In retrospect, did Britain make the right decision by offering financial incentives to Nissan to locate its plant in Sunderland? In Britain, did Nissan find a government with a philosophy that is conductive to foreign direct investment? Explain your answer.

   c) Was it wise on the part of Nissan to ensure that a high percent of the component parts that went into their vehicles at the Sunderland plant be of European origin? In your opinion, how would the outcome of this case have differed if Nissan had insisted that the majority of the component parts be exported from Japan to Britain?

3) Nissan Homepage: {http:www.nissan.co.jp/}

Country Focus: FDI in Vietnam's Infant Auto Industry

1) Summary:

    a) This feature focuses on the reemergence of Vietnam as a participant in global trade. After the conclusion of the war in 1975, Vietnam effectively closed its doors to foreign investors. But the doors have now opened again. Although the government of Vietnam is still officially Communist, in recent years it has pursued an economic liberalization policy that is similar in many respects to that adopted by China. The feature talks about the willingness of Vietnam to accept foreign direct investment and about several companies that have made commitments to build production facilities in Vietnam. In particular, the German car company, Daimler-Benz, is planning to open two production plants in Vietnam in the near future. The feature discussion Daimler-Benz's challenges in implementing this endeavor.

2) Suggested Discussion Questions:

    a) If you were a stockholder of Daimler-Benz, would you feel good about the company's investment in Vietnam? (from strictly an economic standpoint). What are the potential advantages and pitfalls of Daimler'Benz's entry into the Vietnamese market?

    b) Is it realistic on the part of the government of Vietnam to insist on a high level of local content in regard to the component parts that go into Daimler Benz vehicles? Will this requirement discourage other companies from investing in Vietnam? Explain your answer.

    c) What political risk in the United States does a U.S. company face in investing in Vietnam? Is this a significant risk? Explain your answer.

Country Focus: Foreign Direct Investment in Venezuela's Petroleum Industry

1) Summary:

    a) This feature focuses on Venezuela's plan to significantly upgrade its domestic petroleum industry. The plan assigns a key role to foreign investment in Venezuela's oil industry for the first time since the country nationalized all private oil companies in 1976. The feature focuses on Venezuela's reasons for wanting foreign companies to be involved in its initiative. First, the initiative will be very expensive, and Venezuela needs outside capital. However, in addition, the country lacks the technological resources and skills of many of the world's major oil companies. By letting foreign companies participate in its initiative to upgrade its own oil industry, Venezuela hopes to learn new technologies and oil refining techniques to use in the future.

2) Suggested Discussion Questions:

    a) Discuss how this feature illustrates the valuable role that foreign direct investment plays in the global trade picture?

    b) Many protectionist minded people object to foreign direct investment, arguing that a company should provide jobs for its own citizens and not invest abroad. Similarly, people also argue that a government should keep foreign companies "out" in the interest of protecting local jobs. However, after reading this case, one could argue that foreign direct investment in Venezuela's oil initiative could be a "win-win" proposition for all the parties involved. Justify this argument.

CHAPTER 7
REGIONAL ECONOMIC INTEGRATION

Learning Objectives

1. Appreciate the different levels of economic integration that are possible between nations.

2. Understand the economic and political arguments for regional economic integration.

3. Understand the economic and political arguments against regional economic integration.

4. Be familiar with the history, current scope, and future prospects of the world's most important regional economic agreements, including the European Union, the North American Free Trade Agreement, MERCOSUR, and the Asian Pacific Economic Cooperation.

5. Understand the implications for business that are inherent in regional economic integration agreements.

Chapter Summary

In this chapter, the topic of regional economic integration is explored. The levels of regional economic integration discussed (from least integrate to most integrated) include: a free trade area, a customs union, a common market, an economic union, and a full political union. The arguments for and against regional economic integration are provided. Many students will remember some of these arguments from the debate of the ratification of the North American Free Trade Agreement (NAFTA).

The chapter provides information about the major trade blocks of the world, including the European Union, NAFTA, the Andean Group, MERCOSUR, and several other Latin American and Asian trade packs. The implications for business of these trade agreements and others is fully discussed.

Chapter Outline With Lecture Notes and Teaching Tips

1) Introduction - One notable trend in the global economy in recent years has been the accelerated movement toward regional economic integration.

   a) Regional economic integration – Agreement between countries in a geographic region to reduce tariff and nontariff barriers to the free flow of goods, services, and factors of production between each other.

2) Levels of Economic Integration – Several levels of economic integration are possible in theory (see Figure 7.2 in the textbook). From least integrated to most integrated, they are a free trade area, a customs union, a common market, an economic union, and, finally, a full potential union.

   a) Free Trade Area – In a free trade area all barriers to the trade of goods and services among member countries are removed. In a theoretically ideal free trade area, no discriminatory tariffs, quotas, subsidies, or administrative impediments are allowed to distort trade between member nations. Each country, however, is allowed to determine its own trade policies with regard to nonmembers. *Teaching Tip*: An excellent description of the major free trade areas of the world is available at: {http://ps.ucdavis.edu/classes/pol129/SWE/SWEfta.htm}.

   b) Customs Union – The customs union is one step further along the road to full economic and political integration. A customs union eliminates trade barriers between member countries and adopts a common external trade policy.

c) Common Market – Like a customs union, the theoretically ideal common market has no barriers to trade between member countries and a common external trade policy. Unlike in a customs union, in a common market, factors of production also are allowed to move freely between members. Thus, labor and capital are free to move, as there are no restrictions on immigration, emigration, or cross-border flows of capital between markets.

d) Economic Union – An economic union entails even closer economic integration and cooperation than a common market. Like the common market, an economic union involves the free flow of products and factors of production between members and the adoption of a common external trade policy. Unlike a common market, a full economic union also requires a common currency, harmonization of the member countries' tax rates, and a common monetary and fiscal policy.

e) Political Union – In a political union, independent states are combined into a single union. *Teaching Tip*: The International Trade Law Monitor is a site that provides a broad depth of information pertaining international trade law. This site is well worth a visit, and helps acquaint the reader with the legal ramifications of international trade agreements. The site is available at {http://ra.irv.uit.no/trade_law/itlp.html}.

3) The Case for Regional Integration
   a) The Economic Case for Integration – Regional economic integration can be seen as an attempt to achieve additional gains from the free flow of trade and investment between countries beyond those attainable under international agreements such as the WTO.

   b) The Political Case for Integration – Linking neighboring economies and making them increasingly dependent on each other creates incentives for political cooperation between neighboring states.

   c) Impediments to Integration – There are two main impediments to integration. First, although economic integration benefits the majority, it has costs. Although a nation as a whole may benefit significantly from a regional free trade agreement, certain groups may lose. A second impediment to integration arises from concerns over national sovereignty.

4) The Case Against Regional Integration – Although the tide has been running strongly in favor of regional free trade agreements in recent years, some economists have expressed concern that the benefits of regional integration have been oversold, while the costs have often been ignored. They point out that the benefits of regional integration to the participants are determined by the extent of trade creation, as opposed to trade diversion.
   a) Trade Creation – Occurs when high-cost domestic producers are replaced by low-cost producers within the free trade area.

   b) Trade Diversion – Occurs when lower-cost external suppliers are replaced by higher-cost suppliers within the free trade area.

5) Regional Economic Integration in Europe – There are two trade blocks in Europe: the European Union (EU) and the European Free Trade Association. Of the two, the EU is by far the more significant, not just in terms of membership, but also in terms of economic and political influence in the world economy.
   a) Evolution of the European Union – The EU is the product of two political factors: first, the devastation of two world wars on Western Europe and the desire for a lasting peace, and second, the European nations' desire to hold their own on the world's political and economic stage. *Teaching Tip*: The EU maintains an excellent web site at {http://europa.eu.int/index-en.htm}. The site is very substantive, and contains a broad array of information about the historical role and current activities of the EU in the global economy.

58

b) The Single European Act – The Single European Act, adopted by the EU member nations in 1987, committed the EC countries to work toward establishment of a single market by December 31, 1992.

    i) The Stimulus for the Single European Act – The Single European Act was born out of frustration among EC members that the community was not living up to its promise. In the early 1980s, many of the EC's prominent businesses people mounted an energetic campaign to end the EC's economic divisions. The result was the Single European Act, which was independently ratified by the parliaments of each member country and became EC law in 1987.

    ii) The Objectives of the Act – The purpose of the Single European Act was to have a single market in place by December 31, 1992. The changes the act proposed include the following:

        (1) Frontier Controls – Remove all frontier controls between EC countries.

        (2) Mutual Recognition of Standards – Apply the principle of "mutual recognition," which is that a standard developed in one EC country should be accepted in another, provided it meets basic requirements in such matters as health and safety.

        (3) Public Procurement – Open procurement to non-national suppliers.

        (4) Financial Services – Lift barriers to competition in the retail banking and insurance businesses.

        (5) Exchange Controls – Remove all restrictions on foreign exchange transactions between members by the end of 1992.

        (6) Freight Transport – Abolish restrictions on sabotage, the right of foreign truckers to pick up and deliver goods within another member's borders, by the end of 1992.

        (7) Supply-Side Effects – All those changes should lower the costs of doing business in the EC, but the single-market program is also expected to have more complicated supply-side effects.

    iii) Implications – The implications of the Single European Act are potentially enormous. If the EU is successful in establishing a single market, member countries can expect significant gains from the free flow of trade and investment.

c) The Treaty of Maastricht and Its Aftermath – The treaty lays down the main elements of a future European government: a single currency, a common foreign and defense policy, a common citizenship, and an EU parliament with teeth. It

    i) European Monetary Union – As with many of the provisions of the Single European Act, the move to a single currency should significantly lower the costs of doing business in the EU.

d) Enlargement of the European Union – The other big issue that the EU must now grapple with is enlargement.

e) Fortress Europe? – U.S. and Asian countries are concerned that the EU at some point will impose new barriers on imports from outside the EU. The fear is that the EU might increase external protection as weaker members attempt to offset their loss of protection against other EU countries by arguing for limitations on outside competition.

6) Regional Economic Integration in the Americas

a) The North Atlantic Free Trade Agreement (NAFTA) – The free trade agreement between the United States, Canada, and Mexico became law January 1, 1994. It contains the following actions. *Teaching Tip*: The NAFTA Homepage can be accessed at {http://www.nafta.net/naftagre.htm}.

    i) Abolishes within 10 years tariffs on 99 percent of the goods traded between Mexico, Canada, and the United States, removes most barriers on the cross-border flow of services, protects intellectual property rights, removes most restrictions on FDI between the three member countries, allows each country to apply its own environmental standards, provided such standards have a scientific base, establishes two commissions with the poser to impose fines and remove trade privileges when environmental standards or legislation involving health and safety, minimum wages, or child labor are ignored.

    ii) Arguments for NAFTA

        (1) Proponents argue that NAFTA should be viewed as an opportunity to create an enlarged and more efficient productive base for the entire region.

        (2) The international competitiveness of U.S. and Canadian firms that move production to Mexico to take advantage of lower labor costs will be enhanced.
           Teaching Tip: There are many organizations anxious to take advantage of the opportunities offered by NAFTA. As evidence of this, direct your students' attention towards a web site entitled The NAFTA Register {http://www.nafta.net/global/}. The NAFTA Register is a directory of export management companies, export service providers, and trading companies that want to profit from NAFTA by helping buyers and selling take advantage of NAFTA related opportunities.

    iii) Arguments Against NAFTA

        (1) Those who opposed NAFTA claimed that ratification would be followed by a mass exodus of jobs from the United States and Canada into Mexico as employers sought to profit from Mexico's lower wages and less strict environmental and labor laws.
           Teaching Tip: A thoughtful article on the environmental impact of NAFTA is available at {http://lanic.utexas.edu/cswht/NAFTA-environ.html}.

    iv) The Early Experience – It is probably far two early to draw conclusions about the true impact of NAFTA on trade flows and employment.

    v) Enlargement – One big issue now confronting NAFTA is that of enlargement.

  b) The Andean Group – The Andean Group was formed in 1969 when Bolivia, Chile, Ecuador, Columbia, and Peru signed the Cargagena Agreement. The Andean Group was largely based on the EC model, but it has been far less successful at achieving its stated goals.

  c) MERCOSUR – MERCOSUR originated in 1988 as a free trade pact between Brazil and Argentina.
    Teaching Tip: MERCOSUR's Homepage, which includes a broad array of useful information, can be accessed at {http://www.americasnet.com/mauritz/mercosur/english/}.
    Lecture Note: A case study of the effects of MERCOSUR on Uruguay is available at {http://sunsite.scu.eun.eg/untpdc/incubator/ury/tpmon/mercosur.htm}.

  d) Other Latin American Trade Pacts

7) Regional Economic Integration Elsewhere

  a) Association of Southeast Asian Nations – Formed in 1967, ASEAN currently includes Brunei, Indonesia, Malaysia, the Philippines, Singapore, Thailand, and, most recently, Vietnam. The basic objectives of ASEAN are to foster freer trade between member countries and to achieve some cooperation in their industrial policies. Progress has been limited, however.

  b) Asian Pacific Economic Cooperation (APEC) – APEC currently has 18 members including such economic powerhouses as the United States, Japan, and China. The stated aim of APEC is to increase multilateral cooperation in view of the economic rise of the pacific nations and the growing interdependence within the region.
    Teaching Tip: The Homepage of the APEC can be accessed at {http://www.apecsec.org.sg/}. A wealth of information about the APEC is available at this site.

8) Implications for Business
   a) Opportunities
      i) Creation of a single market offers significant opportunities because markets that were formerly protected from foreign competition are opened.
      ii) Additional opportunities arise from the inherent lower costs of doing business in a single market as opposed to 15 national markets in the case of the EU or 3 national markets in the case of NAFTA.
   b) Threats
      i) Just as the emergence of single markets in the EU and North America creates opportunities for business, so it also presents a number of threats. For one thing, the business environment within both groups will become more competitive.
      ii) A further threat to non-EU and/or non-North American firms arises from the likely long-term improvements in the competitive position of many European and North American companies.

Critical Thinking and Discussion Questions

1. NAFTA is likely to produce net benefits for the U.S. economy. Discuss.

   Answer: The proponents argue that NAFTA should be viewed as an opportunity to create an enlarged and a more productive base for the U.S., Canada, and Mexico. As low-income jobs move from Canada and the United States to Mexico, the Mexican economy should be strengthened giving Mexico the ability to purchase higher-cost American products. The net effect of the lower income jobs moving to Mexico and Mexico increasing its imports of high quality American goods should be positive for the American economy. In addition, the international competitiveness of United States and Canadian firms that move production to Mexico to take advantage of lower labor costs will be enhanced, enabling them to better compete with Asian and European rivals.

2. What are the economic and political arguments for regional economic integration? Given these arguments, why don't we see more integration in the world economy?

   Answer: The economic case for regional integration is straightforward. As we saw in Chapter 4, unrestricted free trade allows countries to specialize in the production of goods and services that they can produce most efficiently. If this happens as the result of economic integration within a geographic region, the net effect is greater prosperity for the nations of the region. From a more philosophical perspective, regional economic integration can be seen as an attempt to achieve additional gains from the free flow of trade and investment between countries beyond those attainable under international agreements such as the WTO.

   The political case for integration is also compelling. Linking neighboring economies and making them increasingly dependent on each other creates incentives for political cooperation between neighboring states. Also, the potential for violent conflict between the states is reduced. In addition, by grouping their economies together, the countries can enhance their political weight in the world.

   Despite the strong economic and political arguments for integration, it has never been easy to achieve (on a meaningful level). There are two main reasons for this. First, although economic integration benefits the majority, it has its costs. Although a nation as a whole may benefit significantly from a regional free trade agreement, certain groups may loose. These groups may block a potential form of economic integration is the garner sufficient political clout. The second impediment to integration arises from concerns over national sovereignty.

3. What is the likely effect of creation of a single market within the EU likely to be on competition within the EU? Why?

    Answer: If the EU is successful in establishing a single market, member countries can expect significant gains from the free flow of trade and investment. This will result from the ability of the countries within the EU to specialize in the production of the product that they manufacture the most efficiently, and the have the freedom to trade those product with other EU countries without being encumbered by tariffs and other trade barriers. In terms of competition, the competition between European firms will increase. Some of the most inefficient firms may go out of business, because they will no longer be protected from other European companies by high tariffs, quotas, or administrative trade barriers.

4. How should a U.S. firm that currently exports only to Western Europe respond to the creation of a single market?

    Answer: According to European officials, the creation of a single market in Europe will not have a significant effect on trade with other nations, and the trade barriers that a European single market are likely to impose will not be oppressive. However, common sense says that any prudent firm should take a wait and see approach and watch the developments in Europe closely. Against this backdrop, the U.S. firm that currently exports only to Western Europe might want to think about diversifying its export operations. If a single market is created in Europe, the U.S. firm will be dealing with only one set of conditions (in terms of tariffs, quotas, etc.), and will in effect have all of its eggs in one basket. Diversification into other areas of the world, while retaining its present European markets, seems prudent.

    Another alternative for the U.S. firm to think about is to open a wholly-owned subsidiary in Europe to produce the product that it now exports.

5. How should a firm with self-sufficient production facilities in several EU countries respond to the creation of a single market? What are the constraints on its ability to respond in a manner that minimizes production costs?

    Answer: The firm should respond favorably for several reasons. First, if one or more of it's plants is in operation simply as a result of the need to avoid tariffs or trade barriers, the necessity of keeping those plants open can be reviewed. Second, if several plants remain open, the company can shift the production of a particular product or component part to the plant that can manufacturer it the most efficiently (regardless of country within the single market). The plants will not have to remain self-sufficient, because the trade barriers and other impediments to doing business between the nations in the single market will be removed.

    In terms of the second half of this question, if the single market is achieved like it is now envisioned, there will be no constraints on the ability of a firm to respond in a manner that minimized production costs.

Case Discussion Questions

1. What are the economic costs and benefits to Martin's Textiles of shifting production to Mexico?

   Answer: The economic benefits are compelling. Martin Textiles could replace its $12.50 per hour laborers with labor at a much cheaper rate in Mexico. According to the textbook, in 1991 the average hourly labor costs in Mexico were $2.32. One can only speculate on the economic costs of shifting production to Mexico. Quality may suffer as a result of a less experienced Mexican workforce. In addition, Martin Textiles will incur some additional costs as a result of the need to maintain a sales force in the United States while maintaining manufacturing facilities in Mexico.

2. What are the social costs and benefits to Martin's Textiles of shifting production to Mexico?

   Answer: The potential social costs are compelling. John Martin and his employees will have to go through the emotional turmoil of closing the New York facility and moving the manufacturing operations to Mexico. Probably only a few, if any, of Martin's employees will become expatriate managers at the new facility in Mexico. Also, the environmental laws in Mexico are much more relaxed than the United States. Even if the firm begins its operations in Mexico with good intentions, it will be tempting to operate under the auspices of Mexican rather than U.S. environmental standards, which means that the plant in Mexico will probably be less environmentally friendly than the plant in New York. In terms of benefits, Martin will provide employment for Mexican workers. This will have a positive impact on the Mexican economy. From a broad perspective, as the Mexican economy improves, the people in Mexico will have more money to buy American goods. So, in an indirect manner, by moving to Mexico Martin Textiles may be providing jobs for U.S. workers by increasing the demand for U.S. goods in Mexico.

3. Are the economic and social costs and benefits of moving production to Mexico independent of each other?

   Answer: This question is designed to stimulate classroom discussion or to encourage your students to "think" about this challenging question in preparing a written answer. Clearly, the economic and social costs of moving production to Mexico are not independent of one another. For example, the increased profitability that comes from the lower wage rates in Mexico can only be achieved by laying off the long-time employees in New York.

4. What seems to be the most ethical action?

   Answer: This is the same question that faces many American firms facing the same dilemma. The most ethical approach may be to move the jobs to Mexico, but to do so in a gradual manner. That would ultimately achieve the company's objective of lowering its manufacturing costs, and provide time for Martin's employees to find other jobs. The company could also consider generous severance packages for longtime employees.

5. What would you do if you were John Martin?

Answer: This question is designed to stimulate classroom discussion and/or to encourage your students to "think" about this business dilemma.

Internet Exercise

1) Summary:
    a) This feature acquaints the reader with a number of Internet sites that provide information on regional trade agreements and other forms of regional integration. The addresses for several sites that pertain specifically to the European Union are provided. The exercise portion of the feature instructs the reader to use the Internet to find out several specific pieces of information about the EU and other regional economic trade groups.

2) Additional Material:
    a) In America, NAFTA has been the trade group that has received the most attention and affects America's the most directly. The following are web site addresses that pertain specifically to NAFTA:
        i) NAFTA Homepage: (Sponsored by the U.S. Department of Commerce: {http://iepnt1.itaiep.doc.gov/nafta/nafta2.htm}.
        ii) Study on the Operation and Effect of NAFTA (Compiled by the Office of the U.S. Trade Representative: {http://www.ustr.gov/reports/index.html}.
        iii) NAFTA Net (Sponsored by the North American Forum): {http://www.nafta.net/}
        iv) Mexico Online – The NAFTA Center (Sponsored by the Mexican Business Center): {http://www.mexicool.com/business/nafta1.html}.

Opening Case: Tales From the New Europe

1) Summary:
    a) This feature focuses on the early affects of the implementation of the Single European Act in 1993. Several examples are provided of both the positive effects and the negative effects of the Act on individual Europeans.

2) Suggested Discussion Questions:
    a) From the case, provide examples of both the positive effects and the negative effects of the Single European Act on European citizens.
    b) According to the case, Bernard Cornille, an agent for a French manufacturer of cash machines, had to close his production facility in France and lay off three assistants because the Single European Act paved the way for Spanish and Italian companies to sell cheaper cash machines to Mr. Cornille's customers. Suppose one of the workers that just lost his job asked you the following question. "How can any Act that results in a hard-working person losing his job be good for an entire continent?" How would you answer this question?
    c) How optimistic are you that the provision of the Single European Act will reach their full potential Explain your answer.

Regional Focus: The Creation of a Single European Insurance Market

1) Summary:

a) This feature focuses on the effects of the new rules regarding the insurance market in Europe that have results from the Single European Act. The new rules do two main things. First, they make genuine cross-border trade possible by allowing insurance companies to sell their products anywhere in the EU on the basis of regulations in their home states. Second, insurers throughout the EU will be allowed to set their own rates for all classes of insurance policy. The feature describes the early results of these changes. To date, the changes have produced progress in equalizing insurance rates across Europe, but have not reached their full potential.

2) Suggested Discussion Questions:

a) Describe the overall importance of the Single European Act. Will the full implementation of the changes included in this act have a dramatic impact on free trade in Europe?

b) Why has it been so difficult to equalize insurance rates across Europe? In your opinion, will the insurance industry in Europe ever have a single set of rates for European customers? Why or why not?

Management Focus: Wal-Mart's Expansion Plans in Mexico Run Into Red Tape

1) Summary:

a) This feature focuses on Wal-Mart's early experiences in Mexico. After the passage of NAFTA, Wal-Mart announced an ambitious plan to build Wal-Mart discount stores and Sam's Clubs in Mexico. Consistent with this announcement, in early 1994 four Wal-Mart stores and 10 warehouse-style Sam's Clubs were opened. In the summer of 1994 realty struck. A group of government inspectors made a surprise visit to Wal-Mart's new superstore in Mexico City. The inspectors found thousands of items that they claimed were improperly labeled or lacked Spanish instructions. The remainder of the feature describes other administrative delays and headaches that Wal-Mart has experienced in Mexico.

2) Suggested Discussion Questions:

a) If you were the CEO of Wal-Mart, how enthused would you be about moving forward with your plans to open new stores in Mexico?

b) In Chapter 5, administrative trade policies were defined as bureaucratic rules that are designed to make it difficult for importers to enter a country. Is what Wal-Mart is experiencing in Mexico a form of an administrative trade policy, even if it is an informal one directed towards a company that is already in the country? Can any trade agreement totally prevent what has happened to Wal-Mart in Mexico?

c) What is the lesson to be learned from this case? Explain your answer.

3) Wal-Mart Homepage: {http://www.wal-mart.com/}

CHAPTER 8
THE FOREIGN EXCHANGE MARKET

Learning Objectives

1. Be familiar with the form and function of the foreign exchange market.

2. Understand the different between spot and forward exchange rates.

3. Understand how currency exchange rates are determined.

4. Appreciate the role of the foreign exchange market in insuring against foreign exchange risk.

5. Be familiar with the merits of different approaches toward exchange rate forecasting.

6. Appreciate why some currencies cannot always be converted into other currencies.

7. Understand how countertrade is used to mitigate problems associated with an inability to convert currencies.

Chapter Summary

This chapter focuses on the foreign exchange market. At the outset, the chapter explains how the foreign exchange market works. Included in this discussion is an explanation of the difference between spot exchange rates and forward exchange rates. The nature of the foreign exchange market is discussed, including an examination of the forces that determine exchange rates. In addition, the author provides a discussion of the degree to which it is possible to predict exchange rate movements.

Other topics discussed in the chapter include exchange rate forecasting, currency convertibility, and the implications of exchange rate movements on business. In regard to the later, a number of implications of exchange rates for businesses are contained in the chapter. For instance, it is absolutely critical that international businesses understand the influence of exchange rates on the profitability of trade and investment deals. Adverse changes in exchange rates can make apparently profitable deals unprofitable.

Chapter Outline With Lecture Notes and Teaching Tips

1) Introduction – This chapter has three main objectives. The first is to explain how the foreign exchange market works. The second is to examine the forces that determine exchange rates and to discuss the degree to which it is possible to predict exchange rate movements. The third objective is to map the implications for international business of exchange rate movements and the foreign exchange market. *Lecture Note*: FX Week is an on-line newsletter for foreign exchange specialists. The newsletter provides current information and features about the foreign exchange market that might provide interesting lecture material. The site is available at {http://www.fxweek.com/}.

   a) Foreign Exchange Market – Market for converting the currency of one country into that of another country.

   b) Exchange Rate – Rate at which one currency is converted into another.

2) The Functions of the Foreign Exchange Market

   a) Currency Conversion – The first function of the foreign exchange market is to convert the currency of one country into the currency of another.

Teaching Tip: There are several sites available on the Internet that are "currency converters." These sites provides on-line currency conversion information. An example of one of these sites can be found at {http://www.dna.lth.se/cgi-bin/kurt/rates}.

i) Currency Speculation – Short-term movement of funds from one currency to another in the hopes of profiting from shifts in exchange rates.

ii) Insuring Against Foreign Exchange Risk – A second function of the foreign exchange market is to provide insurance to protect against the possible adverse consequences of unpredictable changes in exchange rates.

(1) Spot Exchange Rate – The spot exchange rate is the rate at which a foreign exchange dealer converts one currency into another currency on a particular day.

(2) Forward Exchange Rate – Two parties agree to exchange currency and execute the deal at some specific date in the future.

(a) Forward Exchange Rate – Rates for currency exchange quoted for 30, 90, or 180 days into the future.

3) The Nature of the Foreign Exchange Market – The foreign exchange market is not located in any one place. Rather, it is a global network of banks, brokers, and foreign exchange dealers connected by electronic communications systems.

a) Features of Particular Note – Two features of the foreign exchange market are of particular note. The first is that the market never sleeps. There are only 3 hours out of every 24 that Tokyo, London, and New York are all shut down. The second feature of the market is the integration of the various trading centers. Direct telephone lines, fax, and computer linkages between trading centers around the globe have effectively created a single market.

Teaching Tip: There is a very entertaining and information "Foreign Currency Aptitude Test" available on-line at {http://www.cme.com/market/cfot/quiz}. The test, which is sponsored by the Chicago Mercantile Exchange, contains 16 multiple-choice questions that are scored on-line.

4) What Determines Exchange Rates? – At the most basic level, exchange rates are determined by the demand and supply of one currency relative to the demand and supply of another.

a) The Law of One Price – Identical products sold in different countries must sell of the same price when their price is expressed in the same currency in competitive markets free of transportation costs and barriers to trade.

b) Purchasing Power Parity – If the law of one price were true for all goods and services, the purchasing power parity (PPP) exchange rate could be found from any individual set of prices. A less extreme version of the PPP theory states that given relatively efficient markets – that is, markets in which few impediments to international trade and investment exist – the price of a "basket of goods" should be roughly equivalent in each country.

c) Money Supply and Price Inflation – In essence, PPP theory predicts that changes in relative prices will result in a change in exchange rates.

d) Empirical Tests of PPP Theory – Extensive empirical testing of the PPP theory has not shown it to be completely accurate in estimating exchange rate changes.

e) Interest Rates and Exchange Rates

i) International Fisher Effect – For any two countries, the spot exchange rate should change in an equal amount but in the opposite direction to the difference in the nominal interest rates between the two countries.

f) Investor Psychology and Bandwagon Effects – There is increasing evidence that various psychological factors, as opposed to macroeconomic fundamentals, play an important role in determining the expectations of market traders as to likely future exchange rates.

5) Exchange Rate Forecasting

a) The Efficient Market School – Many economists believe the foreign exchange market is efficient at setting forward rates. An efficient market is one in which prices reflect all available information. There have been a large number of empirical tests of the efficient market hypothesis. Although most of the early work seems to confirm the hypothesis (suggesting that companies should not waste their money on forecasting services), more recent studies have challenged it.

b) The Inefficient Market School – An inefficient market is one in which prices do not reflect all available information. In an efficient market, forward exchange rates will not be the best possible predictors of future spot exchange rates. If this is true, it may be worthwhile for international businesses to invest in forecasting services (and many do).

c) Approaches to Forecasting

i) Fundamental Analysis – Draws on economic theory to construct sophisticated econometric models for predicting exchange rate movements.

ii) Technical Analysis – Predicts exchange rate movements by using price and volume data to determine past trends, which are expected to continue into the future.

6) Currency Convertibility

a) Convertibility and Government Policy

i) Freely Convertible – Currency able to be used by both residents and nonresidents to purchase foreign currency in unlimited amounts.

ii) Externally Convertible – Currency able to be used by nonresidents only to purchase foreign currency in unlimited amounts.

iii) Nonconvertible – Currency that cannot be converted into a foreign currency.

b) Countertrade – Barterlike agreements by which goods and services can be traded for other goods and services; used in international trade when a country's currency is nonconvertible.
Teaching Tip: A brief, yet informative, article about countertrade can be accessed at {http://www.iccwho.org/html/countertrade.thml}.
Lecture Note: According to the Department of Trade and Industry in the United Kingdom, countertrade is now thought to account for between 10 and 15% of trade worldwide.

7) Implications for Business

a) First, it is absolutely critical that international businesses understand the influence of exchange rates on the profitability of trade and investment deals.

b) International businesses must also understand the forces that determine exchange rates.

c) Complicating this picture is the issue of currency convertibility.

Critical Thinking and Discussion Questions

1. The interest rate on German government securities with one-year maturity is 4 percent, and the expected inflation rate for the coming year is 2 percent. The interest rate on U.S. government securities with one-year maturity is 7 percent, and the expected rate of inflation is 5 percent. The current sport exchange rate for German marks is $1 = DM 1.4. Forecast the spot exchange rate one-year from today. Explain the logic of your answer.

Answer: First, one must determine the nominal interest rate for both countries. The nominal interest rate (i) is the sum of the required "real" rate of interest (r) and the expected rate of inflation over the period of time for which the funds are to be lent (I). More formally, $i = r + I$. Based on the information provided in the question, this means that the nominal interest rate in Germany is 6% and the nominal interest rate in the United States is 12%. According to the International Fisher Effect, if the U.S. nominal interest rate is higher than Germany's, reflecting greater expected inflation, the value of the dollar against the deutsche mark should fall by that interest rate differential in the future.

Thus, since the exchange rate is presently $1 = DM 1.4, a 6% depreciation in the value of the dollar against the deutsche mark would result in an exchange rate of $1 = DM 1.3. (or 1.316 exactly)

2. Two countries, France and the United States, produce just one good: beef. Suppose the price of beef in the United States is $2.80 per pound and in France it is FFr 3.70. (a) According to PPP theory, what should the $/FFr spot exchange rate be?; (b) Suppose the price of beef is expected to rise to $3.10 in the United States to FFr 4.65 in France. What should the one-year forward $/FFr exchange rate be? (c) Given your answers to parts a and b, and given that the current interest rate in the United States is 10 percent, what would you expect the current interest rate to be in France (see the note below pertaining to this question)?

Answer: (a) According to PPP theory, the $/FFr exchange rate = $2.80 (price of a pound of beef in the United States) / FFr 3.70 (price of a pound of beef in France) or $0.75 FFr (i.e., $1 = FFr 1.33); (b) $3.10 (projected price of a pound of beef in the United States) / FFr 4.65 (projected price of beef in France) = $0.66 FFr (i.e. $1 = FFr 1.50); (c) do not use this question.

3. You manufacture wine goblets. In mid-June your receive an order for 10,000 goblets from Germany. Payment of DM 400,000 is due in mid-December. You expect the deutsche mark to rise from its present rate of $1 = DM 1.5 to $1 = DM 1.4 by December. You can borrow marks at 6 percent annually. What should you do?

Answer: There is a problem with the set-up of this question. Do not use the question.

Case Discussion Questions

1. What was the root cause of the fall in the external value of the Russian ruble between 1992 and 1995?

Answer: The root cause of the ruble's fall during this period was Russia's high inflation rate.

2. What must the Russian government do to halt the decline in the value of the ruble?

Answer: The Russian government must take steps to (1) control inflation, and (2) implement meaningful reforms that will provide the world community assurance that the country's economy has stabilized. This will require the Russian government to either end or significantly curtail it subsidies to inefficient Russian industries. In conjunction with this, the government will also have to control the money supply to attenuate inflationary pressures.

3. Why do you think that it is important for a government to promote a stable currency?

Answer: There are at least two important reasons for a government to promote a stable currency. The first reason is that a country's inflation rate, interest rates, and exchange rates are all intimately linked. A stable currency helps keep a country's inflation rate and interest rates in check. In addition, psychological factors must be recognized. As the value of a country's currency starts depreciating against the currency of other countries, sometimes investors panic and the downward spiral in a country's exchange rate is more a reflection of the psychology of currency traders than economic reality. An effort on the part of a government to promote stability in its currency lessens the possibility of this happening.

The second reason for a government to promote a stable currency is to attract international trade and foreign direct investment. Foreign investors are reluctant to invest heavily in a foreign country if they believe that the stability of a country's currency is in question.

4. Do you think the Russian central bank will be able to defend the ruble against speculative pressure and keep it in the trading range announced on July 6, 1995?

Answer: This question is designed to stimulate classroom discussion and/or encourage your students to "think" about this challenging question in preparing a written answer. Despite the resolve of the Russian government, it may be difficult to defend the ruble and keep it within the announced trading range. In the end, only fundamental reforms in the Russian economy and genuine economic progress will save the rubble.

Internet Exercise

1) Summary:
    a) This feature alerts the reader to the availability of up-to-date exchange rate information on the Internet. The Internet addresses for several sites are provided. The exercise portion of the feature asks the reader the use the PACIFIC site to determine today's current exchange rates for his or her country of national origin.
2) Additional Material:
    a) Another excellent exchange rate site is the OANDA currency converter. This site will compute on-line (and free of charge) the current exchange rates between the currencies of 164 different countries.

Opening Case: JAL

1) Summary:
    a) The feature focuses on the currency exchange rate implications of the manner in which Japan Air Lines (JAL) purchases commercial aircraft from Boeing. Because JAP is a Japanese company, the majority of the money that it earns is paid in Japanese yen. However, when JAL purchases aircraft from Boeing, it must covert its yen into dollars to make payment to Boeing. The problem is that JAL must place an order with Boeing approximately five years before the actual plane can be delivered. Along with the order, JAL must pay Boeing a 10 percent deposit. The aircraft that JAL purchase from Boeing involve substantial amounts of money, ranging from $35 million for a 737 to $160 million for a top-of-the line 747-400. Because of this, when purchasing an aircraft from Boeing, JAL uses forward exchange contracts to protect itself against adverse currency movements. The case relates the positive and negative consequences of this policy.

2) Suggested Discussion Questions:

   a) Describe a forward exchange contract? Would JAL be as willing to purchase aircraft from Boeing without the availability of a forward exchange rate market? Why or why not?

   b) In your option, does JAL manage its foreign exchange risk in a prudent manner? Explain your answer?

   c) Explain a scenario in which JAL could be badly hurt if it did not use forward exchange contracts in its relationship with Boeing.

Management Focus: George Soros – The Man Who Moves Markets

1) Summary:

   a) This feature focuses on George Soros, a 65-year old Hungarian-born financier, who is the principal partner of the Quantum Group, which controls a series of hedge funds with assets of around $12 billion. The Quantum Group, which holds a diversified portfolio of assets, is one of the world's largest currency "speculators." The case relates several incidences in which the Quantum Group took major positions in foreign currency exchange rates, and experienced substantial profits and losses. According to the feature, the Quantum Group takes positions that are so large and closely watched, that a major action by the Quantum Group can start a "bandwagon effect" that causes currency movements in the direction that the Quantum Group expects.

2) Suggested Discussion Questions:

   a) Describe what is meant by the term "bandwagon effect."

   b) Describe how an investor can make money by "short selling" one currency against another.

   c) In your opinion, does the Quantum Group serve a useful function or a disruptive function in regard to world currency markets? Make your answer as substantive as possible.

3) Applicable Web Sites:

   a) George Soros Biographical Information: {http://soros.org/gsbio.html}.

Country Focus: Money Supply Growth, Inflation, and Exchange Rates in Bolivia

1) Summary:

   a) This feature focuses on Boliva's economic experiences in the mid-1980s. In the mid-1980s Boliva experienced hyper-inflation – an explosive and seemingly uncontrollable price inflation in which money loses value very rapidly. Between April 1984 and July 1985, Boliva's money supply increased by 17,433 percent, prices increased by 22,908 percent, and the value of the peso against the dollar fell by 24,662 percent. The simultaneous nature of these movements is just what PPP theory would have predicted. In October 1985, the Bolivian government instituted a dramatic stabilization plan which has significantly improved the country's economy.

2) Suggested Discussion Questions:

   a) Explain PPP theory. Describe how the case helps confirm the validity of PPP theory.

   b) How will the tight control of its money supply help Bolivia control inflation? Should Bolivia have taken this action sooner? Why or why not?

   c) Are you optimistic about the economic future of Bolivia? Explain your answer.

CHAPTER 9
THE GLOBAL MONETARY SYSTEM

Learning Objectives

1. Understand the role played by the global monetary system in exchange rate determination.
2. Be familiar with the historical development of the modern global monetary system.
3. Appreciate the differences between a fixed and a floating exchange rate system.
4. Understand why the world's fixed exchange rate regime collapsed in the 1970s.
5. Understand the arguments for and against fixed and floating exchange rate systems.
6. Be familiar with the role played by the International Monetary Fund and the World Bank in the global monetary system.

Chapter Summary

The objective of this chapter is to explain how the international monetary system works and to point out its implications for international business. The chapter begins by reviewing the historical evolution of the monetary system, starting with the gold standard and the Bretton Woods System. The chapter explains the role of the International Monetary Fund (IMF) and the World Bank, both of which were initiated by the Bretton Woods Conference. The fixed exchange rate system that was initiated by the Bretton Woods Conference collapsed in 1973.

The majority of the chapter explains the workings of the international monetary system. The pluses and minuses of fixed exchange rates versus floating exchange rates are discussed. Scholars differ in regard to which system is best. The current role of the IMF and the World Bank is discussed, including the manner in which the IMF has helped nations restructure their debts.

Chapter Outline With Lecture Notes and Teaching Tips

1) Introduction - The objective of this chapter is to explain how the international monetary system works and to point out its implications for international business.
    a) Bretton Woods System - The 1944 Bretton Woods conference established the basic framework for the post World War II international monetary system.
    b) Fixed Exchange Rate - Value of most currencies in terms of U.S. dollars was fixed for long periods and allowed to change only under a specific set of circumstances.
    c) Managed Float System - Value of some currencies is allowed to float freely, but the majority are either managed in some way by government intervention or pegged to another currency.
2) The Gold Standard - The gold standard had its origin in the use of gold coins as a medium of exchange, unit of account, and store of value - a practice that stretches back to ancient times.
    Lecture Note: A very informative and well written explanation of the gold standard is available at {http://www.clev.frb.org/annual/essay.htm#gold}.
    a) Nature of the Gold Standard - The practice of pegging currencies to gold and guaranteeing convertibility is known as the gold standard. For example, under the gold standard one U.S. dollar was defined as equivalent to 23.22 grains of "fine (pure) gold.

b) The Strength of the Gold Standard - The great strength claimed for the gold standard was that it contained a powerful mechanism for simultaneously achieving balance-of-trade equilibrium by all countries.

c) The Period Between the Wars, 1918-39 - The gold standard worked reasonably well from the 1870s until the start of World War I in 1914, when it was abandoned.

3) The Bretton Woods System - In 1944, at the height of World War II, representatives from 44 countries met at Bretton Woods, New Hampshire, to design a new international monetary system. With the collapse of the gold standard and the Great Depression of the 1930s fresh in their minds, these statesmen were determined to build an enduring economic order that would facilitate postwar economic growth. The agreement reached at Bretton Woods established two multinational institutions - the International Monetary Fund (IMF) and the World Bank. The task of the IMF would be to maintain order in the international monetary system and that of the World Bank would be to promote general economic development.

Teaching Tip: A well written, brief history of the rise and fall of the Bretton Woods is available at {http://ps.ucdavis.edu/classes/pol129/SWE/bw2.htm}.

a) The Role of the IMF

i) Discipline - A fixed exchange rate regime imposes discipline in two ways. First, the need to maintain a fixed exchange rate puts a brake on competitive devaluations and brings stability to the world trade environment. Second, a fixed exchange rate regime imposes monetary discipline on countries, thereby curtailing price inflation.

Teaching Tip: The Homepage of the IMF is available at {http://www.imf.org/}.

b) Flexibility - Although monetary discipline was a central objective of the Bretton Woods agreement, it was recognized that a rigid policy of fixed exchange rates would be too inflexible. The IMF stood ready to lend foreign currencies to members to tide them over during short periods of balance-of-payments deficit, when a rapid tightening of monetary or fiscal policy would hurt domestic employment.

c) The Role of the World Bank - The official role of the World Bank is the International Bank for Reconstruction and Development (IBRD). The bank lends money under two schemes. Under the IBRD scheme, money is raised through bond sales in the international capital market. Borrowers pay what the bank calls a market rate of interest - the bank's cost of funds plus a margin for expenses. A second scheme is overseen by the International Development Agency, an arm of the bank created in 1960. IDA loans go only to the poorest countries.

Teaching Tip: The Hompage of the World Bank can be accessed at {http://www.worldbank.org/}.

4) The Collapse of the Fixed Exchange Rate System - The system of fixed exchange rates worked well until the late 1960s, when it began to show signs of strain. The system finally collapsed in 1973, and since then we have had a managed float system.

5) The Floating Exchange Rate Regime - The floating exchange rate regime that followed the collapse of the fixed exchange rate system was formalized in January 1976 when IMF members met in Jamaica and agreed to the rules for the international monetary system that are in place today.

a) The Jamaica Agreement - The purpose of the Jamaica meeting was to revise the IMF's Articles of Agreement to reflect the new reality of floating exchange rates. The three main elements of the Jamaican agreement include the following:

i) Floating rates were declared acceptable.

ii) Gold was abandoned as a reserve asset.

iii) Total annual IMF quotas - the amount member countries contribute to the IMF - were increased to $41 billion.

b) Exchange Rates since 1973 - Since March 1973 exchange rates have become much more volatile and far less predictable than they were between 1945 and 1973. The volatility has been partly due to a number of unexpected shocks to the world monetary system including:

   i) The oil crisis in 1973.

   ii) The loss of confidence in the dollar that followed the rise of U.S. inflation in 1977 and 1978.

   iii) The oil crisis of 1979.

   iv) The unexpected rise in the dollar between 1980 and 1985.

   v) The rapid fall of the U.S. dollar against the Japanese yen and German deutsche mark between 1985 and 1987, and against the yen between 1993 and 1995.

6) Fixed versus Floating Exchange Rates

   a) The Case for Floating Exchange Rates - The case for floating exchange rates has two main elements: monetary policy autonomy and automatic trade balance adjustments.

      i) Monetary Policy Autonomy - It is argued that a floating exchange rate regime gives countries monetary policy autonomy. Under a fixed system, a country's ability to expand or contract its money supply as it sees fit is limited by the need to maintain exchange rate parity. Advocates of a floating exchange rate regime argue that removal of the obligation to maintain exchange rate parity restores monetary control to a government.

      ii) Trade Balance Adjustments - Under the Bretton Woods system, if a country developed a permanent deficit in its balance of trade that could not be corrected by domestic policy, the IMF would agree to a currency devaluation. Critics of this system argue that the adjustment mechanism works much more smoothly under a floating exchange rate regime.

   b) The Case for Fixed Exchange Rates - The case for fixed exchange rates rests on arguments about monetary discipline, uncertainty, and the lack of connection between the trade balance and exchange rates.

      i) Monetary Discipline - The need to maintain a fixed exchange rate parity ensures that governments do not expand their money supplies at inflationary rates.

      ii) Speculation - Critics of a floating exchange rate regime also argue that speculation can cause fluctuations in exchange rates.

      iii) Uncertainty - Speculation also adds to the uncertainty surrounding future currency movements that characterizes floating exchange rate regimes.

      iv) Trade Balance Adjustments - Those in favor of floating exchange rates argue that floating rates help adjust trade imbalances.

   c) Who is Right - This is a matter of debate. We do, however, know that a fixed exchange rate regime modeled along the lines of the Bretton Woods system will not work. It is telling that speculation ultimately broke the system - a phenomenon that advocates of fixed rate regimes claim is associated with floating exchange rates. Nevertheless, a different kind of fixed exchange rate system might be more enduring and might foster the kind of stability that would facilitate more rapid growth in international trade and investment.

7) The IMF and World Bank after Bretton Woods

   Teaching Tip: A book entitled "International Monetary Cooperation Since Bretton Woods" by Harold James is a comprehensive account of the management of the international monetary system from the 1944 Bretton Woods conference to the present day. A review of the book is available at {http://www.oup-usa.org/docs.019510448X.html}.

   a) IMF and the Developing World Debt - The collapse of the Bretton Woods system left the IMF with a diminished role in the international monetary system. As a result, the IMF did what any bureaucracy interested in self-preservation would do; it found a new mission. This new mission was inspired by the OPEC oil price hikes of 1973 and the resulting debt crisis in the developing world.

b) From the IMF Solution to the Brady Plan - Into the breach (of the debt crisis in the developing world) stepped the IMF. Together with several Western governments, particularly that of the United States, the IMF emerged as the key player in resolving the debt crisis with Mexico.

c) The Future of the IMF and the World Bank - The convergence between the World Bank and the IMF points to the possibility of a merger between the IMF and the bank sometime in the future. *Teaching Tip*: The International Monetary Fund maintains a very substantive web site at {http://www.imf.org/external/}. It is very easy to access current information about the IMF at the web site. The site includes current press releases, new briefs, and research reports pertaining to IMF activities.

Lecture Note: The World Bank makes many loans to developing countries. To provide your students an understanding of the types of loans that the World Bank makes, the following is an example of a loan that the World Bank approved on November 20, 1997: Title: Brazil Rural Poverty Alleviation Projects – Paraiba and Maranhao; Loan Amount: $140 million (U.S. dollars). Project Description: These projects will help finance small projects in the States of Paraiba and Maranhao to finance improvements in rural water supply, electricity, roads and bridges, sanitation, community centers and daycare centers, and other farming projects (such as communal irrigation schemes, rearing farm animals). The project will also support training and consultant services and research (information taken from World Bank website at http://www.worldbank.com/}.

8) Implications for Business

a) Currency Management - An obvious implication with regard to currency management is that companies must recognize that the foreign exchange market does not work quite as depicted in Chapter 8. The current system is a managed float system in which government intervention can help drive the foreign exchange market. A second message contained in this chapter is that under the present system, speculative buying and selling of currencies can create volatile movements in exchange rates.

b) Business Strategy - The volatility of the present floating exchange rate regime presents a conundrum for international businesses. Exchange rate movements are difficult to predict, and yet their movement can have a major impact on the competitive position of businesses. One response to the uncertainty that arises from a floating exchange rate regime might be to build strategic flexibility.

c) Corporate-Government Relations - As major players in the international trade and investment environment, businesses can influence government policy towards the international monetary system.

Critical Thinking and Discussion Questions

1. What did the gold standard collapse? Is there a case for returning to some type of gold standard? What is it?

Answer: The gold standard worked reasonably well from the 1870s until the start of World War I in 1914, when it was abandoned. During the war several governments financed their massive military expenditures by printing money. This resulted in inflation, and by the war's end in 1918, price levels were higher everywhere. Several countries returned to the gold standard after World War I. However, the period that ensued saw so many countries devalue their currencies that it became impossible to be certain how much gold a currency could buy. Instead of holding onto another country's currency, people often tried to exchange it into gold immediately, least the country devalue its currency in the intervening period. This put pressure on the gold reserves of various countries, forcing them to suspend gold convertibility. As a result, by the start of World War II, the gold standard was dead.

The great strength of the gold standard was that it contained a powerful mechanism for simultaneously achieving balance-of-trade equilibrium by all countries, as explained in the example provided on pages 294-295 of the textbook. This strength is the basis for reconsidering the gold standard as a basis for international monetary policy.

2. What opportunities might IMF lending policies to developing nations create for international businesses? What threats might they create?

    Answer: The IMF lending policies require the recipient countries to implement governmental reforms to stabilize monetary policy and encourage economic growth. One of the principle ways for a developing nation to spur economic growth is to solicit foreign direct investment and to provide a hospitable environment for the foreign investors. These characteristics of IMF lending policies work to the advantage of international businesses that are looking for investment opportunities in developing countries.

3. Do you think it is in the best interest of Western international businesses to have the IMF lend money to the former Communist states of Eastern Europe to help them transform their economies? Why?

    Answer: Yes. By helping these countries transform their centrally planned economies to market economies, the IMF will help create stronger potential trading partners for Western International Business to invest in.

4. Debate the relative merits of fixed and floating exchange rate regimes. From the perspective of an international business, what are the most important criteria in a choice between the systems? Which system is the more desirable for an international business?

    Answer: The case for fixed exchange rates rests on arguments about monetary discipline, speculation, uncertainty, and the lack of connection between the trade balance and exchange rates. In terms of monetary discipline, the need to maintain fixed exchange rate parity ensures that governments do not expand their money supplies at inflationary rates. In terms of speculation, a fixed exchange rate regime precludes the possibility of speculation. In terms of uncertainty, a fixed rate regime introduces a degree of certainty in the international monetary system by reducing volatility in exchange rates. Finally, in terms of trade balance adjustments, critics question the closeness of the link between the exchange rate and the trade balance.

    The case for floating exchange rates has two main elements: monetary policy autonomy and automatic trade balance adjustments. In terms of the former, it is argued that a floating exchange rate regime gives countries monetary policy autonomy. Under a fixed rate system, a country's ability to expand or contract its money supply as it sees fit is limited by the need to maintain exchange rate parity. In terms of the later, under the Bretton Woods system, if a country developed a permanent deficit in its balance of trade that could not be corrected by domestic policy, the IMF would agree to a currency devaluation. Critics of this system argue that the adjustment mechanism works much more smoothly under a floating exchange rate regime. They argue that if a country is running a trade deficit, the imbalance between the supply and demand of that country's currency in the foreign exchange markets will lead to depreciation in its exchange rate. An exchange rate depreciation should correct the trade deficit by making the country's exports cheaper and its imports more expensive.

It is a matter of personal opinion in regard to which system is better for an international business. We do know, however, that a fixed exchange rate regime modeled along the lines of the Bretton Woods system will not work. Nevertheless, a different kind of fixed exchange rate system might be more enduring and might foster the kind of stability that would facilitate more rapid growth in international trade and investment.

Case Discussion Questions

1. To what extent is the competitive position of Caterpillar against Komatsu dependent on the dollar/yen exchange rate.

   Answer: To a limited degree, the competitive position of Caterpillar is dependent on the dollar/yen exchange rate. If the dollar appreciates against the yen, like it did in the 1980-87 period, it is more difficult for Caterpillar to sell equipment in Japan and easier for Komatsu to sell equipment in the United States. The broader question is the strength of the dollar against all of major currencies versus the strength of the yen against all other major currencies. If the dollar appreciates against all other major currencies and the yen does not, the competitive position of Caterpillar will be significantly worsened relative to Komatsu.

2. If you were the CEO of Caterpillar Tractor, what actions would you take now to make sure there is not repeat of the early 1980s experience?

   Answer: I would continue to lobby the United States government to hold the value of the dollar at a realistic level, and not allow the dollar to appreciate significantly against other major currencies. I would also maintain a currency department and use forward contracts to hedge against exchange rate movements when appropriate.

3. What potential impact can the actions of the IMF and World Bank have on Caterpillar's business? Is there anything that Cat can do to influence the actions of the IMF and World Bank?

   Answer: The IMF and World Bank can lend money to developing nations, and in doing so not only provide the developing nations needed cash but also instill monetary discipline. This helps Caterpillar in two ways. First, some of the money the developing countries receive from the IMF and World Bank may go for construction projects, which creates a market for Caterpillar products. Second, if the IMF and World Bank can help developing nations develop monetary discipline, then the economies of these nations will improve. A stronger nation is more apt to need Caterpillar equipment than a weaker nation.

   In regard to the second half of the question, Caterpillar can act as an advocate for developing nations before the IMF and World Bank, but can do little else on their behalf.

4. As the CEO of Caterpillar, would you prefer a fixed exchange rate regime or a continuation of the current managed float regime? Why?

   Answer: I would prefer a fixed exchange rate regime. That way the competitiveness of my equipment is determined by its merits, rather than exchange rate considerations.

Internet Exercise

1) Summary:

   a) This feature familiarizes the reader with the web sites sponsored by the International Monetary Fund and the World Bank. The exercise portion of the feature asks the reader to visit both sites and search for specified information.

2) Additional Material:

   a) There are a number of additional web sites that are specifically designed to help companies learn about the international monetary system. A sample of these sites are as follows:

      i) U.S. Council on International Banking: {http://www.intlbanking.org/}

      ii) U.S. Federal Reserve Board: {http://www.bog.frb.fed.us/}

      iii) Institute of International Banking Law & Practice, Inc.: {http://www.iiblp.org/}

Opening Case: The Tumbling Peso and the Auto Industry

1) Summary:

   a) This feature focuses on the international auto industry in Mexico. In the euphoria that followed the January 1, 1994, implementation of NAFTA, no industry looked set to gain more than the auto industry. Due to falling trade barriers and booming demand in Mexico, between January and October 1994 U.S. car exports to Mexico increased 500 percent. Based on this and other encouraging developments, several global auto manufacturers began investing in Mexico. Among the biggest foreign investors were Chrysler, Ford, General Motors, Nissan, Mercedes-Benz, and Volkswagen. The feature follows the evolution of the auto industry in Mexico from 1994 to the present day. Several disruptive events have occurred, involving Mexico's economy and currency rates. However, while the short term has been a rough road, the long run may look brighter.

2) Suggested Discussion Questions:

   a) What roles have foreign exchange rates play in the successes and failures of the global auto industry in Mexico?

   b) Have currency speculators been a positive or disruptive influence in the stability of exchange rates in Mexico? Explain your answer.

   c) In your opinion, do global auto companies like Ford and Volkswagen have a bright or dim future in Mexico. Make your answer as substantive as possible.

Country Focus: Yen Shock

1) Summary: What was widely referred to in Japan as "yen shock." in the mid 1990s Japanese firms saw prices and profit margins on exports squeezed relentlessly as the yen climbed against the dollar. This feature discusses the raise of the yen against the dollar, and also provides insightful background into the historic relationship between the Japanese yen and the U.S. dollar.

2) Suggested Discussion Questions:

   a) Describe the role that a country's inflation rate plays in the value of its currency.

   b) What effect did the Japanese recession have on the yen/dollar relationship.

   c) Does the large trade imbalance between the United States and Japan make it harder or easier for the two countries to maintain a relatively stable dollar/yen exchange rate? Explain your answer.

Management Focus: Daimler-Benz Suffers From a Strong Mark

1) Summary:

   a) This feature focuses on the impact of exchange rates on Daimler-Benz, the German automobile and aerospace company. In recent years, the German mark has been appreciating relative to other major currencies. This has hurt the international competitiveness of Dimler-Benz, because the company relies heavily on export sales of products manufacturer in Germany and sold around the world. To further complicate Diamler-Benz's problems, its aerospace division, which accounts for about 20 percent of the group's total sales, receives 74 percent of its income in dollars (airplanes are priced in U.S. dollars), but only 27 percent of its costs are in dollars. This means that an appreciation of the mark against the dollar hits Daimler-Benz particularly hard. The case goes on to describe how Daimler-Benz plans to meet these challenges. In the next several years, the company will be moving a higher percentage of its manufacturing operations out of Germany to avoid the currency exchange implications described above.

2) Suggested Discussion Questions:

   a) What is the root of Daimler-Benz's problems? Does this problem have anything to do with the quality or price of the company's products? If not, if you were the CEO of Daimler-Benz would this frustrate you?

   b) Comment on Daimler-Benz's plans to "work-around" its currency exchange rate problems. Does the company have a viable plan? Explain your answer.

   c) Do you agree with Daimler-Benz's assessment that the appreciation of the mark against the dollar is probably permanent? Why or why not?

3) Homepage for Daimler-Benz: {http://www.mercedes-benz.com/}

CHAPTER 10
GLOBAL STRATEGY

Learning Objectives

1. Be conversant with the concept of strategy.

2. Understand how firms can profit from expanding their activities globally.

3. Be familiar with the different strategies for competing globally.

4. Understand how cost pressures influence a firm's choice of global strategy.

5. Understand how country differences can influence a firm's choice of global strategy.

6. Understand how firms can use strategic alliances to support their global strategy.

Chapter Summary

This chapter focuses on the strategies that firms use to compete in foreign markets. At the outset, the chapter reviews the reasons that firms engage in international commerce, which range from earning a greater return from distinctive skills to realizing location economies by dispersing particular value creation activities to locations where they can be performed most efficiently. A major portion of the chapter is dedicated to the pressures that international firm's face for cost reductions and local responsiveness. These pressures place conflicting demands on firms. On the one hand, cost reductions are best achieved through product standardization and economies of scale. On the other hand, pressures for local responsiveness require firms to modify their products to suite local demands.

The chapter also discusses the four basic strategies that firms utilize to compete in international markets. These strategies include an international strategy, a multidomestic strategy, a global strategy, and a transnational strategy. The advantages and disadvantages of each of these strategies are discussed. The chapter concludes with a discussion of international strategic alliances.

Chapter Outline With Lecture Notes and Teaching Tips

1) Introduction - The primary concern so far in this book has been with aspects of the larger environment in which international businesses compete. Now, our focus shifts from the environment to the firm itself and, in particular, to the actions managers can take to compete more effectively as an international business.

2) Strategy and the Firm

    a) The Firm as a Value Chain - It is useful to think of the firm as a value chain composed of a series of distinct value creation activities, including production, marketing, materials management, R&D, human resources, information systems, and the firm infrastructure. We can categorize these value creation activities as primary activities and support activities.
    Teaching Tip: An insightful article on the strategy, staffing, and structure of a multinational enterprise is available at {http://pacific.commerce.ubc.ca/keith/Lectures/sss.html}.

        i) Primary Activities - The primary activities of a firm have to do with creating the product, marketing and delivering the product to buyers, and providing support and after-sale service to the buyers of the product.

ii) Support Activities - Support activities provide the inputs that allow the primary activities of production and marketing to occur. The materials management function controls the transmission of physical materials through the value chain - from procurement through production and into distribution. The efficiency with which this is carried out can significantly reduce the cost of creating value.

b) The Role of Strategy - A firm's strategy can be defined as the actions that managers take to attain the goals of the firm.

3) Profiting from Global Expansion - Firms that operate internationally are able to: (1) Earn a greater return from their distinctive skills, or core competencies, (2) Realize location economies by dispersing particular value creation activities to locations where they can be performed most efficiently, (3) Realize greater experience curve economies, which reduce the costs of value creation.

a) Transferring Core Competencies - The term core competence refers to skills within the firm that competitors cannot easily match or imitate. These skills may exist in any of the firm's value creation activities. For many firms, global expansion is a way of further exploiting the value creation potential of their skills and product offering by applying those skills and products in a larger market.

b) Realizing Location Economies - Location economies are the economies that arise from performing a value creation activity in the optimal location for that activity, wherever in the world that might be (transportation costs and trade barriers permitting).

i) Creating a Global Web - Refers to the dispersal of the stages of a firm's value chain to those locations around the globe where the value added is maximized or where the costs of value creation are minimized.

ii) Some Caveats - Introducing transportation costs and trade barriers complicates this picture. Due to favorable factor endowments, New Zealand may have a comparative advantage for automobile assembly operations, but high transportation costs would make it an uneconomical location for them. Another caveat concerns the importance of assessing political risks when making location decisions.

c) Realizing Experience Curve Economies - The experience curve refers to the systematic reductions in production costs that have been observed to occur over the life of a product. The experience curve relationship between production costs and output is illustrated in Figure 10.2.

i) Learning Effects - Cost savings that come from learning by doing.

ii) Economies of Scale - Reduction in unit cost achieved by producing a large volume of a product.

iii) Strategic Significance - The strategic significance of the experience curve is clear. Moving down the experience curve allows a firm to reduce its cost of creating value. Serving a global market from a single location is consistent with moving down the experience curve and establishing a low-cost position.

4) Pressures for Cost Reductions and Local Responsiveness - Firms that compete in the global marketplace typically face two types of competitive pressures. They face pressures for cost reductions and pressures to be locally responsive.
Teaching Tip: An article entitled "Forging a Global Appliance" that appeared in CIO magazine (May 1 1995) provides an excellent example of how Whirlpool is coping with the challenge of simultaneously managing cost reductions and local responsiveness. In a nutshell, what Whirlpool is trying to do is to have its engineers worldwide work together to crate several basic designs for its appliances, and then

have each region customize the boilerplate designs to be compatible with local market demands. The full text of this article is available at {http://www.cio.com/archive/050195_group.html}.

a) Pressures for Cost Reductions - Increasingly international businesses are facing pressures for cost reductions.

b) Pressures for Local Responsiveness - Pressures for local responsiveness arise from a number of sources, including:

   i) Differences in consumer tastes and preferences - Strong pressures for local responsiveness emerge when consumer tastes and preferences differ significantly between countries.

   ii) Differences in infrastructure and traditional practices - Pressures for local responsiveness emerge when there are differences in infrastructure and/or traditional practices between countries.

   iii) Differences in distribution channels - A firm's marketing strategies may have to be responsive to differences in distribution channels between countries.

   iv) Host government demands - Economic and political demands imposed by host country governments may necessitate a degree of local responsiveness.

   v) Implications - Pressures for local responsiveness imply that it may not be possible for a firm to realize the full benefits from experience curve and location economies.

5) Strategic Choice - Firms use four basic strategies to compete in the international environment: an international strategy, a multidomestic strategy, a global strategy, and a transnational strategy. The appropriateness of each strategy varies with the extent of pressures for cost reductions and local responsiveness. Figure 10.4 in the text illustrates when each of these strategies is most appropriate.

a) International Strategy - Firms that pursue an international strategy try to create value by transferring valuable skills and products to foreign markets where indigenous competitors lack those skills and products.

b) Multidomestic Strategy - Firms pursuing a multidomestic strategy orient themselves toward achieving maximum local responsiveness.

c) Global Strategy - Firms that pursue a global strategy focus upon increasing profitability by reaping the cost reductions that come from experience curve effects and location economies.

d) Transnational Strategy - This is a hybrid strategy. Christopher Bartlett and Sumantra Ghoshal have argued that in today's environment, competitive conditions are so intense that to survive in the global marketplace firms "must exploit experience-based cost economies and location economies, they must transfer distinctive competencies with the firm, and they must do all of this while paying attention to pressures for local responsiveness." As a result, a transnational strategy is a business strategy that seeks experience-based economies and location economies, transfers distinctive competencies within the firm, and pays attention to pressures for local responsiveness.

   i) Global Learning - Flow of skills and product offerings from home firm to foreign subsidiary and from foreign subsidiary to home firm and from foreign subsidiary to foreign subsidiary.

e) Summary - The advantages and disadvantages of each of the four strategies are summarized in Figure 10.6 in the textbook.

6) Strategic Alliances - The term strategic alliances refers to cooperative agreements between potential or actual competitors. In this textbook, we are concerned specifically with strategic alliances between firms from different countries.

a) The Advantages of Strategic Alliances:

i)   Strategic alliances may facilitate entry into a foreign market.

ii) Alliances allow firms to share the fixed costs (and associated risks) of developing new products or processes.

iii) An alliance is a way to bring together complementary skills and assets that neither company could easily develop on its own.

iv) It can make sense to form an alliance that will help the firm establish technological standards for the industry that will benefit the firm.

b)   The Disadvantages of Strategic Alliances

i)   The can give competitors low-cost routes to new technology and markets.
     Teaching Tip: An internet site that provides information on joint ventures in an international context is available from the University of California at Davis at {http://ps.ucdavis.edu/classes/pol129/SWE/ventures.htm}.

7) Making Alliances Work

a)   Partner Selection - A key to making a strategic alliance work is to select the right ally.

b)   Alliance Structure - Having selected a partner, the alliance should be structured so that the firm's risks of giving too much away to the partner are reduced to an acceptable level.

c)   Managing the Alliance - Once a partner has been selected and an appropriate alliance structure has been agreed on, the task facing the firm is to maximize its benefits from the alliance.

i)   Building Trust - Part of the trick of managing an alliance successfully seems to be to build interpersonal relationships between the firms' managers.

ii) Learning From Partners - After a five-year study of 15 strategic alliances between major multinationals, Gary Hamel, Yves Doz, and C.K. Prahalad concluded that a major determinant of how much a company gains from an alliance is its ability to learn from its alliance partners.

Critical Thinking and Discussion Questions

1.   In a world of zero transportation costs, no trade barriers, and nontrival differences between nations with regard to factor conditions, firms must expand internationally if they are to survive. Discuss.

Answer: In the world described above, firms will survive by basing each value creation activity that it performs at that location where economic, political, and cultural conditions, including relative factor costs, are most conductive to the performance of that activity. Thus, if the best designers for a product live in France, a firm should base its design operations in France. If the most productive labor force for assembly operations is in Mexico, assembly operations should be based in Mexico, and so forth. Firms can only take advantage of these types of opportunities if they expand internationally.

2.   Plot the position of the following firms on Figure 10.3 - Procter & Gamble, IBM, Coca-Cola, Dow Chemical, US Steel, and McDonald's. In each case justify your answer.

Answer: Procter & Gamble would be located in the middle right-hand portion of the graph. This is a position of high pressures for local responsiveness and moderate pressures for cost reductions. P&G sells personal and home care products, which do face pressures for local responsiveness. Although these products are not commodities, there are many competitors in P&G industries, which implies a moderate degree of cost pressures. IBM would be in the upper middle portion of the graph. This is a position of moderate pressure for local responsiveness and high pressure for cost reductions. There is a moderate amount of pressure for local responsiveness for IBM products, due to language differences and differing voltage requirements for electronic products across countries. IBM is in a very competitive industry, and cost pressures are high. Coca-Cola is a commodity type product, and it would be located in the upper left-hand portion of the graph. This is a position of low pressures for local responsiveness and high pressures for cost reductions. Dow Chemical and U.S. Steel would both be located in the upper left-hand portion of the graph. Both Dow and U.S. Steel sell products that are commodity-like by nature. As a result, cost pressures would be high and local responsiveness pressures would be low for these products. Finally, McDonalds would be located in the middle left-hand portion of the graph. Pressures for local responsiveness would be low, and cost reduction pressures would be moderate. McDonalds sells a semi commodity-like product, but not to the same degree as Dow Chemical of U.S. Steel.

3. Are the following global industries or multidomestic industries: bulk chemicals, pharmaceuticals, branded food products, moviemaking, television manufacture, personal computers, airline travel?

Answer: Bulk chemicals are a global industry. Pharmaceuticals are a global industry. Branded food products are a multidomestic industry. Moviemaking is a multidomestic industry that is becoming more global. Many American films, for instance, are released overseas after they finish their run in U.S. theatres. These movies typically have to be modified, however, with foreign language subtitles. The commercial appeal for foreign films in America has yet to develop. Television manufacture is a global industry, as is personal computers. These products do have to be slightly modified to meet the language and voltage requirements of their local markets. Airline travel is a global industry.

4. Discuss how the need for control over foreign operations varies with the strategy and core competencies of a firm. What are the implications of this for the choice of entry mode?

Answer: When a firm's competitive advantage is based on technological competence, or the proprietary nature of its products or services, it usually wants to maintain as much control as possible over its technology and the "trade secrets" that reside within its products and services. As a result, establishing a foreign owned subsidiary is the best foreign entry option. Another option is to export, and maintain regional subsidiaries in foreign markets to handle the marketing and distribution of the product. These options are preferable, because they help a firm maintain control over its technology and products. Entering into licensing agreement, joint ventures, or franchise agreements run a significantly higher risk of losing control.

In contrast, when the competitive advantage of a firm is based on management know-how, this is a difficult competency to copy, so control is not as pervasive of an issue. Firms in this category tend to use a combination of exporting and franchising.

5. What are the main organizational problems likely in the implementation of a transnational strategy?

Answer: A transnational strategy is not an easy one to pursue. The basis of a transnational strategy is to simultaneously pursue cost reductions and local responsiveness. As a result, a transnational company must continually search for ways to improve efficiency and reduce costs. This can be accomplished in part by implementing greater cost efficiencies. The textbook provides several examples of how this is done. For example, Caterpillar Tractor, a transnational company, redesigned its products to use many identical components and invested in a few large-scale component manufacturing facilities at favorable locations to fill global demand and realize scale economies.

Other firms have downsized and implemented outsourcing programs to reduce costs (e.g. Boeing) and have implemented cost-reduction techniques such as just-in time inventory control and total quality management. Achieving local responsiveness at the same time that a firm is focusing on cost reductions is the principle challenge involved with pursuing a transnational strategy. Some firms accomplish this by designing flexible factories that allow them to alter their products (to meet the tastes of individual foreign markets) in a highly efficient manner.

6. What kinds of companies stand to gain the most from entering into strategic alliances with potential competitors? Why?

Answer: The companies that stand to gain the most from entering into strategic alliances with potential competitors are those that (1) need a partner to gain access to a foreign market, (2) need a partner to share the capital requirements necessary to launch a new product or service, and (3) have only a modest amount of proprietary technology that will be placed at risk by entering into a strategic alliance. These attributes benefit a firm without giving too much away, and may provide a firm a tremendous advantage in terms of gaining access to a foreign markets and/or investment capital.

Case Discussion Questions

1. What strategy was IKEA pursuing as it expanded throughout Europe during the 1970s and early 1980s - a multidomestic strategy, a global strategy, or an international strategy?

Answer: IKEA pursued a global strategy throughout Europe during the 1970s and early 1980s.

2. Why do you thing this strategy did not work as well in North America as it did in Europe?

Answer: Probably because the tastes and preferences of IKEA's European customers were more compatible with the Scandinavian design and features of IKEA's products than American tastes and preferences.

3. As of 1995 what strategy is IKEA pursuing? Does this strategy make sense? Can you see any drawbacks with this strategy?

Answer: At least in America, as of 1995 IKEA was pursuing a multidomestic strategy. The drawback of this strategy is that IKEA forfeited some of the economies of scale that it was achieving by pursuing a global strategy. However, IKEA's global strategy apparently was not tenable in America, so the company's only real choices were to modify its products to accommodate the tastes of its American customers or exit the U.S. market.

Internet Exercise

1) Summary:

a) This exercise describes a feature that is included in Digital Equipment's web site. The feature explains the strategic alliances that Digital has with several other companies. The activity that is assigned for the reader is to surf the Digital site to learn more about the company's alliances.

2) Additional Material:

a) For companies that are interested in participating in a joint venture with a foreign firm, there is a web site that helps match interested parties. The site, which is sponsored by the International Business Forum, can be accessed at {http://www.ibf.com/bo/ibbo08jv.htm}.

Opening Case: Its a Mac World

1) Summary:

a) This feature focuses on the phenomenal success that McDonalds has experienced in its efforts to expand in international markets. The features discusses McDonalds's foreign expansion strategy, and the great lengths that the company goes to in its efforts to maintain the quality of its products and services.

2) Suggested Discussion Questions:

a) What is McDonald's core competence? How does McDonalds transfer its core competence to foreign markets?

b) Describe McDonald's foreign market strategy? Is McDonalds pursuing a international strategy, a multidomestic strategy, a global strategy, or a transnational strategy? Defend your answer.

c) Describe a transnational strategy. Regardless of your answer to the question immediately above, make the case that McDonalds is pursuing a transnational strategy?

3) McDonalds Homepage: {http://www.mcdonalds.com/}

Management Focus: Strategy at Swan Optical

1) Summary:

a) This feature follows the case of Swan Optical through its efforts to profit by becoming an international firm. Swan Optical is a manufacturer and distributor of eyewear. Swan began its move toward becoming a multinational in the 1970s, after a strong dollar made U.S. based manufacturing very expensive. To compete with low cost imports, Swan took its own manufacturing operations overseas, first in Hong Kong and then in mainland China. The case describes Swan's experiences in those endeavors, and also discusses Swan's later moves to purchase minority interests in several international eyewear companies.

2) Suggested Discussion Questions:

a) Did Swan have to go global to survive? Explain your answer.

b) Explain why Swan decided to invest in a foreign eyewear firms?

c) Discuss Swan's foreign market strategy. Was the strategy appropriate? Why or why not?

Management Focus: Procter & Gamble's International Strategy

1) Summary:

a) This feature focuses on P&G efforts to introduce products into European and Asian markets. Together with Unilever, P&G is a dominant global force in laundry detergents, cleaning products, and personal care products. P&G expanded abroad after World War II by pursuing an international strategy – transferring brands and marketing policies developed in the United States to Western Europe, initially with considerable success. In the 1970s, however, this strategy started to exhibit some flaws. It became clear that the root cause of P&G problems was its propensity to transfer its

U.S. marketing and product strategies to overseas markets essentially "intact (without taking into consideration the need for local responsiveness). The case goes on to illustrate P&G miscues in this area in several different instances.

2) Suggested Discussion Questions:

a) Based on what you know about P&G (apart from this case), plot P&G's position on Figure 10.3 in the text. According to the information provided in the case, was P&G's strategy in Europe in the early part of the case consistent with where you just placed P&G on the graph? If not, do you believe that P&G's strategy in Europe was flawed? Explain your answer.

b) What do you think that P&G should do to improve its positions in Europe and Asia? Make your answer as substantive as possible.

c) Of the four basic international strategies described in the textbook (global, international, multidomestic, and transnational), which strategy is the most appropriate for the majority of P&G's products? Why?

3) Procter & Gamble Homepage: {http://www.pg.com/}

Management Focus: Anatomy of a Failed Alliance - GM and the Daewoo Group

1) Summary:

a) This feature relates the story of a failed joint venture. In June 1984 General Motors and the Daewoo Group of South Korea signed an agreement that called for each to invest $100 million in a Korean-based 50/50 joint venture that would manufacture the Pontiac LeMans (a subcompact car). The venture started out with good intentions. GM felt that it could benefits from the joint venture by gaining access to South Korea's inexpensive labor, and Daewood felt that it could benefit from the joint venture by gaining access to GM's engineering skills. Unfortunately, as the first LeMans was coming off of the assembly line in 1987, the joint venture was turning sour. In the period between 1984 and 1987, South Korea had lurched toward democracy, and workers throughout the country were demanding better wages. Suddenly, it was cheaper to build LeMans vehicles in German than South Korea. From Daewoo's perspective, GM was treating its Korean partners badly. Daewoo Group Chairman Kim Whooshing complained publicly that GM executives were arrogant and treated him shabbily. The joint venture was dissolved in 1992.

2) Suggested Discussion Questions:

a) Describe the attributes of "making an alliance work" that are discussed in the textbook. Did both GM and Daewoo Group show good faith in each of these areas? Explain your answer.

b) From the information provided in the feature, do you get the impression that GM and Daewoo trusted each other? Did the level of trust in the relationship change over time? What steps could have been taken by GM and Daewoo to enhance the level of trust in the relationship?

c) Make a list of the things that went wrong in this joint venture. Could the joint venture have been saved if the parties involved would have worked harder to preserve the relationship? If not, was the dissolution of the relationship the appropriate thing to do?

3) Homepages:

a) General Motors Homepage: {http://www.gm.com/}

b) Daewoo Group Homepage: {http://www.dwc.co.kr/emain.htm}

CHAPTER 11
ENTERING FOREIGN MARKETS

Learning Objectives

1. Identify the different modes that firms use to enter a foreign market.

2. Understand the advantages and disadvantages of each entry mode.

3. Appreciate the relationship between strategy and a firm's choice of entry mode.

4. Appreciate some pitfalls of exporting.

5. Be familiar with the steps a firm can take to improve its export performance.

6. Have a good grasp of the mechanics of export and import financing.

Chapter Summary

This chapter focuses on the process of entering foreign markets. The six most common foreign entry strategies are discussed. These are: exporting, turnkey projects, licensing, franchising, establishing a joint venture with a host country firm, and setting up a wholly owned subsidiary in the host country. The advantages and disadvantages of each of these strategies is discussed. A nice table is provided on page 369 of the text that sums up this information.

A large portion of the chapter is dedicated strictly to exporting. The promise and pitfalls of exporting are discussed, along with a discussion of the role of export management companies in the internationalization process. The chapter also provides a nice discussion of export financing. In this section, the author discusses the financial devices that have evolved to facilitate exporting including: the letter of credit, the draft (or bill of exchange), and the bill of lading. The chapter ends by providing an example of a typical international trade transaction. This example illustrates the complex nature of international trade transactions.

Chapter Outline With Lecture Notes and Teaching Tips

1) Introduction - This chapter is about entering foreign markets.

   a) Current Status - Evidence suggests the volume of export activity in the world economy, by firms of all sizes, is likely to increase in the foreseeable future. Nevertheless, exporting remains a difficult challenge for many firms.

2) A firm considering entering a foreign market must decide the best means of doing so. These are basically six different ways to enter a foreign market. Each of these entry strategies is discussed below:

   a) Exporting - Most manufacturing firms begin their global expansion as exporters and only later switch to another mode for servicing a foreign market.
   Teaching Tip: Dun and Bradstreet provide two excellent publications on the Internet pertaining to the basics of exporting successfully. The publications are entitled How to Plan for Global Growth and Tips to Help You Export Successfully. The publications are available at {hppt://www.dbisna.com/global/hmenue.htm}.
   Teaching Tip: Your students may wonder how firms U.S. firms find buyers in foreign countries. To find foreign customers, exporters often use '"trade leads" that are provided by organizations

dedicated towards the activity of matching "buyers" and "sellers" in an international context. An example of a site that provides trade leads is the National Trade Data Bank at {http://www.stat-usa.gov/BEN/subject/trade.html}. This service is available on a subscription basis.

Teaching Tip: A site entitled "A Guide to the Best Internet Resources for Small and Medium Sized Exporters" is available at {http://web.ukonline.co.uk/members/jim.hamill/contents.htm}.

   i)   Advantages of Exporting:

      (1) It avoids the often substantial cost of establishing manufacturing operations in the host country.

      (2) Exporting may help a firm achieve experience curve location economies.

   ii) Disadvantages of Exporting:

      (1) Exporting from the firm's home base may not be appropriate if there are lower-cost locations for manufacturing the product abroad.

      (2) High transport costs can make exporting uneconomical.

      (3) Tariff barriers can make exporting uneconomical.

b) Turnkey Projects - In a turnkey project, the contractor agrees to handle every detail of the project for a foreign client, including the training of operating personnel. At completion of the contract, the foreign client is handed the "key" to a plant that is ready for full operation - hence the term turnkey. This is actually a means of exporting process technology to another country.

Lecture Note: Your students might enjoy learning more about companies that identify themselves as firms that engage in "turnkey projects." Examples of these companies include: AJS Design and Contracting, Inc. {http://www.inter-access.com/ajs/index.html} and Construction Specialty Services Inc. {http://www.cssiweb.com/}.

   i)   Advantages of Turnkey Projects:

      (1) It is a way of earning great economic returns from the know-how required to assemble and run a technologically complex process.

      (2) Turnkey Projects may make sense in a country where the political and economic environment is such that a longer-term investment might expose the firm to unacceptable political and/or economic risk.

   ii) Disadvantages of Turnkey Projects:

      (1) First, by definition, the firm that enters into a turnkey deal will have no long-term interest in the foreign country.

      (2) Second, the firm that enters into a turnkey project may create a competitor.

      (3) If the firm's process technology is a source of competitive advantage, then selling this technology through a turnkey project is also selling competitive advantage to potential and/or actual competitors.

c) Licensing - A licensing agreement is an arrangement whereby a licensor grants the rights to intangible property to another entity (the licensee) for a specified time period, and in return, the licensor receives a royalty fee from the licensee. Intangible property includes patents, inventions, formulas, processes, designs, copyrights, and trademarks.

   i)   Advantages of Licensing Agreements:

      (1) In the typical international licensing deal, the licensee puts up most of the capital necessary to get the overseas operations going. Thus, a primary advantage of licensing is that the firm does not have to bear the development costs and risks associated with opening a foreign market.

(2) Licensing is often used when a firm wishes to participate in a foreign market, but is prohibited from doing so by barriers to investment.

(3) Licensing is frequently used when a firm possesses some intangible property that might have business applications, but is does not want to develop those applications itself.

ii) Disadvantages of Licensing Agreements:

(1) First, it does not give a firm the tight control over manufacturing, marketing, and strategy that is required for realizing experience curve and location economies.

(2) Second, competing in a global market may require a firm to coordinate strategic moves across countries by using profits earned in one country to support competitive attacks in another. Licensing severely limits a firm's ability to do this.

(3) Potential loss of proprietary (or intangible) technology or property.

(a) One way of reducing the risk of losing proprietary trade secrets is through the use of cross-licensing agreements. Under a cross-licensing agreement, a firm might license some valuable intangible property to a foreign partner, but in addition to a royalty payment, the firm might also request that the foreign partner license some of its valuable know-how to the firm.

d) Franchising - Is basically a specialized form of licensing in which the franchisor not only sells intangible property to the franchisee, but also insists that the franchisee agree to abide by strict rules as to how it does business.

i) Advantages of Franchising:

(1) Franchising relieves the franchisor of many of the capital requirement of foreign market entry.

ii) Disadvantages of Franchising:

(1) Franchising may inhibit the firm's ability to take profits out of one country to support competitive attacks in another.

(2) A more significant disadvantage of franchising is quality control. The geographic distance of the firm from its foreign franchisees can make poor quality difficult for the franchisor to detect.

e) Joint Ventures - Entails establishment of a firm that is jointly owned by two or more otherwise independent firms. Fuji-Xerox, for example, was set up as a joint venture between Xerox and Fuji Photo.

Teaching Tip: There are a number of organizations that try to help companies find joint venture partners. An example is a British organization called "TradeMatch." Information about TradeMatch is available at their web site at {http://www.expo.co.uk/}.

Teaching Tip: There are also a number of publications available that can help managers make good joint venture decisions. A brief description of a book entitled "International Joint Ventures: A Practical Guide" can be accessed at {http://www.westgroup.com/practice/intllaw/intljoin.htm}.

i) Advantages of Joint Ventures:

(1) A firm can benefit from a local partner's knowledge of the host country's competitive conditions, culture, language, political systems, and business systems.

(2) Second, when the development costs and/or risks of opening a foreign market are high, a firm might gain by sharing these costs and/or risks with a local partner.

(3) In many countries, political considerations make joint ventures the only feasible entry mode.

ii) Disadvantages of Joint Ventures:

(1) First, just as with licensing, a firm that enters into a joint venture risks giving control of its technology to its partner.

(2) Second, a joint venture does not give a firm the tight control over subsidiaries that it might need to realize experience curve or location economies.

(3) Third, shared ownership arrangements can lead to conflicts and battles for control between the investing firms if their goals and objectives change over time, or if they take different views as to what the venture's strategy should be.

f) Wholly Owned Subsidiaries - In a wholly owned subsidiary, the firm owns 100 percent of the stock. Establishing a wholly owned subsidiary in a foreign market can be done two ways. The firm can either set up a new operation in that country or it can acquire an established firm and use that firm to promote its products in the country's market.

   i) Advantages of a Wholly Owned Subsidiary:

   (1) First, when a firm's competitive advantage is based on technological competence, a wholly owned subsidiary will often be the preferred entry mode, since it reduces the risk of losing control over that competence.

   (2) Second, a wholly owned subsidiary gives a firm the tight control over operations in different countries that is necessary for engaging in global strategic coordination (i.e., using profits from one country to support competitive attacks in another).

   ii) Establishing a wholly owned subsidiary is generally the most costly method of serving a foreign market.

3) Selecting an Entry Mode - Although there are trade-offs involved, it is possible to generalize about the optimal choice of entry mode.

   a) Core Competencies and Entry Mode - A distinction can be drawn between firms whose core competency is in technological know-how and those whose core competency is in management know-how.

      i) Technological Know-How - If a high-tech firms sets up operations in a foreign country to profit from a core competency in technological know-how, it will probably do so through a wholly owned subsidiary.

      ii) Management Know-How - Firms that have a competitive advantage based on management know-how typically favor a combination of franchising and subsidiaries to control the franchises within particular countries or regions.

   b) Pressures for Cost Reductions and Entry Mode - The greater the pressures for cost reductions, the more likely a firm will want to pursue some combination of exporting and wholly owned subsidiaries.

4) The Promise and Pitfalls of Exporting - As noted earlier, most firms initially start their international expansion by exporting. Despite the opportunities, studies have shown that while many large firms tend to be proactive about seeking out opportunities for profitable exporting, many medium-sized and small firms tend to be very reactive.

5) Improving Export Performance

   a) Government Information Sources - Most national governments maintain departments that can help firms establish export opportunities. In the U.S., the most comprehensive source of information is probably the U.S. Department of Commerce.

Case Discussion Questions

1. Did Downey Foods' export opportunity occur as a result of proactive action by Downey, or was its strategy reactive?

   Answer: Both. On the one hand, Downey became aware of the penchant on the part of the Japanese people for lobster through a request on the part of the Japanese External Trade Organization to serve his lobster bisque at a trade show. So, the initial idea to export to Japan resulted from this experience. On the other hand, Downey followed up on this experience and aggressively pursued the idea. Many companies are provided ideas and never follow-up on them. To Downey's credit, it did follow-up on the idea to export to Japan, even though it's experience didn't pan out in the way that the company had hoped.

2. Why did Downey experience frustrations when trying to export to Japan? What actions might Downey take to improve its prospects of succeeding in the Japanese market?

   Answer: Downey experienced the administrative trade barriers discussed in Chapter 5. In retrospect, Downey should have found a Japanese partner to help move the processes through the Japanese custom's process.

3. You have been hired by Downey Foods to develop an exporting strategy for the firm. What steps do you think Downey should take to increase the volume of its exports?

   Answer: This question is designed to stimulate classroom discussion and/or encourage your students to think about the type of export program that might be most advisable for Downey. First, because of the problematic nature of exporting food to another country, Downey should find partners in each country to help facilitate the customs approval process. It might also be advisable for Downey to hire an export management company to help it gain access to additional markets.

Internet Exercise

1) Summary:

   a) This exercise alerts the reader to two sites on the World Wide Web that might be of particular interest to exporters. The sites provide a broad array of information pertaining to export related issue. The exercise asks the reader to visit one of the sites described previously, and to summarize the Daily Brief articles concerning exporting.

2) Additional Material:

   a) One international business site that is extremely strong in terms of the breadth and depth of information that it provides is a site sponsored by Michigan State University Center for International Business Education and Research. This site, which can be accessed at {hppt://ciber.bus.msu.edu/busres.htm}, is entitled "International Business Resources on the WWW."

Opening Case: Artais Weather Check

) Summary:

a) This case follows the story of Artais Weather Check, a small Ohio company that produces automated weather observation systems for small airports. For several reasons discussed in the case, Artasi's sales potential in the United States is limited. As a result, the company has sought out export markets as a means of increasing sales. Its experiences have been both positive and negative.

2) Suggested Discussion Questions:

a) Up to this point, Artais has limited its foreign market involvement to exporting. Should the company pursue additional methods of foreign market entry? If so, what additional methods of foreign market entry would you suggest? Why?

b) Based on the information contained in this case, describe some of the challenges that small firms face in competing in export markets. How has Artais dealt with these challenges?

c) In your opinion, is the future for Artais, in terms of its foreign market potential, bright or dim? Explain your answer.

Management Focus: Fuji-Xerox

1) Summary:

a) This feature focuses on the evolution of the joint venture between Xerox (a U.S. manufacturer of photocopiers) and Fuji (a Japanese manufacturer of film products). Initially, Xerox joint ventured with Fuji as a way of gaining access to the Japanese photocopier market. The feature portrays the evolution of the joint venture from the time it was established in 1962 until today. Over the course of time, Fuji's influence over Xerox increased substantially. Fuji recognized the market potential for a small, inexpensive copier in Japan and, over Xerox's objection, designed and introduced a small copier to the Japanese market. The product was a hit. Fuji also championed the use of total quality management and other methods to reduce defect rates and improve quality. As a result of Fuji's successes in these areas, Xerox emulated Fuji and greatly improved its own operations. The feature goes on to discuss the evolution of the copier market in the United States, and the tremendous benefit of the Xerox-Fuji partnership for the Xerox Corporation.

2) Suggested Discussion Questions:

a) Discuss the advantages and disadvantages of a joint venture as a foreign market entry strategy. Which of these advantages and disadvantages manifested themselves in the Fuji-Xerox joint venture?

b) Why did Fuji do a better job at recognizing the market potential for a small, inexpensive copier in the Japanese market than Xerox? What does this tell us about the advantages of having foreign nationals working for a company regardless of its entry strategy>

c) In your opinion, what has made the Fuji-Xerox joint venture one of the most enduring and reportedly successful joint ventures in history between two companies from different countries?

3) Fuji-Xerox Homepage: {http://fujixerox.com/}

Management Focus: Export Strategy at 3M

1) Summary:

a) This feature focuses on 3M's philosophy towards exporting and foreign market entry. In a nutshell what 3M does is enter a new market as an exporter, experiment with a single product on a small scale, gain experience, and then replace exporting with a foreign subsidiary when the sales volume of the product reaches a point where foreign manufacturing is justified. 3M has developed additional rules-of-thumb over the years in regarding to international markets. For example, the firm hires foreign nationals to run its overseas subsidiaries, rather than using a large number of expatriate American managers.

2) Suggested Discussion Questions:

   a) Make a list of the things that 3M does "right" in regard to its approach to international markets. Is this an impressive list? Can other firms learn from 3M's experiences?

   b) Review the three principles that 3M has built its export strategy around. How do these principles help guide 3M's export strategy? Explain your answer.

   c) Discuss 3M's approach to hiring foreign nationals to manage its foreign subsidiaries. Is this a good approach? Why or why not?

3) 3M Homepage: {http://www.mmm.com/}

CHAPTER 12
GLOBAL MARKETING

Learning Objectives

1. Understand why and how it may make sense to vary the attributes of a product across countries.

2. Appreciate why and how a firm's distribution system might vary across countries.

3. Understand why and how advertising and promotional strategies might vary across countries.

4. Understand why and how a firm's pricing strategy might vary across countries.

5. Understand how the globalization of the world economy is affecting new-product development within international business.

Chapter Summary

This chapter focuses on the marketing and R&D activities of global firms. The chapter begins with a review of the four elements that constitute a firm's marketing mix: product attributes, distribution strategy, communication strategy, and pricing strategy. A firm's marketing mix is the set of choice that if offers its customers. Many firms vary their marketing mix from country to country depending on differences cultures, levels of economic development, product and technical standards, the availability of distribution channels, and so forth.

The chapter discusses the strategic implications of each element of the marketing mix for an international firm. The link between marketing and R&D is also discussed. The author stresses the point that selling a product on a global scale may require that a firm vary its products from country to country to satisfy local preferences. This may require a firm to establish R&D centers in different parts of the world, and closely link R&D and marketing in each region to ensure that the company is producing products that its overseas customers will buy.

Chapter Outline With Lecture Notes and Teaching Tips

1) Introduction - In this chapter the focus is on how an international business can perform marketing and R&D activities so it will reduce the costs of value creation and add value by better serving customer needs.
   Teaching Tip: A broad array of international marketing resources is available on the Internet. A very comprehensive menu of these resources, courtesy of Shippensburg University, is available at {http://dylee.keel.econ.ship.edu/intntl/intbus/intmarke.htm}.

2) The Globalization of Markets
   a) Theodore Levitt - A major proponent of the globalization of world markets.
   b) Current status - Although the world is moving towards global markets, the continuing persistence of cultural and economic differences among nations acts as a major brake on any trend toward global consumer tastes and preferences. In addition, trade barriers and differences in product and technical standards also constrain a firm's ability to sell a standardized product to a global market.
   Teaching Tip: There are a number of consulting companies that help firms "go global." You students might be interested in knowing a little bit about these companies. One company is the

Chicago based Quadral Group. The Quadral Group's web site can be accessed at {http://quadralgroup.com/}.

3) Product Attributes - Products sell well when their attributes match consumer needs. If consumer needs were the same the world over, a firm could simply sell the same product worldwide. But consumer needs vary from country to country depending on culture and the level of economic development.

   a) Cultural Differences - Countries differ along a whole range of (cultural) dimensions, including tradition, social structure, language, religion, and education. At the same time, there is some evidence of the trends Levitt talked about. Tastes and preferences are becoming more cosmopolitan.

   b) Economic Differences - Just as important as differences in culture are differences in the level of economic development. Firms based in highly developed countries tend to build a lot of extra performance attributes into their products. Consumers in less developed nations do not usually demand these extra attributes, where the preference is for more basic products.

   c) Product and Technical Standards - Notwithstanding the forces that are creating some convergence of consumer tastes and preferences, Levitt's vision of global markets may still be a long way off due to national differences in product and technological standards.

4) Distribution Strategy - A critical element of a firm's marketing mix is its distribution strategy, the means it chooses for delivering the product to the consumer.

   a) A typical distribution system - Figure 12.2 in the text illustrates a typical distribution system consisting of a channel that includes a wholesale distributor and a retailer. If the firm manufacturers it product in the particular country, it can sell directly to the consumer, to the retailer, or to the wholesaler. The same options are available to a firm that manufacturers outside the country.

   b) Differences Among Countries

      i) Retail Concentration - In some countries the retail system is very concentrated, whereas in other countries it is fragmented. In a concentrated system, a few retailers supply most of the market.

      ii) Channel Length - Refers to the number of intermediaries between the producer and the consumer. If the producer sells directly to the consumer, the channel is very short. If the producer sells through an import agent, a wholesaler, and a retailer, a long channel exists.

      iii) Channel Exclusivity - An exclusive distribution channel is one that is difficult for outsiders to access. Japan's system is often help up as an example of a very exclusive system.

   c) Choosing a Distribution Strategy - A choice of distribution strategy determines which channel the firm will use to reach potential consumers. Since each intermediary in a channel adds its own markup to the products, there is generally a critical link between channel length and the firm's profit margin. However, a long channel also has benefits. One benefit of using a longer channel is that it economizes on selling costs when the retail sector is very fragmented.

5) Communication Strategy - Another critical element in the marketing mix is communicating the attributes of the product to prospective customers. A number of communication channels are available to a firm; they include direct selling, sales promotion, direct marketing, and advertising.

   a) Barriers to International Communication - International communication occurs whenever a firm uses a marketing message to sell its products in another country. The effectiveness of a firm's international communication can be jeopardized by three potentially critical variables:

i) Cultural Barriers - Cultural barriers can make it difficult to communicate messages across cultures. The best way for a firm to overcome cultural barriers is to develop cross-cultural literacy.

ii) Source Effects - Occur when the receiver of the message (i.e. the potential consumer) evaluates the message based on the status or image of the sender.

b) Push versus Pull Strategies - The main decision with regard to communication strategy is the choice between a push strategy and a pull strategy. A push strategy emphasizes personal selling rather than mass media advertising in the promotional mix. A pull strategy depends more on mass media advertising to communicate the marketing message to potential customers. The factors that determine the relative attractiveness of push and pull strategies are shown below.

i) Product Type and Consumer Sophistication - A pull strategy is generally favored by firms in consumer goods industries that are trying to sell to a large segment of the market. In contrast, firms that sell industrial products or other complex products favor a push strategy.

ii) Channel Length - Using direct selling to push a product through many layers of a distribution channel can be very expensive. In such circumstances, a firm may try to pull its product through the channels by using mass advertising to create consumer demand.

iii) Media Availability - A pull strategy relies on access to advertising media. A push strategy is more attractive when access to mass media is limited.

iv) The Push-Pull Mix - In sum, the optimal mix between push and pull strategies depends on product type and consumer sophistication, channel length, and media sophistication.

c) Global Advertising - In recent years there has been much discussion about the pros and cons of standardized advertising worldwide.

i) For Standardized Advertising. The support for global advertising is threefold.

(1) It has significant economic advantages.

(2) There is the concern that creative talent is scarce and that one large effort to develop a campaign will produce better results than 40 or 50 smaller efforts.

(3) Brand names are global.

ii) Against Standardized Advertising. The are two main arguments against globally standardized advertising.

(1) Cultural differences among nations are such tat a message that works in one nation can fail miserably in another.

(2) Country differences in advertising regulations may block implementation of standardized advertising.

iii) Dealing with Country Differences - Some firms have been experimenting with tactics that allow them to capture some of the benefits of global standardization while recognizing differences in countries' cultural and legal environments.

) Pricing Strategy - International pricing strategy is an important component of the overall international marketing mix.

a) Price Discrimination - In an international context, price discrimination exists whenever consumers in different countries are charged different prices for the same product. Two conditions are necessary for profitable price discrimination.

i) First, the firm must be able to keep its national markets separate.

ii) Different price elasticities of demand must exist in different countries.

(1) The Determinants of Demand Elasticity - The elasticity of demand for a product in a given country is determined by a number of factors, of which income level and competitive conditions are perhaps the two most important.

b) Strategic Pricing - The concept of strategic pricing has two aspects, which we will refer to as predatory pricing and experience curve pricing.

    i) Predatory Pricing - Is the use of price as a competitive weapon to drive weaker competitors out of a national market.

    ii) Experience Curve Pricing - Many firms pursuing an experience curve pricing strategy on an international scale price low worldwide in attempting to build global sales volume as rapidly as possible, even if this means taking large losses initially. Such a firm believes that several years in the future, when it has moved down the experience curve, it will be making substantial profits and, moreover, have a cost advantage over its less aggressive competitors.

c) Regulatory Influences on Prices - Firms' abilities to engage in either price discrimination or strategic pricing may be limited by national or international regulations.

    i) Antidumping Regulations - Dumping occurs whenever a firm sells a product for a price that is less than the cost of producing it.

    ii) Competition Policy - Most industrialized nations have regulations designed to promote competition and to restrict monopoly practices.

7) Configuring the Marketing Mix - A firm may vary aspects of its marketing mix from country to country to take into account local differences.
Teaching Tip: In the coming years, the Internet will become an increasingly important part of an international businesses' marketing mix. A site entitled "The Internet and International Marketing" {http://web.ukonline.co.uk/members/jim.hamill/wwwlect.htm} is a ten module on-line course covering effective use of the Internet in international marketing.

8) New Product Development - Firms that successfully develop and market new products can earn enormous returns. Some examples are provided in the textbook.

a) The Location of R&D - Ideas for new products are simulated by the interactions of scientific research, demand conditions, and competitive conditions. Other things being equal, the rate of new-product development seems to be greater in countries where:

    i) More money is spent on basic and applied research and development.

    ii) Demand is strong.

    iii) Consumers are affluent.

    iv) Competition is intense.

b) Linking R&D and Marketing - The need to adequately commercialize new technologies poses special problems in the international business, since commercialization may require different versions of a new product to be produced for different countries. To do this, the firm must build close links between its R&D centers and its various country operations.
Teaching Tip: For anyone interested in doing a better job keeping up with international news, Interactive Global News is an international electronic news source sponsored by Pangaea Communications. The site provides a substantive and thought provoking series of news briefs and commentaries on global business issues. The site is available to the public at {http://www.pangaea.net/ign/news.htm}.

Critical Thinking and Discussion Questions

1. Imagine you are the marketing manager for a U.S. manufacturer of disposable diapers. Your firm is considering entering the European market, concentrating on the major EU countries. Your CEO believes the advertising message that has been effective in the United States will suffice in Europe. Outline some possible objections to this.

   Answer: The countries that make up the European Continent differ along a whole range of dimensions, including social structure, language, religion, and education. In addition, for historic and idiosyncratic reasons, a whole range of cultural differences separate the European countries. As a result of this, it is unlikely that a single advertising message would work across Europe, let along for both the American and European markets.

2. By the end of this century we will have seen the emergence of enormous global markets for standardized consumer products. Do you agree with this statement. Justify your answer.

   Answer: This question is designed to stimulate classroom discussion, or to encourage your students to "think" about this issue in preparing a written answer. There are advocates on both sides of this issue. Theodore Levitt and others argue that modern transportation and communications technologies, such as MTV, are facilitating a convergence of the tastes and preferences of consumers in the more advanced countries of the world. As a result, according to Levitt, the multinational corporation, which operates in a number of countries and adjusts its products to match the tastes of the consumers in each country, is being replaced by the global corporation, which sell the same thing everywhere. Critics argue that Levitt is overstating his case, and that globalization is the exception rather than the rule. Even firms such as McDonald's, which Levitt holds up as the perfect example of a consumer products firm that sells a standardized product worldwide, modifies its menu from country to country in light of local preferences.

3. You are the marketing manager of a food products company that is considering entering the South Korean market. The retail system in South Korea tends to be very fragmented. Moreover, retailers and wholesalers tend to have long-term ties with South Korean food companies, which makes access to distribution channels difficult. What distribution strategy would you advise the company to pursue. Why?

   Answer: The firm should sell to either wholesalers or import agents. Because the retail system in South Korea is very fragmented, it would be very expensive for the firm to make contact with each individual retailer. As a result, it would be more economical for the firm to sell to wholesalers or import agents. Import agents may have long-term relationships with wholesalers, retailers, and/or other import agents. Similarly, wholesalers may have long-standing relationships with retailers and, therefore, be better able to persuade them to carry the firm's product than the firm itself would.

4. Price discrimination is indistinguishable from dumping. Discuss the accuracy of this statement.

   Answer: This statement is inaccurate. In an international context, price discrimination exists whenever consumers in different countries are changed different prices for the same product. In essence, price discrimination involves charging whatever the market will bear; in a competitive market, prices may have to be lower than in a market where the firm has a monopoly. Price discrimination is not illegal or necessarily unethical. It is simply a practice of maximizing profitability based on charging a price that is tenable given the competitive conditions in a particular market (for instance, in a local context, a person pays 50 cents for a 12 ounce can of Coke at the supermarket, and $2.00 for 12 ounces of Coke at a concert or sporting event. This price discrimination occurs because the vendor has a monopoly at the concert or sporting event and can charge a higher price and still attract customers).

Dumping is much different. Technically, dumping occurs whenever a firm sells a product for a price that is less than the cost of producing it. Dumping is a form of predatory pricing that is typically used as a competitive weapon to drive weaker competitors out of a national market.

Case Discussion Questions

1. What was the root cause of P&G's marketing failures in Japan and Poland?

    Answer: The root cause of P&G's marketing failures in Japan and Poland was its propensity to transfer its U.S. marketing and product strategies to these countries "intact" without modifying the strategies to accommodate the tastes and preferences of local consumers. In other words, P&G persistently assumed that "what works in the U.S." would work in its foreign markets as well. Clearly, P&G was mistaken.

2. What strategic and organizational actions do you think P&G should take to increase its sensitivity to national differences and their impact on the marketing mix?

    Answer: From a strategic perspective, P&G should expend more effort learning about the tastes and preferences of its foreign customers before it develops products and marketing campaigns for those markets. Your students may comment that it was naïve for a company as large and experienced as P&G to make the errors in this area that they apparently did. In addition, P&G should hire more foreign nationals to work in its overseas subsidiaries to gain an "insiders" perspective on the products and marketing messages that are likely to work in those markets.

3. How might P&G improve its ability to leverage products and marketing strategies developed in one part of the world and apply them to markets elsewhere?

    Answer: This question is designed to stimulate classroom discussion and/or to encourage your students to "think" about this challenging issue when preparing a written response. Clearly, P&G has learned that it can't assume that a marketing strategy that works in one market will work in another. There may be occasions, however, when P&G can transfer some of what it has done from one market to another culturally and demographically similar market.

Internet Exercise

1) Summary:
    a) This exercise discusses four electronic marketing magazines that are available on the Internet. These magazines contain fashion trends, demographic data, advertising tips, and other forms of

information that helps global managers remain abreast of environmental trends. The exercise asks the reader to explore these four magazines in more detail.

2) Additional Material:

    a) Along with practitioner magazines, a number of academic journals that focus on international marketing issues also have web sites. Some of these sites provide only general information about their respective journal and other sites provide more extensive information including copies of the articles that appear in the journals. The names of a sample of these journals and their web site addresses are as follows:

        i) Journal of International Marketing {http://ciber.bus.msu.edu/jim/}.

        ii) Journal of International Business Studies {http://www.cba.hawaii.edu/aib/pubs/jibs/jibs.htm}.

        iii) European Journal of Marketing {http://www.mcb.co.uk/cgi-bin/journal1/ejm}.

Opening Case: MTV and the Globalization of Teen Culture

1) Summary:

    a) This feature focuses on the phenomenal success of MTV, a music-orientated television station that is broadcast in over 80 countries. MTV's audience is primarily teens and young adults in their early 20s. These are people who are just formulating their tastes and brand preferences, and constitute a perfect market for companies that are trying to sell a global, standardized product. As a result, some of MTV's largest advertisers are Levi Strauss, Procter & Gamble, Johnson & Johnson, Pepsi-Cola, and Apple Computer. These companies use MTV as a medium to reach a global audience and create a "global" appeal for their standardized products. The case expounds upon how MTV is helping "pave the wave" for increased globalization and standardization of products worldwide.

2) Suggested Discussion Questions:

    a) The "Closing Case" that appears at the end of Chapter 12 discusses the misfortunes that P&G experienced by transforming its marketing message for consumer products directly from the United States to parts of Europe and Asia. The message the emerged from this case was that just because a marketing campaign works for P&G in America, that doesn't mean that it will work in other parts of the world. In contrast, the companies that advertise on MTV hope to sell a fairly standardized product to all corners of the world. What is different about P&G's approach in Europe and Asia (as described in the case at the end of the chapter) and what MTV's advertisers are trying to accomplish? Explain your answer.

    b) What type of product lends itself to being advertised on MTV? Can you think of any products that would not be suitable for advertising on MTV? Explain your answer.

    c) MTV has been successful, in part, because music is a global medium. Can you think of any other global mediums? Where else could companies like Levi Strauss, Johnson & Johnson, and Pepsi-Cola advertise to reach a global audience.

3) MTV Homepage: {http://www.mtv.com/}

Management Focus: Global Advertising at Polaroid

1) Summary:

    a) This features focuses on the experiences of Polaroid in developing advertising campaigns for its European markets. In the mid-1970s, Polaroid introduced its SX-70 camera to Europe using an advertising campaign designed in the United States. Despite the objections of the company's European personnel, the commercials were not modified for a European audience. The commercials were not a success, and Polaroid struggled in gaining a foothold in the European market. When

Polaroid changed its strategy and decided to reposition its camera to accommodate a more serious platform, the company changed its attitude towards developing commercials for its European markets. This time, Polaroid let its European personnel help design and implement the commercials, and they have been a phenomenal success.

2) Suggested Discussion Questions:

   a) What was wrong with Polaroid's first attempt at developing an advertising campaign for its European markets? Explain your answer.

   b) Discuss the importance of decentralized decision making in developing advertising campaigns for international markets.

3) Polaroid Homepage: {appt//www.polaroid.com/}

Management Focus: Castrol Oil

1) Summary:

   a) This feature focuses on the strategies and experience of Castrol Oil in marketing its GTX brand of motor oil around the world. Castrol Oil is the lubricants division of the British chemical, oil, and gas concern Burmah Castrol. Castrol Oil's GTX brand of motor oil is marketed as a premium brand. The feature focuses on the company's entries into the lubricants markets in Thailand and Viet Nam. Catrol has a unique strategy of appealing to consumers who drive motorcycles, in hopes of developing brand loyalty and retaining these customers as their countries develop to the point where cars are more common. This strategy worked well in Thailand, and is currently under way in Viet Nam.

2) Suggested Discussion Questions:

   a) In underdeveloped countries like Thailand and Viet Nam, the conventional forms of media that we are accustomed to, like radio and television, are often absent. This problem is particularly pronounced in Viet Nam. Describe how Castrol Oil overcame this challenge. Does their approach seem prudent to you? Explain your answer.

   b) Would you describe Castrol Oil's communications strategy in Viet Nam as a push or a pull strategy? Explain your answer.

   c) Castrol Oil emphasizes a premium pricing strategy. What elements of the company's communications and distributions strategies support this premium pricing strategy?

CHAPTER 13
GLOBAL OPERATIONS MANAGEMENT

Learning Objectives

1. Be familiar with the important influence that operations management can have on the competitive position of an international business.

2. Understand how country differences, manufacturing technology, and product features all affect the choice of where to locate production operations.

3. Appreciate the factors that influence a firm's decision of whether to source component parts from within the company or purchase them from a foreign supplier.

4. Understand what is required to efficiently coordinate a globally dispersed manufacturing system.

Chapter Summary

This chapter explores the issues associated with global operations management. At the outset, the author defines the terms operations, production, and material management, and then goes on to discuss the importance of total quality management (TQM) and ISO 9000. Particular emphasis is placed on the topics of "where" international firms should locate their manufacturing operation and how international firms decided whether to "make-or-buy" component parts. In regard to the former, the author argues that country factors, technological factors, and product factors influence a manufacturers location decision. In regard to make-or-decisions, the author provides a balanced discussion of the advantages and disadvantages of buying components parts (in the world marketplace) opposed to making them in-house.

The chapter concludes with separate discussion of the importance of strategic alliances, just-in-time manufacturing, and information technology to international firms.

Chapter Outline With Lecture Notes and Teaching Tips

1) Introduction

   a) Operations - Activities involved in the procurement of inputs into the production process, the creation of a product, and its delivery to customers. These activities include manufacturing and materials management activities.

   b) Decision Areas - Managers in an international business have to make a number of critical decisions in the operations arena. They have to decide where in the world to locate productive activities, how much production to outsource to foreign suppliers, and how best to coordinate globally dispersed supply and distribution chains.

2) Strategy, Manufacturing, and Materials Management - This chapter focuses on two activities - production and materials management - and attempts to clarify how these activities might be performed internationally to (1) lower the costs of value creation and (2) add value by better serving customer needs.

   a) Production - Activities involved in creating a product.

   b) Materials Management - Activity that controls the transmission of physical materials through the value chain, from procurement through production and into distribution.

c) Logistics - The procurement and physical transmission of material through the supply chain, from suppliers to customers.

d) Strategic Objectives - The manufacturing and materials management functions of an international firms have a number of important strategic objectives. These are:

   i) Lower costs and simultaneously increase product quality.

   ii) Accommodate demands for local responsiveness

   iii) Respond quickly to shifts in customer demands.

e) Total Quality Management (TQM) - Management technique that focuses on the need to improve the quality of a company's products and services. TQM is the main management techniques that companies are utilizing to boost their product quality.

f) ISO 9000 - European standard designed to assure the quality of products and processes.
   Lecture Note: Each year CIO magazine publishes a list of the "Top 100" companies in terms of Supply Chain/Logistics Management. This list may be helpful in locating companies that are heavily involved in this issue. The current list, which includes global corporations such as Caterpillar, Chrysler, Texas Instruments, Toyota, UPS, and Xerox, can be accessed at {http://www.cio.com/CIO/100winners.html#Supply Chain/Logistics Management}.

3) Where to Manufacture - A key decision facing an international firm is where to locate its manufacturing activities to achieve the twin goals of minimizing costs and improving product quality. For the firm that considers international production to be a feasible option, a number of factors must be considered:

a) Country Factors - Other things being equal, a firm should locate its various manufacturing activities where the economic, political, and cultural conditions, including relative factor costs, are more conducive to the performance of those activities. Another country factor is expected future movements in currency exchange rates.

   Teaching Tip: The United States Central Intelligence Agency has compiled a "country profile" on each country in the world. The country profiles are very informative, and may provide useful information to a company that is contemplating doing business in a particular country. The country profiles are available to the public and can be downloaded at {http://fedstats.gov/index20.html}.

   Teaching Tip: For additional information about a particular country, Yahoo provides an easy-to-search bank of linked sources that provide information about almost every country in the world. The site is available at {http://www.yahoo.com/Government/Countries/}.

b) Technological Factors - The type of technology a firm uses in its manufacturing can be pivotal in location decisions. Three characteristics of a manufacturing technology are of interest here:

   i) The level of its fixed costs - In some cases the fixed costs of setting up a manufacturing plant are so high that a firm must serve the world market from a single location or from a very few locations.

   ii) Its minimum efficient scale - The larger the minimum efficient scale of a plant, the greater the argument for centralizing production in a single location or a limited number of locations.

   iii) Its flexibility - When flexible manufacturing technologies are available, a firm can manufacture products customized to various national markets at a single factory at the optimal location.

c) Product Factors - Two product factors impact location decisions.

   i) The first is the product's value-to-weight ratio because of its influence on transportation costs. If the value-to-weight ratio is high, it is practical to produce the product in a single location and export it to other parts of the world. If the value-to-weight ratio is low, there is greater pressure to manufacture the product in multiple locations across the world.

ii) The other product feature that can influence location decisions is whether the product serves universal needs, needs that are the same all over the world. Since there are few national differences in consumer taste and preference for such products, the need for local responsiveness is reduced. This increases the attractiveness of concentrating manufacturing in a central location.

d) Locating Manufacturing Facilities - There are two basic strategies for locating manufacturing facilities: concentrating them in the optimal location and serving the world market from there, and decentralizing them in various regional or national locations that are close to major markets. The appropriate strategic choice is determined by the various country, technological, and product factors discussed in this section. A summary of this material is provided in Table 13.1 in the text.

4) Make-or-Buy Decisions - International businesses face sourcing decisions, decisions about whether they should make or buy the component parts to go into their final product. Make-or-buy decisions are important factors in many firms' manufacturing strategies.
   Teaching Tip: An article entitled "Is the Make-Buy Decision Process a Core Competence"? by Charles H. Fine and Daniel E. Whitney of MIT Center for Technology, Policy, and Industrial Development is available at {http://web.mit.edu/ctpid/www/Whitney/morepapers/make_ab.html}.

   a) The Advantages of Make - The arguments that support making component parts in-house - vertical integration - are fourfold. Specifically, vertical integration may be associated with lower costs, facilitate investments in high specialized assets, protect proprietary technology, and facilitate the scheduling of adjacent processes.

      i) Lower Costs - It may pay a firm to continue manufacturing a product or component part in-house, as opposed to outsourcing it to an independent manufacturer, if the firm is more efficient at that production activity than any other enterprise.

      ii) Facilitating Specialized Investments - When substantial investments in specialized assets are required to manufacture a component, the firm will prefer to make the component internally rather than contract it out to a supplier.

      iii) Proprietary Product Technology Protection - In the case of proprietary technology, to maintain control, the firm might prefer to make such a component part in-house.

      iv) Improved Scheduling - The weakest argument for vertical integration is that production cost savings result from it because it makes planning, coordination, and scheduling of adjacent processes easier.

   b) The Advantage of Buy - The advantages of buying component parts from independent suppliers are that it gives the firm greater flexibility, it can help drive down the firm's cost structure, and it may help the firm to capture orders from international customers.

      i) Strategic Flexibility - The greatest advantage of buying component parts from independent suppliers is that the firm can maintain its flexibility, switching orders between suppliers as circumstances dictate.

      ii) Lower Coasts - Although vertical integration is often undertaken to lower costs, it may end up having the opposite effect and raise costs.

      iii) Offset - Another reason for outsourcing some manufacturing to independent suppliers based in other countries is that it may help the firm capture more orders from that country.

   c) Trade-Offs - It is clear that trade-offs are involved in make-or-buy decisions.

   d) Strategic Alliances with Suppliers - Several international business have tried to reap some of the benefits of vertical integration without the associated organizational problems by entering into strategic alliances with key suppliers.

5) Coordinating a Global Manufacturing System

   a) Materials Management - Which encompasses logistics, embraces the activities necessary to get materials to a manufacturing facility, through the manufacturing process, and out through a distribution system to the end user. The twin objectives of materials management are to achieve this at the lowest possible cost and in a way that best serves customer needs.

     Teaching Tip: Stanford University maintains a web site that is a forum for the dissemination of research and practical advice in the area of global supply chain management. The site supplies current information that can help embellish a lecture on global materials management. The site is available at {http://www-leland.standford.edu/group/scformu/}.

     i) The Power of Just-in-Time (JIT) - The basic philosophy behind JIT systems is to economize on inventory holding costs by having materials arrive at a manufacturing plant just in time to enter the production process, and not before.

     ii) The Role of Information Technology - Information systems play a critical role in modern materials management.

Critical Thinking and Discussion Questions

1. An electronics firm is considering how best to supply the world market for microprocessors used in consumer and industrial electronic products. A manufacturing plant cost approximately $500 million to construct and requires a highly skilled work force. The total value of the world market for this product over the next 10 years is estimated to be between $10 and $15 billion. The tariffs prevailing in this industry are currently low. What kind of manufacturing strategy do you think the firm should adopt - concentrated or decentralized? What kind of location(s) should the firm favor for its plant(s)?

Answer: The firm should pursue a concentrated manufacturing because (1) the tariffs prevailing in the industry are low, (2) the cost of building a plant to produce the microprocessors is high, and (3) the product's value-to-weight ratio is high. All of these factors favor a concentrated vs. a decentralized manufacturing strategy. In terms of location, the company should consider three factors: country factors, technology factors, and product factors. First, in terms of country factors, the firm should locate its plant in a country that has a highly skilled pool of workers available. That criteria probably limits the firm to developed nations. Second, in terms of technology factors, the firm is compelled to limit the number of its manufacturing facilities because of the high cost of constructing a plant. Third, in terms of product factors, the firm can manufacturer its product in a central location due to the relatively high value-weight ratio and the universal appeal of the product.

2. A chemical firm is considering how best to supply the world market for sulfuric acid. A manufacturing plant costs approximately $20 million to construct and requires a moderately skilled work force. The total value of the world market for this product over the new 10 years is estimated to be between $20 and $30 billion. The tariffs prevailing in this industry are moderate. Should the firm favor concentrated manufacturing or decentralized manufacturing? What kind of location(s) should the firm seek for its plant(s)?

Answer: This question is a tougher call than the scenario depicted in Question #1. The firm should probably pursue a limited decentralized manufacturing strategy (meaning that the firm should not set up a plant in every country that it sells to, but should set up plants in several "regions" of the world). This strategy makes sense because (1) The tariffs prevailing in the industry are moderate (rather than low), (2) the cost of constructing a facility is relatively modest ($20 million), and (3) only a moderately skilled work force is needed (which is probably available in many low-cost regions of the world). The firm should select its location based on country factors, technology factors and product factors. In terms of country factors, the firm should find locations where semi-skilled labor is inexpensive. In terms of technology factors, the firm is not constrained by a high fixed costs associated with its product, so technology is not a pervasive issue. Finally, product factors favor the firm locating in several locations throughout the world. The company's product has a low value-weight ratio, making it unattractive to produce the product in a central location and export it across the world.

3. A firm must decide whether to make a component part in-house or to contract it out to an independent supplier. Manufacturing the part requires a nonrecoverable investment in specialized assets. The most efficient suppliers are located in countries with currencies that many foreign exchange analysts expect to appreciate substantially over the next decade. What are the pros and cons of (a) manufacturing the component in-house and (b) outsourcing manufacture to an independent supplier? Which option would you recommend? Why?

Answer: The pros of manufacturing the product in-house are (1) because the part requires a nonrecoverable investment in specialized assets, hiring a supplier to build the part would give the supplier considerable bargaining power in term of price, and (2) manufacturing in-house avoids the risk of losing money on currency transactions. This is a particularly salient issue if the firm believes that the currency in the supplier's country is expected to appreciated against its currency. There are no clear disadvantages of manufacturing the product in-house in this case, except that it requires a larger initial outlay. The typical advantages of outsourcing the production of component parts are (1) strategic flexibility, (2) lower costs, and (3) it may help a firm capture more orders from a foreign country for its finished product. In this particular case, strategic flexibility (i.e. the ability to switch supplier) would not be realized because it is not easy to switch suppliers when nonrecoverable investments are required. Similarly, it might be difficult to achieve costs economies through outsourcing given these special circumstances.

4. Explain how an efficient materials management function can help an international business compete more effectively in the global marketplace.

Answer: Materials management, which encompasses logistics, embraces the activities necessary to get materials to a manufacturing facility, through the manufacturing process, and out through a distribution system to the end user. The twin objectives of materials management are to achieve this at the lowest possible cost and in a way that best serves customer needs, thereby lowering the costs of value creation and helping the firm establish a competitive advantage through superior customer service.

Case Discussion Questions

1. Which change occurred in DEC's operating environment during the 1980s that transformed its high level of vertical integration from a source of competitive strength into a source of high costs?

Answer: Historically, DEC's vertical integration strategy was driven by its desire to keep its proprietary computer technology in-house. This philosophy was consistent with the "closed standard" nature of the computer industry during most of DEC's corporate history. In a closed standard environment, each company produced a unique product and protected its own proprietary technology. What changed in DEC environment was a shift towards an "open standard" environment in which the technical standards necessary to build computers were published, and companies could buy "off-the-shelf" component products to assemble computers. At the same time, technology advanced to the point where PCs and network services, based on "off-the-shelf" standards, were rapidly replacing the demand for DEC's mainframe computers. Unfortunately for DEC, these changes transformed the company's high level of vertical integration from a source of competitive strength to a source of high costs.

2. Why does it make sense for DEC to outsource more activities in the computer industry of the 1990s?

Answer: Today, the technology needed to produce the majority of the component parts that go into a DEC computer is well known, and the parts are available from a number of domestic and offshore suppliers. As a result, DEC may be able to find a supplier that can produce some of its component parts (due to the availability of lower cost semi-skilled labor and/or increased economies of scale in producing a particular part) cheaper than it can.

3. How was DEC able to reduce its annual logistics costs? What was the main source of cost savings?

Answer: DEC did two things to reduce its annual logistics costs. First, the company reduced the number of its manufacturing facilities from 33 to 12. The consolidation of activities in a smaller number of plants reduced the transportation costs of transporting partially assembled products from plant to plant. Second, the company established three major customer regions - Pacific Rim, Americas, and Europe - to be served by plants within their own regions. These changes allowed the company to streamline its global logistics network. There were now far fewer points to ship between, which drove down shipping costs, and the volume of shipping between regions was reduced significantly by the policy that each region become a self-contained entity.

Internet Exercise

1) Summary:
   a) This exercise acquaints the reader with the web site of the National Center for Manufacturing Science. The site includes a number of resources that are of interest to manufacturing and materials management professionals.
2) Additional Material:
   a) Another excellent source of information on global operations management topics is university based web sites. The Massachusetts Institute of Technology (MIT) maintains an excellent site at {http://web.mit.edu/orc/www/}. The Department of Industrial Engineering and Operations Research sponsors another site at the University of California-Berkley. This site can be found at {http://www.ieor.berkeley.edu/}. Another site provides a full menu of operations research "links." This site can be sound at {http://OpsResearch.com/OR-Links/index.html}.

Opening Case: Global Manufacturing and Logistics at Timberland

1) Summary:
   a) This case focuses on Timberland, a New Hampshire based manufacturer of rugged, high-quality shoes. Because of the quality and uniqueness of its shoes, Timberland has experienced rapid growth in both America and international markets. Along with Timberland's growth in sales has come a growth in its system of logistics. Unfortunately, during a large part of its growth era, Timberland did not grow its logistics system very effectively. As a result, by the early 1990s Timberland found itself confronted with an extremely complex global manufacturing and logistics

network. The case describes how Timberland overcame this challenge and how its new logistics and manufacturing system is facilitating, rather than hindering, its global growth initiatives.

2) Suggested Discussion Questions:

   a) What mistakes did Timberland make during the 1980s that resulted in an ineffective global manufacturing and logistics system? How could these mistakes have been avoided during that era?

   b) What role does information technology play in enabling a firm to develop an effective manufacturing and logistics system? Was the importance of effective information technology illustrated by this case? Explain your answer.

   c) Describe Timberland's new approach to global manufacturing and logistic management. Will it work? Justify your answer.

3) Timberland Homepage: {http://www.timberland.com/}

Management Focus: Make-or-Buy Decisions at Boeing

1) Summary:

   a) This feature focuses on the process of generating "make-or-buy" decisions at Boeing. The Boeing Company is the world's largest manufacturer of commercial jet aircraft with a 60 percent share of the global market. Due to decreasing demand for its aircraft and cost constraints on the part of its buyers, Boeing has been forced to find ways to become more price competitive. One strategy that Boeing has utilized is outsourcing. The feature describes Boeing's outsourcing criteria, which involves making a determination whether it is better for Boeing to "make" or "buy" a particular component part. For Boeing this is serious business. On the one hand, Boeing does not want to take unnecessary strategic risks and become too dependent on outside suppliers for critical component parts. On the other hand, Boeing can outsource certain component parts and realize a substantial cost saving. The case illustrates the nature of this dilemma at Boeing.

2) Suggested Discussion Questions:

   a) Describe Boeing's criteria for determining whether a component part should be "outsourced" or whether it should be manufactured in-house. Is Boeing's criteria appropriate? Why or why not?

   b) What could go wrong with Boeing's strategy of outsourcing? Has Boeing taken the necessary precautions? Are there any hazards in the company's strategy?

   c) In the future do you believe that Boeing will be doing more or less outsourcing? Justify your answer.

3) Boeing Homepage: {http://www.boeing.com}

Management Focus: Materials Management at Bose

1) Summary:

   a) This feature focuses on the manner in which Bose Corporation has made its materials management function an important part of its overall competitiveness. Bose's core competence is in its electronic engineering skills, but the company attributes much of its business success to tightly coordinated materials management. Bose purchases most of its electronic and nonelectronic components from independent suppliers scattered around North America, the Far East, and Europe. The case describes the manner in which Bose has capitalized on this strategy by making its materials management function extremely efficient and effective.

2) Suggested Discussion Questions:

   a) Why is materials management so important to Bose? Does Bose give this function an appropriate amount of attention, or is it overemphasized by the company? Explain your answer.

113

b) How important is the role of information technology to Bose's materials management and logistics operations?

3) Bose Homepage: {http://www.bose.com/}

CHAPTER 14
GLOBAL HUMAN RESOURCE MANAGEMENT

Learning Objectives

1. Be familiar with the pros and cons of different approaches to staffing policy in international businesses.

2. Understand why management may fail to thrive in foreign postings.

3. Understand what can be done to increase an executive's change of succeeding in a foreign posting.

4. Appreciate the role that training, management development, and compensation practices can play in effectively managing human resources within an international business.

Chapter Summary

This closing chapter focuses on the challenging topic of global human resource management (HRM). The term expatriate manager is introduced, which refers to a citizen of one country who is working abroad in one of his or her firm's subsidiaries. The task of staffing foreign subsidiaries is discussed. In this area, firms typically pursue either an ethnocentric, polycentric, or geocentric approach. This section is followed with an explanation of the challenges involved in selecting expatriate managers. Expatriate often fail in their overseas assignments for a variety of reasons, ranging from the inability of their spouses to adjust to living overseas to a manager's personal or emotional maturity. Techniques that can be used to reduce expatriate failure are presented and discussed.

The chapter also discussed a number of other HRM topics in the context of global management. The topics of training and management development are discussed, along with performance appraisal and compensation.

Chapter Outline With Lecture Notes and Teaching Tips

1) Introduction

   a) Human Resource Management - Refers to the activities an organization carries out to utilizes its human resources effectively. These activities include determining the firm's human resource strategy, staffing, performance evaluation, management development, compensation, and labor relations.

   b) Challenges Involved - The role of HRM is complex enough in a purely domestic firm, but it is more complex in an international business, where staffing, management development, performance evaluation, and compensation activities are complicated by profound differences between countries in labor markets, culture, legal systems, economic systems, and the like.

   c) Expatriate Manager - An expatriate manager is a citizen of one country who is working abroad in one of the his or her firm's subsidiaries.
   Teaching Tip: There are a number of private HRM firms that provide selection, training and repatriation services for expatriate managers. An example of one of these companies can be found at {http://www.global-dynamics.com/expatria.htm}.
   Lecture Note: According to a new survey by William M. Mercer, Inc. {http://www.relojournal.com/june97/mercer.htm}, the number of expatriate managers living outside their home countries is growing. The majority (90%) of the large multinationals surveyed

predicted that the number of expatriate managers that they employ would increase over the next two years.

2) Staffing Policy - Is concerned with the selection of employees for particular jobs. Research has identified three types of staffing policies in international businesses: the ethnocentric approach, the polycentric approach, and the geocentric approach.

   a) The Ethnocentric Approach - Type of staffing policy in which all key management positions are filled by citizens from the parent firm's home country. Firms pursue an ethnocentric staffing policy for three reasons:

      i) First, the firm may believe there is a lack of qualified individuals in the host country to fill senior management positions.

      ii) Second, the firm may see an ethnocentric staffing policy as the best way to maintain a unified corporate culture.

      iii) Third, if the firm is trying to create value by transferring core competencies to a foreign operation, as firms pursuing an international strategy are, it may believe that the best way to do this is to transfer parent country nationals who have knowledge of that competency to the foreign operation.

      iv) Policy is on the wane - Despite this rationale for pursing an ethnocentric staffing policy, the policy is now on the wane in most international businesses. There are two reasons for this. First, an ethnocentric staffing policy limits advancement opportunities for host country nationals. Second, an ethnocentric policy can lead to "cultural myopia."

   b) The Polycentric Approach - Type of staffing policy in which citizens of the host country are recruited to manage subsidiaries while key management positions at headquarters are filled by citizens from the parent firm's home country.

      i) Advantage of polycentric approach:

         (1) The firm is less likely to suffer from cultural myopia.

         (2) It may be less expensive to implement.

      ii) Disadvantages of the polycentric approach:

         (1) Host country nationals have limited opportunities to gain experience outside their own country and thus cannot progress beyond senior positions in their own subsidiaries.

         (2) A gap can form between host country managers and parent country managers.

   c) The Geocentric Approach - Type of staffing policy in which the best people, regardless of nationality, are sought for key jobs throughout the company.

      i) Advantages of geocentric approach:

         (1) It enables the firms to make the best use of its human resources.

         (2) It enables the firm to build a cadre of international executives who feel at home working in a number of different cultures.

      ii) Disadvantages of geocentric approach:

         (1) Many countries want foreign subsidiaries to employ their citizens. To achieve this goal, they use immigration laws to require the employment of host country nationals is they are available in adequate numbers and have the necessary skills.

         (2) Geocentric staffing policies can be very expensive to implement.

3) The Expatriate Problem - A prominent issue in the international staffing literature is expatriate failure - the premature return of an expatriate manager to his or her home country.

   a) Reasons for expatriate failure (in descending order of importance) for a sample of U.S. multinationals:

      i) Inability of spouse to adjust.

      ii) Manager's inability to adjust.

      iii) Other family problems.

      iv) Manager's personal or emotional maturity.

      v) Inability to cope with larger overseas responsibility.

   b) Reasons for expatriate failure (in descending order of importance) for a sample of Japanese multinationals:

      i) Inability to cope with larger overseas responsibility.

      ii) Difficulties with the new environment.

      iii) Personal of emotional problems.

      iv) Lack of technical competence.

      v) Inability of spouse to adjust.

      Lecture Note: A recent survey by William M. Mercer, Inc., illustrates some of the problems that contribute to expatriate failure. For instance, only 50% of the companies that participated in the survey have structured procedures for selecting candidates for international assignments, fewer than 10% use any form of testing to screen clients, only slightly more than 50% provide expatriates with any form of cultural briefing, and only 45% have a formal repatriation process at the end of the assignment. More examples of issues that contribute to expatriate failure can be found at the Mercer website at {http://www.relojournal.com/june97/mercer.htm}.

      Teaching Tip: A broad array of information about expatriate performance is provided by the Integrated Resources Group at {http://www.expat-repat.com/text/home.html}. This site is well worth a visit and can provide good lecture material.

   c) Expatriate Selection - One way of reducing expatriate failure rates is through improved selection procedures. Mendenhall and Oddou identified four dimensions that seem to predict success in a foreign posting: self-orientation, others-orientation, perceptual ability, and cultural toughness.

      i) Self-Orientation - The attributes of this dimension strengthen the expatriate's self-esteem, self-confidence, and mental well-being.

      ii) Perceptual Ability - This is the ability to understand why people of other countries behave the way they do.

      iii) Cultural Toughness - This dimension refers to the fact that how well an expatriate adjusts to a particular posting tends to be related to the country of assignment.

4) Training and Management Development

   a) Training for Expatriate Managers - Cultural training, language training, and practical training all seem to reduce expatriate failure. However, one study found that only about 30 percent of managers sent on one- to five-year expatriate assignments received training before their departure.

      Teaching Tip: A forum for international trade training is available online at {http://www.fitt.ca/}. Established in 1992, the Forum for International Trade Training (FITT) is a not-for-profit organization mandated by the Canadian government in partnership with private industry to remedy the shortage of people with the skills necessary to succeed in overseas markets.

      i) Cultural Training - Cultural training seeks to foster an appreciation for the host country's culture.

      ii) Language Training - Despite the prevalence of English, an exclusive reliance on English diminishes an expatriate manager's ability to interact with host country nationals.

      iii) Practical Training - Is aimed at helping the expatriate manager and her family ease themselves into day-to-day life in the host country.

  b) Repatriation of Expatriates - A largely overlooked but critically important issue in the training and development of expatriate managers is to prepare them for reentry into their home country organization.

  c) Management Development and Strategy - Management development programs are designed to increase the overall skill levels of managers through a mix of ongoing management education and rotations of managers through a number of jobs within the firm to give them varied experiences.

5) Performance Appraisal

  a) Performance Appraisal Problems - Unintentional bias makes it difficult to evaluate the performance of expatriate managers objectively. In most cases, two groups evaluate the performance of expatriate managers - host nation managers and home office managers - and both are subject to bias.

  b) Guidelines for Performance Appraisal- Several things can reduce bias in the performance appraisal.

      i) First, most expatriates appear to believe more weight should be given to an on-site manager's appraisal than to an off-site manager's appraisal.

      ii) Second, when the policy is for foreign on-site mangers to write performance evaluations, home office managers should probably be consulted before an on-site manager completes a formal termination evaluation.

6) Compensation

  a) National Differences in Compensation - Substantial differences exist in the compensation of executives at the same level in various countries. These differences in compensation practices raise a perplexing question for an international business: should the firm pay executives in different countries according to the prevailing standards in each country, or should it equalize pay on a global basis?

  b) Expatriate Pay - The most common approach to expatriate pay is the balance sheet approach. This approach equalizes purchasing power across countries so employees can enjoy the same standard in their foreign positing that they enjoyed at home.

  c) Components of the typical expatriate compensation package:

      i) Base salary.

      ii) A foreign service premium.

      iii) Allowances of various types.

      iv) Tax differentials.

      v) Benefits.

Critical Thinking and Discussion Questions

1.   What are the main advantages and disadvantages of the ethnocentric, polycentric, and geocentric approaches to staffing policy? When is each approach appropriate?

Answer: The answer to this question is contained in Table 14.1 in the text. An ethnocentric staffing policy is one in which all key management positions are filled by parent country nationals. The advantages of the ethnocentric approach are: (1) Overcomes lack of qualified managers in host country, (2) Unified culture, and (3) Helps transfer core competencies. The disadvantages of the ethnocentric approach are: (1) Produces resentment in host country, and (2) Can lead to cultural myopia. An ethnocentric approach is typically appropriate for firms utilizing an international strategy.

A polycentric staffing policy requires host country nationals to be recruited to manage subsidiaries, while parent country nations occupy key positions at corporate headquarters. The advantages of the polycentric approach are: (1) Alleviates cultural myopia, and (2) It is inexpensive to implement. The disadvantages of the polycentric approach are: (1) Limits career mobility, and (2) Isolates headquarters from foreign subsidiaries. A polycentric approach is typically appropriate for firms utilizing a multidomestic strategy.

A geocentric staffing policy seeks the best people for key jobs throughout the organization, regardless of nationality. The advantages of a geocentric approach are: (1) Uses human resources efficiently, (2) Helps build strong culture and informal management network. The disadvantages of the geocentric staffing policy are: (1) National immigration policies may limit implementation, and (3) It is expensive to implement. A geocentric approach is typically appropriate for firms unitizing a global or transnational strategy.

2. Research suggests that many expatriate employees encounter problems that limit both their effectiveness in a foreign posting and their contribution to the company when they return home. What are the main causes and consequences of these problems, and how might a firm reduce the occurrence of such problems?

The reasons that expatriates fail or are less effective in their jobs than they could be are listed on page 454 of the textbook. For the managers of U.S. multinationals, expatriate failure results from (in descending order of importance): (1) Inability of spouse to adjust; (2) Manager's inability to adjust; (3) Other family problems, (4) Manager's personal or emotional maturity, and (5) Inability to cope with larger overseas responsibilities. There are several steps that a firm can take to reduce the occurrence of such problems. The first step is through the development of appropriate expatriate selection procedures. The second step is through expatriate training, including cultural training, language training, and practical training focused specifically on the country the expatriate manager will be assigned to. Finally, management development programs can help an expatriate manager upgrade his or her skills and personal confidence.

In regard to repatriation, companies can help their expatriate managers by providing them a clear career path to follow when they return from their overseas assignments.

3. What is the link between an international business's strategy and its human resource management policies, particularly with regard to the use of expatriate employees and their pay scale?

There should be a close like between an international business's strategy and its human resource policies. The human resource policies of a company should facilitate rather than undermine the firm's international strategy. For example, compensation is typically not a perverse issue for the overseas employees of a firm pursuing ethnocentric or polycentric staffing policies. In ethnocentric firms the issue can be reduced to that of how much home country expatriates should be paid. As for polycentric firms, the lack of managers' mobility among national operations implies that pay can and should be kept country-specific. However, the issue of compensation is more difficult for firms pursuing a geocentric staffing policy. This policy requires a firm to develop a cadre of international managers. By definition, this cadre may comprise managers of many different nationalities. Should all members of such a cadre be paid the same salary and the same incentive pay? For a U.S.-based firm this would mean rising the compensation for foreign nationals to U.S. levels, which, given the high pay rates prevailing in the United States, could be very expensive. On the other hand, if the firm does not equalize pay, it could cause considerable resentment among foreign nationals who are members of the international cadre and work side by side with U.S. nationals. In general, if a firm is serious about building an international cadre, it may have to pay its international executives the same base salary irrespective of their country or origin or assignment. This is an example of how a firm uses its human resource policies to facilitate its international strategy.

Case Discussion Questions

1. What is the relationship between HRM and strategy at Colgate-Palmolive?

    Answer: Colgate is trying to develop an HRM strategy that facilitates its international strategy. According to the case, Colgate is pursuing a transnational strategy. A transnatonal strategy calls for a geocentric approach to staffing global operations, which is what Colgate is presently doing. Colgate is also trying to develop a compensation program that facilitates its transnational strategy. So far, the compensation program has experienced mixed success. The managers that are selected for the company's international training program are all compensated similarly, which avoids the possibility of resentments over pay developing among this group of managers. However, the locally hired managers (in the host countries) do not receive the same level of compensation as the expatriate managers that come out of the international training program. Colgate needs to find a way to narrow this disparity.

2. How do you think Colgate-Palmolive's international training program might improve its economic performance?

    The international training program provides Colgate with a cadre of managers who have specialized training in international business and who have been fully socialized into the Colgate culture. As these managers move into their overseas assignments, it is less likely that they will make costly mistakes and it is more likely that they will maximize the potential of their overseas assignments than managers who have not had a similar level of training.

3. What potential problem and pitfalls do you see with Colgate-Palmolive's international training program?

    The advantage of the program is that is provides Colgate a group of international managers who have extensive international training and are fully socialized into the Colgate culture. By doing this, Colgate is in effect establishing an "elite" group of managers that have been identified as having high potential to succeed in overseas assignments. The disadvantage of the program is that it can create resentments among locally hired mangers of subsidiaries in overseas markets and other Colgate employees as a result of the generous compensation provided to the "elite" group of managers. Also, the Colgate employees that are "passed over" for admittance to the training program may see their future potential at Colgate as limited, and may leave Colgate to work for another company.

Internet Exercise

1) Summary

   a) This Internet Exercise describes several non-commercial human resource organizations that have a presence on the World Wide Web. These organizations provide a wide variety of useful information to the human resource managers of international firms.

   b) Additional Material:

      i) There are for-profit organizations that provide consulting services to international firms in regard to human resource practices that have a presence on the World Wide Web. You students may find it interesting to learn more about these companies. One Virginia based company, called Global Human Resource Services, can be found at {hppt://www.globalhr.com/}. This company welcomes visitors to its web site with the following message: "Welcome to Global Web Site." A consulting firm founded in 1989, Global's single purpose is to help its clients understand and effectively address their international human resource issues, in order to achieve success." This particular web site has links regarding the company's services in the areas of (1) International HR Policy, (2) Relocation Support Services, and (3) Destination and Host Community Services.

Opening Case: Global Human Resource Management at Coca-Cola

1) Summary

   a) This feature describes how Coca Cola manages the human resource function across its global operations. In essence, the firm using HRM as the glue that binds its widely diverse group of divisions into a cohesive family. This is done in two ways. First, by propagating a common human resources philosophy within the company, and second, by developing a group of internationally minded midlevel executives for future senior management responsibilities.

   The feature goes on to describe the firm's international compensation policy and how Coca Cola continually trains its international managers.

2) Suggested Discussion Questions

   a) Describe the link between strategy and HRM policy at Coca Cola.

   b) Why is it important for Coca-Cola to have a common human resource philosophy within the company? Because Coca-Cola operates in so many diverse markets, wouldn't it be better to develop a separate human resource philosophy within each country? Explain your answer.

   c) Describe Coca-Cola's compensation policy for its group of 500 high level managers with the HRM group. Is this policy appropriate, given Coca-Cola's global strategy? Explain your answer.

Management Focus: Monsanto's Repatriation Program

1) Summary

a) This feature describes Monsanto's repatriation program for its expatriate managers. The program is very sophisticated, and is designed to provide a supportive environment for the company's managers who are returning from overseas assignments. The feature describes the details of the repatriation program, which is a model program for the repatriation of expatriate managers.

2) Suggested Discussion Questions

a) How does Monsanto's repatriation program provide an incentive for high-potential managers to accept overseas assignments?

b) According to the feature, after they return home, Monsanto's expatriate managers are given the opportunity to showcase their experience to their peers, subordinates, and superiors, in special information exchange. Why is this important? What function does this serve in the repatriation process?

c) How does Monsanto's repatriation program help an expatriate manager adjust his personal life to returning home? Is this an important component of a firm's repatriation program?

Management Focus: Executive Pay Policies for Global Managers

1) Summary

a) This feature discusses how several international firms compensate their expatriate managers. The discussion illustrates the fact that there is no one single approach to compensating expatriate managers. This is a complicated issue that companies resolve according to the specifics of their programs.

2) Suggested Discussion Questions

a) Discuss Hewlett-Packard's expatriate compensation program? Does it make sense to establish a different program for short-term expatriates and long-term expatriate managers? Explain your answer.

b) Compare and Contrast Hewlett-Packard's expatriate compensation program with 3M's program. If you were an expatriate manager, which program would you prefer. Why?

1-18.
F
Hard
P.25

Although there are many benefits to globalization, economists argue that increased international trade and cross-border investments will result in higher prices for goods and services.

1-19.
T
Medium
P.25

It is commonly believed that globalization stimulates economic growth, creates jobs, and raises income levels.

1-20.
T
Easy
P.27

The World Trade Organization, established by the GATT negotiations in 1994, was founded to police the world trading system.

Multiple Choice

1-21.
D
Easy
P.4

Commonly referred to as _____, the trend toward a more integrated global economic system has been in place for many years.
a. market standardization
b. cross-border integration
c. nationalization
d. globalization

1-22.
A
Medium
P.5

The two main components of globalization are:
a. the globalization of markets and the globalization of production
b. the globalization of products and the globalization of finance
c. the standardization of technology and the globalization of markets
d. the globalization of finance and the globalization of accounting

1-23.
C
Medium
P.5

The globalization of markets refers to the fact that in many industries historically distinct and separate markets are merging into:
a. several distinct regional markets
b. markets defined by a common culture
c. one huge market
d. markets defined by a common language

1-24.
B
Easy
p.5

The merging of historically distinct and separate national markets into one huge global marketplace is referred to as the _____.
a. melding of markets
b. globalization of markets
c. transformation of commerce
d. integration of markets

1-25.
C
Hard
P.6

The most global of markets is in the area of:
a. services
b. consumer goods
c. industrial goods
d. intellectual capital

1-26.
B
Medium
P.6

The most global of markets are not markets for _____ products – where national differences in tastes and preferences are still often important enough to act as a break on globalization.
a. services
b. consumer goods
c. insurance and banking
d. industrial goods

1-27.
A
Easy
P.6

Globalization results in a greater degree of _____ across markets than would be present otherwise.
a. homogeneity
b. diversity
c. diversification
d. heterogeneity

1-28.
D
Easy
P.6

The globalization of _____ refers to the tendency among many firms to source goods and services from different locations around the globe in an attempt to take advantage of national differences in the cost and quality of factors of production (such as labor, energy, land, and capital).
a. information technology
b. process design
c. markets
d. production

1-29.
C
Medium
p.6

In producing its electronics products, Sony Corporation sources goods and services from different locations around the globe in an attempt to take advantage of national differences in the cost and quality of factors of production. This practice is made possible by the globalization of:
a. process design
b. markets
c. production
d. finance

1-30.
C
Easy
P.8

According to former Secretary of Labor Robert Reich, the propensity of firms to outsource many of their productive activities to different suppliers around the world has resulted in the creation of _____ products.
a. multi-domestic
b. cross-national
c. global
d. cross-cultural

1-31.
D
Hard
P.8

The two macro factors that seem to underlie the trend toward greater globalization are:
a. the increase in global economic stability, and the slowdown in technological change
b. the increase in barriers to the free flow of goods, services, and capital that has occurred since the end of World War II, and global economic stability
c. the decline in barriers to the free flow of goods, services, and capital that has occurred in the past 10 years, and the slowdown in technological change
d. the decline in barriers to the free flow of goods, services, and capital that has occurred since the end of World War II, and technological change

1-32.
A
Medium
P.9

Tyson Foods exports a number of products to consumers in other countries. This practice is referred to as _____.
a. international trade
b. world exchange
c. cross-national barter
d. situational commerce

1-33.
C
Easy
P.9

The exporting of goods or services to consumers in another country is referred to as _____.
a. situational commerce
b. world exchange
c. international trade
d. cross-national barter

1-34.
B
Medium
P.9

Although Gillette is an American company, it has invested substantial business resources in activities outside the United States. This practice is referred to as:
a. transnational commerce
b. foreign direct investment
c. international trade
d. organizational diversification

1-35.
D
Easy
p.9

The investing of resources in business activities outside a firm's home country is referred to as:

a. international trade
b. domestic direct investment
c. transnational barter
d. foreign direct investment

1-36.
C
Medium
P.9

The _____ is a treaty designed to remove barriers to the free flow of goods, services, and capital between nations.

a. Global Agreement on Tariffs and Commerce
b. United Nations Treaty on Trade
c. General Agreement on Tariffs and Trade
d. Multi-National Agreement on Tariffs and Commerce

1-37.
A
Medium
P.9

Under the umbrella of GATT (General Agreement on Tariffs and Trade), there have been eight rounds of negotiations among member states. The most recent round of negotiations was referred to as the _____.

a. Uruguay Round
b. Malaysian Symposium
c. German Round
d. New Zealand Symposium

1-38.
C
Hard
P.9

All of the following were accomplishments of the 1993 Uruguay Round, with the exception of:

a. further reduced trade barriers
b. extended GATT to cover services as well as manufactured goods
c. eliminated tariffs on all consumer goods
d. established a World Trade Organization

1-39.
B
Easy
P.9

The acronym GATT stands for:

a. Global Agreement on Taxation and Tariffs
b. General Agreement on Tariffs and Trade
c. General Agreement on Taxation and Trademarks
d. Global Association of Technology and Trade

1-40.
D
Medium
P.9

The agency established at the 1993 Uruguay Round to police the international trading system is the _____.

a. Global Trade Enforcement Administration
b. World Tariff and Trade Bureau
c. International Trade Enforcement Agency
d. World Trade Organization

1-41.
A
Medium
P.9

Suppose Royal Dutch/Shell, an international oil company, had a complaint about a trade issue. The _____, a governing body established at the Uruguay Round in 1993 to police the international trading system, is an organization that Royal Dutch Shell could take its complaint to.

a. World Trade Organization
b. International Trade Monitoring Bureau
c. World Tariff and Trade Agency
d. International Trade Monitoring Agency

1-42.
D
Hard
P.9

Under the conditions of the 1993 Uruguay agreement, average tariff rates worldwide will approach _____.

a. 1.0 percent
b. 22.0 percent
c. 6.75 percent
d. 3.9 percent

1-43.
D
Hard
P.10

Which of the following statement is consistent with data from the World Trade Organization?

a. the volume of world trade and the volume of world output have remained constant since the 1950s.
b. the volume of world trade has grown slower than the volume of world output since the 1950s.
c. the volume of world trade and the volume of world output have grown at approximately the same rate since the 1950s.
d. the volume of world trade has grown faster than the volume of world output since the 1950s.

1-44.
B
Medium
P.10

According to data from the World Trade Organization, the volume of world trade has grown faster than the volume of world output since the 1950s. This relationship suggests all of the following except:

a. more firms are dispersing different parts of their overall production process to different locations around-the globe to drive down production costs.
b. nations are becoming increasingly self-sufficient for important goods and services
c. FDI is playing an increasing role in the global economy
d. more firms are dispersing different parts of their overall production process to different locations around-the globe to increase quality.

1-45.
A
Medium
P.11

According to our textbook, the growing integration of the world economy is:
a. increasing the intensity of competition in a wide range of manufacturing and service industries
b. decreasing the intensity of competition in manufacturing industries, and increasing the intensity of competition in services
c. increasing the intensity of competition in manufacturing industries, and decreasing the intensity of competition in services
d. narrowing the scope of competition in a wide range of service, commodity, an manufacturing industries

1-46.
D
Easy
P.12

According to our textbook, the single most important innovation has been the development of the _____.
a. telegraph
b. telephone
c. airplane
d. microprossor

1-47.
C
Medium
P.12

The theory that predicts that the power of microprocessor technology doubles an the cost of production falls every 18 months is referred to as:
a. Brennan's Theorem
b. Bailey's Law
c. Moore's Law
d. Ivan's Law

1-48.
D
Easy
P.14

As a result of a variety of innovations, the real costs of information processing ar communication have _____ over the past two decades.
a. fallen slightly
b. increased slightly
c. remained constant
d. fallen dramatically

1-49.
B
Medium
P.15

Although the characteristics of the global economy have changed dramatically over the past 30 years, as late as the 1960s all of the following demographic characteristics were true except:
a. the U.S. dominated the world economy
b. small, U.S. entrepreneurial firms dominated the international business scene
c. the U.S. dominated the world foreign direct investment picture
d. roughly half the world was governed by centrally planned economies of the Communist world

1-50.
A
Hard
P.15

In 1963, the U.S. accounted for _____ of world manufacturing output.
a. 40.3
b. 12.8
c. 65.6
d. 80.0

1-51.
A
Medium
P.16

If we look 20 years into the future, most forecasts now predict a _____ in world output accounted for by developing nations such as China, India, Indonesia, and South Korea, and a _____ in the share enjoyed by rich industrialized countries such as Britain, Japan, and the United States.
a. rapid rise, rapid decline
b. slight rise, slight decline
c. rapid decline, rapid rise
d. rapid rise, slight decline

1-52.
A
Easy
P.16

The following is an example of a developing nation.
a. Thailand
b. Britain
c. Japan
d. United States

1-53.
D
Medium
P.16

All of the following are examples of developing nations with the exception of:
a. China
b. India
c. South Korea
d. Japan

1-54.
B
Hard
P.17

In the 1960s, the two most dominant countries in the world economy were:
a. United States and Japan
b. Britain and the United States
c. United States and Germany
d. Britain and Japan

1-55.
A
Medium
P.17

During the 1970s and 1980s, the foreign direct investment by non-U.S. firms was motivated primarily by the following two factors:
a. the desire to disperse production activities to optimal locations; and the desire to build a direct presence in major foreign markets
b. the desire to disperse production activities to optimal locations, and the desire to influence foreign exchange rates
c. the desire to influence foreign exchange rates, and the desire to influence political developments in foreign countries
d. the desire to build a direct presence in major foreign markets; and the desire to influence political developments in foreign countries

1-56.
D
Easy
P.17

The total cumulative value of foreign investments is referred to as the _____.
a. accumulation of foreign direct investments
b. portfolio of foreign direct investments
c. set of foreign direct investments
d. stock of foreign direct investments

133

1-57.
C
Easy
P.18

The amount of investments made across national boarders each years is called the _____.
a. international foreign direct investment totality
b. inclusive foreign direct investments
c. flow of foreign direct investments
d. totality of foreign direct investments

1-58.
D
Easy
P.19

During the 1990s, the percentage of foreign direct investment inflows accounted for by developing countries has:
a. decreased
b. never been determined
c. remained constant
d. increased

1-59.
D
Easy
P.19

During the 1990s, the percentage of foreign direct investment inflows accounted for by developed countries has:
a. remained constant
b. fluctuated wildly
c. increased
d. decreased

1-60.
C
Medium
P.19

The country that has received the greatest volume of inward FDI in recent years has been _____.
a. Britain
b. South Korea
c. China
d. United States

1-61.
B
Easy
P.19

A _____ enterprise is any business that has productive activities in two or more countries.
a. cross-cultural
b. multinational
c. varied-national
d. diverse-national

1-62.
A
Easy
P.19

General Electric Corporation has productive activities in a number of countries. As a result, it would be appropriate to refer to General Electric as a _____ corporation.
a. multinational
b. diverse-national
c. crossnational
d. varied-national

1-63.
D
Medium
P.19

Since the 1960s, there have been two notable trends in the demographics of the multinational enterprise. These two trends have been:

a. the rise of non-U.S. multinationals and the disappearance of mini-multinationals
b. the decline of non-U.S. multinationals and the decline of mini-multinationals
c. the decline of non-U.S. multinationals and the growth of mini-multinationals
d. the rise of non-U.S. multinationals and the growth of mini-multinationals

1-64.
C
Medium
P.20

The decline of the U.S. in its dominance of the global economy can be explained by two factors. These are:

a. the globalization of the world economy and China's rise to the top rank of economic powers
b. the fall of communism in Eastern Europe and the republics of the former Soviet Union and Japan's rise to the top rank of economic powers
c. the globalization of the world economy and Japan's rise to the top rank of economic powers
d. a decrease in trade barriers worldwide and China's rise in economic power

1-65.
D
Easy
P.20

Mini-multinationals are:

a. multinational firms from relatively small countries
b. multinational firms that have been involved in international business for less than five years
c. multinational firms that operate in three or less foreign countries
d. medium-sized and small multinationals

1-66.
A
Easy
P.20

Apex Engineering is a small firm that operates in several different foreign countries. It would be appropriate to refer to Apex as a:

a. mini-multinational
b. aspiring-multinational
c. insignificant-multinational
d. emerging-multinational

1-67.
A
Medium
P.24

Which of the following statements is not true regarding potential business opportunities in the former Communist nations of Europe and Asia?

a. the economies of most of the former Communist states are very strong
b. many of the former Communist nations of Europe and Asia share a commitment to free market economies
c. as a result of disturbing signs of growing unrest and totalitarian tendencies, the risks involved in doing business in these countries is very high
d. for about half a century these countries were essentially closed to Western international business

1-68.
D
Medium
P.24

Which of the following statements is not true regarding the majority of Latin American countries?

a. governments are selling state-owned enterprises to private investors
b. foreign investment is welcome
c. debt and inflation are down
d. neither democracy nor free market reforms have seemed to take hold

1-69.
C
Easy
P.25

Economists argue that increased international trade and cross-border investments will result in _____ prices for goods and services.

a. higher
b. stable
c. lower
d. unstable

1-70.
A
Medium
P.25

Which of the following is not a benefit of globalization?

a. slows economic growth
b. raises the incomes of consumers
c. lower prices for goods
d. helps to create jobs in all countries that choose to participate

1-71.
D
Medium
P.25

One frequently voiced concern about the effects of globalization is that it may:

a. slow economic growth
b. increase prices for goods
c. lower the income of consumers
d. destroy manufacturing jobs in wealthy advanced economies such as the U.S.

1-72.
C
Hard
P.25

One frequently voiced concern about globalization is that it destroys manufacturing jobs in wealthy advanced economies such as the U.S. The basic thrust of the critics' argument is:

a. developing nations will recruit employees from the more advanced economies, thereby depleting their labor pools
b. globalization increases the pace of the shift from a world economy based on manufactured goods to a world economy based on services
c. falling trade barriers allows firms to move their manufacturing activities offshore to countries where wage rates are much lower
d. the governments of developing countries will heavily subsidize their primary industries, making competing products produced in advanced economies less attractive

1-73.
C
Hard
P.26

Critics use the following argument to suggest that globalization is a contributing factor to an increase in pollution.
a. globalization results in an increase in the amount of activity that takes place in companies that do not have adequate pollution controls
b. globalization results in increased commerce between countries, which results in an increase in the amount of transportation activity (e.g. trains, barges, air cargo, trucks, etc.)
c. firms that operate in countries that have adequate pollution regulations have a tendency to move their manufacturing operations to countries that have less stringent or no pollution controls to avoid the cost of regulation
d. globalization results in increased production, which has the undesirable side-effect of increased pollution

1-74.
D
Easy
P.26

NAFTA stands for:
a. National Alliance For Technology Advancement
b. North Atlantic Free Trade Agency
c. North American Federation of Trade Advocates
d. North American Free Trade Agreement

1-75.
A
Medium
P.27

What is the primary purpose of the World Trade Organization?
a. arbitrate trade disputes
b. act as a "watchdog" for countries that lower their pollution standards in an effort to attract more foreign manufacturing activity
c. set tariffs for countries that signed the GATT agreement
d. monitor the implementation of trade agreements such as NAFTA

1-76.
D
Medium
P.27

In what way can the World Trade Organization (WTO) penalize member countries that are found to be engaged in unfair trade practices?
a. the WTO can impose sanctions on the transgressor
b. the WTO can bring the employees of offending companies to court
c. the WTO can restrict the membership of the offending country in other world organizations such as the United Nations
d. the WTO panel can issue a ruling instructing a member state to change trade policies that violate GATT regulations, and if the policies are not changed, allow other states to impose sanctions

1-77.
A
Easy
P.27

The minimum that a firm has to do to engage in international business is to:
a. export or import
b. invest directly in operations in another country
c. establish joint ventures or strategic alliances with companies in other countries
d. license products to companies in other countries

1-78.
C
Medium
P.30

Managing an international business is different from managing a purely domestic business for all of the following reasons except:

a. countries are different
b. international transactions involve converting money into different currencies
c. the range of problems confronted by a manager in an international business are narrower than those confronted by a manager in a domestic business
d. an international business must find ways to work within the limits imposed by government intervention in the international trade and investment system

1-79.
D
Easy
P.31

The _____ of production makes it increasingly irrelevant to talk about "American" products, "Japanese" products, or "German" products, since these products are made through components parts produced throughout the world.

a. standardization
b. alignment
c. simplification
d. globalization

1-80.
A
Easy
P.31

By the mid-1990s, the U.S. share of world output _____, with major shares of world output being accounted for by Western European and Southeast Asian economies.

a. had been cut in half
b. had increased by 200 percent
c. had fluctuated wildly
d. had remained the same

Essay Questions

1-81.
Easy
P.4

Describe the concept of globalization. What are the major opportunities and challenges that globalization has created for business organization?

Answer: Globalization refers to a fundamental shift that is occurring in the world economy. The world is progressively moving away from a structure in which national economies are relatively isolated from each other, towards a structure in which national economies are merging into one huge interdependent global economic system. This trend is commonly referred to as globalization.

The trend towards globalization is creating many opportunities for businesses to expand their revenues, drive down their costs, and boost their profits. For example, many American firms are now exporting to previously closed foreign markets. By doing so, these firms are simultaneously expanding their sales and driving down their costs through additional economies of scale. Globalization has also created challenges for business organizations. For example, managers now have to grapple with a wide range of globalization related issues. Examples of these issues include: should we export, should we build a plant in a foreign country, should we modify our products to suite the tastes of each of our foreign customers, and how do we respond to foreign competition? These questions often do not have easy answers, but are very important to the future competitiveness of business organizations.

1-82.
Medium
P.5

Describe the two main components of globalization. Explain how each of these components of globalization has helped create the shift towards a more integrated world economy.

Answer: The two main components of globalization are the globalization of markets and the globalization of production. The globalization of markets refers to the fact that in many industries historically distinct and separate national markets are merging into one huge global marketplace. The globalization of production refers to the tendency among many firms to source goods and services from different locations around the world in an attempt to take advantage of national differences in the cost and quality of factors of production (such as labor, energy, and capital).

Both of these components of globalization have helped create the shift towards a more integrated world economy. The globalization of markets has created a "global" interest in many products, such as Coca-Cola, the Sony Walkman, and Levi jeans. This "sharing of interest" in products across national boarders has facilitated the trend towards a more integrated world economy. The globalization of production has resulted in a substantial increase in the number of business relationships between companies from different countries. This increase in the number and intensity of interrelationships between companies from different countries has also facilitated the trend towards a more integrated world economy.

1-83.
Hard
P.9

Describe the meaning of the term "trade barriers"? What measures have been taken by the world community to reduce the impact of trade barriers on international trade?

Answer: Trade barriers are the regulations, tariffs, and other activities that are put in place by governments for the purpose of protecting their domestic industries from "foreign competition." For example, a country may impose a stiff tariff on the import of foreign produced automobiles. That makes it very difficult (i.e. creates a substantial barrier) for foreign produced cars to be sold in their country.

The world community has taken a number of measures to not only lessen the impact of trade barriers on international trade, but to remove trade barriers altogether. The General Agreement on Tariffs and Trade (GATT) has been an ongoing effort to remove and reduce trade barriers worldwide. Under the umbrella of GATT, there have been eight rounds of negotiations among member states, which now number 120, designed to lower and/or reduce all forms of trade barriers. To provide the GATT treaty some teeth, the recently completed Uruguary Round of GATT established the World Trade Organization (WTO) which polices the international trading system. Although the WTO cannot compel a nation to comply with the GATT treaty, it can recommend that other member nations impose sanctions on the offending party.

Other business organizations, governments, trade groups, and not-for-profit organizations are working hard to reduce and remove trade barriers. As mentioned in the textbook, during 1991 alone, 34 countries, rich and poor, made 82 changes to their laws governing investment by foreign businesses in their countries. A total of 80 of the 82 changes have resulted in removing or lessening the impact of some form of trade barrier.

1-84.
Easy
P.19

What is a multinational enterprise? What have been the two most notable trends in multinational enterprises since the 1960s? What is a mini-multinational? Do you expect the role of mini-multinationals to gain momentum or wane in the future? Why?

Answer: A multinational enterprise is any business that has productive activities in two or more countries. There are many multinational enterprises, including General Motors, Sony, General Electric, Exxon, and Toyota. The two most notable trends in multinational enterprises since the 1960s have been (1) the rise of non-U.S. multinationals, particularly Japanese multinationals; and (2) the growth of mini-multinationals.

Mini-multinationals are small and medium-sized international firms. The role of these firms is likely to gain momentum in the future. Many small and medium-sized companies are becoming increasingly involved in international trade, in a variety of different contexts. As these companies expand their international activities, they will increasingly take their place as mini-multinationals on the world stage.

1-85.
Medium
P.25

Discuss the primary advantages and disadvantages of globalization. Do you believe the advantages outweigh the disadvantages? How can the effects of the disadvantages of globalization be reduced?

There are many advantages of globalization. From a broad perspective, globalization creates economic activity (which stimulates economic growth), creates jobs, raises income levels, and provides consumers with more choices in regard to the products and services that are available to them. From the perspective of an individual firm, globalization has the potential to increase revenues (through expanded market potential), drive down costs (through additional economies of scale), and boost profits.

Conversely, critics argue that globalization destroys manufacturing jobs in wealthy countries and contributes to pollution. In regard to destroying manufacturing jobs,

140

the basic thrust of the critics argument is that falling trade barriers allow firms in industrialized countries to move their manufacturing activities offshore to countries where wage rates are much lower. This activity, if it occurs, has the undesirable side-effect of eliminating manufacturing jobs in the industrialized country. In regard to pollution, the critics of globalization argue that globalization encourages firms from advanced nations to move manufacturing facilities offshore to less developed countries to avoid the more stringent pollution controls in place in their home countries. This activity increases worldwide pollution.

The final section of the question is designed to encourage classroom discussion and/or to encourage students to "think" about how these undesirable side-effects of globalization can be reduced.

CHAPTER 2
DIFFERENCES IN POLITICAL ECONOMY

True/False Questions

2-1.
T
Easy
P.40

The term collectivism refers to a system that stresses the primacy of collective goals over individual goals.

2-2.
T
Hard
P.41

Political systems that emphasize collectivism tend to be totalitarian, while political systems that place a high value on individualism tend to be democratic.

2-3.
F
Easy
P.41

There is essentially no relationship between collectivism and socialism.

2-4.
F
Medium
P.43

Individualism is similar to collectivism. In a political sense, individualism refers to a philosophy that an individual should have freedom in his or her economic and political pursuits.

2-5.
T
Medium
P.44

Totalitarianism is a form of government in which one person or political party exercises absolute control over all spheres of human life, and opposing political parties are prohibited.

2-6.
T
Medium
P.45

The four major forms of totalitarianism are: communist totalitarianism, theocratic totalitarianism, tribal totalitarianism, and right-wing totalitarianism.

2-7.
F
Hard
P.45

Tribal totalitarianism is found in states where political power is monopolized by a party, group, or individual that governs according to religious principles.

2-8.
T
Easy
P.47

In a market economy the goods and services that a country produces, and the quantity in which they are produced, is not planned by anyone. Rather, it is determined by the interaction of supply and demand and signaled to producers through the price system.

2-9.
T
Medium
P.47

For a market economy to work, there must be no restrictions on supply.

2-10.
T
Medium
P.48

In a pure command economy, the goods and services that a country produces, the quantity in which they are produced, and the prices at which they are sold are all planned by the government.

2-11.
F
Medium
P.49

Command economies are relatively common among the states of Western Europe, although they are becoming less so. France, Italy, and Sweden can all be classified as command economies.

2-12.
F
Easy
P.51

A copyright grants the inventor of a new product or process exclusive right to the manufacture, use, or sales of that invention.

2-13.
T
Easy
P.51

A patent grants the investor of a new product or process exclusive rights to the manufacture, use, or sale of that invention.

2-14.
F
Medium
P.51

Patents are designs and names, often officially registered, by which merchants or manufacturers designate and differentiate their products (e.g., Christian Dior clothes).

2-15.
F
Medium
P.51

Historically, the enforcement of intellectual property rights has been fairly consistent across countries.

2-16.
T
Medium
P.51

The Paris Convention for the Protection of Industrial Property is an international agreement signed by 96 countries to protect intellectual property rights.

2-17.
T
Easy
P.53

Civil law is based on a very detailed set of laws that are organized into codes.

2-18.
F
Hard
P.57

The Human Development Index is based on three measures: per capita income, life expectancy, and poverty rate.

2-19.
F
Medium
P.60

The process of selling state-owned enterprises to private investors is called downsizing.

2-20.
T
Medium
P.75

The Foreign Corrupt Practices Act is a U.S. law enacted in 1977 that prohibits U.S. companies from making "corrupt" payments to foreign officials for the purpose of obtaining or retaining business.

Multiple Choice

2-21.
C
Easy
P.40

Every country has a political, economic, and legal system. Collectively we refer to these systems as constitution the _____ economy of a country.
a. domestic
b. civic
c. political
d. administrative

2-22.
D
Easy
P.40

England, France, and Germany all have unique political, economic, and legal systems. A country's political, economic, and legal system is collectively referred to as its _____ economy.
a. official
b. formal
c. administrative
d. political

2-23.   A nation's system of government is referred to as its _____ system.
A   a. political
Easy   b. administrative
P.41   c. economic
          d. bureaucratic

2-24.   Political systems can be assessed according to two related dimensions. These
D   are:
Hard   a. the degree to which they emphasize individualism opposed to totalitarian and
P.41   the degree to which they are individualistic verses democratic
          b. the degree to which they are market orientated opposed to production
              orientated and the degree to which they are democratic verses individualistic
          c. the degree to which they are social democrats opposed to communists and the
              degree to which they emphasize collectivism opposed to individualism
          d. the degree to which they emphasize collectivism opposed to individualism and
              the degree to which they are democratic or totalitarian

2-25.   The term _____ refers to a system that stresses the primacy of collective
B   goals over individual goals.
Easy   a. capitalism
P.41   b. collectivism
          c. totalitarian
          d. individualism

2-26.   Which of the following political systems is consistent with the notion that an
B   individuals right to do something may be restricted because it runs counter to "the
Medium   good of society" or "the common good."
P.41   a. totalitarian
          b. collectivism
          c. autocratic
          d. capitalism

2-27.   The group that believed that socialism could be achieved only through violent
A   revolution and totalitarian dictatorship were referred to as:
Medium   a. communists
P.42   b. fascists
          c. political democrats
          d. collectivists

2-28.   The last major Communist power left is _____.
A   a. China
Easy   b. Norway
P.42   c. Australia
          d. Brazil

2-29.
C
Medium
P.42

The group that was committed to achieving socialism by democratic means were referred to as:

a. collectivists
b. communists
c. social democrats
d. fascists

2-30.
D
Hard
P.42

Social democracy has had its greatest influence in the following group of countries:

a. Canada, United States, Mexico, and Spain
b. India, Pakistan, Burma, Nepal, Sri Lanka, and Bhutan
c. Brazil, Chile, Uruguay, Ecuador, Columbia, and French Guiana
d. Australia, Britain, France, Germany, Norway, Spain, and Sweden

2-31.
A
Medium
P.43

Which of the following definitions best describes the concept of individualism?

a. Political philosophy that an individual should have freedom over his or her economic and political pursuits.
b. Political system in which government is by the people, exercised either directly or through elected representatives.
c. Political system that stresses the primacy of collective goals over individual goals.
d. Form of government in which one person or political party exercises absolute control over all spheres of human life and in which opposing political parties are prohibited.

2-32.
A
Easy
P.43

The philosophy that is based on the idea that an individual should have freedom in his or her economic pursuits is called:

a. individualism
b. socialism
c. totalitarianism
d. collectivism

2-33.
D
Easy
P.44

The political system in which government is by the people, exercised either directly or through elected representatives is referred to as:

a. despotism
b. collectivism
c. totalitarianism
d. democracy

2-34.
B
Easy
P.44

_____ is a form of government in which one person or political party exercises absolute control over all spheres of human life, and opposing political parties are prohibited.

a. capitalism
b. totalitarianism
c. democracy
d. collectivism

2-35.
C
Easy
P.44

A political system in which citizens periodically elect individuals to represent them is referred to as a _____.

a. participatory collective
b. totalitarianism democracy
c. representative democracy
d. socialistic democracy

2-36.
D
Medium
P.45

To guarantee that elected representatives can be held accountable for their actions by the electorate, an ideal representative democracy has a number of safeguards. Which of the following is not an example of a safeguard in a ideal respresentative democracy?

a. a fair court system that is independent from the political system
b. universal adult suffrage
c. an individual's right to freedom of expression, opinion, and organization
d. a political police force and armed services

2-37.
C
Medium
P.45

A form of totalitarianism that advocates achieving socialism through totalitarian dictatorship is called _____.

a. tribal totalitarianism
b. collective totalitarianism
c. communist totalitarianism
d. democratic totalitarianism

2-38.
D
Medium
P.45

All of the following are forms of totalitarianism except:

a. tribal
b. theocratic
c. right-wing
d. ancestral

2-39.
B
Medium
P.45

A form of totalitarianism in which political power is monopolized by a party, group or individual that governs according to religious principles is called _____.

a. right-wing totalitarianism
b. theocratic totalitarianism
c. ancestral totalitarianism
d. tribal totalitarianism

2-40.
A
Medium
P.45

In which region of the world is tribal totalitarianism found?
a. Africa
b. Australia
c. South America
d. Asia

2-41.
D
Medium
P.47

Right-wing _____ generally permits individual economic freedom, but restricts individual political freedom on the grounds that it would lead to a rise of communism.
a. socialism
b. collectivism
c. capitalism
d. totalitarianism

2-42.
B
Medium
P.47

The three broad types of economic systems are:
a. market economy, combined economy, and production economy
b. market economy, command economy, and mixed economy
c. combined economy, separate economy, and mixed economy
d. ordinance economy, production economy, and political economy

2-43.
A
Easy
P.47

In a pure _____ economy the good and services that a country products, and the quantity in which they are produced, is not planned by anyone. Rather it is determined by the interaction of supply and demand and signaled to producers through the price system.
a. market
b. ordinance
c. combined
d. command

2-44.
D
Medium
P.48

In a pure command economy the goods and services that a country produces, the quantity in which they are produced, and the prices at which they are sold are all planned by:
a. private industry
b. local trade associations
c. individual entrepreneurs
d. the government

2-45.
C
Easy
P.48

An economic system in which the goods and services produced, the quantity in which they are produced, and the prices at which they are sold are all planned by the government is referred to as a:
a. civic economy
b. administrative economy
c. command economy
d. market economy

2-46.
C
Easy
P.48

In a _____ economy, certain sectors of the economy are left to private ownership and free market mechanisms, while in other sectors there is significant state ownership and government planning.

a. command
b. combined
c. mixed
d. political

2-47.
D
Easy
P.49

The _____ of a country refers to the rules that regulate behavior, along with the processes by which the laws of a country are enforced and through which redress for grievances is obtained.

a. political system
b. administrative system
c. economic structure
d. legal system

2-48.
D
Easy
P.50

_____ rights refer to the bundle of legal rights over the use to which a resource is put and over the use made of any income that may be derived form that resource.

a. Statutory
b. Asset
c. Taxable
d. Property

2-49.
B
Medium
P.51

Which of the following describes the concept of intellectual property?

a. Exclusive legal rights of authors, composers, playwrights, artists, and publishers to publish and dispose of their work as they see fit.
b. Property, such as computer software, screenplays, musical scores, or chemical formulas for new drugs, that is the product of intellectual activity.
c. Designs and names, often officially registered, by which merchants or manufacturers designate and differentiate their products.
d. Document giving the inventor of a new product or process exclusive rights to the manufacturer, use, or sales of that invention.

2-50.
D
Easy
P.51

Suppose you invent a new product and want to obtain the exclusive rights to manufacture the product. To protect yourself, you should apply for a _____ on the product.

a. trust
b. copyright
c. license
d. patent

2-51.
B
Easy
P.51

_____ are the exclusive legal rights of authors, composers, playwrights, artists, and publishers to publish and dispose of their work as they see fit.
a. Patents
b. Copyrights
c. Trusts
d. Licenses

2-52.
A
Medium
P.51

Patents, copyrights, and trademarks are examples of _____ property laws.
a. intellectual
b. administrative
c. official
d. central

2-53.
D
Easy
P.51

"Windows" is a computer operating system that is an exclusive _____ of the Microsoft corporation.
a. sticker
b. hallmark
c. registry
d. trademark

2-54.
C
Easy
P.52

_____ liability involves holding a firm and its officers responsible when a product causes injury, death, or damage.
a. Turnout
b. Contract
c. Product
d. Outcome

2-55.
D
Medium
P.53

There are two main legal traditions found in the world today. These are:
a. administrative law system and civil law system
b. common law system and mutual law system
c. interdependent law system and independent law system
d. common law system and civil law system

2-56.
C
Easy
P.53

A _____ is a document that specifies the conditions under which an exchange is to occur, and details the rights and obligations of the parties involved.
a. patent
b. compact
c. contract
d. treaty

2-57.
A
Medium
P.53

The legal system that is based on a detailed set of laws, organized into codes, that is used in more than 80 countries is referred to as:
a. civil law system
b. criminal law system
c. multi-level system
d. administrative law system

2-58.
C
Medium
P.53

The legal system based on tradition, precedent, and custom that evolved in England over hundreds of years and is now found in Britain's former colonies, including the United States, is called:
a. multi-level legal system
b. civil law system
c. common law system
d. administrative law system

2-59.
C
Hard
P.54

Which of the following statement is true?
a. Civil law tends to be relatively ill-specified.
b. Criminal law is the body of law that governs contract enforcement.
c. Civil law is based on a very detailed set of laws that are organized into codes.
d. The civil law system evolved in England over one hundred years ago. It is now found in most of Britain's former colonies, including the United States.

2-60.
B
Easy
P.55

GDP is an acronym that stands for:
a. gross domestic profile
b. gross domestic product
c. gradual demographic profile
d. general domestic productivity

2-61.
A
Medium
P.57

The United Nations _____ index is based on life expectancy, literacy rates, and whether average incomes are sufficient to meet the basic needs of life in a country,
a. Human Development
b. Standard of Living
c. Quality of Life
d. Economic Development

2-62.
D
Hard
P.57

The United Nations Human Development index is based on the following three measures.
a. standard of living, quality of transportation, and life expectancy
b. access to medical care, access to education, and life expectancy
c. access to education, literacy rates, and whether average incomes, based on PPP estimates, are sufficient to meet the basic needs of life in a country.
d. life expectancy, literacy rates, and whether average incomes, based on PPP estimates, are sufficient to meet the basic needs of life in a country

2-63.
B
Hard
P.57

The Human Development Index is scaled from 0 to 100. Countries scoring less than _____ are classified as low human development (the quality of life is poor).
a. 25
b. 50
c. 75
d. 33.3

2-64.
C
Medium
P.59

There is general agreement that _____ is the engine of long-run economic growth.
a. small business
b. government
c. innovation
d. agriculture

2-65.
D
Easy
P.59

The process through which people create new products, new processes, new organization, new management practices, and new strategies is called:
a. bureaucracy
b. administration
c. development
d. innovation

2-66.
C
Medium
P.60

It has been argued that the economic freedom associated with a _____ economy creates greater incentives for innovation than either a planned or mixed economy.
a. manufacturing
b. commercial
c. market
d. production

2-67.
B
Easy
P.60

The process of selling state-owned enterprises to private investors is called:
a. political-economic divestiture
b. privatization
c. downsizing
d. ownership-transfer

2-68.
D
Easy
P.60

_____ is the process of selling state-owned enterprises to private investors.
a. Downsizing
b. Capitalization
c. Ownership-transfer
d. Privatization

2-69.   Privatization refers to:
A
Medium   a. the selling of state-owned enterprises to private investors
P.60   b. the selling of public corporations to private investors
    c. guarding company secrets from the general public
    d. transferring political power from the government to private citizens

2-70.   Since the late 1980s two major trends have emerged in the political economies of
C   many of the world's national states. These are:
Hard
P.62   a. a wave of communist revolutions have swept the world and there has been a strong move away from free market economies toward more centrally planned economies.
    b. a wave of socialistic revolutions have swept the world and there has been a strong move away from free market economies toward more centrally planned and mixed economies.
    c. a wave of democratic revolutions have swept the world and there has been a strong move away from centrally planned and mixed economies toward more free market economies.
    d. a wave of totalitarian revolutions have swept the world and there has been a strong move away from centrally planned and mixed economies toward more free market economies.

2-71.   Advantages that accrue to early entrants into a business market are referred to
B   as:
Easy
P.71   a. standard-class advantages
    b. first-mover advantages
    c. prime-mover advantages
    d. first-stage advantages

2-72.   _____ accrue to early entrants into a business market.
D
Easy   a. Prime-mover advantages
P.71   b. Standard-class advantages
    c. First-class advantages
    d. First-mover advantages

2-73.   Handicaps suffered by late entrants into a business market are referred to as:
A
Easy   a. late-mover disadvantages
P.71   b. last-class disadvantages
    c. late-mover stumbling blocks
    d. late-mover difficulties

2-74.
A
Medium
P.71

In the language of business strategy, early entrants into potential future economic stars may be able to reap substantial _____ advantages, while late entrants may fall victim to _____ disadvantages.
a. first-mover, late-mover
b. initial-mover, last-mover
c. first-class, final-class
d. economic, financial

2-75.
A
Easy
P.72

The likelihood that political forces will cause drastic changes in a country's business environment that adversely affect the profit and other goals of a particular business enterprise is referred to as:
a. political risk
b. democratic risk
c. administrative risk
d. governmental risk

2-76.
D
Medium
P.72

The likelihood that economic mismanagement will cause drastic changes in a country's business environment that adversely affect the profit and other goals of a business enterprise is called:
a. industrial risk
b. commercial risk
c. legal risk
d. economic risk

2-77.
D
Medium
P.72

_____ is defined as the likelihood that economic mismanagement will cause drastic changes in a country's business environment that adversely affect the profit and other goals of a business enterprise.
a. Financial risk
b. Commercial risk
c. Industrial risk
d. Economic risk

2-78.
A
Easy
P.73

The likelihood that a trading partner will opportunistically break a contract or expropriate property rights is called:
a. legal risk
b. permissible risk
c. constitutional risk
d. legitimate

2-79.
A
Easy
P.75

The _____ is a U.S. law enacted in 1977 that prohibits U.S. companies from making "corrupt" payments to foreign officials for the purpose of obtaining or retaining business.

a. Foreign Corrupt Practices Act
b. Federal Mercenary Practices Act
c. Federal Corrupt Behavior Act
d. Foreign Mercenary Practices Act

2-80.
C
Hard
P.75

The Foreign Corrupt Practices Act is a U.S. law enacted in 1977 that prohibits U.S. companies from:

a. making products in overseas markets that do not comply with the same safety and environmental regulations as domestically produced products.
b. exporting to countries that do not comply with United Nations human rights regulations.
c. making "corrupt" payments to foreign officials for the purpose of obtaining or retaining business.
d. exporting to countries that are not members of the World Trade Organization
e. selling products for corrupt, unethical, or illegal purposes

Essay Questions

2-81.
Medium
P.41

Describe the difference between collectivism and individualism. Are these two ideologies compatible or in direct conflict? Which ideology seems to be gaining ground and which ideology is waning? Is this good news or bad news for international commerce? Explain your answer.

Answer: The term collectivism refers to a political system that stresses the primacy of collective goals over individual goals. The general ideal is that the needs of society as a whole are more important than individual freedoms. As a result, in a collectivist society, an individual's right to do something may be restricted because it runs counter to "the good of the society" or the "common good."

Individualism refers to a philosophy that an individual should have freedom in his or her economic and political pursuits. Moreover, individualism stresses that the interests of the individual should take precedence over the interests of the state.

The ideals exposed by individualism and collectivism are in direct conflict with one another. Over the past two decades, collectivism has been waning and individualism has been gaining steam. A wave of democratic ideals and free market economics is currently sweeping away socialism and communism worldwide. Evidence of this can be seen in Eastern Europe and the republics of the former Soviet Union. According to the author of the textbook, this represents good news for international business, since the pro-business and pro-free trade values of individualism create a favorable environment within which international business can thrive.

2-82. Medium P.44	Draw a distinction between democracy and totalitarianism. Which political system facilitates the development of a free market economic system? Why?

Answer: Democracy and totalitarianism are at different ends of the political spectrum. Democracy refers to a political system in which government is by the people, exercised either directly or through elected representatives. Totalitarianism is a form of government in which one person or political parties exercise absolute control over all spheres of human life, and opposing political parties are prohibited. Most modern democratic states practice what is commonly referred to as representative democracy. In a representative democracy, citizens periodically elect individuals to represent them. There are four major forms of totalitarianism, including communist totalitarianism, theocratic totalitarianism, tribal totalitarianism, and right-wing totalitarianism.

A democratic political system facilitates the development of a free market economy. A democratic system favors the primacy of individual goals over collective goals, which facilitates the development of free markets.

2-83. Medium P.51	What is intellectual property? What is the philosophy behind intellectual property law? Why is it so important to protect intellectual property rights? Are the laws that protect intellectual property rights fairly consistent across nations, or do they vary widely? Is this a problem?

Answer: Intellectual property refer to property, such as computer software, a screenplay, a music score, or the chemical formula for a new drug, that is the product of intellectual activity. The philosophy behind intellectual property law is to reward the originator of a new invention, book, musical record, clothes design, and the like for his or her new idea. Without strict intellectual property laws, there would be very little incentive for an individual to work hard to create these types of items. For instance, a person could work very hard and spend huge amounts of money to create a new animated file, and have someone else duplicate the film for the cost of a film duplicating machine and a blank tape.

Unfortunately, the protection of intellectual property rights varies greatly from country to country. This is a problem. Weak laws or the weak enforcement of intellectual property laws in foreign countries encourages the piracy of intellectual property. This problem is being addressed by the world community, but a satisfactory solution to this problem has yet to be found.

2-84.
Easy
P.59

How important is innovation? Does innovation have a better chance of catching hold in a market economy or a planned economy? Explain your answer.

Answer: There is general agreement that innovation is the engine of long-run economic growth in virtually any country. Innovation has a much better chance of catching hold in a market economy opposed to a planned economy. The individual freedom (and opportunity for personal gain) associated with a market economy (like the economy in the U.S.) creates greater incentives for innovation than either a planned or mixed economy. In a market economy, anyone who has an innovative idea is free to try to develop the idea, and has the potential to reap substantial personal gain. This feature of a market economy provides a powerful incentive for people to work on innovative ideas. In contrast, in a planned economy the state owns all means of production. Consequently there is no incentive or opportunity for entrepreneurial individuals to try to develop valuable new innovations, since it is the state, rather than the individual, that captures all of the gains.

2-85.
Medium
P.73

One major ethical dilemma facing firms from Western democracies is whether they should do business in totalitarian countries that routinely violate the human rights of their citizens. What is the principle argument on both sides of this issue? What is your opinion?

Answer: This question is designed to stimulate classroom discussion and/or encourage your students to think about a difficult ethical issue. The two sides to the debate alluded to above are as follows:

Arguments against Western democracies doing business in totalitarian countries: Some people argue that investing in totalitarian countries provides comfort to dictators and can help prop up repressive regimes that abuse basic human rights. Moreover, these critics argue that without the participation of Western investors in their economies, many repressive regimes would collapse and be replaced by more democratically inclined governments.

Arguments in favor of Western democracies doing business in totalitarian countries: In contrast, there are those who argue that investment by a Western firm, by raising the level of economic development of a totalitarian country, can help change it from within. They note that economic well-being and political well-being often go hand-in-hand.

CHAPTER 3
DIFFERENCES IN CULTURE

True/False Questions

3-1.
T.
Easy
P.84

Culture is a system of values and norms that are shared among a group of people and that when taken together constitute a design for living.

3-2.
F
Medium
P.84

Norms are abstract ideas about what a group believes to be good, right, and desirable.

3-3.
F
Medium
P.85

By definition, nation-states contain a single culture.

3-4.
T
Easy
P.85

Norms that are seen as central to the functioning of a society and to its social life are called mores.

3-5.
T
Easy
P.86

In terms of social structure, Western societies tend to emphasize the primacy of the individual, while groups tend to figure much larger in many other societies.

3-6.
F
Medium
P.90

A caste system is an open system of stratification in which social position is determined by an individual's initiative, abilities, and level of effort.

3-7.
F
Medium
P.90

Social liberty is a term that describes the extent to which individuals can move out of the strata into which they are born.

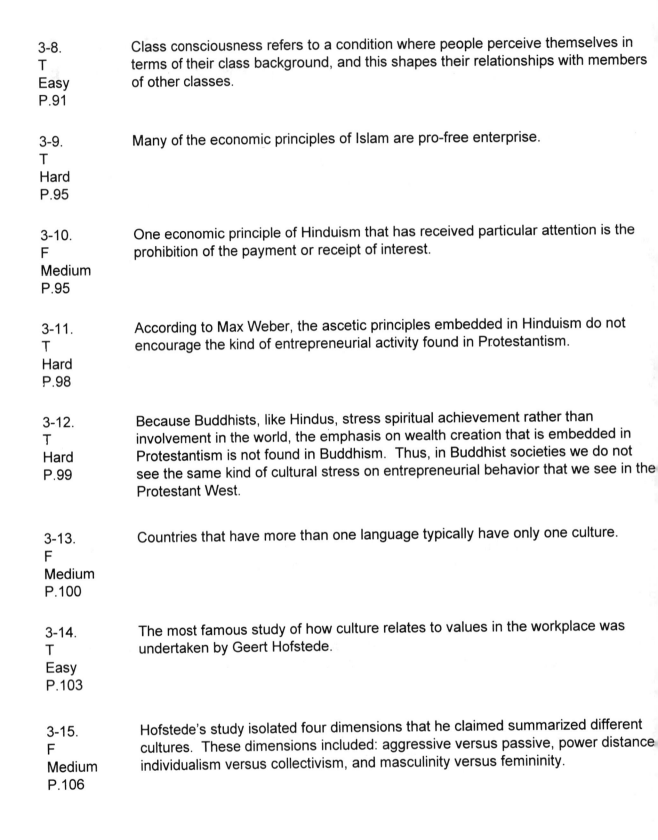

3-8.
T
Easy
P.91

Class consciousness refers to a condition where people perceive themselves in terms of their class background, and this shapes their relationships with members of other classes.

3-9.
T
Hard
P.95

Many of the economic principles of Islam are pro-free enterprise.

3-10.
F
Medium
P.95

One economic principle of Hinduism that has received particular attention is the prohibition of the payment or receipt of interest.

3-11.
T
Hard
P.98

According to Max Weber, the ascetic principles embedded in Hinduism do not encourage the kind of entrepreneurial activity found in Protestantism.

3-12.
T
Hard
P.99

Because Buddhists, like Hindus, stress spiritual achievement rather than involvement in the world, the emphasis on wealth creation that is embedded in Protestantism is not found in Buddhism. Thus, in Buddhist societies we do not see the same kind of cultural stress on entrepreneurial behavior that we see in the Protestant West.

3-13.
F
Medium
P.100

Countries that have more than one language typically have only one culture.

3-14.
T
Easy
P.103

The most famous study of how culture relates to values in the workplace was undertaken by Geert Hofstede.

3-15.
F
Medium
P.106

Hofstede's study isolated four dimensions that he claimed summarized different cultures. These dimensions included: aggressive versus passive, power distance, individualism versus collectivism, and masculinity versus femininity.

3-16.
T
Medium
P.106

According to Hofstede, high power distance cultures are found in countries that let inequalities grow over time into inequalities of power and wealth.

3-17.
F
Medium
P.106

Hofstede's power distance dimension measured the extent to which different cultures socialized their members into accepting ambiguous situations and tolerating uncertainty.

3-18.
T
Medium
P.107

According to Hofstede's Model, Americans are more individualistic and egalitarian than the Japanese.

3-19.
T
Easy
P.112

Acting on the belief in the superiority of one's own ethnic group or culture is referred to as ethnocentric behavior.

3-20.
T
Easy
P.113

The value systems and norms of a country influence the cost of doing business in that country.

Multiple Choice

3-21.
D
Easy
P.84

A _____ is a system of values and norms that are shared among a group of people and that when taken together constitute a design for living.
a. society
b. clique
c. fraternity
d. culture

3-22.
D
Easy
P.84

_____ is that complex whole that includes knowledge, beliefs, art, morals, laws, customs, and other capabilities acquired by people as members of society.
a. Clique
b. Society
c. Organization
d. Culture

3-23.
A
Medium
P.84

Which of the following statements defines the concept of culture?
a. System of values and norms that are shared among a group of people and that when taken together constitute a design for living.
b. Abstract ideas about what a group believes to be good, right, and desirable.
c. Social rules and guidelines that prescribe appropriate behavior in particular situations.
d. Routine conventions of everyday life.

3-24.
B
Medium
P.84

The two central components of culture are:
a. ethics and laws
b. values and norms
c. religious beliefs and family tradition
d. class consciousness and social mobility

3-25.
B
Easy
P.84

A _____ is an abstract idea about what a group believes to be good, right, and desirable.
a. criterion
b. value
c. culture
d. norm

3-26.
A
Easy
P.84

Abstract ideas about what a group believes to be good, right, and desirable are referred to as _____.
a. values
b. norms
c. cultures
d. principles

3-27.
B
Easy
P.84

A _____ is a social rule or guideline that prescribes appropriate behavior in a particular situation.
a. value
b. norm
c. pattern
d. culture

3-28.
B
Easy
P.84

Social rules and guidelines that prescribe appropriate behavior in particular situations are referred to as _____.
a. ethics
b. norms
c. principles
d. models

3-29.
C
Medium
P.84

Social rules and guidelines that prescribe appropriate behavior in particular situations are referred to as _____.
a. values
b. criterions
c. norms
d. patterns

3-30.
B
Easy
P.84

A _____ is a group of people who share a common set of values and norms.
a. cohort
b. society
c. fellowship
d. fraternity

3-31.
C
Hard
P.85

Folkways and mores are forms of _____.
a. conduct
b. culture
c. norms
d. values

3-32.
D
Hard
P.86

Although there are many different aspects of social structure, two main dimensions stand out when explaining differences between cultures. These are:
a. the degree to which the basic unit of social organization is the group; and the degree to which the basic unit of society is a clique
b. the degree to which the basic unit of social organization is the individual; and the degree to which a society is heterogeneous
c. the degree to which the basic unit of social organization is the extended family; and the degree to which the basic unit of society is heterogeneous
d. the degree to which the basic unit of social organization is the individual; and the degree to which a society is stratified into classes or castes

3-33.
B
Easy
P.86

A _____ is an association of two or more individuals who have a shared sense of identity and who interact with each other in structured ways on the basis of a common set of expectations about each other's behavior.
a. assemblage
b. group
c. norm
d. society

3-34.
D
Hard
P.87

According to our textbook, while groups are found in all societies, societies differ according to the degree to which the group is viewed as:
a. the primary means of social mobility
b. the primary means of determining social psychology
c. the primary means of determining social norms
d. the primary means of social organization

3-35.
A
Medium
P.88

In contrast to the Western emphasis on the _____, in many other societies the _____ is the primary unit of social organization.
a. individual, group
b. group, clan
c. coterie, individual
d. clan, group

3-36.
B
Medium
P.89

A central value of the Japanese culture is the importance attached to:
a. individualism
b. group membership
c. personal distinctiveness
d. personal individuality

3-37.
C
Easy
P.89

All societies are stratified on a hierarchical basis into social categories, or:
a. social segments
b. norm based strata
c. social strata
d. norm based associations

3-38.
C
Easy
P.90

The term _____ refers to the extent to which individuals can move out of the strata into which they are born.
a. vertical mobility
b. social potential
c. social mobility
d. vertical potential

3-39.
B
Medium
P.90

The most rigid system of stratification is a _____ system.
a. degree
b. caste
c. cross-cultural
d. class

3-40.
B
Medium
P.90

A _____ system is a closed system of stratification in which social position is determined by the family into which a person is born, and change in that position is usually not possible during an individual's lifetime.
a. rank
b. caste
c. criterion
d. position

3-41.
D
Medium
P.90

Although the number of societies with caste systems has diminished rapidly during the 20th century, one major example still remains. This example is:

a. China
b. Japan
c. Britain
d. India

3-42.
D
Easy
P.90

A _____ system is a form of open stratification in which the position a person has by birth can be changed through his or her own achievements or luck.

a. caste
b. norm
c. category
d. class

3-43.
A
Medium
P.90

British society is divided into three main classes:

a. the upper class, the middle class, and the working class
b. the topmost class, the central class, and the bottom class
c. the preferred class, the medium class, and the lower class
d. the higher class, the central class, and the lower class

3-44.
C
Easy
P.91

_____ consciousness refers to a condition where people perceive themselves in terms of their class background, and this shapes their relationships with members of other classes.

a. Social
b. Rank
c. Class
d. Norm

3-45.
D
Medium
P.91

Many people perceive themselves in terms of their class background, and this shapes their relationships with members of other classes. This form of perception is called:

a. social awareness
b. category mindfulness
c. denominational awareness
d. class consciousness

3-46.
A
Easy
P.92

The system of shared beliefs and rituals that are concerned with the realm of the sacred is referred to as _____.

a. religion
b. persuasion
c. norming
d. divinity

3-47.   The most widely practiced religion in the world is _____.
A   a. Christianity
Medium   b. Buddhism
P.92   c. Islam
         d. Confucianism

3-48.   In 1904, a German sociologist, _____, made a connection between
B   Protestant ethics and "the spirit of capitalism."
Hard   a. Abram Maslow
P.92   b. Max Weber
         c. George Williams
         d. John Wesley

3-49.   In 1904, Max Weber, a German sociologist, made a connection between
B   Protestant ethics and "the spirit of _____."
Medium   a. specialization
P.92   b. capitalism
         c. communism
         d. socialism

3-50.   Which of the following lists correctly identifies the world's major religions by size of
B   following (from highest to lowest)?
Hard   a. Hinduism, Islam, Christianity, Confucianism, Buddhism
P.93   b. Christianity, Islam, Hinduism, Buddhism, Confucianism
         c. Christianity, Hinduism, Islam, Confucianism, Buddhism
         d. Buddhism, Islam, Christianity, Hinduism, Confucianism

3-51.   With 750 million adherents, _____ is the second largest of the world's major
C   religions.
Hard   a. Christianity
P.93   b. Confucianism
         c. Islam
         d. Buddhism

3-52.   Which of the following is not one of the major principles of Islam?
A   a. being pretentious
Medium   b. being generous but not a squanderer
P.94   c. avoiding killing except for justifiable causes
         d. dealing justly and equitably with other

166

3-53.
D
Medium
P.94

The _____ lives in a social structure that is shaped by Islamic values and norms of moral conduct.
a. Buddhist
b. Christian
c. Confucian
d. Muslim

3-54.
C
Medium
P.95

The country in which the Islamic fundamentalists have been the most successful is _____.
a. China
b. India
c. Iran
d. South Korea

3-55.
D
Medium
P.95

Which of the following principles is not consistent with the teachings of the Koran?
a. the protection of the rights of private property
b. earning a legitimate profit through trade economics
c. free enterprise
d. earning profit through the exploitation of others

3-56.
C
Medium
P.95

Islamic countries are likely to be receptive to international business as long as those businesses _____.
a. employ Islamic people
b. have property in an Islamic nation
c. behave in a manner that is consistent with Islamic ethics
d. adhere to Islamic beliefs

3-57.
A
Medium
P.95

One economic principle of _____ that has received particular attention is the prohibition of the payment or receipt of interest, which is considered usury.
a. Islam
b. Christianity
c. Hinduism
d. Confucianism

3-58.
D
Hard
P.96

The world's oldest major religion is:
a. Buddhism
b. Islam
c. Confucianism
d. Hinduism

3-59.
B
Medium
P.97

_____ believe there is a moral force in society that requires the acceptance of certain responsibilities, called *dharma*.
a. Muslims
b. Hindus
c. Christians
d. Confucians

3-60.
A
Medium
P.97

The terms dharma, karma, and nirvana are associated with the _____ religion.
a. Hindu
b. Christian
c. Buddhist
d. Islamic

3-61.
A
Medium
P.98

Under the teachings of _____, the most able individuals in a business organization may find their route to the higher levels of the organization blocked simply because they come from lower casts.
a. Hinduism
b. Christianity
c. Islam
d. Buddhism

3-62.
D
Medium
P.98

_____ was founded in India in the sixth century BC by Shiddhartha Gautama, an Indian prince who renounced his wealth to pursue an ascetic lifestyle and spiritual perfection.
a. Confucianism
b. Islam
c. Christianity
d. Buddhism

3-63.
B
Medium
P.98

Buddhists are found primarily in the following areas:
a. The Middle East and Eastern Africa
b. Central and Southwest Asia, China, Korea, and Japan.
c. Western Europe and North America
d. South America

3-64.
D
Medium
P.99

Individuals that following the teaching of Confucius are found primarily in:
a. North America and Western Europe
b. Eastern Europe and the republics of the former Soviet Union
c. The Middle East and Eastern Africa
d. China, Korea, and Japan

168

3-65.
C
Medium
P.99
The religion that is built around a comprehensive ethical code that establishes guidelines for relationships with others is called _____.
   a. Buddhism
   b. Hinduism
   c. Confucianism
   d. Christianity

3-66.
D
Medium
P.99
The values of loyalty, reciprocal obligations, and honesty are central to the _____ system of ethics.
   a. Buddhist
   b. Islamic
   c. Hindu
   d. Confucian

3-67.
B
Medium
P.101
The most widely spoken language in the world is:
   a. German
   b. English
   c. French
   d. Spanish

3-68.
C
Easy
P.103
The most famous study of how culture relates to values in the workplace was undertaken by _____.
   a. George Williams
   b. Thomas Peters
   c. Geert Hofstede
   d. Michael Porter

3-69.
A
Medium
P.106
Geert Hofstede isolated four dimensions that he claimed summarized different cultures. Which of the following is not one of Hofstede's dimensions?
   a. capitalistic versus socialistic
   b. masculinity versus femininity
   c. power distance
   d. uncertainty avoidance

3-70.
D
Medium
P.106
In his studies, Hofstede isolated four dimensions that he claimed summarized different cultures. These were:
   a. individualism versus collectivism, power distance, tolerant versus intolerant, and aggressive verses passive.
   b. uncertainty avoidance, masculinity versus femininity, individual versus group oriented, forward versus reserved.
   c. aggressive verses passive, tolerant versus intolerant, power distance, and individual versus group oriented.
   d. power distance, individualism versus collectivism, uncertainty avoidance, and masculinity versus femininity

3-71.
B
Easy
P.106

Which of the following is not one of the four dimensions that Hofstede claimed summarized different cultures?
a. uncertainty avoidance
b. aggressive versus passive
c. masculinity versus femininity
d. individualism versus collectivism

3-72.
C
Medium
P.106

Hofstede's _____ dimension focused on how a society deals with the fact that people are unequal in physical and intellectual capabilities.
a. individualism versus collectivism
b. uncertainty avoidance
c. power distance
d. masculinity versus femininity

3-73.
A
Medium
P.106

Hofstede's _____ dimension focused on the relationship between the individual and his or her followers.
a. individualism versus collectivism
b. aggressive versus passive
c. masculinity versus femininity
d. power distance

3-74.
D
Medium
P.106

Hofstede's _____ dimension measured the extent to which different cultures socialized their members into accepting ambiguous situations and tolerating uncertainty.
a. masculinity versus femininity
b. power distance
c. individualism versus collectivism
d. uncertainty avoidance

3-75.
B
Medium
P.106

Hofstede's _____ dimension looked at the relationship between gender and work roles.
a. power distance
b. masculinity versus femininity
c. individualism versus collectivism
d. uncertainty avoidance

3-76.
A
Hard
P.106

According to Hofstede's Model, which group of nations score high on the individualism scale and low on the power distance scale?
a. advanced western nations such as the United States, Canada, and Britain
b. South American nations such as Brazil, Peru, and Ecuador
c. Asian nations such as Japan, South Korea, and Singapore
d. African nations such as Zaire, Sudan, and Chad

3-77.   According to Hofstede's Model, what country stands out as having a culture with
B   strong uncertainty avoidance and high masculinity?
Hard   a. United States
P.106   b. Japan
            c. Australia
            d. Germany

3-78.   Ethnocentrism is a belief in the:
A   a. superiority of one's own ethnic group or culture
Easy   b. superiority of one's own legal system compared to others
P.112   c. superiority of one's own religious beliefs over others
            d. superiority of individualism versus collectivism

3-79.   Acting on the belief in the superiority of one's own ethnic group or culture is
D   referred to as _____ behavior.
Medium   a. collectivist
P.112   b. intolerant
            c. individualistic
            d. ethnocentric

3-80.   Suppose an international executive from Italy consistently acted in a manner that
C   indicated that he believed that his ethnic group and culture is superior to any
Medium   others. If this was the case, the executive would be exhibiting _____
P.112   behavior.
            a. synergistic
            b. plyocentric
            c. ethnocentric
            d. individualistic

Essay Questions

3-81.   Describe what is meant by the term "culture?" Differentiate between the terms
Easy   culture, values, and norms.
P.84

         Answer: Culture can be defined as a system of values and norms that are shared
         among a group of people and that when taken together constitute a design for
         living. Values and norms are the underpinnings of culture. Values are abstract
         ideas about what a group believes to be good, right, and desirable. Put differently,
         values are shared assumptions about how things ought to be. Norms are the
         social rules and guidelines that prescribe appropriate behavior in a particular
         situation.

3-82.
Medium
P.90

Describe the concept of social mobility. Does social mobility vary significantly from society to society? Describe the extremes in terms of a society that has low social mobility and a society that has high social mobility. Would you rather live in a society with a high level or a low level of social mobility? Why?

Answer: Social mobility refers to the extent to which individuals can move out of the strata into which they are born. For instance, in a society with a low level of social mobility, it would be very difficult (if not impossible) for someone that is born into a family of laborers to become a manager. Social mobility varies significantly from society to society. The most rigid system of stratification is a caste system. A caste system is a closed system of stratification in which social position is determined by the family into which a person is born, and change in that position is usually not possible during an individual's lifetime. At the other extreme is the American "class" system (i.e. upper class, middle class, and lower-middle class). In this system, class membership is determined mainly by an individual's own efforts and achievements, rather than his or her family heritage. Thus, an individual in American, through effort and achievement, can move smoothly from the lower-middle class (or the working class) to the upper class.

Your students will undoubtedly say that they would rather live in a society with a high level of social mobility. The clear advantage of such a society is that a person's position is determined by his or her own individual effort.

3-83.
Easy
P.92

What is meant by the Protestant work ethic? What impact has the Protestant work ethic had on the emergence of modern day capitalism?

Answer: In 1904 a German sociologist, named Max Weber, made a connection between Protestant ethics and "the spirit of capitalism." Weber drew this conclusion by observing that, in Western Europe, the business leaders and owners of capital were overwhelmingly Protestant. This relationship led Weber to conclude that there was a link between Protestantism and the emergence of modern capitalism. Weber argued that Protestant ethics emphasized the importance of hard work and wealth creation, which are the essential components of capitalism. Thus, Weber coined the term "Protestant work ethic" to denote the tendency on the part of Protestants to work hard and accumulate wealth, which are the underpinnings of capitalism.

3-84.
Hard
P.106

Hofstede isolated four dimensions that he claimed charaterized the cultures of different countries. Briefly describe each of Hofstede's four dimensions. Should Hofstede's dimensions be used by managers to determine how cultures differ and what that might mean for management practices?

Answer: Hostede's four dimension are: power distance, individualism versus collectivism, uncertainty avoidance, and masculinity versus femininity. Each of these dimensions is briefly described below.

Power Distance: This dimension focuses on how a society deals with the fact that people are unequal in physical and intellectual capabilities. According to Hofstede, high power distance cultures are found in countries that let inequalities grow over time into inequalities of power and wealth. Low power distance cultures are found in societies that try to play down such inequalities as much as possible.

Individualism versus Collectivism: This dimension focuses on the relationship between the individual and his or her fellows. In individualistic societies, the ties between individuals are loose and individual achievement and freedom are highly valued. In societies where collectivism is emphasized, the ties between individuals are tight.

Uncertainty Avoidance: This dimension measures the extent to which different cultures socialize their members into accepting ambiguous situations and tolerating uncertainty. Members of high uncertainty avoidance cultures place a premium on job security, career patterns, retirement benefits, and so on. Lower uncertainty avoidance cultures are characterized by a greater readiness to take risks and less emotional resistance to change.

Masculinity versus Femininity: Finally, this dimension looks at the relationship between gender and work roles. In masculine cultures, sex roles are sharply differentiated and traditional "masculine values," such as achievement and the effective exercise of power, determines cultural ideals. If feminine cultures, sex roles are less sharply distinguished, and little differentiation is made between men and women in the same job.

Hofstede used these dimensions to develop charts that provided descriptive information about cultures. These charts were intended to be used by managers to understand the dynamics of different cultures.

As articulated in the textbook, Hofstede's model has some weaknesses, and should not be used as the sole determinant of how one interfaces with individuals from other cultures. On the other hand, Hofstede's model is a tool that can provide a manager insight that he or she might not otherwise have relative to cultural issues.

3-85.
Medium
P.112

What is ethnocentric behavior? Is ethnocentrism a desirable of an undesirable attribute for the manager of an international firm?

Answer: Ethnocentrism is a belief in the superiority of one's own ethnic group or culture. Often, this leads to behavior that reflects a disregard or contempt for the cultures of other countries. Ethnocentric behavior is not a desirable attribute for the manager of an international firm. International managers must have a healthy respect for other and a balanced perspective.

CHAPTER 4
INTERNATIONAL TRADE THEORY

True/False Questions

4-1.
F
Easy
P.123

Mercantilism is an old and highly regarded doctrine.

4-2.
T
Easy
P.123

Free trade refers to a situation where a government does not attempt to influence through quotas or duties what its citizens can buy from another country or what they can produce and sell to another country.

4-3.
T
Medium
P.123

Adam Smith argued that the invisible hand of the market mechanism, rather than government policy, should determine what a country imports and what it exports.

4-4.
F
Medium
P.124

The theories of Smith, Ricardo, and Heckscher-Ohlin tell us that a country's economy will suffer if its citizens buy certain products from other nations that could be produced at home.

4-5.
T
Hard
P.123

Both the new trade theory and Porter's theory of national competitive advantage can be interpreted as justifying some limited and selective government intervention to support the development of certain export-oriented industries.

4-6.
T
Medium
P.125

The argument for unrestricted free trade is that both import controls and export incentives (such as subsidies) are self-defeating and result in wasted resources.

4-7.
T
Medium
P.125

The new trade theory stresses than in some cases countries specialize in the production and export of particular products not because of underlying differences in factor endowments but because in certain industries the world market can support only a limited number of firms.

4-8.
F
Easy
P.126

A positive-sum game in a situation in which a gain by one country results in a loss by another.

4-9.
T
Easy
P.126

The main tenet of mercantilism was that it is in a country's best interest to maintain a trade surplus, to export more than it imports.

4-10.
F
Hard
P.127

In his 1776 landmark book *The Wealth of Nations*, Adam Smith attacked the mercantilist assumption that trade is a positive-sum game.

4-11.
T
Medium
P.127

Smith's basic argument was that a country should never produce goods at home that it can buy at a lower cost from other countries.

4-12.
F
Hard
P.132

To an even greater degree than the theory of comparative advantage, the theory of absolute advantage suggests that trade is a positive-sum game in which all can gain.

4-13.
T
Medium
P.132

The basic message of the theory of comparative advantage is that the potential world production is greater with unrestricted free trade than it is with restricted free trade.

4-14.
T
Medium
P.135

According to evidence compiled by the World Bank, free trade has a positive effect on economic growth.

4-15.
T
Medium
P.136

Like Ricardo's theory, the Heckscher-Ohlin theory argues that free trade is beneficial. Unlike Ricardo's theory, however, the Heckscher-Ohlin theory argues that the pattern of international trade is determined by differences in factor endowments, rather than differences in productivity.

4-16.
F
Medium
P.136

The Heckscher-Olin theory would predict that the United States should be a primary importer of capital goods.

4-17.
T
Medium
P.136

Most economists prefer the Heckscher-Ohlin theory to Ricardo's theory because it makes fewer simplifying assumptions, and it has been subjected to many empirical tests.

4-18.
T
Medium
P.137

Raymond Vernon's theory of the Product Life-Cycle was based on the observation that for most of the 20th century a very large proportion of the world's new products were developed by U.S. firms and sold first in the U.S. market.

4-19.
T
Medium
P.141

The new trade theorists argue that in those industries where the existence of substantial economies of scale imply that the world market will profitable support only a few firms, countries may export certain products simply because they have a firm that was an early entrant into that industry.

4-20.
F
Medium
P.145

In sum, Porter's argument is that the degree to which a nation is likely to achieve international success in a certain industry is a function of the combined impact of factor endowments, domestic demand conditions, related and supporting industries, and degree of government support.

Multiple Choice

4-21.
C
Easy
P.123

Propagated in the 16th and 17th centuries, _____ advocated that countries should simultaneously encourage exports and discourage imports.
a. ethnocentrism
b. capitalism
c. mercantilism
d. collectivism

4-22.
C
Easy
P.123

Adam Smith advanced the theory of _____.
a. similar opportunity
b. capitalism
c. absolute advantage
d. mercantilism

4-23.
A
Medium
P.123

Which of the following international trade scholars was the first to explain why unrestricted free trade is beneficial to a country?
a. Adam Smith
b. Bertil Ohlin
c. Eli Heckscher
d. Paul Krugman

4-24.
B
Easy
P.123

_____ refers to a situation where a government does not attempt to influence through quotas or duties what its citizens can buy from another country or what they can produce and sell to another country.

a. Autonomous trade
b. Free trade
c. Clear commerce
d. Unencumbered commerce

4-25.
D
Medium
P.123

Which of the following international management scholars argued that the "invisible hand" of the market mechanism, rather than government policy, should determine what a country imports and what it exports?

a. David Ricardo
b. Eli Heckscher
c. Michael Porter
d. Adam Smith

4-26.
A
Medium
P.123

Adam Smith argued that the _____ of the market mechanism, rather than government policy, should determine what a country imports and what it exports.

a. invisible hand
b. blunt force
c. economic realities
d. ups and downs

4-27.
B
Hard
P.123

The theory of comparative advantage, which is based on the work of English economist _____, is described by the author of the textbook as the intellectual basis of the modern argument for unrestricted free trade.

a. Michael Porter
b. David Ricardo
c. Bertil Ohlin
d. Adam Smith

4-28.
B
Medium
P.125

One early response to the failure of the Heckscher-Ohlin theory to explain the observed pattern of international trade was the _____.

a. theory of rising costs
b. product life-cycle theory
c. theory of comparative advantage
d. theory of cultural constraints

4-29.
D
Medium
P.125

The _____ was an early response to the failure of the Hecksher-Ohlin theory to explain the observed pattern of international trade.

a. theory of absolute advantage
b. new trade theory
c. theory of comparative advantage
d. product life-cycle theory

4-30.
C
Medium
P.125

The _____ theory stresses that in some cases countries specialize in the production and export of particular products not because of underlying differences in factor endowments but because in certain industries the world market can support only a limited number of firms.
a. balanced trade
b. Heckscher-Olin
c. new trade
d. product life-Kyle

4-31.
D
Medium
P.125

The theory of _____, developed by Michael Porter, focuses on the importance of country factors such as domestic demand and domestic rivalry in explaining a nation's dominance in the production and export of particular products.
a. new trade
b. absolute advantage
c. comparative advantage
d. national competitive advantage

4-32.
D
Hard
P.125

Which of the following two theories justify some limited and selective government intervention to support the development of certain export-oriented industries?
a. the theory of national competitive advantage and the Heckscher-Ohlin theory
b. the theory of absolute advantage and the new trade theory
c. the Heckscher-Ohlin theory and theory of comparative advantage
d. the new trade theory and theory of national competitive advantage

4-33.
B
Easy
P.126

The first theory of international trade emerged in England in the mid-16th century. Referred to as _____, its principal assertion was that gold and silver were the mainstays of national wealth and essential to vigorous commerce.
a. collectivism
b. mercantilism
c. capitalism
d. economic conservatism

4-34.
C
Medium
P.126

The main tenet of mercantilism was that it was in a country's best interest to maintain a trade _____.
a. balance
b. embargo
c. surplus
d. deficit

4-35.
A
Medium
P.126

The flaw with mercantilism was that it viewed trade as a _____.
a. zero-sum game
b. economic necessity
c. non essential economic activity
d. threat to a government's independence

4-36.
C
Easy
P.126

A situation in which a gain by one party results in a loss by another is called a
_____.
a. transfer of wealth
b. unbalanced scorecard
c. zero-sum game
d. positive-sum game

4-37.
C
Easy
P.126

A _____ is a situation in which a gain by one country results in a loss by another.
a. positive-sum game
b. transfer of wealth
c. zero-sum game
d. unbalanced scorecard

4-38.
B
Easy
P.126

A situation in which all countries can benefit, even if some benefit more than others is called a _____.
a. near equivalent-result game
b. positive-sum game
c. balanced scorecard
d. zero-sum game

4-39.
D
Easy
P.127

In his 1776 landmark book *The Wealth of Nations*, _____ attacked the mercantilist assumption that trade is a zero-sum game.
a. Geert Hofstede
b. Max Weber
c. Michael Porter
d. Adam Smith

4-40.
A
Medium
P.127

In his 1776 landmark book _____, Adam Smith attacked the mercantilist assumption that trade is a zero-sum game.
a. The Wealth of Nations
b. The Free Trade Manifesto
c. A Commentary on Free Trade and Globalization
d. Free Trade and Mercantilism

4-41.
B
Hard
P.127

According to Smith, countries should specialize in the production of goods for which they have an absolute advantage and then:
a. retain these goods for strictly domestic sales
b. trade these goods for the goods produced by other countries
c. sell these goods to the highest domestic or international bidder
d. prohibit the import of these goods from other countries

4-42.
A
Medium
P.127

A situation in which one country is more efficient at producing a product than any other country is referred to as:
a. absolute advantage
b. relative advantage
c. comparative advantage
d. pertinent advantage

4-43.
B
Medium
P.131

In his 1817 book entitled *Principles of Political Economy*, _____ introduced the theory of comparative advantage.
a. Adam Smith
b. David Ricardo
c. Raymond Vernon
d. Max Weber

4-44.
C
Medium
P.131

A situation in which a country specializes in producing the goods it produces most efficiently and buys the products it produces less efficiently from other countries, even if it could produce the good more efficiently itself is referred to as:
a. comprehensive advantage
b. pertinent advantage
c. comparative advantage
d. absolute advantage

4-45.
B
Medium
P.131

According to Ricardo's theory of _____, it makes sense for a country to specialize in the production of those goods that it produces most efficiently and to buy the goods that it produces less efficiently from other countries, even if this means buying goods from other countries that it could produce more efficiently itself.
a. competitive advantage
b. comparative advantage
c. pertinent advantage
d. absolute advantage

4-46.
A
Hard
P.132

According to the textbook, the basic message of the theory of comparative advantage is that:
a. potential world production is greater with unrestricted free trade than it is with restricted trade
b. potential world production is not significantly affected by trade policy
c. potential world production is greater with restricted trade.
d. it makes sense for a country to specialize in the production of those goods that it produces most efficiently and to buy the goods that it products less efficiently from other countries, unless this means buying goods from other countries that it could produce more efficiently itself

4-47.
B
Medium
P.132

According to the textbook, the basic message of the theory of _____ is that potential world production is greater with unrestricted free trade than it is with restricted free trade.
a. mercantilism
b. comparative advantage
c. the Leontief Paradox
d. absolute advantage

4-48.
C
Medium
P.132

To an even greater degree than the theory of absolute advantage, the theory of _____ suggests that trade is a positive-sum game in which all gain.
a. total advantage
b. mercantilism
c. comparative advantage
d. paradoxical advantage

4-49.
D
Medium
P.135

Ricardo's theory stresses that comparative advantage arises from differences in _____ across countries.
a. wage-rates
b. fiscal policy
c. currency exchange rates
d. productivity

4-50.
B
Medium
P.135

Swedish economists _____ and _____ advanced a theory of trade that argued that comparative advantage arises from differences in national factor endowments.
a. Durbin, Coles
b. Hecksher, Ohlin
c. Delhomme, Rivette
d. Mouton, Penn

4-51.
D
Medium
P.135

The theory that argues that comparative advantage arises from differences in national factor endowments was advanced by the Swedish economists _____ and _____.
a. Toussaint, Coles
b. Leblanc, Cormier
c. Wills, Theler
d. Hecksher, Ohlin

4-52. The _____ theory predicts that countries will export those goods that make
C   intensive use of those factors that are locally abundant, while importing goods that
Medium make intensive use of factors that are locally scarce.
P.136
       a. Hecksher-Cormier
       b. Ricardo-Olin
       c. Hecksher-Olin
       d. Carrier-Roller

4-53. Which of the following statements is a fair comparison of the Heckscher-Ohlin
B   theory and the Ricardo theory (i.e. comparative advantage) of free trade?
Hard
P.136 a. both theories argues that the pattern of international trade is determined by
           currency exchange rates
       b. the Heckscher-Olin theory argues that the pattern of international trade is
           determined by trade endowments, while the Ricardo theory argues that the
           pattern of international trade is determined by differences in productivity
       c. both theories argue that the pattern of international trade is determined by
           differences in productivity
       d. the Heckscher-Olin theory argues that the pattern of international trade is
           determined by differences in productivity, while the Ricardo theory argues that
           the pattern of international trade is determined by trade endowments

4-54. According to the textbook, most economists prefer the Heckscher-Ohlin theory to
A   Ricardo's theory (i.e. comparative advantage) because of two factors. These
Medium factors are:
P.136
       a. it makes fewer simplifying assumptions and it has been subjected to many
           empirical tests
       b. it has been subjected to many empirical tests and it has stood the test of time.
       c. it makes fewer simplifying assumptions and it has been acknowledged by the
           World Trade Organization as the better of the two theories
       d. it has been acknowledged as the better of the two theories by the World Trade
           Organization, and it has stood the test of time

4-55. Contrary to what the Heckscher-Ohlin theory would predict, the United States has
B   been a primary importer rather than an exporter of capital goods. This
Easy   phenomenon is referred to as the _____ paradox.
P.136
       a. Theler
       b. Leontief
       c. Cormier
       d. Ricardo

4-56. _____ initially proposed the product life-cycle theory in the mid-1960s.
C
Easy   a. Cormier
P.137 b. Heckscher
       c. Vernon
       d. Smith

4-57.
C
Easy
P.137

Raymond Vernon initially proposed the _____ in the mid-1960s.
a. new trade theory
b. theory of absolute advantage
c. product life-cycle theory
d. theory of comparative advantage

4-58.
C
Medium
P.137

Vernon's product life-cycle theory was based on the observation that for most of the 20th century a very large proportion of the world's new products had been developed by U.S. firms and sold first in the _____ market.
a. Japanese
b. Western European
c. U.S.
d. Canadian

4-59.
D
Medium
p.137

Vernon's product life-cycle theory was based on the observation that for most of the 20th century a very large proportion of the world's new products had been developed by _____ firms and sold first in the U.S. market.
a. Mexican
b. Canadian
c. Western European
d. U.S.

4-60.
C
Medium
P.140

The _____ theory argues that in many industries, because of substantial economies of scale, there are increasing returns to specialization.
a. Leontief's paradox
b. product life0cycle
c. new trade
d. Heckscher-Ohlin

4-61.
D
Medium
P.140

The _____ theory argues that due to the presence of substantial scale economies, world demand will support only a few firms in many industries.
a. Heckscher-Ohlin
b. Leontief's paradox
c. product life-cycle
d. new trade

4-62.
D
Medium
P.140

The theory that argues that due to the presence of substantial scale economies, world demand will support only a few firms in many industries in referred to as the
a. theory of comparative advantage
b. product life-cycle theory
c. theory of absolute advantage
d. new trade theory

4-63.   The theory that argues that due to the presence of substantial scale economies,
C   world demand will support only a few firms in the aircraft industry, is referred to as
Medium   the:
P.140   a. theory of absolute advantage
         b. theory of comparative advantage
         c. new trade theory
         d. product life-cycle theory

4-64.   The economic and strategic advantages that accrue to early entrants in an
A   industry are called:
Easy   a. first-mover advantages
P.141   b. initial-class advantages
         c. early-entrant advantages
         d. first-stage benefits

4-65.   _____ advantages are the economic and strategic advantages that accrue
B   to early entrants into an industry.
Easy   a. Initial-class
P.141   b. First-mover
         c. First-stage
         d. Early-entrant

4-66.   The new trade theorists argue that the United States leads in exports of
D   commercial jet aircraft not because it is better endowed with the factors of
Hard   production required to manufacture aircraft. but because:
P.141   a. U.S. built commercial jet aircraft have the best safety record
         b. the U.S. commercial jet aircraft industry has a lower wage rate than foreign
             competitors
         c. the World Trade Organization has given preferential treatment to the U.S.
             commercial jet aircraft industry
         d. two of the first movers in the industry were U.S. firms

4-67.   New trade theorists stress the role of the following three variables in giving a firm
C   first-mover advantages?
Hard   a. availability of capital, entrepreneurship, and favorable government policies
P.141   b. entrepreneurship, favorable foreign exchange rates, and innovation
         c. luck, entrepreneurship, and innovation
         d. modernization, luck, and the availability of capital

4-68.
B
Easy
P.142

In 1990 _____ of Harvard Business School published the results of an intensive research effort that attempted to determine why some nations succeed and others fail in international competition.

a. Eli Heckscher
b. Michael Porter
c. Bertil Ohlin
d. Raymond Vernon

4-69.
B
Hard
P.142

According to Michael Porter, a nation's position in factors of production such as skilled labor or the infrastructure necessary to compete in a given industry are referred to as:

a. demand endowments
b. factor endowments
c. factor competencies
d. demand conditions

4-70.
C
Medium
P.142

In 1990, Michael Porter of the Harvard Business School, published the results an intensive research effort that attempted to determine why some nations succeed and others fail in international competition. The name of the book was _____.

a. The Comparable Advantage of Trade and Globalization
b. The Wealth of Nations
c. The Competitive Advantage of Nations
d. The Absolute Advantages of Globalization

4-71.
B
Hard
P.142

In his book *The Competitive Advantage of Nations*, Porter thesis was that four broad attributes of a nation shape the environment in which local firms compete, and that these attributes promote or impede the creation of competitive advantage. Which of the following is not one of these attributes?

a. factor endowments
b. customs
c. firm strategy, structure, and rivalry
d. related and supporting industries

4-72.
C
Medium
P.143

In his study dealing with the competitive advantage of nations, Porter argued that in regard to factor endowments, _____ factors are the most significant for competitive advantage.

a. standard
b. basic
c. advanced
d. complementary

4-73.
D
Medium
P.144

In his study dealing with the competitive advantage of nations, Porter argued that in regard to demand conditions, a nation's firms gain competitive advantage if their domestic consumers are _____ and _____.
a. unpretentious, passive
b. modest, passive
c. exacting, unpretentious
d. sophisticated, demanding

4-74.
A
Medium
P.144

Which of the following theorists argued that successful industries within a country tend to be grouped into "clusters" of related industries?
a. Porter
b. Vernon
c. Ricardo
d. Heckscher

4-75.
C
Hard
P.145

In his study, Porter observed that there are a disproportionate number of people with finance backgrounds on the top management teams of many _____ industries.
a. Japanese
b. French
c. United States
d. South Korean

4-76.
D
Medium
P.145

In sum, Porter concluded that the degree to which a nation is likely to achieve international success in a certain industry is a function of the combined impact of factor endowments, domestic demand conditions, related and supporting industries, and _____.
a. domestic wage rates
b. membership in the World Trade Organization
c. availability of capital
d. firm strategy, structure, and rivalry

4-77.
A
Medium
P.145

Porter's "diamond" of the determinants of national competitive advantage includes factor endowments, related and supporting industries, firm strategy, structure, and rivalry, and _____.
a. demand conditions
b. membership in the World Trade Organization
c. domestic wage rates
d. government support

4-78.
C
Medium
P.145

Porter's "diamond" of the determinants of national competitive advantage includes demand conditions, related and supporting industries, firm strategy, structure, and rivalry, and _____.

a. domestic wage rates
b. government support
c. factor endowments
d. membership in the World Trade Organization

4-79.
C
Medium
P.149

According to the new trade theory, firms that establish a _____ advantage with regard to the production of a particular new product may subsequently dominate global trade in that product.

a. initial-class
b. early entrant
c. first-mover
d. initial-entrant

4-80.
C
Hard
P.149

According to the textbook, in it often argued that in recent years _____ firms, rather than their European or North American competitors, seem to have been prepared to undertake the vast investments and bear the years of losses required to build a first-mover advantage.

a. Chinese
b. South Korean
c. Japanese
d. Australian

Essay Questions

4-81.
Easy
P.123

What is meant by the term "free trade." Was Adam Smith an advocate or critic of free trade? Is free trade compatible with the concept of mercantilism? Explain your answer.

Answer: Free trade refers to a situation where a government does not attempt to influence through quotas or duties what its citizens can buy from another country or what they can produce and sell to another country. This concept was supported by Adam Smith, who argued that the "invisible hand" of the market mechanism, rather than government policy, should determine what a country imports and what it exports. The concept of mercantilism is not compatible with the concept of free trade. The main tenet of mercantilism is that it is in a country's best interests to maintain a trade surplus by exporting more than it imports. Consistent with this belief, the mercantilist doctrine advocated government intervention to achieve a surplus in the balance of trade.

188

4-82.
Medium
P.127

Describe Adam Smith's concept of absolute advantage.

Answer: According to Smith, countries should specialize in the production of goods for which they have an absolute advantage and then trade those goods for the goods produced by other countries. For instance, during Smith's time, England had an absolute advantage in the production of textiles, and France had an absolute advantage in the production of wine. According to the concept of absolute advantage, it then only makes sense for England to produce textiles (and export them to France), and France to produce wine (and export it to England). Smith's basic argument, therefore, was that a country should never produce goods at home that it can buy at a lower cost from other countries. Moreover, Smith argued that by specializing in the production of goods in which each has an absolute advantage, both countries benefit by engaging in trade.

4-83.
Medium
P.136

Describe the Heckscher-Ohlin theory of international trade. Is the Heckscher-Olin theory consistent with the notion of free trade? Why or why not?

Answer: The Heckscher-Ohlin theory predicts that countries will export those goods that make intensive use of those factors that are locally abundant, while importing goods that make intensive use of factors that are locally scarce. Thus, the Heckscher-Ohlin theory attempts to explain the pattern of international trade that we see in the world economy. The Heckscher-Ohlin theory is consistent with the notion of free trade. It also has commonsense appeal, and there are many examples of international commerce that are supportive of the theory.

4-84.
Easy
P.141

Describe what is meant by first-mover advantages?

Answer: First mover advantages are the economic and strategic advantages that accrue to early entrants into an industry. Because they are able to gain economies of scale, early entrants may get a lock on the world market that discourages subsequent entry. In other words, the ability of first-movers to reap economies of scale creates a barrier to entry. In the commercial aircraft industry, for example, the fact that Boeing and Airbus are already in the industry and have achieved substantial economies of scale effectively discourages new entrants.

4-85.
Medium
P.143

In an extensive study that was published in a book entitled *The Competitive Advantage of Nations*, Michael Porter concluded that four broad attributes of a nation shape the environment in which local firms compete, and that these attributes promote or impede the creation of competitive advantage. Identify and describe the four attributes advanced by Porter. What did Porter conclude from his analysis?

Answer: The four attributes identified by Porter are as follows:

Factor Endowments: A nation's position in factors of production such as skilled labor or the infrastructure necessary to compete in a given industry.

Demand Conditions: The nature of home demand for the industry's product or service.

Related or Supporting Industries: The presence or absence in a nation of supplier industries and related industries that are internationally competitive.

Firm Strategy, Structure, and Rivalry: The conditions in the nation governing how companies are created, organized, and managed and the nature of domestic rivalry.

Porter speaks of these four attributes as constituting the diamond. He argues that firms are most likely to succeed in industries or industry segments where the diamond is most favorable.

CHAPTER 5
THE GLOBAL TRADING SYSTEM

True/False Questions

5-1.
F
Easy
P.162

A tariff is a tax levied on exports.

5-2.
T
Easy
P.162

Specific tariffs are levied as a fixed charge for each unit of a good imported (for example, $3 per barrel of oil).

5-3.
T
Easy
P.162

Ad Valero tariffs are levied as a proportion of the value of the imported good.

5-4.
F
Medium
P.162

The effect of a tariff is to reduce the cost of imported products relative to domestic products.

5-5.
T
P.164

Tariffs reduce the overall efficiency of the world economy because a protective tariff encourages domestic firms to produce products at home that, in theory, could be produced more efficiently abroad.

5-6.
F
Medium
P.164

The main gains from subsidies accrue to importers, whose international competitiveness is increased as a result of them.

5-7.
Easy
P.164

A subsidy is a government payment to a domestic producer.

5-8.
Medium
P.165

Both import quotas and voluntary export restraints hurt domestic producers.

5-9.
F
Easy
P.165

Quotas benefit consumers.

5-10.
T
Medium
P.165

Local content requirements have been widely used by developing countries to shift their manufacturing base from the simple assembly of products whose parts are manufactured elsewhere into the local manufacture of component parts.

5-11.
T
Medium
P.165

A quota on trade imposed by the exporting country, typically at the request of the importing country, is referred to as a voluntary export restraint.

5-12.
F
Medium
P.166

Administrative trade policies are bureaucratic rules that are designed to make it easy for imports to enter a country.

5-13.
T
Easy
P.167

Perhaps the most common political argument for government intervention in the free flow of trade is that it is necessary for protecting jobs and industries from foreign competition.

5-14.
T
Medium
P.167

Countries sometimes argue that it is important to protect certain industries for reasons of national security.

5-15.
F
Medium
P.167

In general, there are two types of arguments for government intervention into international commerce, technological and sociocultural.

5-16.
T
Medium
P.172

The intellectual case for free trade goes back to the late18th century and the work of Adam Smith and David Ricardo.

5-17.
F
Medium
P.173

In its early years GATT was by most measures unsuccessful.

5-18.
T
Medium
P.174

During the 1980s and early 1990s the world trading system erected by GATT began to be strained as protectionist pressures arose around the world.

5-19.
T
Easy
P.177

The Uruguay Round extended GATT rules to cover intellectual property.

5-20.
F
P.182

Most economists would probably argue that the best interests of international business are served by a free trade stance, including a laissez-faire stance.

Multiple Choice

5-21.
A
Easy
P.162

A _____ is a tax levied on imports.
a. tariff
b. special assessment
c. penalty
d. globalization assessment

5-22.
B
Easy
P.162

A tariff is a tax levied on _____.
a. domestically produced goods
b. imports
c. services
d. exports

5-23.
D
Easy
P.162

A tax that is levied on imports is referred to as a _____.
a. global assessment
b. penalty
c. special assessment
d. tariff

5-24.
C
Medium
P.162

The oldest form of trade policy is a _____.
a. global assessment
b. penalty
c. tariff
d. special assessment

5-25.
C
Medium
P.162

According to the author of the textbook, tariffs cause the most damage to _____, because this group bears the economic brunt of tariffs.
a. trade associations
b. governments
c. consumers
d. producers

5-26.
A
P.162

According to the author of the textbook, tariffs benefit the following two groups:
a. government and producers
b. consumers and trade associations
c. government and consumers
d. producers and consumers

5-27.
A
Easy
P.162

_____ are levied as a fixed charge for each for each unit of a good imported.
a. Specific tariffs
b. General tariffs
c. Ad valorem tariffs
d. Global tariffs

5-28.
C
Easy
P.162

Taxes levied as a fixed charge for each unit of good imported are referred to as:
a. ad valorem tariffs
b. global tariffs
c. special tariffs
d. general tariffs

5-29.
D
Medium
P.162

While _____ tariffs are levied as a fixed charge for each unit of a good imported, _____ tariffs are levied as a proportion of the value of the imported good.
a. general, special
b. ad valorem, special
c. global, special
d. specific, ad valorem

5-30.
B
Medium
P.162

An example of a(n) _____ tariff is the 25 percent tariff the U.S. governmen placed on imported light trucks in the 1980s.
a. general
b. ad valorem
c. special
d. global

5-31.
D
Hard
P.162

According to the author of the textbook, tariffs are unambiguously _____ and _____.
a. pro-producer and pro consumer
b. anti-consumer and pro-producer
c. anti-consumer and anti-producer
d. pro-producer and anti-consumer

5-32.
B
Easy
P.164

A _____ is a government payment to a domestic producer.
a. duty
b. subsidy
c. quota
d. tariff

5-33.
A
Easy
P.164

A government payment to a domestic producer is called a:
a. subsidy
b. tariff
c. duty
d. quota

5-34.
C
Easy
P.164

By lowering costs, _____ help domestic producers to compete against low-cost foreign imports and to gain export markets.
a. duties
b. quotas
c. subsidies
d. tariffs

5-35.
A
Medium
P.164

The main gains from subsidies accrue to _____, whose international competitiveness is increased as a result of them.
a. domestic producers
b. consumers
c. governments
d. importers

5-36.
C
Hard
P.164

According to official national figures, government subsidies to industry in most industrialized countries during the late 1980s amounted to between:
a. 40% and 50% of the value of industrial output
b. 15% and 20% of the value of industrial output
c. 2% and 3.5% of the value of industrial output
d. 10% and 15% of the value of industrial output

5-37.
D
Hard
P.164

Advocates of strategic trade policy favor the use of _____ to help domestic firms achieve a dominant position in those industries where economies of scale are important and the world market is not large enough to profitably support more than a few firms (e.g., aerospace, semiconductors).

a. quotas
b. duties
c. tariffs
d. subsidies

5-38.
B
Easy
P.165

An import quota is a direct restriction on the quantity of some good that may be:
a. subsidized by a country
b. imported into a country
c. exported out of a country
d. produced in a country

5-39.
A
Hard
P.165

Both import quotas and VERs benefit _____ by limiting import competition, but they result in higher prices, which hurts _____.
a. domestic producers, consumers
b. governments, consumers
c. consumers, foreign producers
d. foreign producers, governments

5-40.
C
Easy
P.165

An _____ is a direct restriction on the quantity of some goods that may be imported into a country.
a. specialization quota
b. production quota
c. import quota
d. export quota

5-41.
A
Medium
P.165

A _____ is a quota on trade imposed by the exporting country, typically at the request of the importing country's government.
a. voluntary export restraint
b. involuntary export restraint
c. trade reconciliation
d. refereed export restraint

5-42.
C
Medium
P.165

A quota on trade imposed by the exporting country, typically at the request of the importing country, is called a:
a. involuntary import restraint
b. trade reconciliation
c. voluntary export restraint
d. refereed export restraint

5-43.
D
Hard
P.165

Local content requirements benefit the _____ of component parts, but they raise prices of imported components, which hurts _____.
a. consumers, producers
b. producers, governments
c. consumers, governments
d. producers, consumers

5-44.
B
Easy
P.165

A _____ demands that some specific fraction of a good be produced domestically.
a. international content requirement
b. local content requirement
c. specific content requirement
d. ad valorem content requirement

5-45.
A
Easy
P.165

A government order that some specific fraction of a good be produced domestically is called a:
a. local content requirement
b. ad valorem content requirement
c. international content requirement
d. specific content requirement

5-46.
D
Medium
P.165

If Ford Motor decided to produce cars in Italy, and the Italian government stipulated that 45% of the component parts that went into Ford's vehicles must be produced locally, that requirement would be an example of a:
a. ad valorem content requirement
b. international content requirement
c. specific content requirement
d. local content requirement

5-47.
A
Medium
P.166

For a domestic producer of component parts, local content requirements provide protection in the same way an import quota does _____.
a. by limiting foreign competition
b. by increasing tariffs
c. by eliminating foreign competition
d. by encouraging foreign competition

5-48.
D
Easy
P.166

Bureaucratic rules that are designed to make it difficult for imports to enter a country are referred to as:
a. situational trade policies
b. ad valorem trade policies
c. supplemental trade policies
d. administrative trade policies

5-49.
D
Medium
P.166

An administrative policy is an informal instrument or bureaucratic rule that can be used to restrict imports and boost exports. Such policies benefit _____ but hurt _____.

a. trade associations, producers
b. consumers, producers
c. consumers, trade associations
d. producers, consumers

5-50.
A
Medium
P.166

Consider the following scenario. The Netherlands exports tulip bulbs to almost every country in the world except Japan. The reason is that Japanese customs inspectors insist on checking every tulip bulb by cutting it down the middle (which destroys the bulb). The insistence on the part of the Japanese to inspect the bulbs in this manner (which makes it impractical for the Netherlands to export to Japan) is an example of an:

a. administrative trade policy
b. ad valorem trade policy
c. contingent trade policy
d. supplemental trade policy

5-51.
C
Medium
P.166

At one time, the French government required that all imported videocassette recorders arrive in France through a small customs entry point that was both remote and poorly staffed. This policy, which in effect made it impractical for a foreign company to import videocassette recorders to France, is an example of an

a. supplemental trade policy
b. contingent trade policy
c. administrative trade policy
d. ad valorem trade policy

5-52.
D
Easy
P.166

_____ are bureaucratic rules that are designed to make it difficult for imports to enter a country.

a. Ad valorem trade policies
b. Supplemental trade policies
c. Contingent trade policies
d. Administrative trade policies

5-53.
C
Medium
P.167

In general, there are two types of arguments for government intervention into the free flow of trade. These are:

a. patriotic and sociocultural
b. sociocultural and legal
c. political and economic
d. legal and patriotic

5-54.
D
Medium
P.167

In general, there are two types of arguments for government intervention into the free flow of trade. These are: (1) political and (2)
a. technological
b. sociocultural
c. legal
d. economic

5-55.
C
Medium
P.167

The two main types of arguments for government intervention into the free flow of trade are economic and _____.
a. sociocultural
b. legal
c. political
d. technological

5-56.
A
Easy
P.167

_____ arguments for government intervention into international trade are typically concerned with boosting the overall wealth of a nation.
a. Economic
b. Political
c. Legal
d. Sociocultural

5-57.
C
Medium
P.167

Perhaps the most common political argument for government intervention into the free flow of trade is that:
a. it protects national pride
b. politicians and their constituents tend to think that domestically produced products are superior to products produced in another country
c. it is necessary for protecting jobs and industries from foreign competition
d. it is necessary to maintain domestic economic stability

5-58.
B
Easy
P.168

The _____ argument is by far the oldest economic argument for government intervention into the free flow of trade.
a. mature industry
b. infant industry
c. declining industry
d. proprietary industry

5-59.
A
Easy
P.168

The oldest economic argument for government intervention into the free flow of trade is referred to as the:
a. infant industry argument
b. strategic trade policy argument
c. proprietary industry argument
d. declining industry argument

5-60.
D
Medium
P.168

According to the _____ argument, many developing countries have a potential comparative advantage in manufacturing, but new manufacturing industries there cannot initially compete with well-established industries in developed countries. To allow manufacturing to get a toehold, the argument is that governments should temporarily support new industries (with tariffs, import quotas, and subsidies) until they have grown strong enough to meet international competition.
a. proprietary industry
b. strategic trade policy
c. mature industry
d. infant industry

5-61.
B
Medium
P.168

Primarily as a result of pressure from the developing world, the _____ argument was recognized by the GATT as a legitimate reason for protectionism.
a. declining industry
b. infant industry
c. strategic trade policy
d. mature industry

5-62.
A
Medium
P.169

According to the _____ argument, a government should use subsidies to support promising firms that are active in newly emerging industries.
a. strategic trade policy
b. infant industry
c. declining industry
d. mature industry

5-63.
C
Medium
P.170

The strategic trade policy argument of the new trade theorists advances an _____ justification for government intervention in international trade.
a. technological
b. sociocultural
c. economic
d. political

5-64.
D
Hard
P.170

The _____ arguments of the new trade theorists suggest an economic justification for government intervention in international trade.
a. mature industry
b. declining industry
c. infant industry
d. strategic trade policy

5-65.
C
Medium
P.171

MIT Professor _____ argues that strategic trade policy aimed at establishing domestic firms in a dominant position in a global industry are beggar-thy-neighbor policies that boost national income at the expense of other countries.
a. Geert Hofstede
b. Micheal Porter
c. Paul Krugman
d. David Ricardo

5-66.
A
Medium
P.172

Free trade as a government policy was first officially embraced by Great Britain in 1846, when the British Parliament repealed the _____.
a. Corn Laws
b. Steel Laws
c. Coal Laws
d. Apparel Laws

5-67.
C
Medium
P.173

The General Agreement on Tariffs and Trade (GATT) was established in _____.
a. 1867
b. 1908
c. 1947
d. 1983

5-68.
A
Easy
P.173

Founded in 1947, the _____ was a multilateral agreement whose objective was to liberalize trade by eliminating tariffs, subsidies, import quotas, and the like.
a. General Agreement of Tariffs and Trade
b. World Trade Supervisory Authority
c. United Nations
d. International Trade Organization

5-69.
A
Medium
P.173

The latest round of the GATT agreement, referred to as the _____, was launched in 1986 and completed in December 1993.
a. Uruguay Round
b. German Round
c. Japanese Round
d. Brazilian Round

5-70.
B
Hard
P.174

Which of the following is not one of the main reasons that protectionist pressures arose around the world during the 1980s?
a. many countries found ways to get around GATT regulations
b. the opening of Japanese markets to imports
c. the economic successes of Japan
d. the persistent trade deficit in the United States

5-71.
A
Medium
P.174

One of the best known examples of _____ is the agreement between the United States and Japan, under which Japanese producers promised to limit their auto imports to the United States as a way of defusing growing trade tensions.

a. voluntary export restraint
b. import quotas
c. local content requirement
d. ad valorem tariffs

5-72.
D
Easy
P.175

In 1986 GATT members embarked on their eighth round of negotiations to reduce tariffs. The negotiations were referred to as the _____ Round (so named because they took place in this country).

a. German
b. Australian
c. Brazilian
d. Uruguay

5-73.
B
Easy
P.175

The eighth (and most recent) round of the GATT negotiations was referred to as the:

a. Finland Round
b. Uruguay Round
c. New Zealand Round
d. French Round

5-74.
D
Hard
P.175

Which of the following is not a component of the Uruguay Round agreement?

a. GATT rules will be much clearer and stronger.
b. GATT fair trade and market access rules will be extended to cover a wider range of services.
c. agricultural subsidies will be substantially reduced.
d. tariffs on industrial goods will be increased by more the one-half

5-75.
D
Hard
P.175

Which of the following statement is not a component of the Uruguay Round agreement?

a. tariffs on industrial goods will be reduced by more than one-third
b. barriers on trade in textiles will be significantly reduced over 10 years
c. a World Trade Organization will be created to implement the GATT agreement
d. agricultural subsidies will be substantially increased

5-76.
D
Medium
P.175

The World Trade Organization was created by the _____ of the GATT negotiations.

a. Cyprus Round
b. Canadian Round
c. Norway Round
d. Uruguay Round

5-77.
B
Medium
P.177

As a result of the Uruguay Round agreement, the _____ was created to arbitrate trade disputes and monitor the trade policies of member countries.
a. United Trade Authority
b. World Trade Organization
c. Global Commerce Authority
d. International Trade Authority

5-78.
B
Hard
P.180

As of 1994 roughly _____ of the volume of world trade flows represented trade that occurred between the different subsidiaries of multinational corporations.
a. 75%
b. 33%
c. 25%
d. 10%

5-79.
A
Easy
P.180

The acronym WTO stands for:
a. World Trade Organization
b. World Technology Outlook
c. Western Trade Alliance
d. World Trade Outlook

5-80.
B
Medium
P.181

Which of the following is not a disadvantage of government intervention in trade policy?
a. intervention can be self-defeating, since it tends to protect the inefficient rather than help firms become efficient global competitors
b. intervention in the form of tariffs, quotas, and subsidies can help firms and industries establish a competitive advantage in the world economy
c. intervention is unlikely to be well executed, since it may invite retaliation and trigger a trade war
d. intervention is dangerous, since it may invite retaliation and trigger a trade war

Essay Questions

5-81.
Easy
P.162

What is a tariff? Describe the difference between specific tariffs and ad valorem tariffs.

Answer: A tariff is a tax levied on imports. Specific tariffs are levied as a fixed charge for each unit of a good imported (for example, $500 for each automobile). Ad valorem tariffs are levied as a proportion of the value of the imported good. An example of an ad valorem tariff is the 25 percent tariff that the U.S. government placed on imported light trucks (including pickup trucks, four-wheel-drive vehicles, and minivans) in the late 1980s.

5-82.
Medium
P.166

What are administrative trade policies? Are these trade policies deliberately designed to restrict the flow of imports into a country, or do they simply reflect the complexity of the bureaucracies in many foreign countries? Provide at least one example of an "administrative trade policy."

Answer: Administrative trade policies are bureaucratic rules that are almost always deliberately designed to restrict the flow of a particular import into a country. For instance, a country may design some administrative rule that makes it totally impractical for a foreign company to import a particular product into its country. An example that is provided in the textbook is tulip bulbs. The Netherlands exports tulip bulbs to almost every country of the world except Japan. The reason is that Japanese customs inspectors insist on checking every tulip bulb by cutting it vertically down the middle, which in effect ruins the bulb. Other example are equally as compelling. For example, a country might insist that every VCR that is imported into the country be thoroughly tested to make sure that it will not subject the user to an "electric shock." If it took several weeks for these tests to be completed, it would be very difficult to make money importing VCRs into this country.

Obviously, these types of administrative trade policies are informal tariffs and are designed to block specific imports from entering a country.

5-83.
Easy
P.165

What is a voluntary export restraint? Can countries use voluntary export restraints to avoid trade retaliation? Explain your answer.

A voluntary export restraint is a "voluntary" quota on trade imposed by the exporting company (on itself) typically at the request of the importing country's government. One of the most famous examples is the limitation on auto exports to the United States enforced by the Japanese automobile producers in 1981. In response to direct pressure from the U.S. government, this voluntary export restraint limited Japanese automobile imports to no more than 1.68 million vehicles per year.

Clearly, voluntary export restraints can be used to "head off" higher tariffs, more restrictive formal quotas, and other forms of trade retaliation.

5-84.
Hard
P.166

What are the principle political and economic arguments for government intervention into international trade? Please describe these arguments. In your opinion, which set of arguments are the most compelling?

Answer: *Political Arguments:* The political arguments cover a range of issues, including protecting jobs, protecting industries deemed important for national security, and retaliating against unfair foreign competition. In regard to protecting jobs, this is the most common political argument for government intervention. For example, the Japanese quotas on rice imports are aimed at protecting jobs in that country's agricultural sector. In terms of protecting industries deemed important for national security, countries sometimes argue that it is necessary to protect certain industries (like aerospace, steel, advanced electronics, etc.) because they are important for national security. Finally, in regard to retaliating against foreign competition, some people argue that governments should use the threat to intervene in trade policy as a bargaining tool to help open foreign markets and force trading partners to "play by the rules of the game."

Economic arguments: The economic arguments in favor of government intervention include the infant industry argument and strategic trade policy. The infant industry argument is most often used by developing countries. According to this argument, many developing countries have a potential comparative advantage in manufacturing, but new manufacturing industries there cannon initially compete with well-established industries in developed countries. To allow manufacturing to get a toehold, the argument is that governments should temporarily support new industries (with tariffs, import quotas, and subsidies) until they have grown strong enough to meet international standards. The strategy trade policy argument is more complex, but basically argues that governments should use their trade policies to help certain domestic firms dominate their global industries and gain first-mover advantages, and that it might pay government to intervene in an industry if it helps domestic firms overcome the barriers to entry created by foreign firms that have already reaped first-mover advantages.

The author of the textbook clearly believes that the economic arguments for government intervention into international trade are the most compelling. This question presents an interesting and engaging topic for classroom discussion.

-85.
Medium
.178

The World Trade Organization (WTO) was created by the recently completed Uruguay Round of the GATT negotiations. According to the textbook, has the WTO gotten off to a good start or a poor start? Do you believe that the WTO will be effective in the long run? Why or why not?

Answer: According to the textbook, the early life of the WTO suggests that its policing and enforcement mechanisms are having a positive effect. Countries are using the WTO to settle trade disputes, which represents an important vote of confidence in the organization's dispute resolution procedures. So far, the users of the system have included both developed and developing countries, which is also a promising development. In addition, some powerful developed countries, including the United States, have been willing to accept WTO ruling that have gone against them, which attests to the organization's legitimacy.

The second part of this question – do you believe that the WTO will be effective in the long run – is designed to provide a forum for classroom discussion and/or ask your students to "think" about the role of an organization like the WTO in settling international commerce disputes.

CHAPTER 6
FOREIGN DIRECT INVESTMENT

True/False Questions

6-1.
T.
Easy
P.194

Foreign direct investment occurs when a firm invests directly in new facilities to produce and/or market a product in a foreign country.

6-2.
F
Medium
P.194

The stock of foreign direct investment refers to the amount of FDI undertaken over a given period. The stock of foreign direct investment refers to the total accumulated value of foreign-owned assets at a given time.

6-3.
T
Easy
P.194

Once a firm undertakes FDI it becomes a multinational enterprise.

6-4.
F
Medium
P.195

There has been a rapid decrease in the total volume of FDI over the past 20 years.

6-5.
T
Medium
P.195

Over the past 20 years, there has been decline in the relative importance of the United States as a source for FDI, while several other countries, most notably Japan, have increased their share of total FDI outflows.

6-6.
F
Hard
P.196

The general shift toward democratic political institutions and free market economics has discouraged FDI.

6-7.
T
Medium
P.197

The United States is the largest source country for FDI.

6-8.
F
Medium
P.197

A home country is one that is on the receiving end of foreign direct investment. A host country is a source country for FDI.

6-9.
F
Medium
P.199

Although the world economy is experiencing rapid globalization, the grown of FDI by small and medium-sized firms has been fairly slow.

6-10.
T
Medium
P.201

Granting a foreign entity the right to produce and sell a firm's product in return for a royalty fee on every unit sold is referred to as licensing.

6-11.
T
Medium
P.202

In general, foreign direct investment is more expensive and risky than either licensing or exporting.

6-12.
T
Medium
P.202

FDI is expensive because a firm must establish production facilities in a foreign country or acquire a foreign enterprise.

6-13.
T
Easy
P.202

FDI is risky because of the problems associated with doing business in a different culture where the "rules of the game" may be very different.

6-14.
F
Medium
P.204

There is a branch of economic theory known as internationalization theory that seeks to explain why firms often prefer exporting to foreign direct investment.

6-15.
T
Hard
P.205

A firm will favor FDI over exporting as an entry strategy when transportation cost or trade barriers make exporting unattractive.

6-16.
F
Easy
P.207

The eclectic paradigm has been championed by the British economist John Ferguson.

6-17.
T
Medium
P.210

Many countries have adopted neither a radical policy nor a free market policy toward FDI, but instead a policy that can best be described as pragmatic nationalism.

6-18.
F
Hard
P.211

Three main benefits of inward FDI for a host country are the resource-transfer effect, the technology-transfer effect, and the balance-of-payments effect.

6-19.
T
Easy
P.213

A country's balance-of-payments track both its payments to and its receipts from other countries.

6-20.
T
Medium
P.214

Three main costs of inward FDI concern host countries. These are: the possible adverse effects of FDI on competition within the host nation, adverse effects on the balance of payments, and the perceived loss of national sovereignty and autonomy.

Multiple choice

6-21.
A
Easy
P.194

_____ occurs when a firm invests directly in new facilities to produce and/or market a product in a foreign country.
a. Foreign direct investment
b. Cross-boarder international investment
c. International capital investment
d. Reciprocal foreign investment

6-22.
C
Easy
P.194

FDI is an acronym that stands for:
a. Federation of Direct Investors
b. Federal Diversification Initiative
c. Foreign Direct Investment
d. Formal Direct Internationalization

6-23.
B
Medium
P.194

According to the U.S. Department of Commerce, _____ occurs whenever a U.S. citizen, organization, or affiliated group takes an interest of 10 percent or more in a foreign business entity.
a. cross-boarder international investment
b. foreign direct investment
c. reciprocal foreign investment
d. international capital investment

6-24.   A _____ is a company that conducts business in more than one country.
C
Easy   a. cross-cultural enterprise
P.194   b. synergistic enterprise
         c. multinational enterprise
         d. international conglomerate

6-25.   A company that conducts business in more than one country is referred to as a:
B
Easy   a. synergistic enterprise
P.194   b. multinational enterprise
         c. international conglomerate
         d. foreign direct investment

6-26.   The _____ of foreign direct investment refers to the amount of FDI
A   undertaken over a given period (normally a year). The _____ of foreign
Medium   direct investment refers to the total accumulated value of foreign-owned assets at
P.194   any time.
         a. flow, stock
         b. portfolio, current
         c. stock, flow
         d. stockpile, portfolio

6-27.   The _____ of foreign direct investment refers to the amount of FDI
C   undertaken over a given period (normally a year).
Easy   a. portfolio
P.194   b. stock
         c. flow
         d. register

6-28.   The _____ of foreign direct investment refers to the total accumulated value
D   of foreign-owned assets at a given time.
Easy   a. portfolio
p.194   b. flow
         c. register
         d. stock

6-29.
A
Medium
P.195

Which of the following two statements accurately reflects the trend in foreign direct investments over the past 20 years?

a. there has been a rapid increase in the total volume of FDI undertaken and there has been a change in the importance of various countries as sources for FDI

b. there has been a rapid increase in the total volume of FDI undertaken and the countries that have been instrumental as sources of FDI have remained the same

c. there has been a rapid decrease in the total volume of FDI undertaken and there has been a change in the importance of various countries as sources for FDI.

d. there has been a rapid decrease in the total volume of FDI undertaken and the countries that have been instrumental as sources of FDI have remained the same

6-30.
B
Hard
P.195

The average yearly outflow of FDI increased from about $25 billion in 1975 to a record _____ billion in 1995.

a. $65
b. $315
c. $565
d. $905

6-31.
C
Hard
P.195

Between 1984 and 1995 the total flow of FDI from all countries increased by more than _____, while world trade grew by 82 % and world output by 24 %

a. 75%
b. 300%
c. 700%
d. 1200%

6-32.
D
Medium
P.196

Which of the following factors has not contributed to the increase in FDI over the past several years?

a. dramatic shifts towards free market economies
b. business firms still fear protectionist pressures
c. the globalization of the world economy
d. dramatic shift towards socialist and communist political institutions

6-33.
B
Medium
P.196

Which of the following groups of countries collectively accounted for 58% of total FDI inflows among the top 20 recipient economies from 1985 to 1995.

a. China, Japan, France, and Australia
b. United States, United Kingdom, France, and China
c. China, United States, Canada, and Japan
d. Australia, South Africa, France, and China

6-34.
A
Easy
P.197

A _____ country is one that is on the receiving end of foreign direct investment.
a. host
b. global
c. home
d. residence

6-35.
A
Easy
P.197

A _____ country is a source country for FDI.
a. home
b. residence
c. host
d. global

6-36.
B
Medium
P.197

A _____ country is one that is on the receiving end of foreign direct investment. A _____ country is a source country for foreign direct investment.
a. residence, global
b. host, home
c. global, residence
d. home, host

6-37.
B
Medium
P.198

In terms of absolute dollar amounts, the _____ has been by far the largest recipient of FDI.
a. China
b. United States
c. Russia
d. Japan

6-38.
D
Medium
P.199

The popularity of the United Kingdom as a host country for FDI reflects the fact that many U.S. and Japanese firms see the United Kingdom as a good:
a. base for establishing operations to serve North America
b. base for establishing operations to serve Eastern Europe and the former republics of the Soviet Union
c. base for establishing operations to serve the Northern Pacific and Iceland
d. base for establishing operations to serve the European Union

6-39.
C
Hard
P.199

Which of the following countries has the highest level of FDI per capita?
a. Denmark
b. Japan
c. Singapore
d. United States

6-40.
D
Easy
P.201

A theory of foreign direct investment that combines two other perspectives into a single holistic explanation of FDI is referred to as the:
a. versatile model
b. internationalization model
c. globalization paradigm
d. eclectic paradigm

6-41.
A
Medium
P.201

A theory of _____ that combines two other perspectives in a single holistic explanation is referred to as the eclectic paradigm.
a. foreign direct investment
b. political economy
c. globalization
d. regional economic integration

6-42.
D
Easy
P.201

_____ involves producing goods at home and then shipping them to the receiving country for sale.
a. Foreign direct investment
b. Licensing
c. Franchising
d. Exporting

6-43.
B
Easy
P.201

The practice of producing goods at home and then shipping them to another country for sales is called:
a. franchising
b. exporting
c. licensing
d. foreign direct investment

6-44.
C
Easy
P.201

_____ involves granting a foreign entity the right to produce and sell the firm's product in return for a royalty fee on every unit sold.
a. Franchising
b. Exporting
c. Licensing
d. Foreign Direct Investment

6-45.
B
Easy
P.201

The practice of granting foreign entities the right to produce and sell your own product in return for a royalty fee on every unit sold is called:
a. exporting
b. licensing
c. foreign direct investment
d. importing

6-46.
A
Medium
P.201

_____ involves producing goods at home and then shipping them to the receiving country for sale. _____ involves granting a foreign entity the right to produce and sell the firm's product in return for a royalty fee on every unit sold.

a. Exporting, Licensing
b. Importing, Foreign direct investment
c. Licensing, Exporting
d. Foreign direct investment, Licensing

6-47.
A
Easy
P.204

Much foreign direct investment is undertaken as a response to actual or threatened:

a. trade barriers
b. economic sanctions
c. legal action
d. international appeals

6-48.
A
Medium
P.204

By placing tariffs on imported goods, governments can increase the cost of _____ relative to foreign direct investment and licensing.

a. exporting
b. strategic alliances
c. importing
d. franchising

6-49.
B
Easy
P.204

There is a branch of economic theory known as _____ that seeks to explain why firms often prefer foreign direct investment over licensing as a strategy for entering foreign markets.

a. home market theory
b. internationalization theory
c. host market theory
d. domestic preference theory

6-50.
A
Easy
P.204

_____ explains why firms prefer foreign direct investment over licensing when entering foreign markets.

a. Internationalization theory
b. Home market theory
c. Host market theory
d. Domestic preference theory

6-51.
B
Medium
P.204

Internationalization theory explains why firms prefer _____ over _____ when entering foreign markets.

a. foreign direct investment, exporting
b. foreign direct investment, licensing
c. exporting, foreign direct investment
d. exporting, licensing

6-52.
C
Medium
P.204

Internationalization theory explains why firms prefer foreign direct investment over _____ when entering foreign markets.
a. exporting
b. strategic alliances
c. licensing
d. importing

6-53.
B
Medium
P.204

Internationalization theory explains why firms prefer _____ over licensing when entering foreign markets.
a. joint ventures
b. foreign direct investment
c. exporting
d. importing

6-54.
C
Hard
P.204

According to internationalization theory, licensing has three major drawbacks as a strategy for exploiting foreign market opportunities. Each of the following is a drawback of licensing except:
a. licensing may result in a firm's giving away valuable technological know-how to a potential foreign competitor.
b. licensing does not give a firm the tight control over manufacturing, marketing, and strategy in a foreign country that may be required to maximize its profitability.
c. licensing helps a firm avoid making a direct foreign investment in a foreign country.
d. when a firm's competitive advantage is based not so much on its products as on the management, marketing, and manufacturing capabilities that produce those produces, licensing fails to capture those advantages

6-55.
C
Medium
P.204

A specific disadvantage of _____ is that it may result in a firm giving away valuable technological know-how to a potential foreign competitor.
a. importing
b. foreign direct investment
c. licensing
d. exporting

6-56.
B
Medium
P.204

A specific disadvantage of _____ is that it does not give a firm the tight control over manufacturing, marketing, and strategy in a foreign country that may be required to maximize its profitability.
a. foreign direct investment
b. licensing
c. importing
d. exporting

6-57.
A
Hard
P.205

High transportation costs and/or tariffs imposed on imports help explain why many firms prefer _____ over _____.
a. foreign direct investment or licensing, exporting
b. foreign direct investment or licensing, joint ventures
c. exporting, foreign direct investment or licensing
d. strategic alliances, foreign direct investment or licensing

6-58.
B
Hard
P.205

According to the textbook, a firm will favor FDI over exporting as an entry strategy when:
a. interest rates or government policy make exporting unattractive
b. cultural barriers or interest rates make exporting unattractive
c. transporting costs or trade barriers make exporting unattractive
d. cultural barriers or government policy make exporting unattractive

6-59.
A
Hard
P.205

According to the textbook, a firm will favor _____ over _____ when transportation costs or trade barriers make exporting unattractive.
a. foreign direct investment, exporting
b. foreign direct investment, importing
c. exporting, foreign direct investment
d. licensing, foreign direct investment

6-60.
C
Hard
P.205

According to out textbook, a firm will favor _____ over _____ when it wishes to maintain control over its technological know-how, or over its operations and business strategy.
a. foreign direct investment, exporting
b. licensing, foreign direct investment
c. foreign direct investment, licensing
d. exporting, foreign direct investment

6-61.
A
Medium
P.206

One theory used to explain foreign direct investment patterns is based on the idea that firms follow their domestic competitors overseas. First expounded by _____, this theory has been developed with regard to oligopolistic industries.
a. F.T. Knickerbocker
b. William P. Smith
c. Michael Porter
d. Eli Heckscher

6-62.
A
Easy
P.206

One theory used to explain foreign direct investment patterns is based on the idea that firms follow their domestic competitors overseas. First expounded by F.T. Knickerbocker, this theory has been developed with regard to _____ .
a. oligopolistic industries
b. cartels
c. monopolistic industries
d. syndicated industries

6-63.
C
Easy
P.206

A(n) _____ is an industry composed of a limited number of large firms (i.e. an industry in which four firms control 80 percent of a domestic market)
a. syndicate
b. cartel
c. oligopoly
d. monopoly

6-64.
D
Easy
P.206

An industry composed of a limited number of large firms (i.e. in which four firms control 80 percent of the domestic market), is referred to as a(n):
a. syndicate
b. monopoly
c. cartel
d. oligopoly

6-65.
A
Medium
P.206

Several studies of U.S. enterprises suggest that firms based in _____ industries tend to imitate each other's foreign direct investment patterns.
a. oliogopolistic
b. monopolistic
c. syndicated
d. munificent

6-66.
A
Medium
P.207

The eclectic paradigm has been championed by the British economist _____.
a. John Dunning
b. Edward Luty
c. William Spencer
d. Andrew Ferguson

6-67.
B
Easy
P.207

The _____ has been championed by British economist John Dunning.
a. flexible paradigm
b. eclectic paradigm
c. synergistic model
d. versatile paradigm

6-68.
D
Medium
P.207

Advantages that arise from using resource endowments or assets that are tied to a particular location and that a firm finds valuable to combine with its own unique assets are referred to as:
a. geographic specific preferences
b. unique geographic advantages
c. locale-specific preferences
d. location-specific advantages

6-69.
A
Medium
P.207

By _____, Dunning means the advantages that arise from utilizing resource endowments or assets that are tied to a particular foreign location and that a firm finds valuable to combine with its own unique assets.

a. location-specific advantages
b. locale-specific preferences
c. unique geographic advantages
d. geographic specific preferences

6-70.
A
Easy
P.207

According to _____, firms undertake FDI to exploit resource endowments or assets that are location specific.

a. Dunning
b. Vernon
c. Porter
d. Smith

6-71.
D
Medium
P.208

Knowledge spillovers that occur when companies in the same industry locate in the same area are referred to as:

a. inward overflows
b. cognitive overflows
c. concentric overflows
d. externalities

6-72.
B
Medium
P.209

The _____ theory argues that international production should be distributed among countries according to the theory of comparative advantage.

a. host-country
b. free-trade
c. home-country
d. foreign direct investment

6-73.
A
Medium
P.211

Three main benefits of inward FDI for a host country are the:

a. the resource-transfer effect, the employment effect, and the balance-of-payments effect
b. the capital-transfer effect, the technology effect, and the currency exchange effect
c. the cultural awareness effect, the technology effect, and the balance-of-payments effect
d. the resource-transfer effect, the technology effect, and the currency exchange effect

6-74.
C
Medium
P.211

The three main benefits of inward FDI for a host country are the resource-transfer effect, the employment effect, and the:
a. currency exchange effect
b. economic impact effect
c. balance-of-payments effect
d. technology-transfer effect

6-75.
D
Medium
P.211

The three main benefits of inward FDI for a host country are the employment effect, the balance-of-payments effect, and the:
a. currency exchange effect
b. economic impact effect
c. technology-transfer effect
d. resource-transfer effect

6-76.
D
Easy
P.213

A country's _____ track both its payments to and its receipts from other countries.
a. pulses and minuses account
b. debits and credits account
c. checks and balances account
d. balance-of-payments account

6-77.
A
Medium
P.213

The record of a country's export and import of goods and services is referred to as its:
a. current account
b. foreign account
c. internal account
d. tariff account

6-78.
D
Hard
P.214

Three main costs of inward FDI concern host countries. These are:
a. the employment effect, the perceived loss of national sovereignty and autonomy, and the resource transfer effect
b. the possible adverse effects of FDI on competition with the host country, the resource transfer effect, and the perceived loss of national sovereignty and autonomy
c. the resource transfer effect, the employment effect, and the possible adverse effects of FDI on competition within the host country
d. the possible adverse effects of FDI on competition within the host country, adverse effects on the balance of payments, and the perceived loss of national sovereignty and autonomy

6-79.
C
Medium
P.214

Three main costs of inward FDI concern host countries: the possible adverse effects of FDI on competition within the host nation, adverse effects on the balance of payments, and _____.

a. the resource transfer effect.
b. the technology transfer effect
c. the perceived loss of national sovereignty and autonomy
d. the employment effect

6-80.
C
Medium
P.214

Three main costs of inward FDI concern host countries: the possible adverse effects of FDI on competition within a host nation, the perceived loss of national sovereignty and autonomy, and _____.

a. the resource transfer effect
b. the technology transfer effect
c. the adverse effects on the balance of payments
d. the employment effect

Essay Questions

6-81.
Easy
P.194

What is meant by the term Foreign Direct Investment? Describe the difference between the flow of foreign direct investment and the stock of foreign direct investment.

Answer: Foreign direct investment (FDI) occurs when a firm invests directly in new facilities to produce and/or market a product in a foreign country. To be more precise, the U.S. Department of Commerce describes FDI as follows: FDI occurs whenever a U.S. citizen, organization, or affiliated group takes an interest of 10 percent or more in a foreign business entity.

The flow of foreign direct investment refers to the amount of FDI undertaken over a given period (normally a year). The stock of foreign direct investment refers to the total accumulated value of foreign-owned assets at a given time.

6-82.
Medium
P.199

Is foreign direct investment confined primarily to large firms, or are medium-sized and small firms also involved?

Answer: Most people tend to think of large firms (like General Motors, Mobile, an IBM) when considering the involvement of U.S. firms in FDI. In practice, however the globalization of world markets has been accompanied in large part by the rapi growth in FDI by small and medium-sized firms. FDI by such firms has been driven by a need to stay close to major customers that have gone abroad. Although hard statistics detailing the growth of smaller multinationals are hard to come by, there are many anecdotal examples of the involvement of medium-size and small firms in FDI.

6-83.
Hard
P.207

Describe what is meant by the eclectic paradigm? Who is its principle champion? Does this paradigm make sense as a rationale for FDI?

Answer: The principle champion of the eclectic paradigm is British economist John Dunning. Dunning argues that in addition to other factors, location-specific advantages are also of considerable importance in explaining both the rationale for and the direction of foreign direct investment. By location-specific advantages, Dunning means the advantages that arise from utilizing resource endowments or assets that are tied to a particular foreign location and that a firm finds valuable to combine with its own unique assets. Dunning accepts the arguments of internalization theory, that it is difficult for a firm to license its own unique capabilities and know-how. Therefore, he argues that combining location-specific assets or resource endowments and the firm's own unique capabilities often requires FDI in production facilities.

This paradigm does make sense as a rationale for FDI. For example, as described in the text, an obvious example of Dunning's arguments is natural resources, such as oil and other minerals, which are specific to certain locations. Dunning suggests that to exploit such foreign resources a firm must undertake FDI. Many U.S. oil companies have done this. They have had to invest in refineries in the areas of the world where the oil is located in order to combine their technological and managerial capabilities with this valuable location-specific resources. Another example is California's Silicon Valley, where a substantial portion of the world's R&D in terms of computer technology is taking place. It might make sense for a foreign producer of computer chips to locate their R&D facility in the Silicon Valley to be near this community of computer chip researchers and manufacturers.

6-84.
Medium
P.211

What are the benefits of inward FDI (i.e. FDI coming into a country from foreign sources) for the host country? Are these benefits compelling?

Answer: The three main benefits of FDI for the host country are the resources-transfer effect, the employment effect, and the balance-of-payments effect. These potential benefits are explained in more detail below.

The Resource-Transfer Effect: FDI can make a positive contribution to a host country by supplying capital, technology, and management resources that would otherwise not be available. The provision of these skills by a multinational company (through FDI) may boost s country's intellectual capital and economic growth rate.

The Employment Effects: The beneficial employment effects claimed for FDI is that foreign direct investment brings jobs to a host country that would otherwise not be created there. For instance, the Japanese auto factories in the United States have provided thousands of jobs for U.S. workers.

221

The Balance-of-Payment Effects: The effect of FDI on a country's balance-of-payments account in an important policy issue for most host governments. Governments typically like to see a balance-of-payments surplus rather than a deficit. There are two ways that FDI can help a host country experience a balance-of-payments surplus. First, if the FDI is a substitute for imports of goods or services, it can improve a country's balance of payments. For example, the Japanese auto plants in the U.S. produce cars that act as "substitutes" for Japanese imports. Second, FDI may result in an increase in exports. A portion of the goods and services that are produced as a result of FDI may be exported to other countries.

These arguments are compelling, but must be weighed against the costs of FDI. The arguments against FDI include: the possible adverse effects of FDI on competition within the host nation, adverse effects on the balance-of-payments, and the perceived loss of national sovereignty and autonomy.

6-85.
Medium
P.222

How does a potential host government's attitude toward FDI affect a company's willingness to engage in FDI in that country? Should a host government's attitude toward FDI be a major consideration when making a FDI decision? Why?

Answer: A host government's attitude toward FDI should be an important variable in making decisions about where to locate foreign production facilities and where to make a FDI. According to the author of the textbook, other things being equal, investing in countries that have permissive policies toward FDI is clearly preferable to investing in countries that resist FDI.

However, this issue is not straightforward. Many countries have a rather businesslike stance toward FDI. In such cases, a firm considering FDI usually must negotiate the specific terms of the investment with the host government. Such negotiations typically center on two issues. First, if the host country is trying to attract FDI, the negotiations will typically focus on the kind of incentives the host government is prepared to offer the foreign firm and what the firm will commit in exchange. On the other hand, if the host government is leery of FDI, the central issue is likely to be the concessions the firm will make to be allowed to go forward with its project.

CHAPTER 7
REGIONAL ECONOMIC INTEGRATION

True/False Questions

7-1.
T.
Easy
P.230

One notable trend in the global economy in recent years has been the accelerated movement toward regional economic integration.

7-2.
F
Medium
P.230

By entering into regional agreements, groups of countries aim to increase trade barriers more rapidly than can be achieved under the auspices of the WTO.

7-3.
T
Medium
P.232

As predicted by the theory of comparative advantage, there should be a substantial net gain from regional free trade agreements.

7-4.
T
Easy
P.232

In a free trade area all barriers to the trade of goods and services among member countries are removed.

7-5.
F
Medium
P.232

In a free trade area, the member nations collectively determine their trade policies with regard to nonmembers.

7-6.
T
Medium
P.233

A customs union eliminates trade barriers between member countries and adopts a common external trade policy.

7-7.
F
Medium
P.234

A full common market requires a common currency, harmonization of the member countries' tax rates, and a common monetary and fiscal policy.

7-8.
T
Medium
P.234

In a theoretically ideal common market, labor and capital are free to move, as there are no restrictions on immigration, emigration, or cross-border flows of capital between markets.

7-9.
F
Medium
P.234

Although the European Union is the best known, a number of successful common markets exist throughout the world.

7-10.
T
Medium
P.234

An economic union involves the free flow of products and factors of production between members and the adoption of a common external trade policy.

7-11.
F
Easy
P.234

Most attempts to achieve regional economic integration have been successful.

7-12.
F
Easy
P.235

Because international institutions such as the WTO have been moving the world toward a free trade regime, success has been almost total.

7-13.
T
Medium
P.235

Regional economic integration can be seen as an attempt to achieve additional gains from the free flow of trade and investment between countries beyond those attainable under international agreements such as the WTO.

7-14.
F
Hard
P.236

Trade diversion occurs when high-cost domestic producers are replaced by low-cost producers within the free trade area.

7-15.
T
Easy
P.237

A regional free trade agreement will benefit the world only if the amount of trade it creates exceeds the amount it diverts.

7-16.
T
Medium
P.237

There are now two trade blocs in Europe: the European Union and the European Free Trade Association.

7-17.
F
Hard
P.241

To signify the importance of the Single European Act, the European Union decided to change its name to the European Community once the act took effect.

7-18.
T
Medium
P.247

Movement of production from the United States to Mexico (made more attractive by the passage of NAFTA) is most likely to occur in low-skilled, labor-intensive manufacturing industries where Mexico might have a comparative advantage,

7-19.
T
Easy
P.248

According to the textbook, the first year after NAFTA turned out to be a positive experience for all three member nations.

7-20.
F
Hard
P.253

The basic objectives of ASEAN are to foster freer trade between member countries and to achieve some cooperation in their industrial policies. So far, progress towards these objectives has been excellent.

Multiple Choice

7-21.
A
Easy
P.230

An agreement between countries in a geographic region to reduce tariff and nontariff barriers to the free flow of goods, services, and factors of production between each other is referred to as:
a. regional economic integration
b. cross-cultural economic integration
c. geographic economic-political integration
d. cross-cultural economic-political integration

7-22.
B
Easy
P.230

By _____ we mean agreements between groups of countries in a geographic region to reduce, and ultimately remove, tariff and nontariff barriers to the free flow of goods, services, and factors of production between each other.
a. geographic economic-political integration
b. regional economic integration
c. cross-cultural economic integration
d. cross-cultural economic-political integration

7-23.
C
Hard
P.230

According to the World Trade Organization, between 1990 and 1996 the number of regional trade agreements increased from _____.
a. 5 to 42
b. 25 to 36
c. 38 to 80
d. 65 to 112

7-24.
D
Medium
P.230

Nowhere has the movement toward regional economic integration been more successful than in _____.

a. Africa
b. South America
c. Asia
d. Europe

7-25.
D
Medium
P.231

Which of the following statement is not accurate in regard to the European Union?

a. members of the European Union have plans to establish a single currency
b. members of the European Union are moving toward a closer political union
c. members of the European Union are discussing enlargement of the EU from the current 15 countries to include another 15 Eastern European states
d. members of the European Union are discussing a common language

7-26.
A
Easy
P.231

The following three countries recently implemented the North American Free Trade Agreement (NAFTA)

a. United States, Canada, and Mexico
b. United States, Mexico, and Brazil
c. Chile, Brazil, and Mexico
d. United States, Argentina, and Mexico

7-27.
C
Hard
P.231

The free trade area known as MERCOSUR consists of the following four countries.

a. Mexico, Columbia, Paraguay, and Uruguay
b. Chile, Brazil, Uruguay, and Columbia
c. Argentina, Brazil, Paraguay, and Uruguay
d. Chile, Mexico, Columbia, and Paraguay

7-28.
A
Medium
P.232

As predicted by the theory of comparative advantage, there should be a _____ from regional trade agreements.

a. substantial net gain
b. minor net gain
c. no economic impact
d. substantial net loss

7-29.
C
Hard
P.232

Which of the following selections accurately depicts the levels of economic integration from least integrated to most integrated?

a. common market, economic union, full political union, free trade area, and customs union
b. common market, economic union, full political union, free trade area, and customs union
c. free trade area, customs union, common market, economic union, and full political union
d. full political union, free trade area, common market, customs union, and economic union

7-30.
A
Medium
P.232

Which of the following selections accurately depicts the levels of economic integration from most integrated to least integration?

a. full political union, economic union, common market, customs union, and free trade area
b. free trade area, common market, customs union, full political union, and economic union
c. common market, economic union, full political union, customs union, and free trade area
d. economic union, common market, full political union, free trade area, and customs union

7-31.
C
Medium
P.232

The most enduring free trade area in the world is the:

a. Asian Free Trade Association
b. MERCOSUR
c. European Free Trade Association
d. North American Trade Association

7-32.
B
Hard
P.232

The European Free Trade Association currently includes the following three countries:

a. Ireland, Iceland, and Denmark
b. Norway, Iceland, and Switzerland
c. Finland, Great Britain, and Denmark
d. Sweden, Norway, and Finland

7-33.
D
Easy
P.232

In a theoretically ideal _____, no discriminatory tariffs, quotas, subsidies, or administrative impediments are allowed to distort trade between member nations. Each country, however, is allowed to determine its own trade policies with regard to nonmembers.

a. common market
b. economic union
c. political union
d. free trade area

7-34.
D
Medium
P.233

A _____ eliminates trade barriers between member countries and adopts a common external trade policy.

a. free trade area
b. global union
c. tariff union
d. customs union

7-35.
C
Hard
P.233

The Andean Pact is a _____.

a. political union
b. free trade area
c. customs union
d. economic union

7-36.
D
Easy
P.233

NAFTA stands for:

a. North Asian Free Trade Agreement
b. North African Free Trade Association
c. North Atlantic Free Trade Agreement
d. North American Free Trade Association

7-37.
B
Medium
P.234

Like a customs union, the theoretically ideal _____ has no barriers to trade between member countries and a common external trade policy.

a. free trade area
b. common market
c. tariff union
d. external market

7-38.
C
Medium
P.234

A common market includes all of the following characteristics except:

a. factors of production are allowed to move freely between members
b. there are no restrictions on immigration between members
c. full economic integration
d. there are no restrictions on the cross-border flow of capital between members

7-39.
A
Medium
P.234

Which of the following is not an attribute of a common market?

a. harmonization of the member countries' tax rates
b. there are no restrictions on the cross-border flow of capital between member nations
c. there are no restrictions on immigration between member nations
d. factors of production are allowed to move freely between member nations

7-40.
A
Medium
P.234

The European Union is currently a _____.

a. common market
b. customs union
c. economic union
d. political union

Like the common market, an _____ involves the free flow of products and factors of production between members and the adoption of a common external trade policy.
a. free trade area
b. economic union
c. global union
d. customs union

The _____, which is playing an every more important role in the EU, has been directly elected by citizens of the EU countries since the late 1970s.
a. North Atlantic Parliament
b. North Atlantic Trade Commission
c. European Parliament
d. European Trade Commission

Because many governments have accepted part or all of the case for intervention, unrestricted free trade and FDI have proved to be:
a. only an ideal
b. a reality
c. a goal which should be realized soon
d. a goal that there is no rationale for

The two main reasons that have made economic integration difficult to achieve are cost and:
a. concerns over national sovereignty
b. concerns over immigration and emigration
c. concerns over the safety of travel from one nation to another
d. concerns over economic stability

The two main reasons that have made economic integration difficult to achieve are concerns over economic integration and:
a. concerns over costs
b. concerns over economic stability
c. concerns over immigration and emigration
d. concerns over the safety of travel from one nation to another

_____ occurs when high-cost domestic producers are replaced by low-cost producers within the free trade area.
a. Trade alteration
b. Trade qualification
c. Trade diversion
d. Trade creation

7-47.
C
Medium
P.236

The phenomenon that occurs when high-cost domestic producers are replaced by low-cost producers within the free trade are is called:
a. trade alteration
b. trade qualification
c. trade creation
d. trade diversion

7-48.
A
Medium
P.237

_____ occurs when lower-cost external suppliers are replaced by higher-cost suppliers within the free trade area.
a. Trade diversion
b. Trade qualification
c. Trade synergy
d. Trade creation

7-49.
A
Medium
P.237

The phenomenon that occurs when lower-cost external suppliers are replaced by higher-cost suppliers within the free trade area is called:
a. trade diversion
b. trade creation
c. trade synergy
d. trade qualification

7-50.
C
Hard
P.237

_____ occurs when high-cost domestic producers are replaced by low-cost producers. _____ occurs when lower-cost external suppliers are replaced by higher-cost suppliers within the free trade area.
a. Trade synergy, Trade qualification
b. Trade qualification, Trade synergy
c. Trade creation, Trade diversion
d. Trade diversion, Trade creation

7-51.
A
Hard
P.237

There are now two trade blocs in Europe. These are the:
a. European Union and the European Free Trade Association
b. European Federation and the North Atlantic Trade Block
c. North Atlantic Trade Block and the European Union
d. European Federation and the European Trade Association

7-52.
B
Medium
P.237

There are now two trade blocs in Europe. The European Union and the _____.
a. North Atlantic Federation
b. European Free Trade Association
c. North Atlantic Trade Block
d. European Federation

230

7-53.
D
Medium
P.237

There are now two trade blocs in Europe. The European Free Trade Association and the _____.
a. North Atlantic Federation
b. European Federation
c. North Atlantic Trade Block
d. European Union

7-54.
B
Hard
P.238

The original forerunner of the EU, the _____ was formed in 1951 by Belgium, France, West Germany, Italy, Luxembourg, and the Netherlands.
a. European Union
b. European Coal and Steel Community
c. European Agricultural and Energy Union
d. European Textiles and Agricultural Community

7-55.
C
Hard
P.238

The European Coal and Steel Community was the original forerunner of the _____.
a. European Federation
b. North Atlantic Treaty Organization
c. European Union
d. North Atlantic Trade Area

7-56.
A
Medium
P.238

With the signing of the Treaty of Rome in 1957, the _____ was established.
a. European Community (or Union)
b. European Free Trade Association
c. European Coal and Steel Community
d. European Textiles and Coal Community

7-57.
C
Hard
P.238

How many countries are members of the European Union?
a. 4
b. 9
c. 15
d. 36

7-58.
D
Easy
P.238

The acronym EC stands for:
a. Eastward Community
b. Eastern Europe Community
c. Eastern Conference
d. European Community

7-59.
B
Easy
P.238

The acronym EU stands for:
a. Eastern Europe Union
b. European Union
c. Eastward Union
d. Eastern Union

7-60.
B
Medium
P.240

The purpose of the _____ was to have a single market in place by December 31, 1992.

a. North Atlantic Sovereignty Act
b. Single European Act
c. European Primacy Act
e. European Sovereignty Act

7-61.
A
Medium
P.240

The purpose of the Single European Act was to:

a. have a single market in place by December 31, 1992
b. establish a common currency among European Union Nations
c. establish common tax laws among European Union Nations
d. have a single government in place by December 31, 1992

7-62.
C
Medium
P.241

To signify the importance of the _____, the European Community decided to change its name to the European Union once the act took effect.

a. European Unification Act
b. European Common Commerce Act
c. Single European Act
d. European Free Trade Act

7-63.
D
Medium
P.241

To signify the importance of the Single European Act, the _____ decided to change its name to the European Union once the act took effect.

a. North Atlantic Community
b. North Atlantic Trade Federation
c. European Federation
d. European Community

7-64.
D
Medium
P.245

In 1988 the governments of the United States and Canada agreed to enter in a _____, which went into effect on January 1, 1989.

a. economic union
b. common market
c. political union
d. free trade agreement

7-65.
A
Easy
P.246

The agreement that is designed to abolish within 10 years tariffs on 99 percent of the goods traded between Mexico, Canada, and the United states is called the:

a. North American Free Trade Agreement
b. American Federation
c. American Community
d. North Atlantic Trade Federation

7-66.
C
Medium
P.247

According to the textbook, one likely short-term effect of NAFTA will be that many U.S. and Canadian firms will move some production to Mexico to take advantage of:
a. cheaper transportation costs
b. lower interest rates
c. lower labor costs
d. a higher skilled labor force

7-67.
B
Medium
P.247

The principle argument of those that opposed NAFTA centered around the feat that ratification would result in:
a. higher interest rates in the U.S.
b. many U.S. jobs transferred to Mexico
c. the move towards a common currency for NAFTA member nations
d. retaliation from the European Union

7-68.
A
Medium
P.251

The _____ was formed in 1969 when Bolivia, Chile, Ecuador, Columbia, and Peru signed the Cartagena Agreement.
a. Andean Group
b. Bolivian Group
c. NW South America Group
d. South American Federation of Independent States

7-69.
C
Hard
P.251

The Andean Group was formed in 1969 when _____ signed the Cartagena Agreement.
a. Bolivia, Chile, Argentina, French Guiana, and Venezuela
b. Brazil, Venezuela, Argentina, and Peru
c. Bolivia, Chile, Ecuador, Colombia, and Peru
d. Argentina, Chile, Ecuador, Columbia, and Guyana

7-70.
D
Hard
P.251

The initial principles of The Andean Group included all of the following except:
a. internal tariff reduction program
b. common external tariff
c. transportation policy
d. common currency among member nations

7-71.
C
Medium
P.251

MERCOSUR originated in 1988 as a free trade pact between _____.
a. Mexico and Brazil
b. Peru and Brazil
c. Brazil and Argentina
d. Venezuela and Peru

7-72.
D
Medium
P.251

MERCOSUR originated in 1988 as a free trade pact between Brazil and _____.

a. Mexico
b. Peru
c. Columbia
d. Argentina

7-73.
A
Medium
P.251

MERCOSUR originated in 1988 as a free trade pact between Argentina and _____.

a. Brazil
b. Mexico
c. Peru
d. Columbia

7-74.
B
Hard
P.253

Formed in 1967, ASEAN currently includes:

a. Indonesia, Hong Kong, Singapore, Taiwan, Thailand, Malaysia, and Japan
b. Brunei, Indonesia, Malaysia, Philippines, Singapore, Thailand, and Vietnam
c. Japan, Taiwan, Hong Kong, Singapore, China, Thailand, and Malaysia
d. Brunei, Indonesia, Hong Kong, Thailand, Cambodia, Malaysia, and Japan

7-75.
B
Hard
P.253

The most recent country to become a member of ASEAN is:

a. China
b. Vietnam
c. Brunei
d. Japan

7-76.
B
Medium
P.254

The United States, Japan, and China are among 18 members of an trade organization referred to as:

a. AAFTC (American Asian Free Trade Congress)
b. APEC (Asia Pacific Economic Cooperation)
c. USAEU (United States Asian Economic Union)
d. ANAEPC (Asian-North American Economic and Political Coop)

7-77.
B
Hard
P.254

APEC currently has _____ including such economic powerhouses as the United States, Japan, and China.

a. 6
b. 18
c. 25
d. 44

7-78.   According to the textbook, currently the most significant developments in regional
C   economic integration are taking place in _____.
Medium   a. Europe and South America
P.255   b. Asia and North America
             c. Europe and North America
             d. Asia and South America

7-79.   According to the textbook, currently the most significant developments in regional
A   economic integration are taking place in Europe and:
Medium   a. North America
P.255   b. South America
             c. Asia
             d. The Middle East

7-80.   The term "Fortress Europe" refers to:
B   a. the military prowess of European nations
Medium   b. the perception that the European Union is designed to protect the European
P.255   continent from the import of foreign produced goods
             c. the unwillingness of European nations to consider forming trade relationships
             d. the economic stability of the European continent

Essay Questions

7-81.   Describe the concept of regional economic integration. Do you believe that
Easy   regional economic integration is a good thing? Explain your answer.
P.230

         Answer: Regional economic integration refers to agreements made by groups of
         countries in geographic regions to reduce, and ultimately remove, tariff and
         nontariff barriers to the free flow of goods, services, and factors of production
         between each other. The North American Free Trade Agreement, which is an
         agreement between the United States, Mexico, and Canada to reduce and
         eliminate tariffs between the three countries, is an example of regional economic
         integration.

         Ask your students to comment on whether regional economic integration is a good
         thing. In general, the observers of international trade believe that regional
         economic integration is a positive development. Countries that have participated
         in regional trade agreements have typically experienced nontrival gains in trade
         from other member countries. In addition, as predicted by the theory of
         comparative advantage (explained in Chapter 4), there should be a substantial net
         gain from regional trade agreements.

7-82.
Hard
P.232

Please briefly explain the following forms of economic integration: free trade area, customs union, common market, economic union, and full political union. Provide an example of each form of economic integration.

Answer: *Free Trade Area*: In a free trade area, all barriers to the trade of goods and services among member countries are removed. In a theoretically ideal free trade area, no discriminatory tariffs, quotas, subsidies, or administrative impediments are allowed to distort trade between member nations. Each country, however, is allowed to determine its own trade policies with regard to nonmembers. The European Free Trade Association, involving Norway, Iceland, and Switzerland, is an example of a free trade area.

Customs Union: A customs union eliminates trade barriers between member countries and adopts a common external policy. The Andean Pack, which involves Bolivia, Columbia, Ecuador, and Peru, is an example of a customs union.

Common Market: A common market eliminates trade barriers between member countries and adopts a common external policy. In addition, factors of production are also allowed to move freely between member countries. Thus, labor and capital are free to move, as there are no restrictions on immigration, emigration, or cross-border flows of capital between members. Hence, a much closer union is envisaged in a common market than a customs union. The European Union is currently a common market, although its goal is full economic union.

Economic Union: An economic union eliminates trade barriers between members nations, adopts a common external policy, and permits factors of production to move freely between member countries. In addition, a full economic union requires a common currency, harmonization of the member countries' tax rates, and a common monetary and fiscal policy. There are no true economic unions in the world today.

Political Union: A political union is the bringing together of two or more previously separate countries into essentially one country. As a result, all of the components of an economic union would apply, in addition to the political coupling of the countries involved. The United States is an example of a political union, in which previously separate "states" combined into one country. If Puerto Rico ever becomes the 51st state, the political coupling of the present United States with Puerto Rico would be an example of a political union

7-83.
Medium
P.236

What are the primary impediments to integration? Are these impediments difficult to overcome? Explain your answer.

Answer: Even though there may be a clear rationale for economic integration, there are two impediments that make integration difficult in many cases. First, although economic integration typically benefits the majority of the people in a country, certain groups may lose. For example, according to the author of the textbook, as a result of the 1994 establishment of NAFTA some Canadian and U.S. workers in such industries as textiles, which employ low-cost, low-skilled labor, will lose their jobs as Canadian and U.S. firms move their production to Mexico. As a result, even though the population as a whole may gain as a result of an agreement like NAFTA, these individuals may lose. If these individuals have enough political clout, they may be able to stop a NAFTA type agreement.

The second impediment to integration arises from concerns over national sovereignty. For example, for a full economic union to become a reality, the countries involved have to establish a common currency. The citizens of many countries view their currencies as symbols of national sovereignty and pride. As a result, the desire to maintain a sovereign currency may prohibit a country from joining an economic union. Similar examples prevent countries from entering into all of the forms of regional integration.

In many cases, these impediments to integration are very difficult to overcome. For instance, it is very easy to sympathize with someone who might lose their job as the result of a trade agreement. Similarly, many people become very intransigent on issues involving national sovereignty, which make some forms of regional integration almost impossible to achieve.

7-84.
Medium
P.243

What is meant by the term "Fortress Europe?" Is this term fair, or is it an exaggeration?

Answer: There are presently two trade blocks in Europe: the European Union (EU) and the European Free Trade Association (EFTA). The EFTA has three members, including Norway, Iceland, and Switzerland. The European Union has 15 members, with more countries trying to get in. The fear on the part of non-European nations is that as regional integration in Europe continues to spread and deepen, the European countries will become more dependent upon one another and more protectionist in terms of their trade practices with other parts of the world. Thus, the term "Fortress Europe."

It is too early to tell whether this characterization is fair or not. What is particularly worrisome to Asia and the West, is that the EU, in particular, might increase external protection as weaker members attempt to offset their loss of protection against other EU countries by arguing for limitations on outside competition.

7-85.
Medium
P.245

Describe the arguments for and against the North American Free Trade Agreement (NAFTA). In your opinion, is the recent ratification of NAFTA a positive development or a negative development for the citizens of the countries involved?

Answer: This question is designed to provide a forum for classroom discussion and/or to ask students' to think about the pluses and minuses of the NAFTA. In general, the proponents of NAFTA have argued that NAFTA should be seen as an opportunity to create an enlarged and more efficient productive based for the entire North American region. The proponents concede that some lower-income jobs will move from the United States and Canada to Mexico. However, they argue that in the end, this will benefit all three countries involved because the movement of jobs to Mexico will create employment and economic growth, and as Mexico's economy grows the demand for U.S. and Canadian products in Mexico will increase. In addition, the international competitiveness of U.S. and Canadian firms that move production to Mexico to take advantage of lower labor costs will be enhanced, enabling them to better compete against Asian and European rivals.

Those that oppose NAFTA claim that U.S. and Canadian citizens will lose their jobs in alarming numbers as low-income positions are moved to Mexico to take advantage of lower wage rates. To date, the movement of jobs from the U.S. and Canada has not reached the numbers that NAFTA's critics envisioned. Environmentalists have also voiced concerns about NAFTA. Because Mexico has more lenient environmental protection laws than either the U.S. or Canada, there is a concern that U.S. and Canadian firms will relocate to Mexico to avoid the cost of protecting the environment. Finally, there is continued opposition in Mexico to NAFTA from those who fear a loss of national sovereignty. Mexican critics fear that NAFTA will allow their country to be dominated by U.S. and Canadian multinationals, and use Mexico as a low-cost assembly site, while keeping their higher-paying jobs in their own countries.

CHAPTER 8
THE FOREIGN EXCHANGE MARKET

True/False Questions

8-1.
T
Easy
P.264

Without the foreign market exchange, international trade and international investment on the scale that we see today would be impossible.

8-2.
T
Easy
P.264

An exchange rate is simply the rate at which one currency is converted into another.

8-3.
F
P.266

In international trade, the risk of not getting paid for a product that is exported from one country to another is referred to foreign exchange risk.

8-4.
F
Hard
P.267

Currency speculation typically involves the short-term movement of funds from one currency to another in the hopes of profiting from shifts in interest rates.

8-5.
F
Medium
P.268

When a U.S. tourist in Edinburgh goes to a bank to convert her dollars in pounds, the exchange rate is the forward exchange rate.

8-6.
T
Medium
P.269

Spot exchange rates change daily as determined by the relative demand and supply for difference currencies.

8-7.
T
Easy
P.270

A forward exchange occurs when two parties agree to exchange currency and execute the deal at some specific date in the future.

8-8.
F
Medium
P.271

In recent years the foreign exchange market has been in decline, reflecting a general slowdown in the volume of cross-border trade and investment.

8-9.
F
Medium
P.272

Arbitrage is the process of buying a currency high and selling it low.

8-10.
T
Easy
P.273

At the basic level, exchange rates are determined by the demand and supply of one currency relative to the demand and supply for another.

8-11.
T
P.273

The law of one price states that identical products sold in different countries must sell for the same price when their price is expressed in the same currency in competitive markets free of transportation costs and barriers to trade.

8-12.
F
Easy
P.274

An efficient market has significant impediments to the free flow of goods and services.

8-13.
T
Hard
P.279

According to the International Fisher Effect, for any two countries, the spot exchange rate should change in an equal amount but in the opposite direction to the difference in the nominal interest rates between the two countries.

8-14.
F
Medium
P.282

Technical analysis draws on economic theory to construct sophisticated econometric models for predicting exchange rate movements.

8-15.
T
Medium
P.282

Fundamental analysis uses price and volume data to determine past trends, which are expected to continue into the future.

8-16.
F
Medium
P.281

An efficient market in one in which prices do not reflect all available information.

8-17.
T
Medium
P.283

A currency is said to be externally convertible when only nonresidents may convert it into foreign currency without limitations.

8-18.
F
Medium
P.283

A country's currency is said to be freely convertible when neither residents nor nonresidents are allowed to convert it into a foreign currency.

8-19.
F
Medium
P.283

The majority of the countries in the world have currency that is freely convertible.

8-20.
T
Easy
P.284

Countertrade refers to a range of barterlike agreements by which goods and services can be traded for other goods and services.

Multiple Choice

8-21.
A
Easy
P.264

The _____ is a market for converting the currency of one country into that of another.
a. foreign exchange market
b. cross-cultural interchange
c. financial barter market
d. monetary replacement market

8-22.
B
Easy
P.264

The rate at which one currency is converted into another is called the

_____.
a. replacement percentage
b. exchange rate
c. resale rate
d. interchange ratio

8-23.
A
Easy
P.264

An _____ is simply the rate at which one currency is converted into another.
a. exchange rate
b. resale rate
c. interchange ratio
d. replacement percentage

8-24.
C
Medium
P.265

One function of the foreign exchange market is to provide some insurance against the risks that arise from changes in exchange rates, commonly referred to as:
a. foreign market hazard
b. global jeopardy
c. foreign exchange risk
d. commerce uncertainty

8-25.
D
Medium
P.266

The foreign exchange market serves two main functions. These are:

a. collect duties on imported products and convert the currency of one country into the currency of another
b. insure companies against foreign exchange risk and set interest rates charged to foreign investors
c. collect duties on imported products and set interest rates charged to foreign investors
d. convert the currency of one country into the currency of another and provide some insurance against foreign exchange risk

8-26.
A
Medium
P.266

The foreign exchange market converts the currency of one country into the currency of another and:

a. provides some insurance against foreign exchange risk
b. collects duties on imported products
c. sets interest rates charged to foreign investors
d. arbitrates disputes between trade partners

8-27.
B
Medium
P.266

The foreign exchange market provides some insurance of foreign exchange risk and:

a. arbitrates disputes between trade partners
b. converts the currency of one country into the currency of another
c. collects duties on imported products
d. set interest rates charged to foreign investors

8-28.
C
Hard
P.266

Which of the following correctly matches a country with its currency?

a. South Korea, the pound
b. France, the deutsche mark
c. Japan, the yen
d. Great Britain, the franc

8-29.
D
Hard
P.266

Which of the following correctly matches a country with its currency?

a. Japan, franc
b. South Korea, the deutsche mark
c. Canada, the yen
d. Great Britain, the pound

8-30.
C
Medium
P.266

Which of the following is the currency of Japan?

a. dollar
b. deutsche mark
c. yen
d. pound

8-31. Which of the following is the currency of France?
A
Medium   a. franc
P.266   b. deutsche mark
            c. dollar
            d. pound

8-32. The _____ is the rate at which the market converts one currency into
C   another.
Medium   a. international conversion factor
P.267   b. world barter factor
            c. foreign exchange rate
            d. global replacement percentage

8-33. _____ typically involves the short-term movement of funds from one
B   currency to another in the hopes of profiting from shifts in exchange rates.
Easy   a. Capital venturing
P.267   b. Currency speculation
            c. Monetary risk taking
            d. Investment contemplation

8-34. Currency speculation typically involves the _____ movements of funds from
D   one currency to another in the hopes of profiting from shifts in exchange rates.
Medium   a. medium-term
P.267   b. long-term
            c. historical
            d. short-term

8-35. When two parties agree to exchange currency and execute the deal immediately,
C   the transaction is referred to as a _____.
Easy   a. point-in-time exchange
P.268   b. temporal exchange
            c. spot exchange
            d. forward exchange

8-36. The _____ is the rate at which a foreign exchange dealer converts one
A   currency into another currency on a particular day.
Medium   a. spot exchange rate
P.268   b. reference point exchange rate
            c. point-in-time exchange rate
            d. forward exchange rate

8-37.
D
Medium
P.270

A _____ exchange occurs when two parties agree to exchange currency and execute the deal at some specific date in the future.
a. reverse
b. spot
c. hedge
d. forward

8-38.
D
Medium
P.270

_____ exchange rates represent market participants' collective predictions of likely spot exchange rates at specified future dates.
a. Reciprocal
b. Hedge
c. Reverse
d. Forward

8-39.
A
Medium
P.270

An exchange in which two parties agree to exchange currency and execute the deal at some specific date in the future is called a:
a. forward exchange
b. hedge exchange
c. reverse exchange
d. spot exchange

8-40.
A
Easy
P.270

Rates for currency exchange quoted for 30, 90, or 180 days into the future are referred to as _____.
a. forward exchange rates
b. foreign exchange quotes
c. united trade rates
d. generic exchange quotes

8-41.
C
Hard
P.271

When the dollar buys more francs on the spot market than the 30-day forward market, we say the dollars is selling at a _____. Conversely, when the dollars buys less francs on the spot market than the 30-day forward market, we say the dollar is selling at a _____.
a. premium, discount
b. handicap, bonus
c. discount, premium
d. subsidy, handicap

8-42.
A
Hard
P.271

The most important trading centers for the foreign exchange market are in:
a. London, New York, and Tokyo
b. San Paulo, New York, and Paris
c. San Francisco, Tokyo, and Singapore
d. New York, Hong Kong, and Paris

8-43.
B
Hard
P.271

The largest trading center in the foreign exchange market is _____ .
a. Hong Kong
b. London
c. San Paulo
d. Paris

8-44.
D
Easy
P.272

The process of buying a currency low and selling it high is called:
a. forward exchange
b. skimming
c. profiteering
d. arbitrage

8-45.
C
Easy
P.272

_____ is the process of buying a currency low and selling it high.
a. Situational exchange
b. Inward exchange
c. Arbitrage
d. Skimming

8-46.
A
Hard
P.273

Most economic theories suggest that three import factors have an important impact on future exchange rate movements in a country's currency. These factors are:
a. the country's price inflation, its interest rate, and its market philosophy
b. the country's rate of GNP, its unemployment rate, and its economic policy
c. the country's participation in the World Trade Organization, its monetary policy, and its market philosophy
d. the country's rate of economic growth, its participation in the World Trade Organization, and its economy policy

8-47.
C
Medium
P.273

The three factors that have the most important impact on future exchange rate movement include the country's price inflation, its market philosophy, and its _____ .

a. rate of economic growth
b. unemployment rate
c. interest rate
d. participation in the World Trade Organization

8-48.
A
Medium
P.273

The three factors that have the most important impact on future exchange rate movement include the country's interest rate, its market philosophy, and its _____ .

a. price inflation
b. participation in the World Trade Organization
c. unemployment rate
d. rate of economic growth

8-49.
A
Medium
P.273

The _____ states that in competitive markets free of transportation costs and barriers to trade, identical products sold in different countries must sell for the same price when their price is expressed in terms of the same currency.
a. law of one price
b. principle of consistent pricing
c. model of fair pricing
d. principle of equitable pricing

8-50.
C
Medium
P.273

PPP theory stands for:
a. Productivity Power Premium theory
b. Process Productivity Predictor theory
c. Purchasing Power Parity theory
d. Personal Power Predictor theory

8-51.
B
Easy
P.274

A(n) _____ has no impediments to the free flow of goods and services.
a. classical market
b. efficient market
c. traditional market
d. inefficient market

8-52.
A
Medium
P.274

A(n) _____ is one in which prices reflect all available information.
a. efficient market
b. inefficient market
c. traditional market
d. classical market

8-53.
D
Easy
P.274

A market that has no impediments to the free flow of goods and services is called a(n) _____ market.
a. inefficient
b. classical
c. tolerant
d. efficient

8-54.
A
Medium
P.274

A _____ is a market in which few impediments to international trade and investment exist.
a. relatively efficient market
b. consistently inefficient market
c. absolutely free market
d. absolutely closed

8-55.
D
Hard
P.274

If the law of one price were true for all goods and services, the _____ exchange rate could be found from any individual set of prices.
a. stability power similarity (SPS)
b. purchasing ability adeptness (PAA)
c. buying prowess equality (BPE)
d. purchasing power parity (PPP)

8-56.
D
Hard
P.274

The PPP theory of exchange rate changes yields relatively accurate predictions of _____ trends in exchange rates, but not of _____ movements.
a. short-term, long-term
b. short-term, intermediate-term
c. intermediate-term, long-term
d. long-term, short-term

8-57.
B
Hard
P.274

In essence, the _____ theory predicts that changes in relative prices will result in a change in exchange rates.
a. buying power equality (BPE)
b. purchasing power parity (PPP)
c. stability power similarity (SPS)
d. buying prowess equality (BPE)

8-58.
B
Medium
P.274

In essence, purchasing power parity predicts that changes in relative prices will result in a change in _____ rates.
a. unemployement
b. exchange
c. interest
d. gross domestic product

8-59.
A
Medium
P.276

PPP theory predicts that changes in _____ will result in a change in exchange rates.
a. relative prices
b. interest rates
c. unemployment rates
d. statutory prices

8-60.
B
Hard
P.278

According to the textbook, PPP theory does not seem to be a particularly good predictor of exchange rate movements for time spans of:
a. one year or less
b. five years or less
c. ten years or less
d. twenty years or less

8-61. For time periods of _____, PPP theory does not seem to be a particularly
C   good predictor of exchange rate movements.
Hard   a. twenty years or less
P.278   b. ten years or less
        c. five years or less
        d. one year or less

8-62. The PPP theory seems to best predict exchange rate changes for countries with:
C   a. very low rates of inflation and developed capital markets
Hard   b. very low rates of inflation and underdeveloped capital markets
P.278   c. very high rates of inflation and underdeveloped capital markets
        d. very high rates of inflation and developed capital markets

8-63. Economic theory tells us that _____ rates reflect expectations about likely
C   future inflation rates.
Medium a. currency
P.279   b. exchange
        c. interest
        d. unemployment

8-64. The _____ states that for any two countries, the spot exchange rate should
C   change in an equal amount but in the opposite direction to the difference in the
Medium nominal interest rates between the two countries.
P.279   a. Worldwide James Effect
        b. Universal Phillips Effect
        c. International Fisher Effect
        d. Global Miller Effect

8-65. The International Fisher Effect states that for any two countries, the _____
B   exchange rate should change in an equal amount but in the opposite direction to
Medium the difference in the nominal interest rates between the two countries.
P.279   a. reciprocal
        b. spot
        c. forward
        d. inward

8-66. The _____ market school argues that forward exchange rates do the best
A   possible job of forecasting future spot exchange rates, so investing in exchange
Medium rate forecasting services would be a waste of time.
P.281   a. efficient
        b. closed
        c. inefficient
        d. free

8-67.
D
Hard
P.281

The _____ market school argues that companies can improve the foreign exchange market's estimate of future exchange rates by investing in forecasting services.
a. inefficient
b. free
c. open
d. efficient

8-68.
B
Medium
P.281

A(n) _____ market is one in which prices do not reflect all available information.
a. efficient
b. inefficient
c. free
d. closed

8-69.
B
Hard
P.281

In an _____ market, forward exchange rates will not be the best possible predictors of future spot exchange rates.
a. closed
b. inefficient
c. efficient
d. reciprocal

8-70.
B
Medium
P.282

_____ draws on economic theory to construct sophisticated econometric models for predicting exchange rate movements.
a. Principal investigation
b. Fundamental analysis
c. Primary evaluation
d. Technical analysis

8-71.
D
Medium
P.283

_____ uses price and volume data to determine past trends, which are expected to continue into the future.
a. Principal investigation
b. Primary evaluation
c. Fundamental analysis
d. Technical analysis

8-72.
C
Medium
P.283

The type of analysis that predicts exchange rate movements by using price and volume data to determine past trends is called:
a. fundamental analysis
b. primary evaluation
c. technical analysis
d. principal investigation

8-73.
B
Easy
P.283

A country's currency is said to be _____ when the country's government allows both residents and nonresidents to purchase unlimited amounts of foreign currency with it.

a. technically convertible
b. freely convertible
c. externally convertible
d. nonconvertible

8-74.
B
Medium
P.283

A country's currency is said to be freely convertible when the country's government:

a. allows residents to purchase unlimited amounts of a foreign currency with it and allows nonresidents to purchase a limited amount of a foreign currency with it
b. allows both residents and nonresidents to purchase unlimited amounts of foreign currency with it
c. allows only residents to purchase foreign currency with it
d. allows both residents, nonresidents, and foreign governments to purchase limited amounts of foreign currency with it

8-75.
A
Medium
P.283

A currency is said to be _____ when only nonresidents may convert it into a foreign currency without any limitations.

a. externally convertible
b. freely convertible
c. technically convertible
d. nonconvertible

8-76.
B
Medium
P.283

A currency is _____ when neither residents nor nonresidents are allowed to convert it into a foreign currency.

a. freely convertible
b. nonconvertible
c. externally convertible
d. technically convertible

8-77.
B
Hard
P.284

A government restricts the convertibility of its currency to protect the country's _____ and to halt any capital flight.

a. membership in the World Trade Organization
b. foreign exchange reserves
c. political stature
d. national sovereignty

8-78.   _____ refers to a range of barterlike agreements by which goods and
C   services can be traded for other goods and services.
Easy   a. Separate trade
P.284   b. Reciprocal trade
        c. Countertrade
        d. Alternative trade

8-79.   If an American grain company exported corn to Russia, and instead of receiving
A   nonconvertible Russian currency in exchange for the corn received Russian crude
Medium oil, that would be an example of _____.
P.284   a. countertrade
        b. synergistic trade
        c. separate trade
        d. reciprocal trade

8-80.   According to a study cited in the textbook, _____ of world trade in 1985
B   involved some form of countertrade agreement.
Hard   a. 5 to 10 percent
P.284   b. 20 to 30 percent
        c. 40 to 50 percent
        d. 70 to 80 percent

Essay Questions

8-81.   What are the functions of the foreign exchange market? Would international
Easy   commerce be possible without its existence?
P.264

Answer: The foreign exchange market is a market for converting the currency of
one country into that of another. For example, an American exporter that gets paid
by a German importer in deutsche marks can convert the deutsche marks to
dollars on the foreign exchange market. The two main functions of the foreign
exchange market are currency conversion and insuring against foreign exchange
risk. In terms of currency conversion, the market has four primary functions for
international businesses: (1) converting payments a company receives in foreign
currencies into the currency of its home country; (2) converting the currency of a
company's home country into another currency when they must pay a foreign
company for its products and services in their currency; (3) international
businesses may use foreign exchange markets when they have spare cash that
they wish to invest for short terms in money markets (of another country); and (4)
currency speculation. The second function of the foreign exchange market is to
provide insurance to protect against the possible adverse consequences of
unpredictable changes in exchange rates. This can be accomplished through the
use of a forward exchange.

It is difficult to image how international commerce would work without the existence of the foreign exchange market. Without it, international trade would have to be completed on the basis of barter, rather than currency exchange. As suggested by the author of the textbook, the foreign exchange markets is the lubricant that enables companies based in countries that use different currencies to trade with each other.

8-82.
Medium
P.266

Explain the difference between spot exchange rates and forward exchange rates. Briefly explain how the forward exchange market works.

Answer: The spot exchange rate is the rate at which a foreign exchange dealer converts one currency into another currency on a particular day. Thus, when a Japanese tourist in Orlando goes to a bank to convert yen into dollars, the exchange rate is the spot rate for that day. Spot exchange rates change daily, based on the relative supply and demand for different currencies.

Forward exchange rates are rates for currencies quoted for 30, 90, or 180 days into the future (in some cases, it is possible to get forward exchange rates for several years into the future). Forward exchange rates are available because of the volatile and problematic nature of the spot exchange market. Suppose a U.S. importer agreed to paid a Japanese exporter $100 a piece for a large quantity of cameras. The day of the agreement, the exchange rate for dollars and yen was 1:1 (1 dollar for 1 yen). The U.S. importer planed to sell the cameras for $125, guaranteeing himself a profit of $25 per camera. Further suppose that the payment is not due to the Japanese exporter for 30 days, and during the 30 day waiting period, the dollar unexpectedly depreciates against the yen, forcing the exchange rate to one dollar for every .75 yen. Per the original agreement, the U.S. importer still has to pay the Japanese importer 100 yen per camera, but now the exchange rate is not 1 dollar per yen, but is 1 dollar per .75 yen. As a result, the U.S. importer has to pay $1.33 to buy the equivalent of 1 yen. Now, instead o making $25 per camera ($125 selling price - $100 purchase price), the U.S. importer will lose $8 per camera ($125 selling price - $133 purchase price influenced by currency fluctuations). To avoid this potential problem, the U.S. importer could have entered into a 30-day forward exchange transaction with a foreign exchange dealer at, say, 1 dollar for every .95 yen (the forward rate will typically be somewhat lower than the spot rate). By doing this, the importer is guaranteed that he or she will not have to pay more than 1.05 dollars for every 1 yen, which would still guarantee the importer a $20 per profit on the cameras.

8-83.
Medium
P.280

Explain how the psychology of investors and bandwagon effects can have an impact on the movement in exchange rates. Do you believe that bandwagon effects really happen? Explain your answer.

Answer: As noted by the author of the textbook, empirical evidence suggests that empirical explanations are not particular good at explaining short-term movements in exchange rates. One reason for this may be the impact of investor psychology on short-run exchange rate movements. Investors, because they are human beings, do not always make decisions based on a rational analysis of the facts. Sometimes investors imitate the actions of someone that is very influential, even if there is no logical reason to do so. Investors also trade based on "hunches" or speculation, which is more psychological in nature than rational. A bandwagon effect in when investors in increasing numbers start following the lead of someone who may be pushing the value of a currency up or down due to psychological reasons. As a bandwagon effect builds up, the expectations of investors become a self-fulfilling prophecy, and the market moves in the way the investors expected.

Ask your students if they believe bandwagon effects actually happen in practice. Most students will say that they do, and have vivid examples to support their conclusions.

3-84.
Hard
P.282
In the context of forecasting exchange rate movements, describe the difference between fundamental analysis and technical analysis. Which approach is preferred by economists? Why?

Answer: Fundamental analysis draws on economic theory to construct sophisticated econometric models for predicting exchange rate movements. The variables contained in these models typically include relative money supply growth rates, inflation rates, and interest rates. In addition, they may include variables related to a countries' balance-of-payments positions. In contrast, technical analysis uses price and volume data to determine past trends, which are expected to continue into the future. This approach does not rely on a consideration of economic fundamentals. Technical analysis is based on the premise that there are analyzable market trends and waves and that previous trends and waves can be used to predict future trends and waves.

Since there is no theoretical rationale for the assumption of predictability that underlies technical analysis, most economists compare technical analysis to fortune-telling, and prefer fundamental analysis. However, despite this skepticism, technical analysis has gained favor in recent years.

3-85.
Medium
P.284
Explain the concept of countertrade. When does countertrade make sense? How does countertrade help solve the nonconvertability problem?

Answer: Countertrade refers to a range of barterlike agreements by which goods and services can be traded for other goods and services. Countertrade makes sense when a country's currency is nonconvertible. For example, the Russian ruble in nonconvertible. What that means it that if a U.S. exporter sold grain to a Russian importer and was paid in rubles, the U.S. exporter could not take the rubles to a bank and have them converted into dollars. The rubles are only of value in Russia. To get around this limitation, the U.S. exporter and the Russian importer might enter into a countertrade agreement, in which the U.S. exporter accepts some type of goods or services in exchange for the grain rather than Russian rubles. For instance, the Russian importer could use rubles to buy Russian crude oil, and exchange the crude oil for the grain. The U.S. exporter could then sell the crude oil for American dollars, and benefit from the transaction.

CHAPTER 9
THE GLOBAL MONETARY SYSTEM

True/False Questions

9-1.
F
Easy
P.293

The Bretton Woods system called for floating exchange rates against the U.S. dollar.

9-2.
T
Medium
P.293

The Bretton Woods system of fixed exchange rates collapsed in 1973. Since then the world has operated with a managed float system.

9-3.
F
Easy
P.294

The practice of pegging currencies to gold and guaranteeing convertibility is known as the metals standard.

9-4.
T
Medium
P.294

The great strength claimed for the gold standard was that it contained a powerful mechanism for simultaneously achieving balance-of-trade equilibrium by all countries.

9-5.
F
Medium
P.296

The agreement reached at Bretton Woods established two multinational institutions - The World Trade Organization and the World Bank

9-6.
T
Medium
P.296

As stipulated by the Bretton Woods agreement, the task of the IMF was to maintain order in the international monetary system.

9-7.
T
Hard
P.297

Although monetary discipline was a central objective of the Bretton Woods agreement, it was recognized that a rigid policy of fixed exchange rates would be too inflexible.

9-8.
T
Hard
P.297

The system of adjustable parities allows for the devaluation of a country's currency by more than 10% if the IMF agrees that the country's balance of payments is in "fundamental disequilibrium."

9-9.
F
Medium
P.298

The official name of the World Bank is the International Bank for Credit and Commerce

9-10.
T
Hard
P.298

Most economists trace the breakup of the fixed exchange rate system to the U.S. macroeconomic policy package of 1965-1968.

9-11.
F
Medium
P.300

The Bretton Woods agreement had an Achilles' heel: the system could not work if its key currency, the British pound, was under speculative attack.

9-12.
T
Hard
P.300

The purpose of the Jamaica meeting was to revise the IMF's Articles of Agreement to reflect the new reality of floating exchange rates.

9-13.
T
Medium
P.303

Under a floating exchange rate regime, market forces have produced a volatile dollar exchange.

9-14.
F
Medium
P.304

The case for fixed exchange rates has two main elements: monetary policy autonomy and automatic trade balance adjustments.

9-15.
T
Medium
P.305

It is argued that a floating exchange rate regime gives countries monetary policy autonomy.

9-16.
T
Medium
P.305

Advocates of a floating exchange rate regime argue that removal of the obligation to maintain exchange rate parity restores monetary control to a government.

9-17.
F
Hard
P.306

Under the Bretton Woods system, if a country developed a permanent deficit in its balance of trade that could not be corrected by domestic policy, the World Bank would agree to a currency devaluation.

9-18.
T
Medium
P.306

The case for fixed exchange rates rests on arguments about monetary discipline, speculation, uncertainty, and the lack of connection between the trade balance and exchange rates.

9-19.
F
Hard
P.306

Critics of a floating exchange rate regime argue that speculation causes stability in exchange rates

9-20.
T
Medium
P.307

Those in favor of floating exchange rates argue that floating rates help adjust trade imbalances.

Multiple Choice

9-21.
B
Easy
P.293

The Bretton Woods system called for _____ exchange rates against the U.S. dollar.
a. variable
b. fixed
c. floating
d. fluctuating

9-22.
B
Medium
P.293

Under the exchange rate system established by the Bretton Woods agreement, the value of most currencies in terms of _____ was fixed for long periods and was allowed to change only under a specific set of circumstances.
a. British pound
b. U.S. dollars
c. Japanese yen
d. German deutsche mark

9-23.
A
Medium
P.293

The Bretton Woods conference created two major international institutions. These are:
a. the International Monetary Fund and the World Bank
b. the World Trade Organization and the United Nations
c. the World Currency Exchange and the World Bank
d. the Bretton Woods Monetary Fund and the World Trade Organization

9-24.
D
Medium
P.293

The International Monetary Fund and the _____ were created by the Bretton Woods conference.
a. Bretton Woods Monetary Fund
b. World Currency Exchange
c. World Trade Organization
d. World Bank

9-25.
C
Medium
P.293

The World Bank and the _____ were created by the Bretton Woods conference.
a. Bretton Woods Monetary Fund
b. World Currency Exchange
c. International Monetary Fund
d. Global Trade Organization

9-26.
A
Medium
P.293

As stipulated by the Bretton Woods conference, the goal of the International Monetary Fund was to:
a. maintain order in the international monetary system
b. establish a world currency
c. promote development
d. set interest rates in members nations

9-27.
D
Easy
P.293

The acronym IMF stands for:
a. International Monopoly Function
b. Interval Monetary Fluctuations
c. Interagency Monetary Function
d. International Monetary Fund

9-28.
B
Medium
P.293

As stipulated by the Bretton Woods conference, the goal of the World Bank was to:
a. maintain order in the international monetary system
b. promote development
c. set interest rates in member states
d. establish a world currency

9-29.
D
Easy
P.293

Under a _____, some currencies are allowed to float freely, but the majori of currencies are either managed in some way by government intervention or pegged to another currency.
a. random monetary system
b. regulated standard system
c. monitored spot market
d. managed float system

9-30.
A
Medium
P.293

The Bretton Woods system of fixed exchange rates collapsed in 1973. Since then the world has operated with a:

a. managed float system
b. random monetary system
c. regulated standard system
d. monitored spot market

9-31.
B
Easy
P.294

The practice of pegging currencies to gold and guaranteeing convertibility was referred to as the _____.

a. premium standard
b. gold standard
c. metal standard
d. federal reserve standard

9-32.
D
Easy
P.294

The _____ is a monetary standard that pegs currencies to gold and guarantees convertibility to gold.

a. metal standard
b. federal reserve standard
c. premium standard
d. gold standard

9-33.
A
Medium
P.294

The great strength claimed for the gold standard was that it contained a powerful mechanism for simultaneously obtained _____ for all countries.

a. balance-of-trade equilibrium
b. economic stability
c. interest rate parity
d. equal tariff levels

9-34.
B
Medium
P.294

A country is said to be a balance-of-trade equilibrium when:

a. the income that its residents earn from the export of manufactured goods equals the income that its residents earn from the export of services
b. the income that its residents earn from exports is equal to the money that its residents pay for imports
c. the income that its residents earn from exports in the current fiscal year is equal to the income that its residents earned from exports in the previous fiscal year
d. the income that its residents earn from the export of raw materials is equal to the income that its residents earn from the export of manufactured goods

9-35.
B
Hard
P.295

The gold standard broke down in the _____ as countries engaged in competitive devaluations.
a. 1910s
b. 1930s
c. 1950s
d. 1970s

9-36.
C
Easy
P.296

In 1944, at the height of World War II, representatives from 44 countries met at _____ to design a new international monetary system.
a. Richmond, Virginia
b. San Francisco, California
c. Bretton Woods, New Hampshire
d. Morris Plains, New Jersey

9-37.
B
Hard
P.296

In _____, representatives from 44 countries met at Bretton Woods, New Hampshire to design a new international monetary system.
a. 1922
b. 1944
c. 1957
d. 1981

9-38.
C
Easy
P.296

The Bretton Woods system of fixed exchange rates was established in 1944. The central currency of this system was the:
a. French Franc
b. German Deutsche Mark
c. U.S. Dollar
d. British Pound

9-39.
D
Medium
P.296

A fixed exchange rate regime imposes discipline in two ways: (1) the need to maintain a fixed exchange rate puts a brake on competitive devaluations and brings stability to the world trade environment and (2) a fixed exchange rate regime imposes
a. social discipline on countries, thereby increasing the standard of living
b. economic discipline on countries, thereby increasing gross national product
c. political discipline on countries, thereby curtailing global opportunism
d. monetary discipline on countries, thereby curtailing price inflation

9-40.
B
Medium
P.297

An increase in money supply typically leads to an increase in:
a. employment
b. price inflation
c. gross national product
d. national standard of living

9-41.
A
Medium
P.297

Fixed exchange rates are seen as a mechanism for achieving the following two objectives:
a. controlling inflation and economic discipline
b. controlling unemployment and political discipline
c. controlling economic stability and increasing gross national product
d. controlling political stability and economic discipline

9-42.
B
Medium
P.297

Fixed exchange rates are seen as a mechanism for achieving the following two objectives: (1) controlling inflation and (2)
a. increasing the standard of living
b. economic discipline
c. political stability
d. increasing gross national product

9-43.
A
Medium
P.297

_____ are seen as a mechanism for controlling inflation and imposing economic discipline on countries.
a. Fixed exchange rates
b. Floating exchange rates
c. Global exchange rates
d. Transnational exchange rates

9-44.
D
Hard
P.297

Two major features of the International Monetary Fund (IMF) Articles of Agreement fostered flexibility into the monetary system. These features included (1) IMF facilities and (2):
a. IMF export assistance
b. fixed parities
c. a return to the gold standard
d. adjustable parities

9-45.
A
Medium
P.297

Two major features of the International Monetary Fund (IMF) Articles of Agreement fostered flexibility into the monetary system. These features included (1) adjustable parities and (2):
a. IMF facilities
b. IMF export assistance
c. a return to the gold standard
d. fixed parities

9-46.
A
Hard
P.297

The IMF's system of adjustable parities, under the auspices of the Bretton Woods agreement, allowed for the devaluation of a country's currency by more than _____ if the IMF agreed that the country's balance of payments is in fundamental disequilibrium.

a. 10%
b. 20%
c. 40%
d. 50%

9-47.
B
Easy
P.298

The International Bank for Reconstruction and Development (IBRD) is the official name for the:

a. World Trade Organization
b. World Bank
c. International Monetary Fund
d. Global-Regional Bank

9-48.
C
Hard
P.298

In the context of the global monetary system, the IBRD stands for the _____.

a. International Bank for Rents and Deposits
b. International Bureau for Restraining Devaluations
c. International Bank for Reconstruction and Development
d. International Bureau for Research and Development

9-49.
D
Medium
P.298

The official name of the World Bank is the:

a. Global Bank for the Financing of Trade and Development
b. International Bank for Sustained Economic Stability
c. Global Bank for the Promotion of Trade
d. International Bank for Reconstruction and Development

9-50.
A
Medium
P.298

The initial mission of the World Bank was to:

a. help finance the building of Europe's economy by providing low-interest loans
b. help small businesses establish export operations
c. provide letters of credit on behalf of first-time exporters
d. provide development loans for developing countries in Asia

9-51.
B
Medium
P.298

Helping finance the building of Europe's economy after World War II by providing low-interest loans was the initial mission of:

a. The World Trade Organization
b. The World Bank
c. The European National Bank
d. The International Monetary Fund

9-52.
C
Hard
P.298

Which of the following statements accurately depicts what happened to the Bretton Woods system of fixed exchange rates?

a. the system never got off the ground, and collapsed in the late 1940s
b. the system worked well for about a decade, then collapsed in the mid-1950s
c. the system began to show signs of strain in the 1960s, and finally collapsed in 1973
d. the system remained in place until the early 1990s when an international conference was convened in Finland to develop a managed float system

9-53.
C
Easy
P.298

The Bretton Woods system of fixed exchange rates collapsed in 1973, and since then we have had a:

a. stepwise fixed rate exchange system
b. more rigid and enforceable fixed exchange rate system
c. managed float system
d. combination of managed float systems and fixed exchange rate systems

9-54.
A
Medium
P.300

In the context of the global money system, in August 1971 President Nixon made the following two announcements: (1) a new 10 percent tax on imports would remain in effect until the trading partners of the U.S. agreed to revalue their currency against the dollar and (2)

a. the dollar was no longer convertible into gold
b. the U.S. would no longer support the World Bank
c. the U.S. planned to devalue its currency by 20 percent
d. the U.S. planned to called for a second Bretton Woods conference

9-55.
A
Medium
P.300

The _____ exchange rate regime that followed the collapse of the fixed exchange rate system was formalized in January 1976 when IMF members met in Jamaica and agreed to the rules for the international system that are in place today.

a. floating
b. quasi-fixed
c. open
d. closed

9-56.
D
Medium
P.300

The floating exchange rate regime that followed the collapse of the fixed exchange rate system was formalized in January 1976 when IMF members met in _____ and agreed to the rules for the international system that are in place today.

a. Ireland
b. Hong Kong
c. Spain
d. Jamica

9-57.
B
Medium
P.300

The three main elements of the Jamaica Agreement were:

a. the International Monetary Fund was established; gold was abandoned as a reserve asset; and floating rates were declared unacceptable
b. floating rates were declared acceptable; gold was abandoned as a reserve asset; and total annual IMF quotas were increased to $41 billion
c. floating rates were declared unacceptable; the International Monetary Fund was abolished; and the World Bank was established
d. fixed rates were declared acceptable, gold was accepted as a reserve asset; and the total annual IMF quotas were increased to $41 billion

9-58.
A
Medium
P.300

Which of the following was not one of the main elements of the Jamaica Agreement?

a. the establishment of the International Monetary Fund
b. floating rates were declared acceptable
c. total annual IMF quotas were increased to $41 billion
d. gold was abandoned as a reserve asset

9-59.
C
Hard
P.301

The _____ represents the exchange rate of the U.S. dollar against a weighted basket of the currencies of 15 other industrial countries.

a. Nelson's Assurance Index
b. Phillips Security Index
c. Morgan Guaranty Index
d. Stanley Obligation Index

9-60.
B
Hard
P.302

The so called "Group of Five" major industrialized nations includes:

a. Germany, China, United States, and France
b. Great Britain, France, Japan, Germany, and the United States
c. United States, Japan, China, Brazil, and Germany
d. France, Germany, Japan, China, and the United States

9-61.
D
Hard
P.302

The 1995 Plaza Accord, which was sponsored by the financial ministers of the Group of Five major industrial countries, concluded that it would be desirable if:

a. most major currencies appreciated vis-a-vis the Japanese yen
b. the World Bank converted to a private organization
c. the nations of the world returned to the gold standard
d. most major currencies appreciated vis-a-vis the U.S. dollar

9-62.
A
Medium
P.304

The case for floating exchange rates has two main elements. These are:

a. monetary policy autonomy and automatic trade balance adjustments
b. sporadic trade balance adjustments and monetary policy autonomy
c. the impracticality of the gold standard and monetary policy control
d. monetary policy control and sporadic trade balance adjustments

9-63.
C
Medium
P.304

The case for floating exchange rates has two main elements: (1) monetary policy autonomy and (2)
a. sporadic trade balance adjustments
b. the impracticality of the gold standard
c. automatic trade balance adjustments
d. monetary policy control

9-64.
B
Medium
P.304

Automatic trade balance adjustments and _____ are the two main elements in the case for floating exchange rates.
a. sporadic trade balance adjustments
b. monetary policy autonomy
c. a return to the gold standard
d. monetary policy control

9-65.
D
Medium
P.305

It is argued that a _____ exchange rate regime gives countries monetary policy autonomy.
a. restricted
b. forward
c. fixed
d. floating

9-66.
B
Hard
P.305

Under a _____ exchange rate regime, a country's ability to expand or contract its money supply as it sees fit is limited by the need to maintain exchange rate parity.
a. forward
b. fixed
c. narrow
d. floating

9-67.
B
Hard
P.305

Advocates of a _____ exchange rate regime argue that removal of the obligation to maintain exchange rate parity restores monetary control to a government.
a. fixed
b. floating
c. narrow
d. forward

9-68.
A
Medium
P.306

Under the Bretton Woods system, if a country developed a permanent deficit in its balance of trade that could not be corrected by domestic policy, the IMF would agree to a:
a. currency devaluation
b. increase in employment
c. increase in output
d. increase in interest rates

265

9-69.
B
Medium
P.306

The case for fixed exchange rates rests on arguments about monetary discipline, speculation, the lack of connection between the trade balance and exchange rates, and _____.
a. trade balance adjustments
b. uncertainty
c. the impracticality of the gold standard
d. monetary policy autonomy

9-70.
A
Medium
P.306

The case for fixed exchange rates rests on arguments about monetary discipline, uncertainty, the lack of connection between the trade balance and exchange rates, and _____.
a. speculation
b. the impracticality of the gold standard
c. monetary policy autonomy
d. trade balance adjustments

9-71.
C
Hard
P.308

No major industrial country has borrowed funds from the IMF since the:
a. mid-1950s
b. mid-1960s
c. mid-1970s
d. mid-1980s

9-72.
A
Medium
P.308

Which of the following was not a factor that choked off economic growth in the developing world in the early 1980s?
a. falling short-term interest rates worldwide
b. poor macroeconomic management
c. poor use of the loan funds
d. a slowdown in the growth rate of the Industrialized West

9-73.
C
Hard
P.309

In the early 1980s, the IMF intervened to settle an international debt crisis involving Mexico's inability to service its foreign debt. The IMF's agreement with Mexico, designed to resolve the crisis, involved the following three elements: (1) rescheduling of Mexico's old debt; (2) a commitment from the Mexican government to abide by a set of IMF-dictated macroeconomic prescriptions for its economy; and (3)
a. a commitment from the Mexican government to lower interest rates
b. debt forgiveness for Mexico by its largest five creditors
c. new loans to Mexico from the IMF, the World Bank, and commercial banks
d. a commitment from the Mexican government to remove all trade barriers

9-74.
B
Medium
P.309

The first country that applied for debt relief under the Brady Plan was:
a. Brazil
b. Mexico
c. Argentina
d. Canada

9-75.
D
Hard
P.309

The Brady Plan was named after:

a. Citibank Chairman Stephen Brady
b. World Bank Chairman Andrew Scott Brady
c. International Monetary Fund Chairman William Brady
d. U.S. Treasury Secretary Nicholas Brady

9-76.
C
Medium
P.309

The plan that required the IMF, the World Bank and the Japanese government to each contribute $10 billion to a fund that would be used to help debt strapped countries reduce their debt was called the:

a. World Bank Reduction Plan
b. Phillips Plan
c. Brady Plan
d. Unified Plan

9-77.
A
Hard
P.310

Under the original Bretton Woods agreement, the _____ was to provide short-term loans and the _____ was to provide long-term loans.

a. IMF, World Bank
b. United Nations, World Trade Organization
c. World Bank, IMF
d. World Trade Organization, United Nations

9-78.
C
Medium
P.311

The current foreign exchange system can be best described as a _____.

a. managed variable-rate system
b. completely autonomous system
c. managed float system
d. managed fixed-rate system

9-79.
B
Medium
P.311

According to the textbook, under the present foreign exchange system, speculative buying and selling of currencies can create _____ movements in exchange rates.

a. virtually no
b. very volatile
c. very stable
d. fixed

9-80.
B
Medium
P.312

According to the textbook, the IMF and World Bank are increasingly insisting that countries that come to them for significant borrowings adopt IMF or World Bank mandated _____.

a. currency valuations
b. macroeconomic policy
c. interest rates
d. tariffs

Essay Questions

9-81.
Easy
P.296

Describe what happened at the 1944 Bretton Woods conference. Are the monetary principles established by the Bretton Woods conference still in effect today?

Answer: In 1944, at the height of World War II, representatives from 44 countries met at Bretton Woods, New Hampshire, to design a new international monetary system. The purpose of the conference was to build an economic order that would facilitate postwar economic growth and cooperation. Three primary initiatives resulted from the conference:

a) The establishment of the International Monetary Fund (IMF).

b) The establishment of the World Bank.

c) A call for the establishment of a set of fixed currency exchange rates that would be policed by the IMF.

d) A commitment not to use devaluation as a weapon of competitive trade policy.

The task of the IMF would be to maintain order in the international monetary system, and the World Bank was designed to promote general economic development. In regard to currency exchange rates, all countries were to fix the value of their currency in terms of gold but were not required to exchange their currencies for gold. Only the U.S. dollar remained convertible into gold - at a price of $35 per ounce. Each other country decided what it wanted its exchange rate to be vis-a-vis the dollar and then calculated the gold par value of its currency based on that selected dollar exchange rate. All participating countries agreed to try to maintain the value of their currency within 1 percent of the par value.

Today, the IMF and the World Bank still play a role in the international monetary system. The system of fixed exchange rates established at Bretton Woods worked well until the late 1960s, when it began to show signs of strain. The system finally collapsed in 1973, and since then we have had a managed float system.

9-82.
Medium
P.298

Describe the role of the World Bank in the international community. How does the World Bank contribute to the overall stability of the global monetary system?

Answer: The World Bank was established by the 1944 Bretton Woods agreement. The official name for the World Bank is the International Bank for Reconstruction and Development (IBRD). The bank's initial mission was to help finance the building of Europe's war torn economy by providing low-interest loans. As it turned out, the role of the World Bank in Europe was overshadowed by the Marshall Plan, under which the U.S. lent money directly to European nations to help them rebuild in the aftermath of World War II. As a result, the bank turned its attention to lending money for development in Third World nations.

Although the World Bank does not play a direct role in monetary policy, it contributes to the global money system by providing low interest loans to developing countries. These loans, which are used for such things as public-sector projects (i.e. power stations, roads, bridges, etc.), agricultural development, education, population control, and urban development, are intended to promote economic development and increase the standard of living in developing countries.

As the result of some disappointment in regard to loaning money to countries that do not practice sound economy policy, the World Bank has recently devised a new type of loan. In addition to providing funds to support specific projects, the bank will now also provide loans for the government of a nation to use as it sees fit in return for promises on macroeconomic policy.

9-83.
Hard
P.304

Describe the difference between fixed and floating exchange rates. Which is better? Explain your answer.

Answer: Under a fixed rate system the value of a currency is fixed (usually in terms of U.S. dollars) and is only allowed to change under a specific set of circumstances. The value of a fixed rate system is that it introduces monetary discipline (on a country level), discourages currency speculation, reduces uncertainty (in regard to future currency movements), and, according to the proponents of fixed rates, has little or no effect on trade balance adjustments. In contrast, under a floating rate system, currencies are allowed to float freely (in practice, the majority of floating rate systems are either managed in some way by government intervention or are pegged to another currency). The benefits of a floating rate system is that it gives countries monetary policy autonomy and, according to the proponents, provides a way for countries to correct trade deficits (i.e. an exchange rate depreciation should correct a trade balance by making a country's exports cheaper and its imports more expensive).

There is no right or wrong answer to this question - we simply don't know which system is better. We do know that a fixed rate system modeled along the lines of the Bretton Woods system will not work. Conversely, advocates of a fixed rate system argue that speculation is a major disadvantage of floating rates. Perhaps a modified fixed rate system will producc the type of economic stability that will contribute to greater growth in international trade and investments.

9-84.
Medium
P.311

How do exchange rates affect individual international businesses? Do international businesses like stable rates or volatile rates? Explain your answer.

Answer: The volatility of the present system of floating exchange rates is a problem for international businesses. Exchange rates are difficult to predict, and introduce a major source of "uncertainty" in international trade that is unnerving for many businesses. For example, a company like Case Tractor may build a high quality product in the U.S. and make a profit by exporting it to Japan. But if the Japanese yen depreciates against the U.S. dollar, the relative cost of the tractor in Japan will go up. This will either lower the demand for the tractor in Japan or force Case to lower its price (and accept a lower profit).

The majority of international businesses would probably prefer stability in exchange rates. As depicted above, exchange rate fluctuations introduce uncertainty into the international business process, which is uncertain enough to begin with. Imagine how frustrating it must be for the mangers of firms like Case Tractor, who may lose sales in an international market or suffer declines in profitability that has nothing to do with the quality of their products, but hinge solely on currency rate volatility.

9-85.
Medium
P.312

What can international business organizations do to help shape global monetary policy and encourage growth in international trade and investment?

Answer: This question is designed to encourage classroom discussion and/or to encourage students to "think" about how international businesses can play a constructive role in shaping monetary policy and increase international trade and investment. Obviously, businesses can lobby their respective governments to encourage steps that minimize currency volatility and maximize international business opportunities. In addition, businesses can act prudently in terms of their individual trade practices, and by doing so, lessen the chance that nations will use their currencies (through devaluation) to protect their local industries. Finally, businesses can help sponsor international forums (like the World Bank) that facilitate the growth in international trade and investment.

CHAPTER 10
GLOBAL STRATEGY

True/False Questions

10-1.
T
Easy
P.323

There are two basic strategies for improving a firm's profitability - a differentiation strategy and a low cost strategy.

10-2.
T
Easy
P.324

It is useful to think of the firm as a value chain composed of a series of distinct value creation activities.

10-3.
F
Medium
P.324

The primary activities in a firm's value chain includes human resources, materials management, and manufacturing.

10-4.
T
Easy
P.325

A firm's strategy can be defined as the actions that managers take to attain the goals of the firm.

10-5.
T
Medium
P.325

Firms that operate internationally are typically able to earn a greater return from their distinctive skills, or core competencies.

10-6.
F
Medium
P.326

The term core competence refers to skills within a firm that competitors can easily match.

10-7.
T
Medium
P.328

Economies that arise from performing a value creation activity in the optimal location for the activity are referred to as location economies.

10-8.
T
Easy
P.329

The experience curve refers to the systematic reductions in production costs that have been observed to occur over the life of a product.

10-9.
F
Hard
P.330

Moving down the experience curve causes a firm to increase its cost of creating value.

10-10.
T
Easy
P.330

The reduction in unit costs achieved by producing a large volume of a product is referred to as economies of scale.

10-11.
T
Medium
P.332

Firms that compete in the global market typically face two types of competitive pressure. They face pressures to be locally responsive and pressures for cost reductions.

10-12.
F
Hard
P.334

According to Theodore Levitt, consumer demands for local customization are on the increase worldwide.

10-13.
F
Medium
P.337

Firms that pursue a multidomestic strategy focus upon increasing profitability by reaping the cost reductions that come from experience curve effects and location economies.

10-14.
T
Easy
P.337

Global firms tend not to customize their product offering and marketing strategy to local conditions.

10-15.
T
Hard
P.338

A global strategy makes most sense in those cases where there are strong pressures for cost reductions, and where demands for local responsiveness are minimal.

10-16.
T
Medium
P.340

A transnational strategy is a business strategy seeks experience-based economies and location economies, transfers distinctive competencies within the firm, and pays attention to pressures for local responsiveness.

10-17.
F
Easy
P.342

A lack of local responsiveness is a distinct disadvantage of a multidomestic strategy.

10-18.
T
Medium
P.342

A transnational strategy is difficult to implement due to organizational problems.

10-19.
T
Easy
P.342

A strategic alliance is a cooperative agreement between potential or actual competitors.

10-20.
F
Medium
P.344

Despite the challenges involved, the success rate for international strategic alliances is remarkably good.

Multiple Choice

10-21.
B
Easy
P.324

According to the textbook, it is useful to think of the firm as a _____ composed of a series of distinct activities, including production, marketing, materials management, R&D, human resources, information systems, and the firm infrastructure.
a. functional stream
b. value chain
c. inertia chain
d. momentum machine

10-22.
A
Easy
P.324

The _____ activities of a firm have to do with crating the product, marketing and delivering the product to buyers, and providing support and after-sales service to the buyers of the product.
a. primary
b. subordinate
c. ancillary
d. support

10-23.
A
Medium
P.324

In the context of value chain analysis, the primary activities of a firm include:
a. manufacturing, marketing & service, and sales
b. infrastructure (structure and leadership), human resources, and R&D
c. R&D, sales, and materials management
d. manufacturing, human resources, and materials management

10-24.
D
Hard
P.324

In the context of value chain analysis, the support activities of a firm include:

a. human resources, management information systems, materials management, and accounting
b. accounting, infrastructure, R&D, and materials management
c. manufacturing, marketing and service, R&D, and management information systems
d. human resources, materials management, infrastructure, R&D

10-25.
C
Easy
P.325

A firm's _____ can be defined as the actions that managers take to attain the goals of the firm.

a. systems
b. value chain
c. strategy
d. operations

10-26.
D
Easy
P.325

Actions that managers take to attain the firm's goals are referred to as _____.

a. value chain activities
b. operations
c. systems
d. strategies

10-27.
D
Easy
P.326

The term _____ refers to skills within a firm that competitors cannot easily match.

a. discriminate attributes
b. indigenous properties
c. value chain
d. core competenceies

10-28.
A
Easy
P.326

The skills within a firm that competitors cannot easily match or imitate are called:

a. core competencies
b. discriminate attributes
c. value chain
d. indigenous properties

10-29.
D
Easy
P.328

Economies that arise from performing a value creation activity in the optimal location for that activity are called _____.

a. site expediencies
b. location synergies
c. site commerce
d. location economies

10-30.
C
Medium
P.328

Suppose General Motors decided to manufacture brakes in Ireland, because a detailed analysis of country specific advantages indicated that Ireland is the optimal place in the world to produce brakes. In this example, General Motors is capturing _____ by manufacturing brakes in Ireland.

a. location synergies
b. site expediencies
c. location economics
d. site commerce

10-31.
B
Medium
P.328

According to our textbook, a firm creates a _____ by dispersing the stages of its value chain to those locations around the globe where the value added in maximized or where the costs of value creation are minimized.

a. international mesh
b. global web
c. disperse chain
d. integrate circle

10-32.
A
Easy
P.329

The _____ refers to the systematic reductions in production costs that have been observed to occur over the life of a product.

a. experience curve
b. forward advantage
c. positive-sum result
d. managed advantage

10-33.
C
Medium
P.329

If Goodyear Tire Corporation experienced systematic reductions in the products costs of a particular product over the life of the product, they would be realizing _____ effects.

a. managed production
b. forward advantage
c. experience curve
d. value chain

10-34.
A
Easy
P.330

_____ refer to cost savings that come from learning by doing.

a. Learning effects
b. Exponential effects
c. Ancillary effects
d. Indirect effects

10-35.
C
Easy
P.330

The term _____ refers to the reduction in unit cost achieved by producing a large volume of a product.

a. volume synergies
b. captured savings
c. economies of scale
d. rent effects

10-36.
D
Medium
P.330

If Honda noticed that the unit costs of Honda Accords went down as the number of Accord's produced went up, Honda would be realizing the benefits of _____.
a. captured savings
b. volume synergies
c. rent effects
d. economies of scale

10-37.
C
Hard
P.333

Among global firms, which of the following is not a factor that is driving pressures for local responsiveness?
a. differences in distribution channels
b. differences in infrastructure and traditional practices
c. similarities in consumer tastes and preferences
d. host government demands

10-38.
A
Hard
P.333

Which of the following is not a factor that is driving pressures for local responsiveness among global firms?
a. similarities in distribution channels
b. host government demands
c. differences in infrastructure and traditional practices
d. differences in consumer tastes and preferences

10-39.
C
Medium
P.333

Differences in consumer tastes and preferences, differences in infrastructure and traditional practices, differences in distribution channels, and host government demands are factors pressuring firms to be sensitive to _____ in their international strategies.
a. cost containment
b. global standardization
c. local responsiveness
d. integrating more "commodity" like features

10-40.
A
Medium
P.335

Firms use four basic strategies to compete in the international environment. These are:
a. an international strategy, a multidomestic strategy, a global strategy, and a transnational strategy
b. a cross-cultural strategy, a trade block strategy, a regional strategy, and a world strategy
c. a domestic-based strategy, an international-focused strategy, a local/regional-based strategy, and a cultural-based strategy
d. an international strategy, a regional strategy, a global strategy, and a world strategy

10-41.
B
Medium
P.335

In the international environment, firms used four basic strategies. These are: an international strategy, a multidomestic strategy, a global strategy, and a _____ strategy.
a. local/regional
b. transnational
c. cross-cultural
d. trade block

10-42.
C
Medium
P.335

Firms use four basic strategies to compete in international markets: an international strategy, a global strategy, a transnational strategy, and a _____ strategy.
a. trade block
b. cross-cultural
c. multidomestic
d. local/regional

10-43.
D
Medium
P.336

The appropriateness of the strategy that a firm uses in an international market varies with the extent of pressures for _____ and _____.
a. cost reductions; availability of financing.
b. price concessions; quality improvements
c. availability of financing; product standardization
d. cost reductions; local responsiveness

10-44.
A
Medium
P.336

The appropriateness of the strategy that a firm uses in an international market varies with the extent of pressures for cost reductions and _____.
a. local responsiveness
b. availability of financing
c. trade block membership
d. price concessions

10-45.
B
Hard
P.336

When cost pressures are low and the pressures for local responsiveness are high a _____ strategy is the most appropriate.
a. global
b. multidomestic
c. transnational
d. international

10-46.
B
Hard
P.336

A _____ strategy makes most sense when there are high pressures for cost reductions and high pressures for local responsiveness
a. international
b. transnational
c. global
d. multidomestic

10-47.
C
Hard
P.336

A _____ strategy makes sense when there are low pressures for local responsiveness and low pressures for cost reductions.
a. multidomestic
b. global
c. international
d. transnational

10-48.
D
Medium
P.336

Firms that pursue a _____ strategy try to create value by transferring valuable skills and products to foreign markets where indigenous competitors lack those skills and products.
a. multidomestic
b. transnational
c. global
d. international

10-49.
B
Medium
P.337

A(n) _____ strategy makes sense if a firm has a valuable core competence that indigenous competitors in foreign markets lack and if the firm faces relatively weak pressures for local responsiveness and cost reductions.
a. multidomestic
b. international
c. global
d. transnational

10-50.
A
Medium
P.337

Firms pursuing a _____ strategy orient themselves toward achieving maximum local responsiveness.
a. multidomestic
b. transnational
c. global
d. international

10-51.
A
Medium
P.337

Firms pursuing a multidomestic strategy orient themselves toward achieving maximum:
a. local responsiveness
b. product standardization
c. cost containment
d. product visibility

10-52.
D
Medium
P.337

Unlike international firms, _____ firms extensively customize both their product offerings and their marketing strategy to different national conditions.
a. transnational
b. trade block
c. global
d. multidomestic

10-53.
B
Medium
P.337

Firms that pursue a _____ strategy have a tendency to establish a complete set of value creation activities - including production, marketing, and R&D - in each major national market in which they do business.
a. transnational
b. multidomestic
c. international
d. global

10-54.
B
Medium
P.337

Firms that pursue a _____ strategy focus upon increasing profitability by reaping the cost reductions that come from experience curve effects and location economies.
a. transnational
b. global
c. multidomestic
d. international

10-55.
B
Medium
P.338

A _____ strategy makes most sense in those cases where there are strong pressures for cost reductions, and where demands for local responsiveness are minimal.
a. international
b. transnational
c. multidomestic
d. global

10-56.
C
Easy
P.340

The flow of skills and product offerings from home firm to foreign subsidiary and from foreign subsidiary to home firm and from foreign subsidiary to foreign subsidiary is referred to as _____.
a. knowledge assimilation
b. technical transfer
c. global learning
d. skills and product offerings transfer

10-57.
D
Easy
P.340

_____ is the flow of skills and product offerings from home firm to foreign subsidiary and from foreign subsidiary to home firm and from foreign subsidiary to foreign subsidiary.
a. Skills and product offerings transfer
b. Technical transfer
c. Knowledge assimilation
d. Global learning

10-58.
B
Medium
P.340

A business strategy that seeks experience-based cost economies and location economies, transfers distinctive competencies within the firm, and pays attention to pressures for local responsiveness is referred to as a _____ strategy.
a. international
b. transnational
c. global
d. multidomestic

10-59.
A
Medium
P.340

Firms that pursue a _____ strategy are trying to simultaneously achieve low cost and differentiation advantages.
a. transnational
b. multidomestic
c. global
d. international

10-60.
D
Medium
P.341

According to Bartlett and Ghoshal, the _____ strategy is the only viable international strategy.
a. international
b. multidomestic
c. global
d. transnational

10-61.
D
Hard
P.342

An inability to realize location economies, an failure to exploit experience curve effects, and a failure to transfer distinctive competencies to foreign markets are disadvantages of the _____ strategy.
a. international
b. transnational
c. global
d. multidomestic

10-62.
A
Medium
P.342

Which of the following two international strategies are disadvantaged by a lack of local responsiveness?
a. global and international
b. multidomestic and transnational
c. transnational and global
d. multidomestic and international

10-63.
A
Hard
P.342

A lack of local responsiveness, an inability to realize location economies, and a failure to exploit experience curve effects are disadvantages of a _____ strategy.
a. international
b. global
c. multidomestic
d. transnational

10-64.
A
Hard
P.342

The ability to exploit experience curve effects and to exploit location economies are advantages of a _____ strategy.
a. global
b. multidomestic
c. international
d. transnational

10-65.
B
Hard
P.342

The ability to exploit experience curve effects, exploit location economies, customize product offerings and marketing in accordance with local responsiveness, and reap benefits of global learning are advantages of a _____ strategy.
a. multidomestic
b. transnational
c. international
d. global

10-66.
B
Easy
P.342

The term _____ refers to cooperative agreements between potential or actual competitors.
a. tactical union
b. strategic alliance
c. political affiliation
d. economic association

10-67.
D
Easy
P.342

Cooperative agreements between potential or actual competitors are called:
a. economic associations
b. tactical unions
c. trade unions
d. strategic alliances

10-68.
A
Easy
P.342

_____ are cooperative agreements between potential or actual competitors.
a. Strategic alliances
b. Tactical unions
c. Economic associations
d. Trade unions

10-69.
D
Medium
P.343

Which of the following is not an advantage of a strategic alliance?
a. alliances help facilitate entry into foreign markets
b. allows a firm to share the fixed costs of developing new product or services with another firm
c. provides a forum for firms to bring together complementary skills and assets that neither company could easily develop on its own
d. helps a firm guard its proprietary technology

10-70.
C
Hard
P.344

One recent study of 49 international strategic alliances found that _____ ran into serious managerial and financial troubles within two years of their formation.

a. 1/4
b. 1/2
c. 2/3
d. 3/4

10-71.
C
Medium
P.344

According to the textbook, the success of a strategic alliance is a function of three factors. These are: partner selection, alliance structure, and _____.

a. similarity in size of the alliance partners
b. geographic distance between the alliance partners
c. the manner in which the alliance is managed
d. government support

10-72.
D
Medium
P.344

The success of a strategic alliance is a function of three factors. These are: alliance structure, the manner in which the alliance is managed, and _____.

a. geographic distance between the alliance partners
b. similarity in size of the alliance partners
c. government support
d. partner selection

10-73.
B
Medium
P.344

The success of a strategic alliance is a function of three factors. These are:

a. alliance governance, level of planning, and the manner in which the alliance is managed
b. partner selection, alliance structure, and the manner in which the alliance is managed
c. alliance governance, alliance leadership, and level of planning
d. partner selection, geographic distance between the alliance partners, and government support

10-74.
B
Hard
P.345

The four safeguards against opportunism by alliance partners include:

a. retaining a CPA to audit the alliance's books, agreeing to share valuable skills and technologies, seeking credible commitments, and shared leadership in alliance activities
b. walling off critical technology, establishing contractual safeguards, agreeing to swap valuable skills and technologies, and seeking credible commitments
c. restricting the alliance to activities outside the partner's distinctive competencies, maintaining an atmosphere of secrecy, shared leadership in alliance activities, and seeking credible commitments
d. establishing contractual safeguards, maintaining an atmosphere of secrecy, retaining a CPA to audit the alliance's books, and shared leadership in alliance activities

10-75.
A
Medium
P.345

The four safeguards against opportunism by alliance partners include: walling off critical technology, establishing contractual safeguards, agreeing to swap valuable skills and technologies, and _____.
a. seeking credible commitments
b. maintaining an atmosphere of secrecy
c. retaining a CPA to audit the alliance's books
d. restricting the alliance to activities outside the partner's

10-76.
A
Medium
P.348

According to the textbook, there are three important antecedents to maximizing the benefits of strategic alliances. These are:
a. make allowances for cultural differences, building trust, and learning from partners
b. joint planning, complete disclosure of proprietary technology, limiting the number of alliance partners
c. restricting the alliance to issues dealing with the core competencies of the alliance partners, complete disclosure of proprietary technology, and learning from partners
d. joint planning, building trust, and limiting the number of alliance partners

10-77.
C
Medium
P.348

There are three important antecedents to maximizing the benefits of strategic alliances. These are: making allowances for cultural differences, learning from partners, and _____.
a. limiting the number of alliance partners
b. restricting the alliance to issues dealing with the core competencies of the alliance partners
c. building trust
d. complete disclosure of proprietary technology

10-78.
B
Medium
P.348

According to the textbook, the three most important antecedents to maximizing the benefits of strategic alliances include: building trust, learning from partners, and _____.
a. limiting the number of alliance partners
b. making allowances for cultural differences
c. complete disclosure of proprietary technology
d. restricting the alliance to issues dealing with the core competencies of the alliance partners

10-79.
C
Hard
P.349

After a five-year study of 15 strategic alliances between major multinationals, Gary Hamel, Yves Doz, and C.K. Prahalad concluded that a major determinant of how much a company gains from an alliance is:
a. its ability to enhance its reputation
b. its ability to realize cost savings
c. its ability to learn from alliance partners
d. its ability to achieve greater economies of scale

10-80.   _____is a major determinant of how much a company gains from an
A   alliance, according to a five-year study of 15 strategic alliances between major
Hard   multinationals completed by Gary Hamel, Yves Doz, and C.K. Prahald.
P.349
a. The ability to learn from alliance partners
b. The ability to achieve greater economies of scale
c. The ability to enhance its reputation
d. The ability to realize cost savings

Essay Questions

10-81.   Describe the concept of "core competence." What types of core competencies
Easy   are the most valuable for penetrating foreign markets?
P.3326

Answer: The term core competence refers to the skills within the firms that
competitors cannot easily match or imitate. These skills may exist in any of the
firm's value creation activities (i.e. manufacturing, marketing, sales, materials
management, etc.). These skills typically enable a firm to produce a product or
service that competitors find difficult to duplicate. For instance, Home Depot has a
core competence in managing home improvement superstores. Home Depot's
competitors have found this core competence difficult to imitate.

Core competencies are the most valuable as a tool for helping firms enter foreign
markets when they are unique, when the value placed on them by consumers is
great, and when there are very few capable competitors with similar skills and/or
products in foreign markets. According to the textbook, firms with unique and
valuable skills can often realize enormous returns by applying those skills, and the
products they produce, to foreign markets where indigenous competitors lack
similar skills and products.

10-82.   What is the experience curve? How can an involvement in overseas markets help
Medium   a firm capture experience curve advantages more rapidly?
P.329

Answer: The experience curve refers to the systematic reductions in production
costs that have been observed to occur over the life of a product. In general, the
experience curve suggests that as a firm produces more of a particular product,
the unit price of the product drops. This phenomenon occurs because of learning
effects and economies of scale. Learning effects refer to the cost savings that
come from learning by doing. Economies of scale refers to the reduction in unit
costs achieved by producing a large volume of a product as a result of the ability
to spread fixed costs over a larger volume.

Firms can typically move down the experience curve (i.e. realize a reduction in
production costs by selling more of a product) faster through involvement in
overseas markets. The simple logic is that by going global, a firm expands its
customer base and is able to sell a higher volume of its product. By selling a

higher volume of its product, a firm can experience learning effects and economies of scale benefits more rapidly.

10-83.
Medium
P.332

Firms that compete in global markets often face pressures for local responsiveness. Describe what is meant by local responsiveness, and identify the underlying reasons that local responsiveness pressures exist.

Answer: Many firms enter global markets with the idea of selling essentially the same product in each market that they enter. This approach becomes problematic when the citizens of a particular country ask that the product be customized to fit their particular needs. When the consumer in a country ask that a product be modified to suite their particular tastes, they are in effect asking the international company to be "locally responsive" to their needs. This is where the term local responsiveness comes from.

Pressures for local responsiveness arise from a number of sources. These sources include: (1) Differences in consumer tastes and preferences across markets; (2) Differences in infrastructure and traditional practices across markets; (3) Differences in distribution channels across markets; and (4) Host government demands.

10-84.
Medium
P.335

Describe the four basic strategies that firms use to compete in international markets. Which strategy is the best?

Answer: The four basic strategies that firms use to compete in international markets are: an international strategy, a multidomestic strategy, a global strategy, and a transnational strategy. Each of the strategies is briefly described below.

International Strategy - Firms that pursue an international strategy try to create value by transferring valuable skills and products to foreign markets where indigenous competitors lack those skills and products. These firms tend to centralize product development functions at home, and establish manufacturing and marketing functions in each major country in which they do business. An international strategy makes sense if a firm has a valuable core competence that indigenous competitors in foreign markets lack and if the firm faces relatively weak pressures for local responsiveness and cost reductions. Typically, local responsiveness is fairly modest.

Multidomestic Strategy - Firms pursuing a multidomestic strategy orient themselves toward achieving maximum local responsiveness. These firms tend to transfer skills and products developed at home to foreign markets. Consistent with their strategy of local responsiveness, however, they tend to establish a complete set of value creation activities - including production, marketing, and R&D - in each major market in which they do business. A multidomestic strategy makes sense when there are high pressures for local responsiveness and low pressures for cost reductions. The high cost structure associated with the duplication of production facilities makes this strategy inappropriate in industries where cost pressures are intense.

Global Strategy - Firms that pursue a global strategy focus upon increasing profitability by reaping the cost reductions that come from experience curve effects and location economies. That is, they are pursuing a low cost strategy. The majority of the value chain activities for a global firm are concentrated in a few favorable locations. Global firms are not very locally responsive. Instead, they prefer to market a standardized product worldwide. This strategy makes most sense in those cases where there are strong pressures for cost reductions, and where demands for local responsiveness are minimal.

Transnational Strategy - A transnational strategy is an ambitious strategy in which a firm tries to simultaneously exploit experience-base cost economies and location economies, transfer distinctive competencies within the firm, and pay attention to pressures for local responsiveness. This type of strategy makes sense when a firm faces high pressures for cost reductions and high pressures for local responsiveness. Barlett and Ghoshal admit that building an organization that is capable of supporting a transnational strategic posture is complex and difficult. In essence, a transnational strategy requires a firm to simultaneously achieve cost efficiencies, global learning, and local responsiveness. These are contradictory demands which are difficult to achieve at the same time in practice.

Which strategy is the best? There is no compelling answer to this question. The most advantageous strategy is the one that best complements a firm's distinctive competencies and its ultimate goals and objectives.

10-85.
Medium
P.344

Under what circumstances is entering into strategic alliances a risky undertaking?

Answer: This question is designed to encourage classroom discussion and/or to encourage students to "think" about the potential hazards of alliance formation. There are many compelling reasons to enter into a strategic alliance with another company. For example, an American firm may find the Japanese market tough to crack without finding a Japanese company to partner with. Similarly, if a company like General Motors decided to speed up its R&D in the area of electric cars, it would be awful tempting to develop an alliance with a foreign producer like Honda or Mazda to share the development expense. The primary disadvantage of entering into strategic alliances is that they often compel firms to share sensitive proprietary information with their alliance partners. This practice can give a potential competitor a low cost route to new technology and markets.

CHAPTER 11
ENTERING FOREIGN MARKETS

True/False Questions

11-1.
F
Easy
P.358

Evidence suggests the volume of export activity in the world economy, by firms of all sizes, is likely to decrease in the foreseeable future.

11-2.
T
Easy
P.359

Most manufacturing firms begin their global expansion as exporters.

11-3.
T
Medium
P.360

In a turnkey project, the contractor agrees to handle every detail of the project for a foreign client, including the training of operating personnel.

11-4.
=
Medium
P.361

Turnkey projects are most common in industries that use simple, inexpensive production-process technologies.

11-5.
T
Medium
P.361

A primary advantage of licensing is that the firm does not have to bear the development costs and risks associated with opening a foreign market.

1-6.
=
Easy
P.362

A primary advantage of licensing is total control over technology.

1-7.
=
Medium
.363

Whereas licensing is pursued primarily by manufacturing firms, franchising is employed primarily by service firms.

11-8.
T
Medium
P.363

A primary advantage of franchising is low development costs and risks.

11-9.
F
Easy
P.363

Franchising, as a mode of foreign market entry, is most often used by manufacturing companies.

11-10.
T
Medium
P.364

One of the most significant disadvantages of franchising is quality control.

11-11.
T
Easy
P.366

A joint venture entails establishment of a firm that is jointly owned by two or more otherwise independent companies.

11-12.
F
Medium
P.366

Research suggests that joint ventures with local partners face a high risk of being subject to nationalization or other forms of government interference.

11-13.
T
Medium
P.366

A primary advantage of joint ventures is the sharing of development costs and risks.

11-14.
T
Medium
P.367

One of the primary advantages of a wholly owned subsidiary is that it gives the firm tight control over operations in different countries that is necessary for engaging in global strategic coordination.

11-15.
T
Easy
P.370

The competitive advantage of many service firms is based on management know how.

11-16.
T
Medium
P.371

Studies have shown that while many large firms tend to be proactive about seeking out opportunities for profitable exporting, many medium-sized and small firms are very reactive.

11-17.
F
Medium
P.376

A stamp of credit worthiness, which is issued by a bank at the request of an exporter, states the bank will pay a specified sum of money to a beneficiary, normally the exporter, on presentation of particular, specified documents.

11-18.
F
Medium
P.378

A bill of lading, sometimes referred to as a bill of exchange, is the instrument normally used in international commerce for payment.

11-19.
T
Easy
P.378

International practice is to use drafts to settle trade transactions.

11-20.
F
Easy
P.378

A sight draft allows for a delay in paying - normally 30, 60, 90, or 120 days.

Multiple Choice

11-21.
C
Hard
P.358

In the United States, _____ of companies with annual revenues of less than $100 million said they exported products in 1993.
a. 12%
b. 26%
c. 49%
d. 66%

11-22.
C
Easy
P.359

Most manufacturing firms being their global expansion through _____.
a. establishing a joint venture with a host country firm
b. licensing
c. exporting
d. turnkey projects

11-23.
A
Medium
P.359

Exporting has two distinct advantages. These are:

a. it avoids the often substantial cost of establishing manufacturing operations in the host country; and it may help a firm achieve experience curve and location economies
b. access to local partner's knowledge; and politically acceptable
c. ability to earn returns from process technology skills in countries where FDI is restricted; and politically acceptable
d. access to a local partner's knowledge and it may help a firm achieve experience curve; and location economies

11-24.
C
Medium
P.359

Exporting has two distinct advantages: it avoids the often substantial cost of establishing manufacturing operations in the host country and _____.

a. it provide a firm the ability to earn returns from process technology skills in countries where FDI is restricted
b. it is politically acceptable
c. it may help a firm achieve experience curve and location economies
d. it provides a firm access to local partner's knowledge

11-25.
D
Medium
P.359

Exporting has two distinct advantages: it may help a firm achieve experience curve and location economies and _____.

a. it provides a firm access to a local partner's knowledge
b. it is politically acceptable
c. it provides the firm the ability to earn returns from process technology skills in countries where FDI is restricted
d. it avoids the often substantial cost of establishing manufacturing operations in the host country

11-26.
B
Medium
P.359

All of the following are disadvantages of exporting except?

a. high transportation costs can make exporting uneconomical
b. it may help a firm achieve experience curve economies
c. tariff barriers can make exporting uneconomical
d. exporting from a firm's home bases may not be appropriate if there are lower-cost locations for manufacturing the product abroad

11-27.
A
Medium
P.359

High transport costs, trade barriers, and problems with local marketing agents are disadvantages of _____.

a. exporting
b. franchising
c. licensing
d. turnkey projects

11-28.
D
Medium
P.359

Consider the following scenario: Tucker Manufacturing wants to sell its products overseas, but only if it can act on its own and manufacturer its product in a central location. Based on these objectives, the appropriate foreign entry mode for Tucker is:

a. wholly owned subsidiary
b. franchising
c. licensing
d. exporting

11-29.
D
Easy
P.360

In a _____ project, the contractor agrees to handle every detail of the project for a foreign client, including the training of operating personnel.

a. beginning to end
b. A to Z
c. front-to-back
d. turnkey

11-30.
A
Medium
P.360

Creating efficient competitors and lack of long-term market presence are disadvantages of _____.

a. turnkey projects
b. licensing
c. franchising
d. exporting

11-31.
C
Medium
P.360

Turnkey projects are a means of exporting _____ to other countries.

a. commodities
b. manufacturing goods
c. process technology
d. services

11-32.
D
Medium
P.360

Suppose Mobil Oil, a U.S. company, was contracted by a Saudi Arabian company to build a oil refinery in Saudi Arabia, and the contract specified that Mobil would handle every aspect of the construction of the refinery, including the training of the operating personnel. This type of project is referred to as a:

a. front to back
b. beginning to end
c. A to Z
d. turnkey project

11-33.
A
Hard
P.360

Turnkey projects are most common in the following industries:

a. chemical, pharmaceutical, petroleum refining, and metal refining
b. textiles, shoes, leather products, and linens
c. cars, trucks, construction equipment, and farm implements
d. lumber, furniture, paper, and pulp

11-34.
B
Medium
P.361

Which of the following foreign market entry mode takes advantage of a firm's competency in the area of assembling and running technologically complex projects?
a. franchising
b. turnkey project
c. exporting
d. licensing

11-35.
C
Easy
P.361

A _____ agreement is an arrangement whereby a licensor grants the rights to intangible property to another entity for a specified time period in exchange for royalties.
a. franchising
b. turnkey
c. licensing
d. exporting

11-36.
C
Hard
P.361

Lack of control over technology, inability to realize location and experience curve economies, and an inability to engage in global strategic coordination are distinct disadvantages of _____.
a. turnkey projects
b. exporting
c. licensing
d. wholly owned subsidiaries

11-37.
C
Hard
P.361

Which of the following is not an argument in favor of licensing as a means of foreign market entry?
a. the firm does not have to have capital to open markets overseas
b. a firm wants to participate in a foreign market, but is prohibited from doing so by barriers to investment
c. the firm possesses some intangible property that might have business applications and wants to develop that technology or those applications itself
d. the firm does not have to bear the development costs and risks associated with opening a foreign market

11-38.
B
Medium
P.361

Suppose 3M Corporation granted a South Korean company the rights to manufacture "Post-It-Notes" in South Korean in exchange for a royalty fee. This type of arrangement is referred to as a:
a. franchising agreement
b. licensing agreement
c. turnkey project
d. wholly owned subsidiary

11-39.
A
Easy
P.361

Patents, inventions, formulas, processes, designs, copyrights, and trademarks are examples of _____ property.
a. intangible
b. discernible
c. tangible
d. nondescript

11-40.
C
Medium
P.362

Under a _____ agreement, a firm might license some valuable intangible property to a foreign partner, but in addition to a royalty payment, the firm might also request that the foreign partner license some of its valuable know-how to the firm.
a. inter-licensing
b. reciprocal-licensing
c. cross-licensing
d. parity-licensing

11-41.
A
Medium
P.362

An arrangement whereby a company grants the right to intangible property to another firm for a specified time period in exchange for royalties and a license from the foreign partners for some of its technological know-how is referred to as _____.

a. cross-licensing agreement
b. reciprocal licensing agreement
c. parity licensing agreement
d. inter-licensing agreement

11-42.
B
Medium
P.363

Other than licensing, the form of foreign market entry that results in a firm in the host country paying a royalty to the firm that has the rights to a product or service is called _____.
a. joint venture
b. franchising
c. exporting
d. wholly owned subsidiary

11-43.
D
Easy
P.363

_____ is basically a specialized form of licensing in which the franchiser not only sells intangible property to the franchisee, but also insists that the franchisee agree to abide by strict rules as to how it does business.
a. Leasing
b. Chartering
c. Exporting
d. Franchising

11-44.
D
Medium
P.363

Low development costs and risks are distinct advantages of:
a. wholly owned subsidiaries and exporting
b. exporting and turnkey projects
c. joint ventures and wholly owned subsidiaries
d. franchising and licensing

11-45.
A
Medium
P.363

Which of the following two modes of foreign market entry typically involves a royalty payment made by the firm in the host country?
a. licensing and franchising
b. setting up a wholly owned subsidiary in the host country and exporting
c. exporting and establishing a joint venture with a host country firm
d. turnkey projects and establishing a joint venture with a host country firm

11-46.
A
Hard
P.363

Lack of control over quality and the inability to engage in global strategic coordination are distinct disadvantages of _____.
a. franchising
b. exporting
c. wholly owned subsidiaries
d. turnkey projects

11-47.
C
Medium
P.364

One of the most significant disadvantages of franchising is _____.
a. high financial risks
b. high development costs
c. quality control
d. the need for coordination of manufacturing to achieve experience curve and location economies

11-48.
D
Easy
P.366

A _____ entails establishment of a firm that is jointly owned by two or more otherwise independent firms.
a. licensing agreement
b. wholly owned subsidiary
c. franchise
d. joint venture

11-49.
C
Medium
P.366

If Texaco and a Russian firm established a jointly owned entity for the purpose of exploring for oil in Northern Siberia, that would be an example of a:
a. turnkey project
b. wholly owned subsidiary
c. joint venture
d. franchise

11-50.
B
Medium
P.366

If Honda and Ford established a jointly owned entity for the purpose of building cars to export to Eastern Europe, that would be an example of a _____ form of foreign market entry.
a. wholly owned subsidiary
b. joint venture
c. turnkey project
d. franchise

11-51.
B
Medium
P.366

The most typical joint venture is:
a. 80/20, in which there are two partners and one partner holds a substantial majority share
b. 50/50, in which there are two partners and each partner holds an equal share
c. 25/25/25/25, in which there are four partners and each partner hold an equal share
d. 51/49, in which there are two partners and one partner holds a slight majority share

11-52.
C
Medium
P.366

What is the preferred mode of foreign market entry for a high-tech firms that wants to (1) minimize the risk of losing control over its technological competence; and (2) maintain tight control over its operations?
a. licensing
b. franchising
c. wholly owned subsidiary
d. turnkey operation

11-53.
D
Medium
P.367

Suppose Eastman Kodak decided to build a manufacturing plant in Poland and, in an effort to maintain maximum control, decided to operate the plant completely on its own. This is an approach to foreign market entry referred to as:
a. joint venture
b. turnkey operation
c. exporting
d. wholly owned subsidiary

11-54.
B
Easy
P.367

In a wholly owned subsidiary, the firm owns _____ of the stock.
a. the majority
b. 100%
c. 51%
d. the minority

11-55.
B
Hard
P.367

Protection of technology, the ability to engage in global strategic coordination and the ability to realize location and experience economies are distinct advantages of _____.

a. franchising
b. wholly owned subsidiary
c. exporting
d. licensing

11-56.
D
Hard
P.369

If a firm's competitive advantage is based on control over proprietary technological know how, which of the following foreign entry modes should be avoided?

a. exporting and joint ventures
b. turnkey projects and franchising
c. wholly owned subsidiaries and franchising
d. joint ventures and licensing

11-57.
A
Medium
P.369

If a high-tech firm sets up operations in a foreign country to profit from a core competency in technological know-how, the most advantageous entry mode is:

a. wholly owned subsidiary
b. turnkey operation
c. franchising
d. licensing

11-58.
C
Easy
P.372

In the United States, the most comprehensive source of information for export advice is the:

a. World Trade Organization
b. U.S. Department of State
c. U.S. Department of Commerce
d. United Nations

11-59.
A
Easy
P.372

In the United States, the _____ is the most comprehensive source of information for export advice.

a. U.S. Department of Commerce
b. U.S. Department of State
c. United Nations
d. World Trade Organization

11-60.
B
Medium
P.373

_____ are export specialists that act as the export marketing department or international department for their client firms.

a. Export accounting agencies
b. Export management companies
c. Overseas marketing companies
d. International intermediaries

11-61.
C
Hard
P.373

Export management companies normally accept two types of export assignments: they start export operations for a firm with the understanding that the firm will take over operations after they are well established, or:

a. they perform start-up with the understanding that the export management company will remain committed for a period of at least ten years
b. they perform start-up with the understanding the export management company will remain committed for a period of at least five years
c. they perform start-up with the understanding that the export management company will have continuing responsibility for selling the firm's products
d. they perform start-up with the understanding the export management company will acquire an equity interest in the exporting firm

11-62.
D
Hard
P.375

Which of the following was not mentioned in the textbook as a strategy for effective exporting?

a. it is important to hire local personnel to help the firm establish itself in a foreign market
b. particularly for a new exporter, it helps to hire an export management company
c. in many countries it is important to devote a lot of attention to building strong and enduring relationships with local distributors and/or customers
d. it often makes sense to focus on a large number of markets initially

11-63.
A
Medium
P.375

Three mechanisms for financing exports and imports include:

a. the letter of credit, the draft, and the bill of lading
b. the open note, the bill of cargo, and the stamp of credit worthiness
c. the stamp of credit worthiness, the open note, and the bill of cargo
d. the guaranteed note, the letter of credit, and the bill of shipping

11-64.
D
Medium
P.375

Three mechanisms for financing exports and imports include the letter of credit, the draft, and the _____.

a. the open note
b. the stamp of credit worthiness
c. the guaranteed note
d. bill of lading

11-65.
A
Medium
P.375

Three mechanisms for financing exports and imports include the draft, the bill of lading, and the _____.

a. letter of credit
b. open note
c. stamp of credit worthiness
d. guaranteed note

11-66.
D
Medium
P.375

Three mechanisms for financing exports and imports include the letter of credit, the bill of lading, and the _____.
a. open note
b. stamp of credit worthiness
c. continuous note
d. draft

11-67.
B
Medium
P.375

Issued by a bank at the request of an importer, a _____ states the bank will pay a specified sum of money to a beneficiary, normally the exporter, on presentation of particular, specified documents
a. stamp of credit worthiness
b. letter of credit
c. bill of lading
d. draft

11-68.
C
Medium
P.375

A _____ is a document issued by a bank and states the bank will pay a specified sum of money to a beneficiary, normally an exporter, on presentation of particular, specified documents.
a. certificate of credit worthiness
b. bill of lading
c. letter of credit
d. draft

11-69.
C
Medium
P.378

A _____, sometimes referred to as a bill of exchange, is the instrument normally used in international commerce for payment.
a. open note
b. stamp of credit worthiness
c. draft
d. bill of lading

11-70.
A
Medium
P.378

The instrument normally used in international commerce for payment is referred to as a _____.
a. draft
b. stamp of credit worthiness
c. bill of lading
d. open note

11-71.
A
Medium
P.378

International practice is to use _____ to settle trade transactions.
a. drafts
b. letters of credit
c. open notes
d. credit vouchers

11-72.
B
Easy
P.378

Drafts fall into two categories. These are:
a. inspection drafts and duration drafts
b. sight drafts and time drafts
c. credit drafts and cash drafts
d. inspection drafts and cash drafts

11-73.
C
Easy
P.378

Drafts fall into two categories: sight drafts and _____ drafts.
a. duration
b. credit
c. time
d. inspection

11-74.
B
Medium
P.378

In the context of drafts used in international commerce for payment, a _____ draft allows for a delay in payment - normally 30, 60, 90, or 120 days.
a. duration
b. time
c. sight
d. inspection

11-75.
C
Medium
P.378

In the context of drafts used in international commerce for payment, a _____ draft is payable on presentation to the drawee.
a. duration
b. inspection
c. sight
d. time

11-76.
B
Easy
P.379

The _____ is issued to the exporter by the common carrier transporting the merchandise.
a. acceptance certificate
b. bill of lading
c. bill of tender
d. stamp of receipt

11-77.
C
Medium
P.379

A bill of laden serves three purposes. These are:
a. it is a certificate of authenticity, proof of insurance, and a contract
b. it is proof of payment, a certificate of tariff payment, and a contract
c. it is a receipt, a contract, and a document of title
d. it is a certificate of authenticity, a letter of credit, and a document of title

11-78.
A
Medium
P.379

A bill of laden serves three purposes: it is a receipt, a contract, and _____.
a. a document of title
b. a letter of credit
c. it is proof of insurance
d. it is proof of customs clearance

11-79.
B
Medium
P.379

A bill of laden serves three purposes: it is a contract, a document of title, and
_____.

a. it is proof of customs clearance
b. a receipt
c. a letter of credit
d. it is proof of environmental safety

11-80.
C
Medium
P.379

A bill of laden serves three purposes: it is a receipt, a document of title, and
_____.

a. it is proof of insurance
b. it is proof of customs clearance
c. a contract
d. a letter of credit

Essay Questions

11-81.
Easy
P.359

What are the six different ways for a firm to enter a foreign market? Provide a
brief description of each of these foreign market entry strategies.

Answer: The six different ways for a firm to enter a foreign market include:

A. Exporting – involves manufacturing a product in a central location and shipping
it to foreign markets for sale.

B. Turnkey projects – in a turnkey project, a contractor from one country handles
every detail of the design, construction, and start-up of a facility in a foreign
country, and then hands the foreign client the key to a facility that is ready for
operation.

C. Licensing – in a licensing agreement, a company from one country grants the
rights to intangible property (such as patents, processes, and trademarks) to a
company in another country in exchange for a royalty fee.

D. Franchising – is a specialized form of licensing in which the franchiser sells
intangible property (normally processes and trademarks) to a franchisee, but
also insists that the franchisee agree to abide by strict rules as to how it does
business. The McDonalds Corporation, for example, has been very successful
in selling franchises to both domestic and foreign franchisees.

E. Joint Ventures – entails establishing a firm that is jointly owned by two or more
otherwise independent firms.

F. Wholly Owned Subsidiary – this form of foreign market entry entails setting up
a new operation (or acquiring an existing company) in a foreign country.

11-82. From the perspective of a domestic firm, what are the advantages and
Medium disadvantages of licensing the rights to the company's production process and
P.361   trademark to a firm in a foreign country? What are some of the ways that a firm
        can reduce the risk of losing its proprietary know-how to foreign companies
        through licensing agreements?

Answer: The primary advantage of licensing is that the firm does not have to bear
the development costs and risks associated with opening a foreign market. As a
result, licensing is a very attractive option for firms that lack the capital or risk
bearing ability to open overseas markets. Licensing is also an attractive option
when a firm is interested in pursuing a foreign market but does not want to commit
substantial resources to an unfamiliar or potentially volatile foreign market.
Licensing is also used when a firm wishes to participate in a foreign market, but is
prohibited from doing so by barriers to investment. Finally, licensing is used when
a firm possesses some intangible property (like its trademark) but does not want
to pursue a potential application itself. For example, Coca-Cola has licensed its
familiar trademark to clothing manufacturers, which have incorporated the design
into their clothing.

There are three main drawbacks to licensing. First, if a firm licenses any of its
proprietary know-how (such as its production processes) to another company, it
risks losing control over this knowledge by permitting access to it by another firm.
According to the textbook, many firms have made the mistake of thinking they
could maintain control over their know-how within the framework of a licensing
agreement. Second, licensing is not an effective way of realizing experience
curve and location economies by manufacturing a product in a centralized
location. If these attributes are important to a firm, licensing may be a poor
choice. Finally, competing in a global market may require a firm to coordinate
strategic moves across countries by using profits from one country to support
competitive attacks in another. Licensing severely limits a firm's ability to do this.
A licensee is unlikely to allow a multinational firm to use its profits (beyond the
royalty payments) to support a different licensee operating in another country.

A licensor can reduce the risk of losing proprietary know-how to a foreign partner
by entering into a cross-licensing agreement. Under a cross-license agreement, a
firm licenses some valuable intangible property (such as a production process) to
a foreign partner, but in addition to royalty payments, the firm also requires the
foreign partner to license some of its valuable know-how to the firm. Cross-
licensing agreements enable firms to hold each other "hostage," thereby reducing
the risk they will behave in an opportunistic manner toward each other.

11-83. What is meant by the term "wholly owned subsidiary?" Under what circumstances
Medium is the establishment of a wholly owned subsidiary an appropriate foreign entry
P.367   strategy?

301

Answer: A wholly owned subsidiary is a company that is completely owned by another company. One choice that a firm has for entering a foreign market is to setup a new operation in that market or purchase an existing firm. In either case, if the original company owns 100% of the new operation, it is "wholly owned subsidiary" of the original firm.

Establishing a wholly owned subsidiary as a entry strategy into a foreign market is appropriate when a firm's competitive advantage is based on technological competence. By establishing a wholly owned subsidiary, a firm reduces the risk of losing control over that competence. This is a particularly important concern for firms that have important proprietary technology. Other forms of foreign market entry, such as licensing and joint venture, do a poorer job of protecting a firm's proprietary technology.

Establishing a wholly owned subsidiary may be appropriate for two additional reasons. First, expanding via the wholly owned subsidiary route gives a firm tight control over its operations in various countries. This strategy maximizes a firm's potential to engage in global strategic coordination (i.e., using profits from one country to support competitive attacks in another). Second, a wholly owned subsidiary strategy may be required if a firm is trying to realize location and experience curve economies.

11-84.
Easy
P.373

What is an export management company? What should a company do before it hires an export management company to help with its export operations?

Answer: An export management company (EMC) is a firm that specializes in helping other firms initiate and manage their export operations. EMCs typically accept two types of assignments. First, they can start exporting operations for a firm with the understanding that the firm will take over operations after they are well established. Second, they can perform start-up export operations for a firm with the understanding that they will maintain an ongoing relationship with the company. EMC are valuable because they specialize in export operations, which often involves a lot of export specific paperwork, knowledge, and networking. By using an EMC, a firm can move much quicker than it could if it had to learn all of the export specific regulations itself, and had to start from scratch in terms of making contacts in foreign countries.

Studies have revealed that there is a wide variation in the quality of EMCs. While some perform their functions very well, others appear to add little value to the exporting companies. Therefore, an exporter should carefully review a number of EMCs, and check references from an EMC's past clients, before deciding on a particular EMC.

11-85.
Medium
P.376

Describe the mechanisms for financing export and imports. Do you belief that the complexity of export financing deters small firms from becoming involved in exporting? Explain your answer.

Answer: There are three principle mechanisms used to finance exports and imports. These are: the letter of credit, the draft (or bill of exchange), and the bill of lading. The following is a description of each one of these items.

Letter of Credit: A letter of credit is issued by a bank at the request of an importer. The letter of credit states the bank will pay a specified sum of money to a beneficiary, normally the exporter, on presentation of particular, specified documents. This process is reflected in the following example. If Goodyear Tire sold 10,000 tires to a company in France, the French company could go to a bank and request a letter of credit to assure Goodyear that it will get paid. If the French company is creditworthy, the bank would issue a letter of credit. The letter of credit would stipulate that upon receipt of the 10,000 tires by the French Company, the bank would pay Goodyear the agreed upon amount. This type of arrangement helps the system of international commerce work. Without some assurance of payment, a company like Goodyear may be reluctant to ship products to a foreign company that it is not very familiar with.

Draft: A draft, sometimes referred to as a bill of exchange, it the instrument normally used in international commerce for payment. A draft is simply an order written by an exporter instructing an importer, or an importer's agency, to pay a specified amount of money at specified time.

Bill of Lading: The third critical document for financing international trade is the bill of lading. The bill of lading is issued to the exporter by the common carrier transporting the merchandise. It serves three purposes: it is a receipt, a contract, and a document of title. As a receipt, the bill of laden indicates the carrier has received the merchandise described on the face of the document. As a contract, it specifies that the carrier is obligated to provide a transportation service in return for a certain charge. As a document of title, it can be used to obtain payment or a written promise of payment before the merchandise is released to the importer. The bill of laden can also function as collateral against which funds may be advanced by the exporter to its local bank before or during shipment and before final payment by the importer.

Does the complexity of this system discourage small businesses from becoming more actively involved in exporting? Probably This question provides a platform for classroom discussion.

CHAPTER 12
GLOBAL MARKETING

True/False Questions

12-1.
T.
Easy
P.389

A global marketing strategy, which views the world's consumers as similar in their tastes and preferences, is consistent with the mass production of a standardized output.

12-2.
F
Medium
P.389

Academic research has long maintained that a major factor of success for new-product introductions is the closeness of the relationship between finance and R&D.

12-3.
T
Easy
P.389

The four elements of a firm's marketing mix include product attributes, distribution strategy, communication strategy, and pricing strategy

12-4.
T
Medium
P.390

According to the textbook, globalization seems to be the exception rather than the rule in many industrial markets.

12-5.
F
Medium
P.393

The main differences among countries' distribution systems are retail concentration, channel breadth, and channel depth.

12-6.
T
Medium
P.394

Developed countries tend to have greater retail concentration than developing countries.

12-7.
F
Hard
P.394

A country that is characterized by a high percentage of car ownership, a high percentage of households with refrigerators and freezers, and a high percentage of two-income households, will most likely have a low level of retail concentration.

12-8.
T
Medium
P.395

The most important determinant of channel length is the degree to which the retail system is fragmented.

12-9.
T
Medium
P.395

Countries with fragmented retail systems also tend to have long channels of distribution.

12-10.
T
Medium
P.396

Since each intermediary in a channel adds its own markup to the products, there is generally a critical link between channel length and the firm's profit margin.

12-11.
T
Easy
P.397

International communication occurs whenever a firm uses a marketing message to sell its product in another country.

12-12.
F
Easy
P.398

A pull strategy emphasized personal selling rather than mass media advertising in the promotional mix.

12-13.
F
Hard
P.398

A push strategy is generally favored by firms in consumer goods industries that are trying to sell to a large segment of the market.

12-14.
T
Medium
P.399

Push strategies tend to be emphasized for industrial products and/or complex new products.

12-15.
T
Medium
P.399

The longer the distribution channel, the more intermediaries there are that must be persuaded to carry the product for it to reach the consumer.

12-16.
F
Easy
P.401

In an international context, predatory pricing exists whenever consumers in different countries are charged different prices for the same product.

12-17.
T
Medium
P.402

Arbitrage occurs when an individual or business capitalizes on a price differential between two countries by purchasing the product in the country where prices are low and reselling it in the country where prices are high.

12-18.
T
Medium
P.403

The elasticity of demand for a product in a given country is determined by a number of factors, of which income level and competitive conditions are perhaps the two most important.

12-19.
T
Easy
P.407

Dumping occurs whenever a firm sells a product for a price that is less than the cost of producing it.

12-20.
F
Medium
P.410

Other things being equal, the rate of new-product development seems to be greater in countries where demand is strong, consumers are affluent, and competition is weak.

Multiple Choice

12-21.
C
Easy
P.389

A critical aspect of the _____ function is identifying gaps in the market so that new products can be developed to fill those gaps.
a. materials management
b. finance
c. marketing
d. operations

12-22.
A
Medium
P.389

The four elements that constitute a firm's marketing mix include:
a. product attributes, distribution strategy, communication strategy, and pricing strategy
b. transportation strategy, warehousing strategy, availability of financing, and pricing strategy
c. promotions strategy, pricing strategy, availability of financing, and distribution strategy
d. product attributes, promotions strategy, communication strategy, and transportation strategy

12-23.
C
Medium
P.389

The four elements that constitute a firm's marketing mix include product attributes, distribution strategy, communications strategy, and:
a. availability of financing
b. warehousing strategy
c. pricing strategy
d. advertising strategy

12-24.
D
Medium
P.389

A firm's marketing mix includes distribution strategy, communications strategy, pricing strategy, and _____.
a. advertising strategy
b. warehousing strategy
c. availability of financing
d. pricing strategy

12-25.
A
Easy
P.390

Levitt has argued that, due to the advent of modern communications and transport technology, consumer tastes and preferences are becoming _____, which is creating global markets for standardized consumer products.
a. global
b. localized
c. cross-regional
d. individualistic

12-26.
A
Hard
P.393

According to the textbook, the most important aspect of a countries' cultural differences is the impact of:
a. tradition
b. language
c. geographic location
d. the availability of natural resources

12-27.
B
Easy
P.393

A critical element of a firm's marketing mix is its _____ strategy, which is the means it chooses for delivering the product to the consumer.
a. materials management
b. distribution
c. logistics
d. communication

12-28.
D
Medium
P.393

In terms of their distribution strategies, countries differ along three main dimensions. These are:
a. end-user identification, channel integration, and transportation strategy
b. customer concentration, channel breadth, and warehousing strategy
c. wholesale concentration, channel depth, and transportation strategy
d. retail concentration, channel length, and channel exclusivity

12-29.
B
Medium
P.393

The main differences among countries' distribution systems are threefold: retail concentration, channel length, and _____.
a. transportation strategy
b. channel exclusivity
c. channel depth
d. warehousing strategy

12-30.
A
Medium
P.393

The main differences among countries' distribution systems are threefold: channel length, channel exclusivity, and _____.
a. retail concentration
b. preferred mode of transportation
c. warehousing strategy
d. wholesale concentration

12-31.
B
Medium
P.394

In terms of retail concentration, developed countries tend to have a higher degree of concentration than developing countries for all of the following reasons except:
a. increases in car ownership
b. a tradition of established local neighborhoods in which people walk to stores
c. number of households with refrigerators and freezers
d. number of two-income households that accompany development

12-32.
A
Easy
P.395

Channel _____ refers to the number of intermediaries between the product (or manufacturer) and the consumer.
a. length
b. exclusivity
c. distance
d. reach

12-33.
B
Easy
P.395

The number of intermediaries between the product (or manufacturer) and the consumer is referred to as:
a. channel distance
b. channel length
c. channel exclusivity
d. channel reach

12-34.
C
Hard
P.395

Which of the following countries is characterized by fragmented retail systems with long channels of distribution?
a. United States
b. Germany
c. Japan
d. Great Britain

12-35.
A
Hard
P.395

_____ is a country that is characterized by fragmented retail systems with long channels of distribution.
a. Japan
b. Great Britain
c. Germany
d. United States

12-36.
A
Easy
P.395

A choice of _____ strategy determines which channel the firm will use to reach potential consumers.
a. distribution
b. transportation
c. communications
d. operations

12-37.
A
Easy
P.397

Direct selling, sales promotion, direct marketing, and advertising are all apart of a firm's _____ strategy.
a. communications
b. distribution
c. product
d. operations

12-38.
D
Easy
P.397

Direct selling, sales promotion, direct marketing, and _____ are all part of a firm's communications strategy.
a. pricing
b. reengineering
c. warehousing
d. advertising

12-39.
B
Easy
P.397

_____ communications occurs whenever a firm uses a marketing message to sell its products in another country.
a. Diversified
b. International
c. Multi-domestic
d. Functional

12-40.
D
Medium
P.397

The effectiveness of a firm's international communication can be jeopardized by three potentially critical variables. These are:
a. technological barriers, geographic barriers, and political barriers
b. economic factors, political-legal barriers, and noise levels
c. technological factors, source effects, and noise levels
d. cultural barriers, source effects, and noise levels

12-41.
C
Medium
P.397

The effectiveness of a firm's international communication can be jeopardized by three potentially critical variables. These are source effects, noise levels, and _____.

a. geographic barriers
b. technological factors
c. cultural barriers
d. political barriers

12-42.
D
Medium
P.397

Three potentially critical variables can jeopardize the effectiveness of a firm's international communications efforts. These are: cultural barriers, noise levels, and:

a. geographic factors
b. technological barriers
c. political barriers
d. source effects

12-43.
C
Medium
P.397

_____ occur when the receiver of the message (i.e. the potential customer) evaluates the message based on the status or image of the sender.

a. Synergistic effects
b. Temporal effects
c. Source effects
d. Direct effects

12-44.
A
Medium
P.397

The types of effects that occurs when the receiver of a message (i.e. the potential customer) evaluates the message based on the status or image of the sender are referred to as:

a. source effects
b. concentric effects
c. temporal effects
d. direct effects

12-45.
C
Easy
P.398

In the context to barriers to international communication, _____ refer(s) to the number of other messages competing for a potential consumer's attention.

a. alternative signals
b. source effects
c. noise
d. channels effects

12-46.
D
Easy
P.398

In regard to communication strategy, a _____ strategy emphasizes personal selling rather than mass media advertising in the promotional mix.

a. reverse
b. pull
c. forward
d. push

12-47.
A
Easy
P.398

In regard to communication strategy, which of the following strategies emphasizes personal selling rather than mass media advertising in the promotional mix?
a. push
b. pull
c. reverse
d. forward

12-48.
B
Easy
P.398

Which of the following communications strategies relies primarily on mass media advertising rather than personal selling?
a. forward
b. pull
c. push
d. reverse

12-49.
C
Medium
p.398

The three main factors that determine the relative attractiveness of push and pull strategies include:
a. advertising cost, product type relative to consumer sophistication, and channel exclusivity
b. geographic dispersion of buyers, channel length, and channel exclusivity
c. product type relative to consumer sophistication, channel length, and media availability
d. channel exclusivity, advertising cost, and cultural diversity of buyers

12-50.
B
Medium
P.398

The three main factors that determine the relative attractiveness of push and pull strategies include channel length, media availability, and _____.
a. channel exclusivity
b. product type relative to consumer sophistication
c. cultural diversity of buyers
d. advertising costs

12-51.
A
Medium
P.398

According to the textbook, three factors that determine the relative attractiveness of push and pull strategies include product type relative to consumer sophistication, channel length, and _____.
a. media availability
b. channel exclusivity
c. advertising costs
d. cultural diversity of buyers

12-52.
A
Medium
P.398

A _____ strategy is generally favored by firms in consumer goods industries that are trying to sell to a large segment of the market.
a. pull
b. conditional
c. reverse
d. push

12-53.
B
Medium
P.398

A pull strategy is generally favored by:
a. firms in durable goods industries that are trying to sell to a small segment of the markets
b. firms in consumer goods industries that are typing to sell to a large segment of the market
c. firms in commodities industries that are trying to sell to foreign governments
d. firms in service industries that are typing to sell to a large segment of the market

12-54.
D
Medium
P.398

A push strategy is favored by firms that sell:
a. services
b. commodities
c. consumer products or other standardized products
d. industrial products or other complex products

12-55.
A
Medium
P.398

A _____ strategy is favored by firms that sell industrial products or other complex products.
a. push
b. pull
c. reverse
d. disperse

12-56.
C
Medium
P.399

In the context of communications strategy, push strategies tend to be emphasized:
a. for industrial products and/or complex new products, when distribution channels are short, and when few print or electronic media are available
b. for commodities, when distribution channels are short, and when international markets are attractive for the product
c. for consumer goods, when distribution channels are long, and when sufficient print and electronic media are available to carry the marketing message
d. for services, when distribution channels are long, and when international markets are attractive for the product

12-57.
B
Medium
P.399

In the context of communications strategy, pull strategies tend to be emphasized:
a. for commodities, when distribution channels are short, and when international markets are available for the product
b. for consumer goods, when distribution channels are long, and when sufficient print and electronic media are available to carry the marketing message
c. for services, when distribution channels are long, and when international markets are available for the product
d. for industrial products and/or complex new products, when distribution channels are short, and when few print or electronic media are available

12-58.
A
Medium
P.399

Push strategies tend to be emphasized for industrial products and/or complex new products, when distribution channels are short, and when _____.
a. few print or electronic media are available
b. international markets are available for the product
c. sufficient print and electronic media are available
d. distribution channels are difficult to access

12-59.
A
Medium
P.399

Pull strategies tend to be emphasized for _____.
a. consumer goods
b. commodities
c. industrial goods
d. services

12-60.
B
Medium
P.399

Push strategies tend to be emphasized for _____.
a. services
b. industrial products and/or complex new products
c. commodities
d. consumer goods

12-61.
D
Easy
P.400

Which of the following is not a justification for global advertising?
a. it has significant economic advantages
b. because creative talent is scarce, one large effort to develop a campaign will produce better results than 40 or 50 smaller efforts
c. many brands are global
d. cultural differences among nations are such that a message that works in one nation can fail in another

12-62.
C
Medium
P.400

There are two main arguments against global advertising. These are:
a. many brands are global; country differences in advertising regulations may block implementation of global messages
b. because creative talent is scarce, one large effort to develop a campaign will produce better results than 40 or 50 smaller efforts; it has significant economic advantages
c. cultural differences among nations are such that a message that works in one nation can fail in another; country differences in advertising regulations may block implementation of global messages
d. many brands are global; it has significant economic advantages

12-63.
A
Medium
P.401

In an international context, _____ exists whenever consumers in different countries are charged different prices for the same product.
a. price discrimination
b. global pricing
c. predatory pricing
d. standardized pricing

12-64.
B
Medium
P.401

If a consumer in Italy paid $45,000 for a Lexus and a consumer in Great Britain paid $ 60,000 for the identical vehicle, that would be an example of:
a. standardized pricing
b. price discrimination
c. global pricing
d. predatory pricing

12-65.
B
Hard
P.402

Two conditions are necessary for profitable price discrimination. These are:
a. the firm must sell a standardized product; and the firm must be able to keep its national markets separate
b. the firm must be able to keep its national markets separate; and the existence of different price elasticities of demand in different countries must exist
c. the firm must rely upon substantial economies of scale; and the firm cannot be a member of a major trade block
d. the firm must sell highly differentiated products; and the existence of different prices elasticities of demand in different countries must exist

12-66.
D
Medium
P.403

Two conditions are necessary for profitable price discrimination: the firm must be able to keep its national markets separate and:
a. the firm must be able to keep its national markets separate
b. the firm must rely upon substantial economies of scale
c. the firm must sell highly differentiated products
d. the existence of different price elasticities of demand in different countries must exist

12-67.
C
Hard
P.403

According to the textbook, the elasticity of demand for a product in a given country is determined at least in part by the following two important factors:
a. geographic location and economic stability
b. currency rates and interest rates
c. income level and competitive conditions
d. tax rates and standard of living

12-68.
A
Medium
P.406

The use of price as a competitive weapon to drive weaker competitors out of a national market is called:
a. predatory pricing
b. pillaging pricing
c. forward pricing
d. noncompetitive pricing

12-69.
A
Medium
P.406

If a manufacturer of specialized medical equipment used price as a competitive weapon to drive competitors out of a national market, that would be an example of:
a. predatory pricing
b. pillage pricing
c. reverse pricing
d. forward pricing

12-70.
C
Medium
P.406

_____ is the use of price as a competitive weapon to drive weaker competitors out of a national market.
a. Synergy
b. Pillaging
c. Predatory
d. Reverse

12-71.
B
Easy
P.407

In the context of strategic pricing, _____ occurs whenever a firm sells a product for a price that is less than the cost of producing it.
a. insourcing
b. dumping
c. price reengineering
d. outsourcing

12-72.
D
Easy
P.407

Selling a product for a price that is less than the cost of producing it is called:
a. outsourcing
b. reverse pricing
c. price reengineering
d. dumping

12-73.
B
Medium
P.407

If a Japanese steel manufacture sold steel in the U.S. for a price that was less than the cost of producing the steel, that would be an example of _____.
a. reverse pricing
b. dumping
c. outsouring
d. price reengineering

12-74.
A
Hard
P.407

A country is allowed to bring antidumping actions against an importer under Article 6 of GATT as long as two criteria are met. These are:
a. sales are made at less than fair market value; and when material injury is done to a domestic industry
b. the importer is not participant in the GATT Agreement; and when no advance notice of the dumping action was provided
c. when material injury is done to a domestic industry; and the alleged dumping has taken place for more then six months
d. sales are made at less than fair market value; and the importer is a participant in the GATT Agreement

12-75.
C
Medium
P.407

Under Article 6 of the GATT Agreement, a country is allowed to bring antidumping actions against an importer as long as two criteria are met: sales are made at less than fair market value and when _____.
a. the importer is a participant in the GATT Agreement
b. the alleged dumping has taken place for more than 6 months
c. material injury is done to a domestic industry
d. the importer is not a participant in the GATT Agreement

316

12-76.
C
Medium
P.407

Under Article 6 of the GATT Agreement, a country is allowed to bring antidumping charges against an importer as long as two criteria are met: material injury is done to a domestic industry and when _____.
a. the importer is not a participant in the GATT Agreement
b. the alleged dumping has taken place for more than 60 days
c. sales are made at less than fair market value
d. the importer is a participant in the GATT Agreement

12-77.
B
Medium
P.410

Which of the following is not a characteristic of countries where new-product development is strong?
a. competition is intense
b. demand is weak
c. consumers are affluent
d. more money is spent on basic and applied research and development than in countries where new-product development is weak

12-78.
A
Medium
P.410

Countries where new-product development is strong have all of the following characteristics except:
a. competition is weak
b. more money is spent on basic and applied research and development than in countries where new-product development is weak
c. consumers are affluent
d. demand is strong

12-79.
A
Medium
P.410

Countries where new-product development is strong have all of the following characteristics except:
a. consumers are poor
b. competition is intense
c. demand is strong
d. more money is spent on basic and applied research and development than in countries where new-product development is weak

12-80.
D
Hard
P.411

According to the textbook, one estimate of R&D effectiveness suggested that _____ of all research and development projects either fail to produce a marketable product or produce a product that fails to earn an economic return in the marketplace.
a. 10-22
b. 38-44
c. 60-66
d. 80-88

Essay Questions

12-81.
Easy
P.389

Describe what is meant by the term "marketing mix." What factors cause a firm to vary its marketing mix across markets?

Answer: Marketing mix is a term that describes the set of choices that a firm offers to its customers. The four elements that constitute a firm's marketing mix are product attributes, distribution strategy, communication strategy, and pricing strategy. Many international businesses vary their marketing mix from country to country to take into account local differences. The potential differences between countries cover a wide range of factors, including culture, economic conditions, competitive conditions, product and technical standards, distribution systems, government regulations, and the like. According to the author of the textbook, as a result of the cumulative effects of these differences, it is rare to find a firm operating in an industry where it can adopt the same marketing mix worldwide.

12-82.
Medium
P.391

What are the factors that influence a firm's ability to sell the same product worldwide? Ideally, is it better for a firm to sell the same product worldwide or would a firm rather customize its products for each individual market?

Answer: The three main factors that limit the ability of a firm to sell the same product to all of overseas markets are cultural differences across markets, economic differences across markets, and product and technical standards that differ from country to country.

Cultural Differences Across Markets: In regard to cultural differences across markets, countries vary along a wide range of dimensions. These dimensions include social structure, language, religion, tradition, education, physical stature, and forms of recreation. As a result, consumers in different countries have different tastes and preferences. For example, Japanese people tend to be smaller in stature than Americans. Consequently, American apparel manufacturers must be sensitivity to that when exporting clothing products to Japan. On the other hand, there is some evidence that tastes are converging worldwide, on a number of levels. For instance, Coca-Cola is a near global product, and its taste varies little worldwide. McDonalds Hamburgers are very similar worldwide, as are Levi Jeans and other apparel products. These examples, however, are the exception rather than the rule. In general, cultural differences across markets make it difficult to sell the same product worldwide.

Economic Differences Across Markets: Just as important as differences in culture are differences in the level of economic development across markets. Firms based in highly developed countries such as the U.S. tend to build a lot of extra performance attributes into their products because their customers want them. Conversely, consumers in developing countries (who have much less buying power) are typically content with much plainer products. This factor makes it difficult to sell the same product worldwide.

Product and Technical Standards Differences Across Markets: Differing product standards mandated by governments can rule out mass production and marketing of a standardized product in many settings. For instance, many appliance that are made for North American consumers cannot be plugged into the wall and run in Europe because of differing voltage requirements. Hundreds of these types of examples exist, which require exporters to customize their products to be suitable for individual foreign markets.

Whether firms prefer product standardization or customization is a difficult question. It is easy to quickly jump to the conclusion that a standardized product would be preferable, because it lends itself to economies of scale across the marketing mix. However, products that must be customized for individual markets have the benefit of representing a "best fit" between the consumer and the product. This may enable a firm to charge a higher price, and recapture some of the economies of scale advantages of a standardized product.

12-83.
Medium
p.393

Explain what is meant by distribution strategy. What are the main differences among countries' distribution systems? Ultimately, how does a firm determine its distribution strategy in individual foreign markets?

Answer: A firm's distribution strategy is the way that it gets it product in the hands of consumers. Wholesale, retail, and direct sales are examples of distribution strategies. An international firm's distribution strategy is limited by the nature of the distribution systems that are available in its host countries. The main differences among countries' distribution systems are threefold: retail concentration, channel length, and channel exclusivity. Retail concentration refers to the number of retailers that supply a particular market. In some countries the retail system is very concentrated, and in other countries it is very fragmented. In a concentrated system, a few retailers supply most of the market. In a fragmented system, no one retailer has a major market share. In Germany, for example, four retail chains control 65 percent of the market for food products. This is an example of a very concentrated system. Channel length refers to the number of intermediaries between the producer and the consumer. If the producer sells directly to the consumer, the channel is very short. If the producer sells through several agents and wholesalers, the channel is very long. The most important determinant of channel length is the degree to which the retail system is fragmented. Fragmented retail systems tend to promote the growth of wholesales to serve retailers, which lengthens channels. Finally, channel exclusivity refers to how difficult the channel is to penetrate. For example, it is often difficult for a new firm to get access to shelf space in U.S. grocery stores because retailers tend to prefer to carry the products of long-established manufacturers like Procter & Gamble and General Mills. Channel exclusivity is very high in Japan, which makes the Japanese market so difficult to penetrate effectively. In Japan, relationships between manufacturers, wholesalers, and retailers often go back decades. Many of these relationships are based on the understanding that distributors will not carry the products of competing firms.

Ultimately, a firm's choice of distribution strategy in its international markets is influenced by which channels are available (i.e. channel exclusivity may eliminate some choices) and by the relative costs and benefits of each remaining alternative. The relative costs of each remaining alternative are affected by the three factors discussed above. For instance, if a food products company entered a foreign market that has very long, exclusive channels (which is often the case when the market if fragmented), selling to wholesalers might make the most economic sense. It would be difficult (if not impossible) for the importer to obtain shelf space in local supermarkets without the help of local wholesalers. Conversely, if the channels were short (which is often the case in highly concentrated markets), the importer may be able to sell directly to the retailer.

12-84.
Medium
P.398

In regard to communication strategy, what is the difference between a push versus a pull strategy? Provide an example of an appropriate application of a push strategy and an example of an appropriate application of a pull strategy.

Answer: The main decision with regard to communications strategy is the choice between a push and a pull strategy. A push strategy emphasizes personal selling rather than mass media advertising in the promotional mix. A pull strategy depends more on mass media advertising to communicate the marketing message to potential customers.

A push strategy is favored by firms that sell industrial products or other complex products. One of the strengths of direct selling is that it allows the firm to educate potential customers about the features of the product. Push strategies also tend to be emphasized (somewhat by default) when distribution channels are short and when few print or electronic media are available. An example of when a push strategy would be appropriate is a machine tool company that is selling a new manufacturing robotics product. The direct selling nature of the push strategy would provide the firm a forum to educate their potential customers relative to the merits of the new product.

A pull strategy is generally favored by firms in consumer goods industries that are trying to sell to a large segment of the market. For such firms, mass communication has cost advantages, and direct selling is rarely used. Pull strategies are also used when distribution channels are long. In most cases, using direct selling to push a product through many layers of a distribution channel would be impractical. As a result, a pull strategy, which makes use of print or electronic media to get its message across, is much more practical. An example of when a pull strategy would be appropriate is a soft drink company marketing its product in a new country that has fairly long distribution channels but sufficient media available.

12-85.
Medium
P.406

Discuss the concept of predatory pricing. Is predatory pricing ethical? What, if anything, should governments do to limit the influence predatory pricing by importers on domestic industries? Explain your answer.

Answer: This question is designed to stimulate classroom discussion and/or encourage students to "think" about the ethics of predatory pricing. Predatory pricing is the use of price as a competitive weapon to drive weaker competitors out of a national market. Once the competitors have left the market, the firm can raise prices and enjoy high profits. For such a pricing strategy to work, the firm must normally have a profitable position in another national market, which it can use to subsidize aggressive pricing in the market it is trying to monopolize. Many Japanese firms have been accused of pursuing this strategy, along with firms from other countries.

Predatory pricing can run afoul of antidumping regulations. Technically, dumping occurs when a firm sells a product for a price that is less than the cost of producing it. Dumping can result in retaliatory tariffs. For instance, in 1988 the Busch administration placed a 25 percent duty on the imports of Japanese light trucks into the U.S. Should other measures be used to protect domestic industries from predatory pricing by foreign importers. This question may provide an interesting forum for classroom discussion.

CHAPTER 13
GLOBAL OPERATIONS MANAGEMENT

True/False Questions

13-1.
T
Easy
P.421

Materials management is the activity that controls the transmission of physical materials through the value chain, from procurement through production and into distribution.

13-2.
T
Medium
P.422

The choice of an optimal manufacturing location must consider country factors, technological factors, and product factors.

13-3.
F
Medium
P.422

Total quality management takes as its central focus the need to improve the quality of a company's logistics and materials management functions.

13-4.
T
Easy
P.422

A standard designed to assure the quality of products and processes is referred to as ISO 9000.

13-5.
F
Easy
P.425

The concept of economies of scale tells us that as plant output expands, unit costs increase.

13-6.
T
Medium
P.425

Flexible manufacturing technologies allow a company to produce a wider varity of end products at a unit cost that at one time could be achieved only through the mass production of a standardized output.

13-7.
F
Medium
P.427

Flexible manufacturing technologies are unique in their ability to help companies produce highly standardized products for a global clientele.

13-8.
T
Easy
P.427

A product with a high value-to-weight ratio is expensive and does not weigh very much.

13-9.
F
Hard
P.427

The arguments for concentrating production at a few choice locations are strong when fixed costs are substantial, the minimum efficient scale of production is high, and flexible manufacturing technologies are not available.

13-10.
T
Hard
P.427

The arguments for concentrating production at one or a few locations are not as compelling when fix costs are low, the minimum efficient scale of production is low, and flexible manufacturing technologies are not available.

13-11.
T
Easy
P.428

Needs that are the same all over the world are called universal needs.

13-12.
T
Medium
P.428

Concentrating a firm's manufacturing facilities in an optimal location and serving the world market from that single location makes sense when trade barriers are low.

13-13.
F
Medium
P.428

Decentralizing a firm's manufacturing facilities in various regional or national markets that are close to major markets makes sense when the product's value-to-weight ratio is high.

13-14.
T
Easy
P.429

The decision about whether a firm should make or buy the component parts that go into the final product is referred to as a sourcing decision.

13-15.
T
Easy
P.430

A piece of equipment that can be used for only one purpose is referred to as a specialized asset.

13-16.
F
Hard
P.431

The strongest argument for vertical integration is that production cost savings result from it because vertical integration makes planning, coordination, and scheduling of adjacent processes easier.

13-17. Proprietary product technology is technology unique to a firm.
T
Easy
P.431

13-18. The greatest advantage of buying component parts from independent suppliers is
T that the firm can maintain its flexibility.
Medium
P.432

13-19. The benefits of manufacturing components in-house seem to be greatest when
T highly specialized assets are involved, when vertical integration is necessary for
Hard protecting proprietary technology, or when the firm is simply more efficient than
P.435 external suppliers at performing a particular activity.

13-20. In the context of materials management and operations, JIT stands for Just-In-
F Transit.
Easy
P.437

Multiple Choice

13-21. The process of creating a product is called _____.
D   a. materials management
Easy b. bureaucracy
P.421 c. administration
      d. production

13-22. _____ is the activity that controls the transportation of physical materials
A   through the value chain, from procurement through production and into
Easy distribution.
P.421 a. Materials management
      b. Production
      c. Operations
      d. Bureaucracy

13-23. The activity that controls the transportation of physical materials through the value
C   chain, from procurement through production and into distribution is called:
Easy a. bureaucratic management
P.421 b. transportation management
      c. materials management
      d. conveyance management

325

13-24.
B
Easy
P.422

Materials management includes _____, which refers to the procurement and physical transmission of material through the supply chain, from suppliers to consumers.
a. interchange
b. logistics
c. reciprocation
d. conveyance

13-25.
A
Easy
P.422

The procurement and physical transmission of material through the supply chain, from suppliers to customers, is referred to as:
a. logistics
b. conveyance
c. interchange
d. reciprocation

13-26.
C
Medium
P.422

Which of the following is not a result of improved quality control?
a. greater product quality means lower warranty costs
b. increased product quality means lower scrap costs
c. increased product quality means higher rework
d. productivity increases because time is not wasted manufacturing poor-quality products that cannot be sold

13-27.
D
Easy
P.422

The main management technique that companies are utilizing to boost their product quality is:
a. logistics
b. materials management
c. reengineering
d. total quality management

13-28.
C
Easy
P.422

_____ is the main management technique that companies are utilzing to boost their product quality.
a. Total feature management
b. Logistics
c. Total quality management
d. Materials management

13-29.
D
Medium
P.422

Saving time by not producing poor quality products that cannot be sold, lowering rework costs, lowering scrap costs, and lowering warranty costs are the intended results of:
a. total feature management
b. reengineering
c. logistics
d. total quality management

13-30.
B
Easy
P.422

The TQM concept was developed by a number of American consultants such as:
a. Martin Wolf, R.B. Weber, and Raymond Vernon
b. W. Edwards Deming, Joseph Juran, and A.V. Feigenbaum
c. J.H. Dunning, M. McQueen, and Michael Porter
d. Paul Krugman, Raymond Vernon, and Michael Porter

13-31.
B
Easy
P.422

In Europe, the European Union requires that the quality of a firm's manufacturing processes and products be certified under a quality standard known as _____ before the firm is allowed access to the European marketplace.
a. total quality management
b. ISO 9000
c. BT 12000
d. reengineering

13-32.
C
Medium
P.422

ISO 9000 is a standard designed to assure the quality of products and products entering the:
a. North American Free Trade Agreement marketplace
b. Andean Group marketplace
c. European Union marketplace
d. MERCOSUR marketplace

13-33.
B
Medium
P.423

The key decision factors that pertain to where an international firm locates its manufacturing facilities can be grouped under three broad headings. These are:
a. political factors, economic factors, and legal factors
b. country factors, technological factors, and product factors
c. product factors, service factors, and labor factors
d. language factors, cultural factors, and transportation factors

13-34.
C
Medium
P.423

The key decision factors that pertain to where an international firm locates its manufacturing facilities can be grouped under three broad headings. These are country factors, technological factors, and _____ factors.
a. political
b. economic
c. product
d. labor

13-35.
C
Medium
P.423

Country factors, product factors, and _____ factors are the broad headings that contain the key decision factors that pertain to where an international firm locates its manufacturing facilities.
a. labor
b. economic
c. technological
d. political

13-36.
A
Medium
P.423

Technological factors, product factors, and _____ factors are the broad headings that contain the key decision factors that pertain to where an international firm locates its manufacturing facilities.

a. country
b. political
c. economic
d. legal

13-37.
A
Medium
P.424

Three characteristics of a manufacturing technology that are particularly interesting to international firms when making manufacturing location decisions are: (1) the level of its fixed costs, (2) its minimum efficient scale, and (3)

a. its flexibility
b. its variable costs
c. the technological sophistication of the manufacturing process
d. the cost of moving manufacturing executives overseas

13-38.
B
Medium
P.424

Three characteristics of a manufacturing technology that are particularly interesting to international firms when making manufacturing location decisions are: (1) the level of its fixed costs, (2) its flexibility, and (3)

a. the cost of moving manufacturing executives overseas
b. its minimum efficient scale
c. its variable costs
d. the technological sophistication of the manufacturing process

13-39.
C
Easy
P.424

In some cases the _____ costs of setting up a manufacturing plant are so high that a firm must serve the world market from a single location or from a very few locations.

a. changeable
b. reoccurring
c. fixed
d. variable

13-40.
A
Easy
P.425

The concept of economies of scale tells us that as plant output expands, unit cost _____.

a. decrease
b. increase
c. remain the same
d. expand exponentially

13-41. Manufacturing technologies designed to reduce setup times, increase use of
B   individual machines through better scheduling, and improve quality control at all
Medium stages of manufacturing is called:
P.425   a. multifaceted production
        b. lean production
        c. lateral production
        d. temporal production

13-42. _____ is a manufacturing technology designed to reduce setup times,
A   increase use of individual machines through better scheduling, and improve
Easy   quality control at all stages of manufacturing.
P.425   a. Lean production
        b. Lateral production
        c. Temporal production
        d. Multifaceted production

13-43. According to the textbook, _____ manufacturing technologies provide a
D   company the ability to produce a wider variety of end products at a unit cost that at
Medium one time could be achieved only through the mass production of a standardized
P.425   output.
        a. multifaceted
        b. lateral
        c. side by side
        d. flexible

13-44. Recent research suggests that the adoption of _____ manufacturing
B   technologies may actually increase efficiency and lower unit costs relative to what
Medium can be achieved by the mass production of a standardized output.
P.425   a. lateral
        b. flexible
        c. multifaceted
        d. side by side

13-45. All of the following are advantages of flexible manufacturing except:
D   a. improved efficiency
Medium b. flexible manufacturing technologies allow companies to customize products to
P.427   suite the unique demands of small consumer groups
        c. increase customer responsiveness
        d. flexible manufacturing technologies help firms standardize products for
            different national markets

13-46. In terms of making a location decision, when fixed costs are substantial, the
B minimum efficient scale of production is high, and flexible manufacturing
Medium technologies are available, it makes sense to:
P.427
a. manufacture the product in every country in which it is sold
b. concentrate production at a few choice locations
c. spread production over as many locations as possible
d. outsource production to a third party

13-47. The arguments for concentrating production at one or a few locations are not
A compelling when:
Hard
P.427
a. fixed costs are low, the minimum efficient scale of production is low, and
flexible manufacturing technologies are not available
b. fixed costs are high, the minimum efficient scale of production is high, and
flexible manufacturing technologies are available
c. fixed costs are low, the minimum efficient scale of production is high, and
flexible manufacturing technologies are not available
d. fixed costs are moderate, the minimum efficient scale of production is high,
and flexible manufacturing technologies are available

13-48. Two product factors impact location decisions. These are:
A
a. the product's value-to-weight ratio and whether the product serves universal
Medium needs
P.427
b. the product's shape and the product's weight
c. the product's content and the product's point-of-origin
d. the product's technological sophistication and the product's shape

13-49. Two product factors impact location decisions. These are (1) the product's value-
B to-weight ratio and (2)
Medium a. the product's technological sophistication
P.427
b. whether the product serves universal needs
c. the product's weight
d. the product's shape

13-50. Two product factors impact location decisions. These are (1) whether the product
A serves universal needs and (2)
Medium a. the product's value-to-weight ratio
P.427
b. the product's point-of-origin
c. the product's weight
d. the product's shape

13-51.
B
Easy
p.

Needs that are the same all over the world are referred to as _____ needs.

a. specific
b. universal
c. domestic
d. individualistic

13-52.
D
Easy
P.428

_____ needs are the same all over the world.

a. Precise
b. Individualistic
c. Domestic
d. Universal

13-53.
A
Hard
P.428

Which of the following two factors correctly depict the manufacturing attributes of a product that has universal needs?

a. since there are few national differences in consumer taste and preferences for such products, the need for local responsiveness is reduced, manufacturing should be concentrated at an optimal location
b. since there are many national differences in consumer taste and preferences for such products, the need for local responsiveness is reduced, manufacturing should be concentrated at an optimal location
c. since there are few national differences in consumer taste and preferences for such products, the need for local responsiveness is increased, manufacturing should take place in each major market in which the firm is active
d. since there are many national differences in consumer taste and preferences for such products, the need for local responsiveness is increased, manufacturing should take place in each major market in which the firm is active

13-54.
C
Medium
P.428

The most attractive manufacturing strategy for producing universal needs is to:

a. manufacture the product in each major market in which the firm is active
b. manufacture the product in at least one location on each continent in which the product is sold
c. concentrate manufacturing at an optimal location
d. concentrate manufacturing in a market that is part of a major trade block

13-55.
C
Medium
P.428

There are two basic strategies for locating manufacturing facilities. These are:

a. concentrating them in the optimal location and serve the world market from there and, concentrate them in markets that are parts of major trade blocks
b. locate at least one manufacturing facility in each continent in which the firm is active and, concentrate manufacturing at an optimal location
c. concentrate them in the optimal location and serve the world market from there and, decentralizing them in various regional or national locations that are close to major markets
d. concentrate them in markets that are part of major trade blocks and, centralizing them at a single location

13-56.
B
Medium
P.428

There are two basic strategies for locating manufacturing facilities. These are: (1) concentrating them in the optimal location and serving the world from there, and (2)

a. concentrate them in markets that are part of major trade blocks
b. decentralizing them in various regional or national locations that are close to major markets
c. centralizing them to a single location
d. locate at least one manufacturing facility in each continent in which the firm is active

13-57.
A
Hard
P.428

Placing manufacturing facilities in one concentrated location makes sense for all of the following reasons except:

a. trade barriers are high
b. the product serves universal needs
c. important exchange rates are expected to remain relatively stable
d. the production technology has high fixed costs or a high minimum efficient scale or a flexible manufacturing technology exists.

13-58.
C
Hard
P.428

Placing manufacturing facilities in one concentrated location makes sense for all of the following reasons except:

a. the product serves universal needs
b. trade barriers are low
c. important exchange rates are expected to be volatile
d. differences in factor costs, political economy, and culture have a substantial impact on the costs of manufacturing in various countries

13-59.
A
Hard
P.428

Decentralization of the location of a firm's manufacturing locations makes sense for all of the following reasons except:

a. trade barriers are low
b. volatility in important exchange rates is expected
c. the production technology has low fixed costs, low minimum efficient scale or a flexible manufacturing technology exists
d. the product does not serve universal needs

13-60.
B
Hard
P.428

Decentralization of a firm's manufacturing locations makes sense for all of the following reasons except:

a. trade barriers are high
b. the product's value-to-weight ratio is high
c. the production technology has low fixed costs
d. the product serves universal needs

13-61.
A
Easy
P.429

Decisions about whether a firm should make or buy the component parts that go into the final product are called _____ decisions.
a. sourcing
b. synergistic
c. end-user
d. feedforward

13-62.
A
Hard
P.430

The arguments that support making component parts in-house (i.e. vertical integration) are fourfold:
a. lower costs, facilitates investments in highly specialized assets, protects proprietary product technology and, facilitates the scheduling of adjacent processes
b. greater flexibility, helps a firm capture orders from international customers, facilitates investments in highly standardized assets and, facilitates the scheduling of adjacent processes
c. helps a firm capture orders from international customers, lower costs, facilitates investments in highly standardized assets and, facilitates the scheduling of adjacent processes
d. lower costs, greater flexibility, facilitates the scheduling of adjacent customers and, facilitates investments in highly specialized assets

13-63.
B
Medium
P.430

The arguments that support vertical integration include: lower costs, facilitates investments in highly specialized assets, protects proprietary technology and:
a. helps the firm capture orders from international customers
b. facilitates the scheduling of adjacent processes
c. greater flexibility
d. facilitates investment in highly standardized assets

13-64.
A
Medium
P.431

In general, when substantial investments in specialized assets are required to manufacture a component, a firm will:
a. prefer to make the component internally rather than contract it out to a supplier
b. find a alternative method of manufacturing the component
c. contract out the production of the component rather than make it internally
d. discontinue making the product that the component goes into

13-65.
C
Medium
P.431

Proprietary product technology is technology that is:
a. widely shared among firms
b. unique to a country
c. unique to the firm
d. unique to a particular industry

13-66.
D
Hard
P.432

The advantages of buying component parts from independent suppliers are that it gives the firm the following advantages:

a. it may help the firm to capture orders from international customers, facilitates the scheduling of adjacent processes and, greater flexibility
b. greater flexibility, facilitates the scheduling of adjacent processes and, protects proprietary production technology
c. facilitates investments in highly specialized assets, protects proprietary product technology and, facilitates the scheduling of adjacent processes
d. greater flexibility, it can help drive down the firm's cost structure and, it may help the firm to capture orders from international customers

13-67.
A
Medium
P.432

The advantages of buying component parts from independent suppliers includes: (1) it gives the firm greater flexibility, (2) it can help drive down the firm's cost structure, and (3)

a. it may help the firm to capture orders from international customers
b. it facilitates the scheduling of adjacent processes
c. if facilitates investments in highly specialized assets
d. it protects proprietary production technology

13-68.
B
Medium
P.432

The advantages of buying component parts from independent suppliers includes: (1) it can help drive down the firm's cost structure, (2) it may help the firm to capture orders from international customers, and (3)

a. it protects proprietary production technology
b. it leads to greater flexibility
c. it facilitates investments in highly specialized assets
d. it facilitates the scheduling of adjacent processes

13-69.
D
Medium
P.432

The advantages of buying component parts from independent suppliers includes: (1) it gives the firm greater flexibility, (2) it may help the firm to capture orders from international customers, and (3)

a. it protects proprietary production technology
b. it facilitates the scheduling of adjacent processes
c. it facilitates investments in highly specialized assets
d. it can drive down the firm's cost structure

13-70.
C
Hard
P.435

According to the textbook, the benefits of manufacturing components in-house seem to be greatest when all of the following factors are involved except:

a. when highly specialized assets are involved
b. when the firm is simply more efficient than external suppliers at performing a particular activity
c. when maximum flexibility is necessary
d. when vertical integration is necessary for protecting proprietary technology

13-71.
A
Medium
P.435

Many Japanese automakers have cooperative relationships with their suppliers that go back for decades. These types of relationships are referred to as:
a. strategic alliances
b. firm-to-firm cooperative arrangements
c. integral forms of integration
d. operating arrangements

13-72.
C
Medium
P.436

In general, the trends toward just-in-time systems (JIT), computer-aided design (CAD), and computer-aided manufacturing (CAM) seem to have increased pressures for firms to establish _____ relationships with their suppliers.
a. strictly arms-length
b. intermediate term
c. long-term
d. short-term

13-73.
A
Easy
P.436

_____, which encompasses logistics, embraces the activities necessary to get materials to a manufacturing facility, through the manufacturing process, and out through a distribution system to the end user.
a. Materials management
b. Bureaucracy
c. Production
d. Wares operations

13-74.
C
Hard
P.436

According to the textbook, for the typical manufacturing firm, material costs account for between _____ percent of revenues depending on the industry.
a. 15-25
b. 30-40
c. 50-70
d. 80-90

13-75.
C
Easy
P.437

The basic philosophy behind _____ systems is to economize on inventory holding costs by having materials arrive at a manufacturing plant "just in time" to enter the production process.
a. management by objectives
b. reengineering
c. just-in-time
d. total quality management

13-76.   The basic philosophy behind just-in-time systems (JIT) is to:
D   a. economize on costs by paying suppliers just-in-time to avoid late charges
Medium   b. economize on training costs by providing training to employees just-in-time for
P.437   them to implement new strategies
            c. economize on personnel costs by hiring the right number of people just-in-time
                to meet organizational needs
            d. economize on inventory holding costs by having materials arrive at a
                manufacturing plant just-in-time to enter the production process.

13-77.   In the context of materials management, the acronym JIT stands for:
D   a. Jobber-In-Training
Easy   b. Job-In-Transit
P.437   c. Joint-In-Transpiration
            d. Just-In-Time

13-78.   A drawback of a _____ system is that it leaves a firm without a buffer stock
B   of inventory.
Medium   a. total-quality management
P.437   b. just-in-time
            c. management by objectives
            d. reengineering system

13-79.   In the context of materials management, the acronym EDI stands for:
D   a. Electronic Data Intelligence
Easy   b. Eliminate Distribution Intermediaries
P.438   c. Eastern Distribution Interchange
            d. Electronic Data Interchange

13-80.   EDI stands for:
B   a. Eliminate Distribution Intermediaries
Easy   b. Electronic Data Interchange
P.438   c. Eastern Distribution Interchange
            d. Electronic Data Intelligence

Essay Questions

13-81.   Discuss the overall objectives of international firms in terms of manufacturing and
Medium   materials management.
P.422

            Answer: International firms have four principle objectives in the area of
            manufacturing and materials management. The first two objectives are to lower
            costs and increase quality. In this respect, international firms are no different than
            their strictly domestic counterparts. Cost reductions can be realized through
            improved efficiency and through eliminating defective products from both the

supply chain and the manufacturing process. Implementing Just-In-Time manufacturing is an important step in achieving these objectives. Quality improvement can be realized through a number of initiatives, including total quality management (TQM) and ISO 9000 certification.

The second two objectives that are shared by the majority of international firms in this area relate directly to their international efforts. First, a firm's manufacturing and materials management functions must be able to accommodate demands for local responsiveness. For instance, an American exporter may have to vary the design of a product that is manufactured and sold in the U.S. to meet European standards. Second, a firm's manufacturing and materials management function must be able to respond quickly to shifts in consumer demand. For instance, if a trend developed in Asia towards a preference for lower-fat foods, the importers of food products to Asia that respond to this trend the most rapidly would have a substantial advantage.

13-82.
Hard
P.423

How does an international firm decide where to locate its manufacturing activities? Include in your answer a discussion of country factors, technological factors, and product factors.

Answer: The key factors involved in making location decisions, which entail the dual considerations of minimizing costs and increasing quality, can be grouped under three broad headings: country factors, technological factors, and product factors.

Country Factors: This is a large area of consideration, which encompasses a lot of factors. As described throughout the textbook, the advantage of producing in one country opposed to another varies along a number of dimensions. In Chapter 4, for example, we saw that due to differences in factor costs, certain countries have a comparative advantage for producing certain products. In Chapters 2 and 3 we saw how differences in political economy and national culture influence the desirability of location decisions. In this regard, all other things being equal, a firm should locate its manufacturing activities in countries that have hospitable political, economy, and factor cost environments.

Other country specific factors play a role in location decisions. These factors include formal and informal trade barriers and rules and regulations regarding foreign direct investment. Another country factor is expected movements in currency exchange rates. Adverse changes in exchange rates can quickly alter a country's attractiveness as a manufacturing site. Firms should consider the potential living conditions of their expatriate managers when making locations decision, and also the quality of the local labor pool.

Technological Factors: The three primary factors that drive location decisions in terms of technology are a manufacturing activity's level of fixed costs, its minimum efficient scale, and its flexibility. In terms of fixed costs, when the fixed costs of setting up a manufacturing operation are high, a firm must serve the world market from a single location or from a few locations. This is the case with aircraft manufacturing, for example. On the other hand, when fixed costs are low, a firm can scatter its manufacturing activities throughout the world to better accommodate local markets. In terms of minimum efficient scale, the larger the minimum efficient scale of a plant, the greater is the argument for centralized production at a single location. This factor motivates companies like Caterpillar Tractor, which makes heavy construction equipment in huge plants, to locate in a single location. Finally, in regard to flexibility, when flexible manufacturing technologies are available, a firm can manufacture products customized to various national markets at a single factory at the optimal location.

Product Factors: Two product features impact location decisions. The first is the product's value-to-weight ratio because of its influence on transportation costs. If a product has a high value-to-weight ratio, like semiconductors, it can be shipped around the world, and the shipping cost would represent only a small portion of the total cost of the product. Conversely, a product with a low value-to-weight ratio, like soft drinks, almost have to be mixed and bottled in the location in which they are sold, because the cost of shipping a 50 cent can of Coke from one country to another would represent a significant part of the value of the product. The second product consideration pertains to whether the product serves universal needs. If so, the need for local responsiveness is reduced, and the product can be produced at its ideal location.

As this discussion indicates, location decisions are complex for international firms. A consideration and weighing of all of the issues involved will result in the best overall decision.

13-83.
Medium
P.429

What are Make-or-Buy Decisions? What are the advantages of make versus buy and visa-versa? Are these decisions harder for international opposed to strictly domestic firms? Explain your answer.

Answer: A make-or-buy decision pertains to whether a business should make or buy the component parts that go into its final product. In other words, should a firm vertically integrate to manufacture its own component parts or should it purchase the parts from outside suppliers? For many firms, the make-or-buy decision is a difficult one, because there are good arguments to support either position.

The Advantages of Make: The arguments that support making component parts in-house (i.e. vertical integration) include: lower costs, facilitating specialized investments, proprietary product technology protection, and improved scheduling. In terms of lower costs, it may pay a firm to manufacture its own component parts if no cheaper source (assuming quality remains consistent) is available. In terms of facilitating specialized investments, when a firm needs a component part that is highly customized and specialized, it is often best for the firm to manufacturer the part itself. Having a supplier manufacture the part would be awkward, because the supplier would rely strictly on one buyer to purchase the part and the buyer would typically have only the one supplier to furnish the part. In terms of protecting proprietary product technology, the more involvement that a firm has with suppliers, the more likely it is that proprietary information will be lost. As a result, a firm that has highly sensitive proprietary technology may be ahead to produce its own component products. Finally, improved scheduling can result from producing in-house rather than relying upon suppliers. The author of the textbook indicates that this is the weakest argument for vertical integration.

The Advantages of Buy: The advantages of buying component parts from independent suppliers is that it gives the firm greater flexibility, it can help drive down the firm's cost structure, and it may help the firm to capture orders from international customers. In regard to flexibility, by outsourcing the manufacture of its component parts, a firm can switch suppliers as circumstances dictate. This could provide a firm a substantial advantage in a rapidly changing environment. In terms of costs, using suppliers to manufacture component parts allows a firm to narrow its scope, and the resulting administrative overhead costs may be smaller. Finally, an advantage of buying rather than making component parts is that the relationships that are established through buying parts may lead to sales of the firm's final product. For example, if an American firm negotiated the purchase of component parts from several Brazilian firms, that would put the American firm in a position to develop a network of contacts in Brazil that might ultimately result in sales of its finished product.

The make-buy decision is harder for international firms than domestic firms because their decision set is simply more complex. For instance, it may appear desirable to purchase parts from a foreign supplier, but what about political stability in the supplier's country, foreign exchange risk, and the host of other questions that must be answered in international trade?

13-84.
Medium
P.435

Discuss the advantages of entering into strategic alliances with suppliers? In general, is alliance formation a good idea for international firms?

Answer: This question is designed to elicit classroom discussion. It is also a good "thought" question for an exam. The number of strategic alliances between firms from different countries is growing and is becoming an increasingly important option for international firms. For example, in recent years we have seen an alliance between Kodak and Canon, under which Canon builds photocopiers to be sold by Kodak.

There are a number of advantages and disadvantages of alliances that may be pointed out by students. The advantages include a sharing of production costs and risks, along with joint marketing and R&D. Also, the long-term relationship that develops between the alliance partners may engender trust and be beneficial for both firms. On the other hand, many of the disadvantages of using suppliers rather than producing products in-house apply to strategic alliances. For instance, proprietary technology may be lost to an alliance partner. This represents a compelling disadvantage of strategic alliances, particularly if the alliance partners are in the same industry.

There is no right or wrong answer to the question of whether alliances are good or bad for international businesses. This topic, however, provides an excellent forum for classroom discussion.

13-85.
Easy
P.437

Describe the concept of "Just-In-Time" manufacturing. What are the advantages and disadvantages of the Just-In-Time system?

Answer: The basic philosophy behind just-in-time (JIT) manufacturing is to economize on inventory holding costs by having materials arrive at a manufacturing plant "just in time" to enter the product process. This results in potential cost savings and quality improvements. The cost savings come from speeding up inventory turnover, thus reducing inventory holding costs, as well as warehousing and storage costs. In addition, JIT systems can lead to quality improvements. Under a JIT system, parts enter the manufacturing process immediately. This allows defective inputs to be spotted right away. The problem can then be traced to the supply source and fixed before more defective parts are produced. The disadvantage of a JIT system is that it leaves a firm without a buffer stock of inventory. As a result, a labor dispute at a supplier's plant or a disruption in the transportation system (such as the UPS strike) could leave a manufacturer without adequate component parts.

True/False Questions

14-1.
T
Easy
P.448

Human resource management refers to the activities an organization carries out to utilize its human resources effectively.

14-2.
F
Easy
P.448

The role of HRM has a similar level of complexity for a domestic and an international firm.

14-3.
T
Medium
P.449

An expatriate manager is a citizen of one country who is working abroad in one of the firm's subsidiaries.

14-4.
F
Easy
P.449

Compensation policy is concerned with the selection of employees for particular jobs.

14-5.
T
Medium
P.449

Staffing policy can be a tool for developing and promoting corporate culture.

14-6.
F
Medium
P.450

A geocentric staffing policy is one in which all key management positions are filled by parent company nationals.

14-7.
T
Medium
P.451

One advantage of adopting a polycentric approach to staffing is that a firm is less likely to suffer from cultural myopia.

14-8.
T
Easy
P.453

Expatriate failure represents a failure of the firm's selection policies to identify individuals who will not thrive abroad.

14-9.
F
Hard
P.454

According to a study conducted by R.L. Tung, European-based multinationals experience a much higher expatriate failure rate than either Japanese or United States multinationals.

14-10.
F
Medium
P.455

In regard to expatriate selection and performance, Mendenhall and Oddou believe that domestic performance potential and overseas performance potential are the same thing.

14-11.
F
Medium
P.456

According to research conducted by R.L. Tung, the vast majority of firms use formal procedures and psychological tests to determine whether the personality traits and relational abilities of potential expatriate managers are suitable for overseas assignments.

14-12.
F
Hard
P.457

A recent survey by Windam International, a HRM management consulting firm, found that spouses were included in preselection interviews for foreign postings nearly 90 percent of the time.

14-13.
T
Medium
P.457

Historically, most international businesses have been more concerned with training than with management development.

14-14.
T
Easy
P.1

Management development programs help build a unifying corporate culture by socializing new managers into the norms and value systems of the firm.

14-15.
T
Medium
P.461

Typically, managers from both the host nation and the home office are involved in assessing the performance of an expatriate manager.

14-16.
F
Medium
P.461

According to the textbook, almost all expatriates believe that a position in a foreign country is beneficial to their careers.

14-17.
T
Easy
P.462

Substantial differences exist in the compensation of executives at the same level in various countries.

14-18.
T
Medium
P.464

According to the textbook, an expatriate's total compensation package may amount to three times what he or she would cost the firm in a home country posting.

14-19.
F
Medium
P.465

Four types of allowances are often included in an expatriate's compensation package: relocation allowances, travel allowances, training allowances, and discretionary allowances.

14-20.
T
Easy
P.466

Unless a host country has a reciprocal tax treaty with the expatriate's home country, the expatriate may have to pay income tax to both the home and the host country governments.

Multiple Choice

14-21.
C
Easy
P.448

Human resource management refers to the activities an organization carries out to utilize its _____ effectively.
a. customers
b. external stakeholders
c. human resources
d. suppliers

14-22.
A
Easy
P.448

_____ management refers to the activities an organization carries out to utilize its human resources effectively.
a. Human resource
b. External stakeholder
c. Positive-sum
d. Personnel psychology

14-23.
B
Easy
P.448

The activities an organization carries out to utilize its human resources effectively is referred to as:
a. positive-sum management
b. human resource management
c. stakeholder management
d. personnel psychology management

14-24.
D
Medium
P.448

The activities which include determining the firm's human resource strategy, staffing, performance evaluation, management development, compensation, and labor relations are referred to as:
a. personnel psychology management
b. stakeholder management
c. positive-sum management
d. human resource management

14-25.
D
Easy
P.449

A(n) _____ manager is a citizen of one country who is working abroad in one of his or her firm's subsidiaries.
a. ethnocentric
b. cross-divisional
c. cross-cultural
d. expatriate

14-26.
C
Easy
P.449

A citizen of one country who is working abroad in one of his or her firm's subsidiaries is called an:
a. ethnocentric manager
b. cross-cultural manager
c. expatriate manager
d. cross-divisional manager

14-27.
A
Medium
P.449

Kenneth Johnson works for Apple Computer (a U.S. based firm) but is assigned to Apple's sales office in Japan. Under these circumstances, Mr. Johnson would be called an _____ manager.
a. expatriate
b. cross-divisional
c. ethnocentric
d. cross-cultural

14-28.
B
Easy
P.449

_____ is concerned with the selection of employees for particular jobs.
a. Compensation policy
b. Staffing policy
c. Performance appraisal policy
d. Training policy

14-29.
C
Easy
P.449

The policy concerned with the selection of employees for particular jobs is referred to as:
a. compensation policy
b. organization policy
c. staffing policy
d. internal stakeholder policy

14-30.
A
Medium
P.449

The term corporate culture refers to an organization's _____.
a. norms and value systems
b. compensation system
c. standing among its peer firms
d. policies, rules, and regulations

14-31.
A
Hard
P.449

An individual whose behavioral style, beliefs, and value system are consistent with that of the company that she works for is said to be compatible with her company's:
a. corporate culture
b. corporate structure
c. corporate resources
d. corporate bureaucracy

14-32.
D
Medium
P.449

Research has identified three types of staffing policies in international businesses: (1) the ethnocentric approach, (2) the polycentric approach, and (3) the
a. networkcentric approach
b. intercentric approach
c. globalcentric approach
d. geocentric approach

14-33.
A
Medium
P.449

The three types of staffing policies in international business are:
a. the ethnocentric approach, the polycentric approach, and the geocentric approach
b. the globalcentric approach, the networkcentric approach, and the geocentric approach
c. the geocentric approach, the networkcentric approach, and the polycentric approach
d. the intercentric approach, the polycentric approach, and the networkcentric approach

14-34.
B
Medium
P.449

The three types of staffing policies in international business are the polycentric approach, the geocentric approach, and the _____ approach.
a. networkcentric
b. ethnocentric
c. intercentric
d. globalcentric

14-35.
A
Medium
P.450

An _____ staffing policy is one in which all key management positions are filled by parent company nationals.
a. ethnocentric
b. intercentric
c. polycentric
d. geocentric

14-36. An ethnocentric staffing policy is one in which all key management positions are
C filled by:
Medium   a. host company nationals
P.450   b. the best people available, regardless of whether they are parent company
            nationals or host company nationals
         c. parent company nationals
         d. contract employees typically obtained from a consulting firm

14-37. Which of the following is not a reason for pursuing an ethnocentric staffing policy?
B   a. if a firm is trying to create value by transferring core competencies to a foreign
Hard   operation, it may believe that the best way to do this is to transfer parent
P.450   country nationals who have knowledge of that competency to the foreign
            operation
         b. the firm may believe there is a lack of qualified individuals in its own parent
            company to fill senior management positions
         c. the firm may see an ethnocentric staffing policy as the best way to maintain a
            unified corporate culture
         d. the firm may believe there is a lack of qualified individuals in the host country
            to fill senior management positions

14-38. There are two reasons that the ethnocentric staffing policy is on the wane in most
A   international businesses. These are:
Medium   a. an ethnocentric staffing policy limits advancement opportunities for host
P.451   country nationals and an ethnocentric policy can lead to "cultural myopia"
         b. an ethnocentric staffing policy is the most expensive of the alternatives and an
            ethnocentric policy limits advancement opportunities for parent country
            personnel
         c. an ethnocentric staffing policy limits the cultural awareness of parent company
            personnel and an ethnocentric policy can lead to "cultural myopia"
         d. an ethnocentric staffing policy is the most expensive of the alternatives and an
            ethnocentric policy limits the cultural awareness of parent company personnel

14-39. A _____ staffing policy requires host country nationals to be recruited to
D   manage subsidiaries, while parent company nationals occupy key positions at
Medium corporate headquarters.
P.451   a. intercentric
         b. geocentric
         c. ethnocentric
         d. polycentric

14-40.
A
Hard
P.451

A polycentric staffing policy requires _____ to be recruited to manage subsidiaries, while _____ occupy key positions at corporate headquarters.
  a. host country nationals, parent country nationals
  b. parent country nationals, contract employees from an international employment firm
  c. parent country nationals, host country nationals
  d. contract employees from an international employment firm, host country nationals

14-41.
C
Medium
P.451

A _____ staffing policy seeks the best people for key jobs throughout the organization.
  a. intercentric
  b. ethnocentric
  c. geocentric
  d. polycentric

14-42.
C
Medium
P.452

Which of the following is not an advantage of a geocentric approach to staffing for international businesses?
  a. uses human resources efficiently
  b. helps build a strong culture
  c. inexpensive to implement
  d. helps build a strong informal management network

14-43.
D
Medium
P.452

Which of the following international strategies is most compatible with an ethnocentric staffing policy?
  a. transnational strategy
  b. global strategy
  c. multidomestic strategy
  d. international strategy

14-44.
B
Medium
P.452

Which of the following international strategies is most compatible with an polycentric staffing policy?
  a. international strategy
  b. multidomestic strategy
  c. global strategy
  d. transnational strategy

14-45.
A
Medium
P.452

Which of the following two international strategies are most compatible with an geocentric staffing policy?
  a. global and transnational
  b. multidomestic and transnational
  c. international and multidomestic
  d. global and multidomestic

14-46.
A
Hard
P.453

Two of the three common international staffing policies rely on extensive use expatriate managers. These are:
a. ethnocentric, geocentric
b. polycentric, intercentric
c. ethnocentric, intercentric
d. polycentric, geocentric

14-47.
B
Easy
P.453

The premature return of an expatriate manager to his of her home country is referred to as:
a. expatriate relief
b. expatriate failure
c. expatriate rotation
d. expatriate timing

14-48.
C
Easy
P.453

_____ is the premature return of an expatriate manager to his or her home country.
a. Expatriate rotation
b. Expatriate timing
c. Expatriate failure
d. Expatriate relief

14-49.
B
Hard
P.453

One estimate of the costs of expatriate failure is that the average cost per failure to the parent company can be as high as _____ time the expatriate's annual domestic salary plus the cost of relocation.
a. 1.5
b. 3
c. 5
d. 7

14-50.
B
Hard
P.454

According to a study conducted by R.L. Tung, _____ of U.S. multinationals experience expatriate failure rates of 10 percent or more.
a. 91%
b. 76%
c. 44%
d. 17%

14-51.
C
Medium
P.454

Which of the following was not identified by R.L. Tung as a reason for expatriate failure among U.S. expatriate managers?
a. inability of spouse to adjust
b. difficulties with new environment
c. poor pay
d. personal or emotional problems

14-52.
D
Hard
P.454

The results of a study by R.L. Tung indicated that the most consistent reason cited by European expatriates for expatriate failure among their group was:
a. personal or emotional problems
b. inability to cope with larger overseas responsibilities
c. poor pay
d. the inability of the manager's spouse to adjust to a new environment

14-53.
B
Hard
P.455

A recent study by International Orientation Resources, an HRM consulting firm, found that 60% of expatriate failures occur because of three reasons. These reasons are:
a. the inability to cope with larger overseas responsibility, the lack of technical competence, and the manager's personal or emotional maturity.
b. the inability of a spouse to adjust, the inability of the manager to adjust, and other family problems
c. poor pay, the inability of a spouse to adjust, and the lack of technical competence
d. the inability to cope with larger overseas responsibilities, the inability of the manager to adjust, and other family problems

14-54.
C
Medium
P.455

A recent study by International Orientation Resources, an HRM consulting firm, found that 60% of expatriate failures occur because of three reasons. These reasons are (1) the inability of a spouse to adjust, (2) the inability of the manager to adjust, and (3):
a. inadequate compensation
b. the inability to cope with larger overseas responsibilities
c. other family problems
d. the lack of technical competence

14-55.
A
Medium
P.455

A recent study by International Orientation Resources, an HRM consulting firm, found that 60% of expatriate failures occur because of three reasons. These reasons are the (1) inability of a spouse to adjust, (2) other family problems, and (3):
a. the inability of the manager to adjust
b. inadequate compensation
c. the lack of technical competence
d. the inability to cope with larger overseas responsibilities

14-56.
A
Medium
P.455

Mendenhall and Oddou identified four dimensions that seem to predict success in expatriate selection. These are:
a. self-orientation, others-orientation, perceptual ability, and cultural toughness
b. cognitive ability, subjective ability, positive affect, and cultural awareness
c. self-orientation, cognitive ability, subjective ability, and cultural toughness
d. subjective ability, others-orientation, perceptual ability, and cultural awareness

14-57.
B
Medium
P.455

Mendenhall and Oddou identified four dimensions that seem to predict success in expatriate selection: (1) self-orientation, (2) others-orientation, (3) perceptual ability, and _____.
a. cognitive ability
b. cultural toughness
c. subjective ability
d. global-orientation

14-58.
C
Medium
P.455

Mendenhall and Oddou identified four dimensions that seem to predict success in expatriate selection: (1) others-orientation, (2) perceptual ability, (3) cultural toughness, and (4) _____.
a. global-orientation
b. cognitive ability
c. self-orientation
d. subjective ability

14-59.
D
Medium
P.455

According to Mendenhall and Oddou, the attribute of _____ strengthens an expatriate's self-esteem, self-confidence, and mental well-being.
a. cultural toughness
b. perceptual ability
c. others-orientation
d. self-orientation

14-60.
A
Medium
P.456

According to Mendenhall and Oddou, the attribute of _____ enhances the expatriate's ability to interact effectively with host country nationals.
a. others-orientation
b. self-orientation
c. cultural toughness
d. perceptual ability

14-61.
C
Medium
P.456

According to Mendenhall and Oddou, the attribute of _____ provided an expatriate the ability to understand why people of other countries behave the way they do, that is, the ability to empathize with them.
a. cultural toughness
b. self-orientation
c. perceptual ability
d. others-orientation

14-62.
A
Hard
P.456

Only _____ of the firms in the study conducted by R.L. Tung used formal procedures and psychological tests to assess the personality traits and relational abilities of potential expatriates.
a. 5%
b. 15%
c. 30%
d. 45%

350

14-63.
A
Easy
P.458

The type of training that seeks to foster an appreciation for the host country's culture is called:

a. cultural training
b. technical training
c. language training
d. practical training

14-64.
B
Easy
P.458

The type of training that is aimed at helping an expatriate managers and his or her family ease themselves into day-to-day life in the host country is called:

a. cognitive training
b. practical training
c. technical training
d. cultural training

14-65.
D
Hard
P.459

According to one study of repatriated employees, _____ didn't know what their position would be when they returned home.

a. 10-20 %
b. 25-35 %
c. 45-55 %
d. 60-70 %

14-66.
B
Medium
P.459

_____ programs are designed to increase the overall skill levels of managers through a mix on ongoing management education and rotations of managers through a number of jobs within the firm to give them varied experiences.

a. Organizational development
b. Management development
c. Technical development
d. Personnel development

14-67.
C
Medium
P.463

The most common approach to expatriate pay is the _____.

a. merit approach
b. correspondence approach
c. balance sheet approach
d. parity approach

14-68.
A
Medium
P.463

In regard to expatriate pay, the _____ equalizes purchasing power across countries so employees can enjoy the same living standard in their foreign posting that they enjoyed at home.

a. balance sheet approach
b. standard of living approach
c. merit approach
d. correspondence approach

14-69.
A
Medium
P.463

In regard to expatriate pay, the balance sheet approach accomplishes two objectives. These are:

a. equalizes purchasing power across countries so employees can enjoy the same living standard in their foreign posting that they enjoyed at home, and provides financial incentives to offset qualitative differences between assignment locations

b. relieves an employee of the burden of paying taxes on income earned overseas, and provides an employee a standard 25% increase in pay for taking an overseas assignment

c. equalizes purchasing power across countries so employees can enjoy the same living standard in their foreign posting that they enjoyed at home, and relieves an employee of the burden of paying taxes on income earned overseas

d. provides financial incentives to offset qualitative differences between assignment locations, and provides an employee a standard 25% increase in pay for taking an overseas assignment

14-70.
D
Easy
P.463

The _____ attempts to provide expatriates with the same standard of living in their host countries as they enjoy at home plus a financial inducement for accepting an overseas assignment.

a. merit approach
b. correspondence approach
c. parity approach
d. balance sheet approach

14-71.
D
Medium
P.464

A _____ is extra pay the expatriate receives for working outside his or her country of origin.

a. parity adjustment
b. expatriate special circumstance
c. allowance
d. foreign service premium

14-72.
A
Medium
P.464

The extra pay an expatriate receives for working outside his or her country of origin is referred to as a:

a. foreign service premium
b. allowance
c. expatriate special circumstance
d. parity adjustment

14-73.
D
Medium
P.464

The form of compensation that compensates an expatriate for having to live in a unfamiliar country isolated from family and friends is referred to as a:

a. expatriate special circumstance
b. allowance
c. parity adjustment
d. foreign service premium

14-74.
B
Medium
P.465

Four types of allowance are often included in an expatriate's compensation package. These are:

a. travel allowances, emergency allowances, training allowances, relocation allowances
b. hardship allowances, housing allowances, cost-of-living allowances, and education allowances
c. emergency allowances, hardship allowances, training allowances, cost-of-living allowances
d. housing allowances, travel allowances, cost-of-living allowances, and relocation allowances

14-75.
D
Medium
P.465

Four types of allowances are often included in an expatriate's compensation package: a hardship allowance, a housing allowance, a cost-of-living allowance, and a _____ allowance.

a. training
b. relocation
c. travel
d. education

14-76.
C
Medium
P.465

Four types of allowances are often included in an expatriate's compensation package: a housing allowance, a cost-of-living allowance, an education allowance, and a _____ allowance.

a. training
b. relocation
c. hardship
d. travel

14-77.
C
Medium
P.466

In regard to the types of allowances often included in an expatriate's compensation package, a _____ allowance is paid when the expatriate is being sent to a difficult location.

a. education
b. housing
c. hardship
d. cost-of-living

14-78.
D
Medium
P.465

In regard to the types of allowances often included in an expatriates compensation package, a _____ allowance is often paid to ensure that the expatriate will enjoy the same standard of living in the foreign posting as at home.

a. housing
b. education
c. hardship
d. cost-of-living

14-79.   Unless a host country has _____ with the expatriate's home country, the
D   expatriate may have to pay income tax to both the home and host country
Medium   governments.
P.466   a. a positive balance of trade
           b. a trade treaty
           c. diplomatic relations
           d. a reciprocal tax treaty

14-80.   When a reciprocal tax treaty is not in force, the firm typically:
C   a. pays one-third of the expatriate's income tax in the host country
Medium   b. pays one-half of the expatriate's income tax in the host country
P.466   c. pays the expatriate's income tax in the host country
           d. requires the expatriate to pay his or her own income tax in the host country

Essay Questions

14-81.   Describe the concept of human resources management. What extra challenges
Easy   confront an international business in this area?
P.448

           Answer: Human resource management (HRM) refers to the activities an
           organization carries out to utilize its human resources effectively. These activities
           include staffing, training and management development, performance appraisal,
           compensation, labor relations, and determining the firm's human resources
           strategy. To maximize human resources effectiveness, all of these activities
           should be performed with the firm's overall strategy, goals, and objectives in mind.

           International businesses are faced with a number of extra challenges in this area.
           These extra challenge result primarily from the fact that countries differ in terms of
           their cultures, customs, philosophies of management, compensation systems, etc
           As a result, a firm must adjust its HRM program (to varying degrees) to be
           compatible with each country that it does business in. In addition, selecting
           expatriate managers it is a challenge. A expatriate manager must have the
           technical skills necessary to do the job, along with a personal disposition and a
           family situation that is conductive to living in a foreign country for an extended
           period of time. The relatively high expatriate failure rate experience by U.S.
           multinationals attests to the difficulty of this challenge. Finally, international
           businesses must decided how to structure their overseas operations, which
           involves determining the appropriate roles of parent country and host country
           management personnel.

14-82.   Discuss the differences between an ethnocentric approach, a polycentric
Hard   approach, and a geocentric approach to staffing for international businesses.
P.450   What is the rationale behind each of these approaches? How does a firm's
           staffing policy relate to the strategy that it is pursuing in a foreign country?

Answer: *Ethnocentric Approach*: An ethnocentric staffing policy is one in which all key management positions are filled by parent country nationals. Firms pursue an ethnocentric staffing policy for three reasons. First, the firm may believe there is a lack of qualified individuals in the host country to fill senior management positions. Second, the firm may see an ethnocentric staffing policy as the best way to maintain a unified corporate culture. For instance, many Japanese firms prefer that their foreign operations be headed up by Japanese managers, because these managers will be intimately familiar with the firm's culture and values. Third, if the firm is trying to create value by transferring core competencies to a foreign operation, it may feel that the best way to do this is to transfer parent country nationals who have knowledge of that competency to the foreign operation.

Polycentric Approach: A polycentric staffing policy requires host country nationals to be recruited to manage foreign operations, while parent country nationals occupy key positions at corporate headquarters. The principle advantage of adopting a polycentric approach is that the firm is less likely to suffer from cultural myopic. Host country managers are unlikely to make the mistakes arising from cultural misunderstandings that expatriate managers are subject to. Another advantage of the polycentric approach is that it is less expensive than other approaches to implement. By hiring host country personnel to fill management positions, the firm will not incur a significant amount of expatriate expense.

Geocentric Approach: A geocentric staffing policy tries to identify the best people available for management jobs, regardless of nationality. There are several advantages to this approach. First, it enables the firm to make the best personnel selections possible, without regard to nationality. In other words, a firm is not handcuffed in regard to who it can hire because of a candidate's nationality. Second, a geocentric policy enables the firm to build a cadre of international executives who feel at home working in a number of different cultures. This is a critical consideration if the firm has future international business expansion in mind. The multicultural composition of the management team that results from geocentric staffing tends to reduce cultural myopic and enhances local responsiveness.

A firm's staffing policy does related to the overall global strategy it is trying to pursue (global strategy was covered in Chapter 10). Overall, an ethnocentric approach is compatible with an international strategy, a polycentric approach is compatible with a multidomestic strategy, and a geocentric approach is compatible with both global and transnational strategies. Large international businesses may pursue a combination of these strategies to achieve the optimal staffing policy/international strategy mix.

14-83.
Medium
P.449

What is an expatriate manager? What are some of the steps that an international business can take to enhance the success of their expatriate manager program?

Answer: An expatriate manager is a citizen of one country who is working abroad in one of his or her firm's subsidiaries. For example, if a manager for Disney (an American company) was moved from Orlando, Florida to Paris, France to work at Euro Disney, he or she would be an expatriate manager.

Selecting expatriate managers is a challenge because an individual who takes an assignment in a foreign country must have both the technical skills necessary to do the job and the personality disposition and family situation conductive to living and working overseas. The success of an expatriate program begins with the proper "selection" of expatriate personnel. Mehdenhall and Oddou have identified four dimensions that seem to predict success in foreign postings: self-orientation, others-orientation, perceptual ability, and cultural toughness. These factors should be considered in expatriate selection. Expatriate selection should be followed by expatriate training and management development. The training should include cultural training, language training, and practical training focused on living in a foreign country. Expatriates should also be prepared for repatriation. Upon returning home, a former expatriate manager can find himself or herself without a clear job or career path if repatriation is not an ongoing consideration during the expatriate period.

Other HRM issues should be carefully designed to accommodate the complex issues involved in employing expatriate managers. These issues include performance appraisal and compensation. Firms should work hard to reduce bias in performance appraisals, by both parent company and host country supervisors. Compensation programs should be thoughtfully prepared to adequately compensate expatriate managers for overseas assignments.

14-84.
Medium
P.457

What are management development programs? How can international businesses use management development programs as a strategic tool?

Answer: Management development programs are designed to increase the overall potential of employees by providing them training and a variety of experiences. For instance, a management development program might involve regularly scheduled educational programs, training, workshops covering a wide range of issues, and a program of rotating employees through foreign assignments to provide them international experience.

As a strategic tool, management development programs can play an important role in international businesses. These program can help a firm build a corporate culture that is sensitive to international business issues. In addition, in house company training programs, workshops, and off-site training can foster a sense of unity among the employees as well as the development of technical skills. In addition, the introduction of company songs, uniforms, T-shirts, and other firm specific initiatives can help build a manager's identification with the company and company spirit.

All of these initiatives can help build unity among the employees and the units of a firm, which may be particularly important for international businesses that have a number of disperse locations.

Management development programs are designed to increase the overall skill levels of managers through a mix of ongoing management education and rotations of managers through a number of jobs within the firm to give them varied experiences.

14-85.
Medium
P.462

Discuss the issue of expatriate compensation. Suppose you worked for a firm that transferred you from the United States to a developing country in Asia or South America. How do you think you should be compensated relative to your peers in similar jobs at home?

Answer: This question is designed to encourage classroom discussion and/or to encourage students to "think" about how expatriate managers should be compensated. The issue of expatriate compensation is a difficult one. Substantial differences exist in the compensation of executives at the same level in various countries. These differences raise the question: should a firm pay its expatriate managers the prevailing wage rate in the country that they are working in, or should a firm pay all of its expatriate managers at the same level of responsibility a similar amount of pay? There is no standard answer to this question. The most common approach to expatriate pay is the balance sheet approach. This approach equalizes purchasing power across countries so employees can enjoy the same standard of living in their foreign postings that they enjoyed at home. In addition, this approach provides financial incentives to offset qualitative differences between assignment locations.

Consistent with this approach, the components of the typical expatriate compensation package are a base salary, a foreign service premium, allowances of various types, tax differentials, and benefits. In some cases, expatriates receive extra "hardship" allowances for living is a particularly difficult location. All together, an expatriate's compensation package may amount to three times what he or she would receive at home. Bear in mind, however, that the expatriate may be living and working in a difficult overseas assignment.

Ask your students to comment on this issue. It provides an interesting forum for classroom discussion.